AN ARMY OF TRIBES

An Army of Tribes

British Army Cohesion, Deviancy and Murder in Northern Ireland

Edward Burke

Liverpool University Press

First published 2018 by
Liverpool University Press
4 Cambridge Street
Liverpool
L69 7ZU

British Library Cataloguing-in-Publication data
A British Library CIP record is available

ISBN: 978-1-78694-097-1 cased
ISBN: 978-1-78694-103-9 limp

Typeset by Carnegie Book Production, Lancaster
Printed and bound in Poland by BooksFactory.co.uk

Contents

Preface

In July 2012, I decided to walk on or close to the 303 miles of the Irish border for charity. I had recently returned from a year and a half in Afghanistan, where security restrictions and high fences had limited my movements. I was rewarded with walks along twisting boreens arched with canopies of ash, scrambles over sentinel hills such as Cuilcagh or Slieve Gullion and long pauses at the dark, still loughs of the Ulster marches. Battle sites were also strewn across my path: I walked through or past places such as the Barnesmore gap, Benburb and Moyry pass. These were often remarkably serene places. It is very difficult to find anything but peace at 'Bloody Pass', the Upper Lough Erne site of a massacre of Jacobite soldiers after the Battle of Newtownbutler in 1689. I was treated with an immense kindness and not a little curiosity during my hike along the border. In quieter moments people would relate to me some darker stories. Standing on a wind-stripped hill in west Tyrone, a Catholic farmer told me how his only neighbour, serving in the local Ulster Defence Regiment battalion, would lie in wait at night in a field behind his house to taunt his elderly mother with sectarian abuse. Grievance and violence in such a setting were extremely intimate, with complicated, often highly localised, motives. As I walked and tried to get my head around such accounts, I became increasingly curious as to how British soldiers made sense of such a political and social landscape, what were the accepted narratives and 'truths' that enabled them to function, to do 'a job' and emotionally respond to casualties during this most violent of periods in the recent Troubles? Too often, at least in Irish Nationalist narratives, the British Army has been unhelpfully demonised; atrocities inevitably lead to the top and everything was planned from the outset. The divergent motivations, experiences and emotions of soldiers in different units are lost in such accounts.

An iconic image of the British Army in Northern Ireland in 1972 is that of a Scottish Highlander, his glengarry hat sloped to the side of his head, left thumb in his belt, tear gas gun cocked by his right hip, and all the time glowering at a crowd. This image has come to encapsulate the animosity and threatening attitude of the Army to the people of Northern Ireland. Philip Jones Griffiths, the Magnum photographer who took the picture, thought so: the caption included the word 'disdain'. However, a closer analysis of the lives, interests and humour of soldiers – young and obsessed by westerns featuring John Wayne and Clint Eastwood (during pre-Northern Ireland training in Kent an Argyll and Sutherland Highlander 'borrowed' a horse so that he ride 'cowboy style', rifle pointing skyward at his side back to his platoon) – makes one look again at the picture. Perhaps the soldier is simply having a laugh. Maybe he is threatening the crowd and having a joke at the same time. We do not know. It is better to suspend judgement.

A selective narrative sympathetic to two regiments that are a particular focus of this study, the Scots Guards and the Argyll and Sutherland Highlanders, would only highlight incidents that reflect well and win sympathy for these regiments, such as when the Argylls saved the lives of Bernadette McAliskey and her husband after they had been shot in their home by Loyalist paramilitaries, the fire discipline under provocation of the Scots Guards in Londonderry and Belfast, the Scots Guardsman who went absent without leave in order to find his girlfriend in Newtownstewart who had been abducted, beaten, tarred and feathered by the IRA, the similar treatment meted out to Nancy McCumiskey in Glassdrumman, County Armagh, whose family made the mistake of giving tea and sandwiches to passing Argyll soldiers (she was dragged from her family's car, tied to the church railing and tarred and feathered before a congregation gathered to attend mass).

Similarly, it is easy to find incidents that reflect badly on both regiments: the murders of Michael Naan and Andrew Murray in Newtownbutler by Argyll soldiers; the Scots Guards' collective punishment and sectarian taunting of the population in the Brandywell area of Derry are two such examples. This study attempts to leave nothing out. It is not possible, for example, to explain why Michael Naan and Andrew Murray were murdered without examining the climate of fear and sectarian mistrust in South Fermanagh in 1972. I eventually discovered that the two most plausible catalysts for the murders were a missing Argyll soldier, presumed captured, tortured and killed, and the local denunciation of Michael Naan as a senior IRA commander, partly as a result of a land dispute between him and a part-time, local UDR commander. Both of these key 'push factors' appear to have been ignored or unknown to investigators at the time. As well as being perpetrators of murder, the Argylls were also used and misled by locals in South Fermanagh.

Some former soldiers were suspicious of my motives: why would an Irishman, from the Republic of Ireland, want to study the British Army, if not to malign its reputation? My contacts with, and respect for, the British Army, gained during my time as an analyst with the European Union Police Mission in Afghanistan, did help to alleviate some, but not all, of these concerns. Some interviewees were willing to give me the benefit of the doubt; others were not. My own experience of conflict in my previous professional life has given me a lot of sympathy for the complexity of counterinsurgency operations and the capacity of soldiers for remarkable acts of kindness and, much more rarely, cruelty. I did not forget this lesson when listening to the accounts given by former soldiers who served in Northern Ireland, who were unfailingly hospitable and generous during my encounters with them. My aim has not been to eulogise or demonise but to better understand their motives, behaviour and actions. The Scots Guards Association and the Argyll and Sutherland Highlanders Association have never sought to control my research conclusions, even though they granted me access to their regimental archives and informed interested veterans about my research. They have their own accounts of what happened in Northern Ireland during their tours in 1971 and 1972. This is mine; they will probably approve of some parts and strongly disagree with others.

Acknowledgements

Alison Welsby and her colleagues at Liverpool University Press have been endlessly supportive and patient during the research and writing of this book. Similarly, Rachel Chamberlain and the team at Carnegie Book Production did an excellent job preparing the book for publication. I am also indebted to my former PhD supervisor, Professor Richard English, for the outstanding guidance and encouragement he has given me over many years. I am also grateful to my second Supervisor, Dr Sibylle Scheipers, for her many valuable insights and advice. My examiners, Professor Sir Hew Strachan and the late Professor Keith Jeffery, were both exacting and encouraging. Dr Tim Wilson has been a remarkable source of knowledge and good humour. I am also in the debt of Professor Nick Rengger, Dr Kieran McConaghy, Dr Neale Gregg, Air Commodore (retd) Nick Randle, Dr Tom Smith, Dr Frank Ledwidge, Professor Wyn Rees, Dr Bettina Renz, Dr Andrew Mumford, Dr Rory Cormac, Mrs Elaine Watts and Dr Nick Brooke for their advice and support. A number of people at the Handa Centre for the Study of Terrorism and Political Violence (CSTPV) and the wider School of International Relations at the University of St Andrews, including Mrs Julie Middleton and Mrs Gillian Brunton, have been rocks of professionalism and sound advice. I am very grateful to my colleagues at the University of Nottingham and the University of Portsmouth for their advice, friendship and support. I have also received a lot of guidance from outside the University of St Andrews, the University of Nottingham and the University of Portsmouth including from, among others, Professor Sönke Neitzel, Professor Sir Simon Wessely, Professor Eunan O'Halpin, Dr Jan Honig, Dr Huw Bennett, Professor Peter Jackson, Dr Martin McCleery, Dr Connal Parr, Mr Sonny Jackson, Mr Anthony Hanrahan BL, Mr Peter Malone, Professor Anthony King and Professor Graham Walker. At the Public Record Office of Northern Ireland, Lynsey Gillespie and her colleagues were always polite and helpful. The Military Archives of Ireland at Cathal Brugha Barracks in Dublin diligently helped me sift through the archives of the Irish Defence Forces and the Department of Defence. I am very grateful to the staff of the library at the University of St Andrews, the McClay library at Queen's University Belfast, the Linen Hall library and Land Registry of Northern Ireland in Belfast, the Cardinal O'Fiaich Library in Armagh and Cavan County and Enniskillen libraries for their support during my research. The Scots Guards Association, the Regimental Headquarters of the Scots Guards at Wellington Barracks, the Argyll and Sutherland Highlanders Association, the Regimental Museum of the Royal Scots Dragoon Guards, the Royal Artillery Museum, Woolwich, the Queen's Royal Lancers and Nottinghamshire Yeomanry Museum, have all been exceptionally helpful throughout my research. I am especially grateful to all those who made themselves available for interview, many of whom shared invaluable files and notes from the time. Any errors are mine alone. This book is dedicated to my family, the greatest gift I will ever know.

Abbreviations

1 Argylls	1st Battalion, Argyll and Sutherland Highlanders
1 GREN GDS	1st Battalion, Grenadier Guards
1 PARA	1st Battalion, The Parachute Regiment
1 Scots Guards/1 SG	1st Battalion, Scots Guards
2 Light Infantry	2nd Battalion, The Light Infantry
2 PARA	2nd Battalion, The Parachute Regiment
2 Scots Guards/2 SG	2nd Battalion, Scots Guards
3 Brigade	3rd Infantry Brigade
3 PARA	3rd Battalion, The Parachute Regiment
8 Brigade	8th Infantry Brigade
16/5 Lancers	16th/5th The Queen's Royal Lancers
22 SAS	22nd Special Air Service Regiment
39 Brigade	39th Infantry Brigade
ALS	Army Legal Service
ASH	The Argyll and Sutherland Highlanders
ASU	IRA Active Service Unit
ATO	ammunition technical officer
AVRE	Armoured Vehicle Royal Engineers
BAOR	British Army on the Rhine
CDCC	Central Citizens' Defence Committee
CESA	Catholic Ex-Servicemen's Association
CLFNI	Commander Land Forces Northern Ireland
CO	commanding officer
COIN	counterinsurgency
COPFS	Crown Office and Procurator Fiscal Service, Scotland
CPA	Conservative Party Archive, Oxford University
CRD	Conservative Research Department
CSM	Company Sergeant Major
DAC	Divisional Action Committees

DEFE	Ministry of Defence File Series, National Archives
DFA	Department of Foreign Affairs
DPP	Director of Public Prosecutions
EOD	Explosive Ordnance Disposal
EOKA	Ethniki Organosis Kyprion Agoniston
FCO	Foreign and Commonwealth Office
FLOSY	Front for the Liberation of South Yemen
GAA	Gaelic Athletic Association
Gdsmn	guardsman
GOC	General Officer Commanding Northern Ireland
GPMG	general-purpose machine gun
GSW	gunshot wound
HET	Historical Enquiries Team
HQNI	Headquarters Northern Ireland
HV	high velocity
IED	improvised explosive device
Intsum	Intelligence Summary
IRA	Provisional Irish Republican Army
IWM	Imperial War Museum, London
JSC	joint security committee
LAW	Loyalist Association of Workers
LDV	Loyalist Defence Volunteers
LF	left flank
LHCMA	Liddell-Hart Centre for Military Archives, King's College London
LMG	light machine gun
LRNI	Land Registry of Northern Ireland
MACP	military aid to the civil power
MAI	Military Archives of Ireland, Cathal Brugha Barracks
MC	Military Cross
MI5	Security Service
MI6	Secret Intelligence Service
MoD	Ministry of Defence
MRF	Military Reaction Force
NAI	National Archives of Ireland
NAM	National Army Museum
NAS	National Archives of Scotland

Abbreviations

NAVCOMMSTA	US Naval Communications Station
NCO	non-commissioned officer
NICRA	Northern Ireland Civil Rights Association
NIO	Northern Ireland Office
NITAT	Northern Ireland Training and Advisory Teams
NLF	Yemeni National Liberation Front
OBE	Order of the British Empire
OC	officer commanding
OIRA	Official Irish Republican Army
OP	observation post
PHC1	Prisoner Holding Centre 1 (Holywood Barracks)
PRONI	Public Record Office of Northern Ireland
PSNI	Police Service of Northern Ireland
QOH	Queen's Own Highlanders
QRF	quick reaction force
RF	right flank
RMAS	Royal Military Academy Sandhurst
RMASH	Regimental Museum of the Argyll and Sutherland Highlanders
RMP	Royal Military Police
RPG	rocket propelled grenade
RSDG	Royal Scots Dragoon Guards
RSDGA	Royal Scots Dragoon Guards Association
RSM	Regimental Sergeant Major
RUC	Royal Ulster Constabulary
RUSI	Royal United Services Institute
RVH	Royal Victoria Hospital
SAS	Special Air Service
SBS	Special Boat Squadron
SDLP	Social Democratic and Labour Party
SIB	Special Investigation Branch
Sitrep	situation report
SLR	self-loading rifle
SMG	sub-machine gun
SSNI	Secretary of State for Northern Ireland
TAC HQ	Tactical Headquarters
TNA	National Archives of the United Kingdom
Tpr	trooper
UDA	Ulster Defence Association

UDR	Ulster Defence Regiment
USC	Ulster Special Constabulary
UUC	Ulster Unionist Council
UUP	Ulster Unionist Party
UVF	Ulster Volunteer Force
UWC	Ulster Workers Council
VBIED	vehicle-borne improvised explosive device
VCP	vehicle checkpoint
WO	War Office

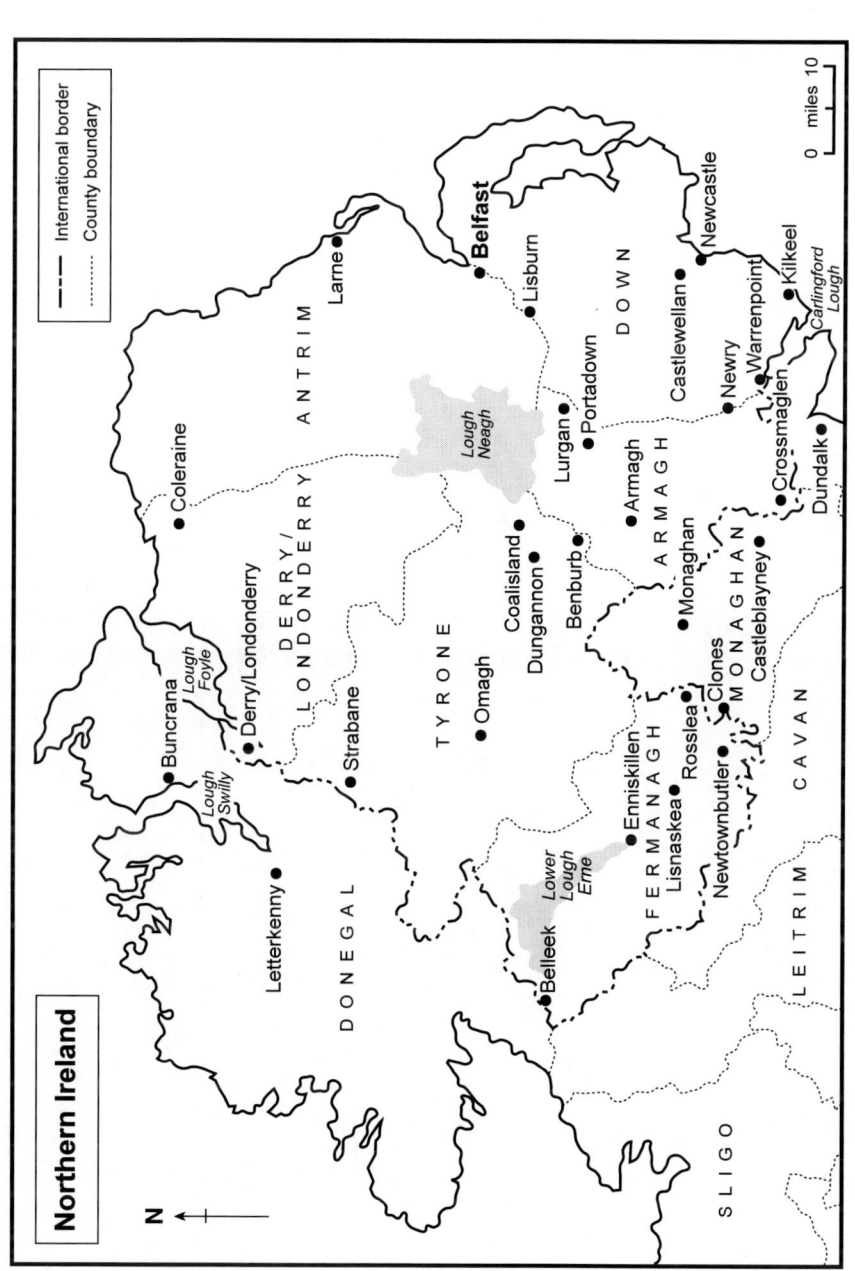

Northern Ireland

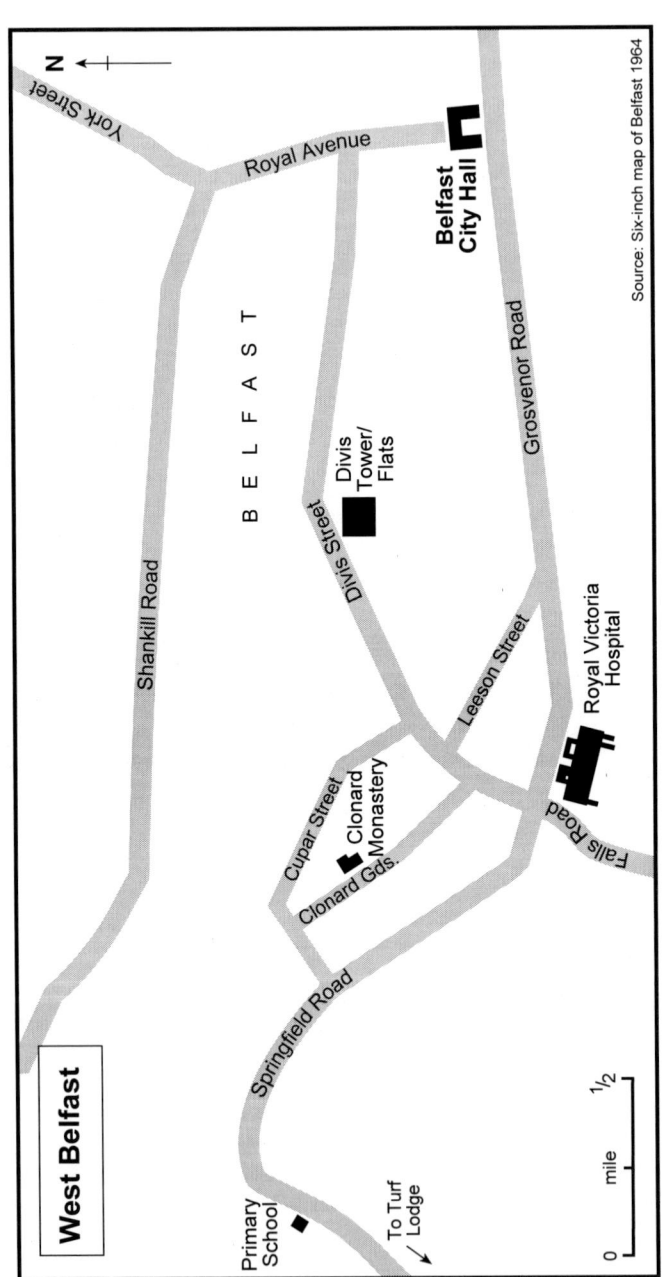

West Belfast

N

York Street
Royal Avenue
Shankill Road
BELFAST
Divis Tower/Flats
Divis Street
Belfast City Hall
Grosvenor Road
Leeson Street
Cupar Street
Clonard Monastery
Clonard Gds.
Royal Victoria Hospital
Falls Road
Springfield Road
Primary School
To Turf Lodge

0   ½   mile

Source: Six-inch map of Belfast 1964

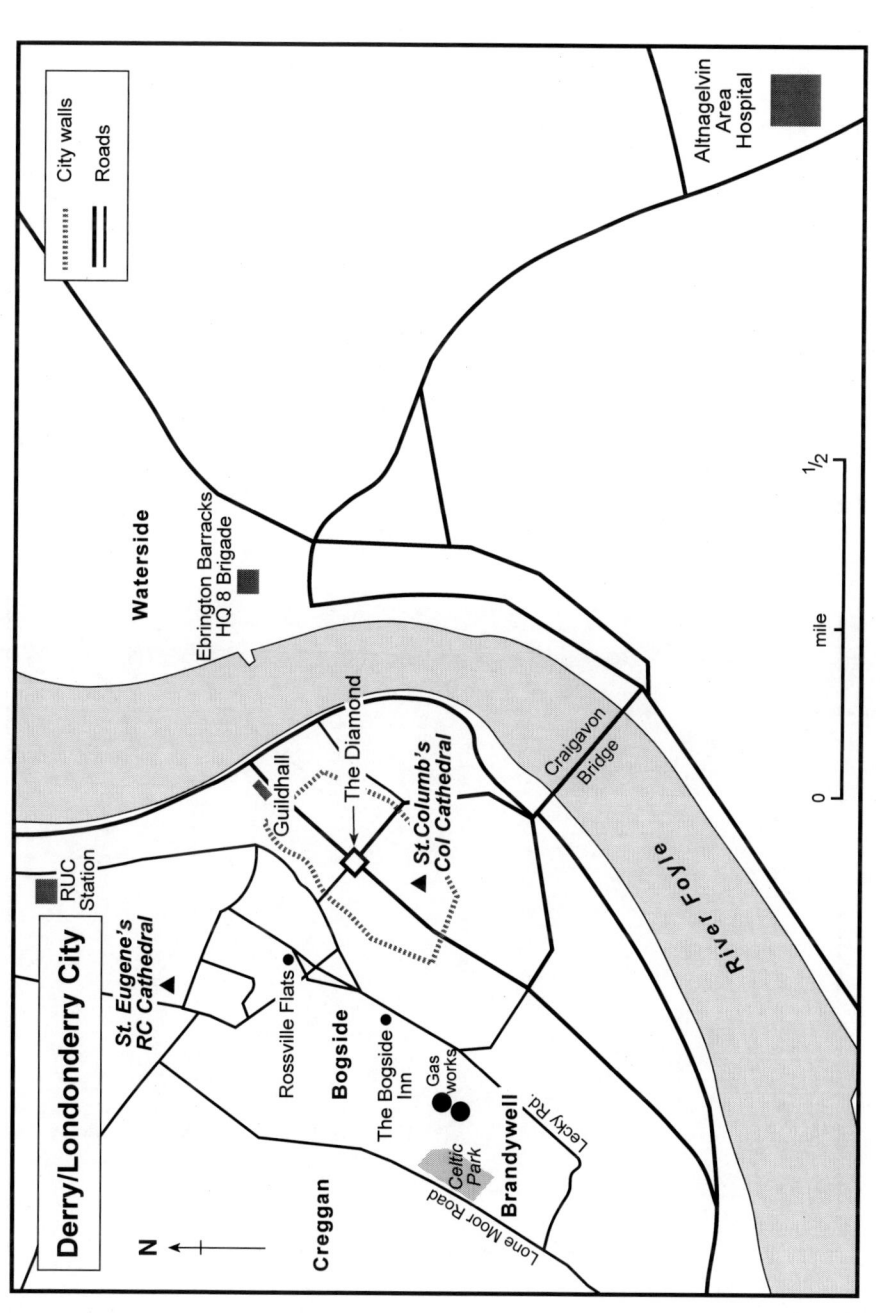

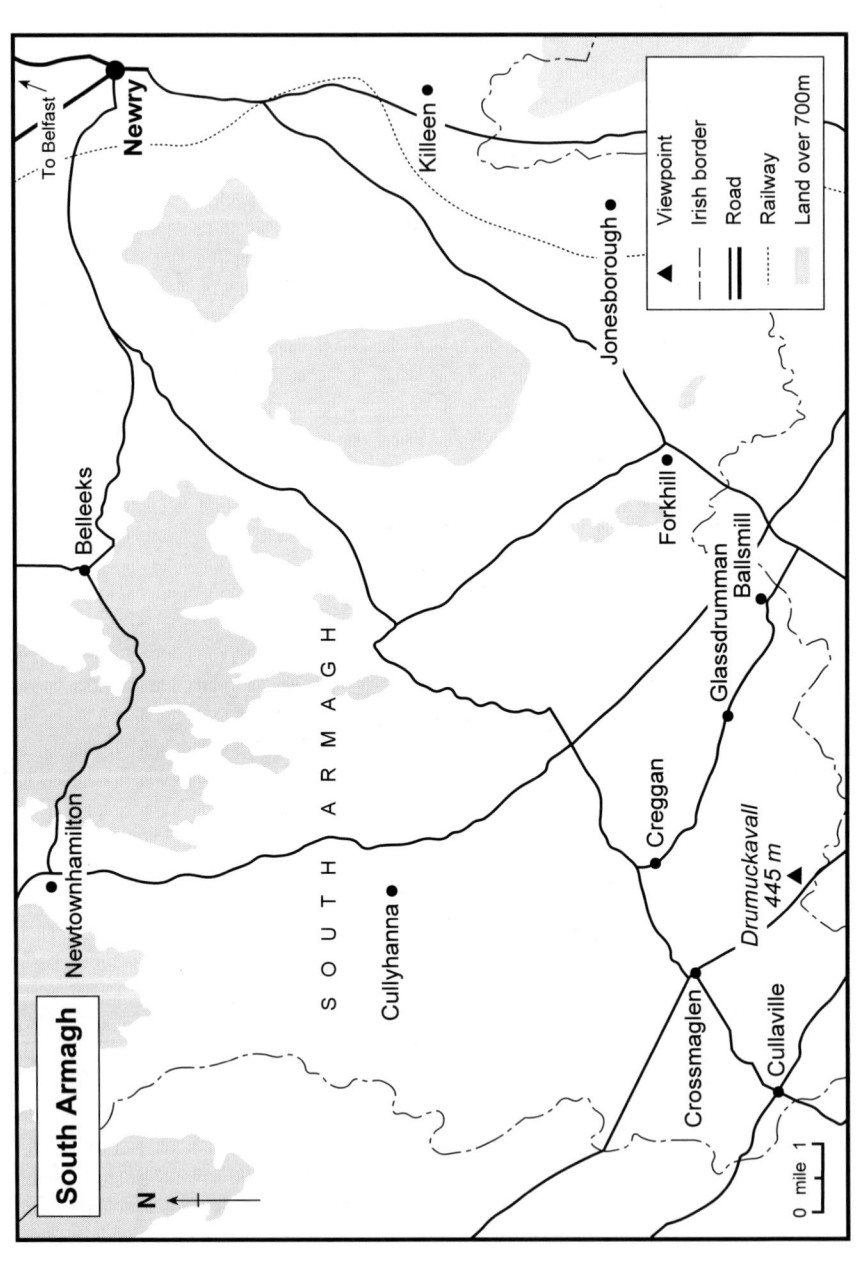

South Armagh

N

To Belfast

Newry

Killeen

Jonesborough

Belleeks

Forkhill

Glassdrumman
Ballsmill

Newtownhamilton

S O U T H   A R M A G H

Creggan

Cullyhanna

Drumuckavall
445 m

Crossmaglen

Cullaville

Viewpoint
Irish border
Road
Railway
Land over 700m

0   mile   1

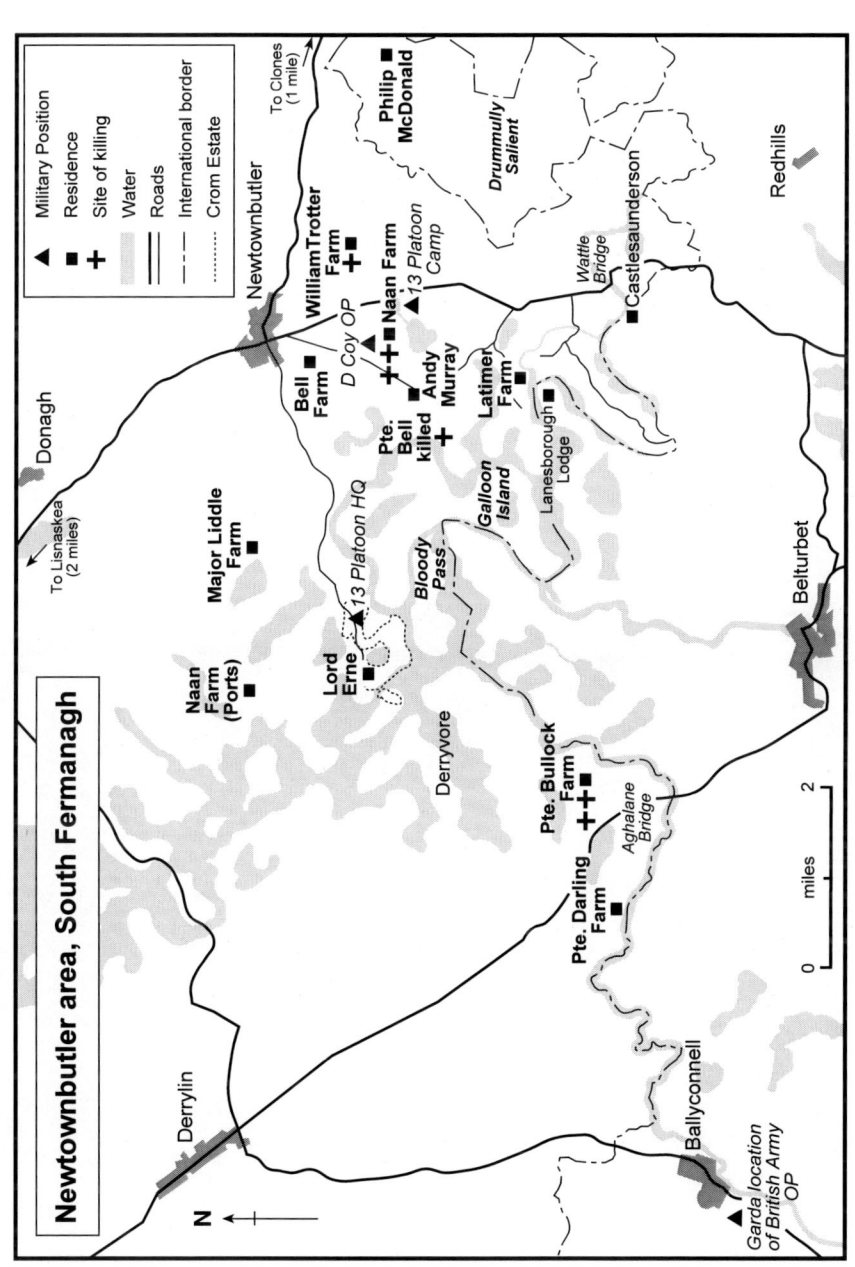

Newtownbutler area, South Fermanagh

Military Position ▲
Residence ■
Site of killing +
Water
Roads
International border
Crom Estate

Donagh

Newtownbutler

To Clones
(1 mile)

Philip
McDonald ■

Drummully
Salient

William Trotter
Farm ■
+ ■ Naan Farm
D Coy OP ▲
▲ 13 Platoon Camp

Bell
Farm ■

Castlesaunderson ■

Wattle
Bridge

Redhills

+ + ■ Andy
Murray

Pte.
Bell
killed +

Latimer
Farm ■

Major Liddle
Farm ■

To Lisnaskea
(2 miles)

13 Platoon HQ ▲

Galloon
Island

Lanesborough
Lodge ■

Naan
Farm
(Ports) ■

Lord
Erne ■

Bloody
Pass.

Derryvore

Belturbet

Pte. Bullock
Farm
+ +

Aghalane
Bridge

Derrylin

Pte. Darling
Farm ■

0   miles   2

N ←

Ballyconnell

Garda location
of British Army
OP ▲

Introduction

> The aim is not to show how the decisions of a few generals affected thousands of soldiers but, rather, how the decisions of thousands of soldiers affected a few generals.[1]

> 'The Army is a collection of semi-nomadic tribes', said a gunner brigadier. A cavalry general spoke of the different combat arms as 'collections of wigwams round a totem pole which they spent their time polishing'.[2]

Michael Howard, one of Britain's leading thinkers on military affairs and strategy, was reluctant to describe the conflict in Northern Ireland as a 'war', preferring to see it as 'an emergency'. Howard's limited definition was politically motivated: he wished to minimise Irish Republican Army (IRA) violence as a domestic 'law and order' issue. Howard was understandably concerned that if the public was told that Britain was 'at war' in Northern Ireland, an expectation would grow for either an all-out victory, meaning an escalation of State violence, or withdrawal – exactly the type of short-term duality that played into the hands of the IRA.[3] Moreover, war, with all its horrors, is also not something that should be contemplated within one's own country, against one's own people. The author Elizabeth Bowen, writing about the earlier Anglo-Irish conflict of 1919–1921, captured a similar hesitancy to apply language reserved for international wars to an insurgency within the borders of the United

---

1 T. Ashworth, *Trench Warfare, 1914–1918: The Live and Let Live System* (London: Macmillan, 1980), 13.

2 A. Beevor, *Inside the British Army* (London: Corgi Books, 1991), 308.

3 M. Howard, 'Mistake to Declare this "a War"', *RUSI Journal* 146(6) (2001), 1–4.

Kingdom – 'Oh but one wouldn't call it a war … If anyone would, we would clean these beggars out in a week.'[4]

Britain, at least, had a short memory when it came to conflict within the British Isles. The vice chief of the general staff of the Army during the early years of Operation Banner,[5] Lieutenant General Sir Cecil 'Monkey' Blacker, recalled that the fatal shooting of a solider in Londonderry in early 1971 profoundly shocked the Army (and British society more widely):

> Looking back over more than twenty years, across the gulf which has since swallowed thousands of lives to the point when such news hardly earns a comment, I still remember the cold chill of horror which struck me – here, unbelievably, here in Great Britain, in one of our streets in our own country, a British soldier had been killed in action.[6]

Despite a general distaste for waging war at home, the conflict in Northern Ireland during 1971 and 1972 does meet the minimal criteria to be described as a war. Carl von Clausewitz described war, in its bare essence, as 'an act of force to compel our enemy to do our will'.[7] Martin Edmonds later provided a useful expansion of Clausewitz's original definition: 'War … may be defined as the use of violence, or physical coercion, by a state, society or a group against another to achieve a desired objective. It is a physical means employed by one group or society against another and, as such, it is not, nor ever can be, independent of their internal affairs.'[8]

---

4 E. Bowen, *The Last September* (London: Vintage, 1998), 38.

5 Operation Banner was the name given by the British Armed Forces to their campaign in Northern Ireland (1969–2007).

6 Blacker had served as Commander of 39 Infantry Brigade in Northern Ireland in the early 1960s; he was a former commanding officer of an Irish Cavalry Regiment, the 5th Inniskilling Dragoon Guards. Nevertheless, he was also capable of being profoundly surprised by the place. C. Blacker, *Monkey Business: The Memoirs of General Sir Cecil Blacker* (London: Quiller Press, 1993), 171.

7 Carl von Clausewitz, *On War*, edited and translated by M. Howard and P. Paret (Princeton, NJ: Princeton University Press, 1989), 75.

8 M. Edmonds, *Armed Services and Society* (Leicester: Leicester University Press, 1988), 1.

Clausewitz argued that war leads to a natural escalation and that 'to introduce the principle of moderation into the theory of war itself would always lead to a logical absurdity'.[9] But in reality Clausewitz admits that natural theory is usually trumped by political reality; a state will normally be unwilling to expend more resources than it believes the objective is worth and will limit its efforts or sue for peace instead of unquestioningly escalating its efforts until war becomes total or all-consuming. Clausewitz counsels that, 'If we were to think purely in absolute terms, we could avoid every difficulty by a stroke of the pen and proclaim with inflexible logic that, since the extreme must always be the goal, the greatest effort must always be exerted. Any such pronouncement would be an abstraction and would leave the real world unaffected'.[10]

The lowest-end of Clausewitz's definition of 'war' was what he called 'a threatening attitude meant to support negotiations, a mild attempt to gain some small advantage before sitting back and letting matters take their course, or a disagreeable obligation imposed by an alliance, to be discharged with as little effort as possible'.[11] Moreover, the more limited the military intervention, the more political the conflict, in that 'war will be driven further from its natural course'.[12] Guerrilla tactics and wars of insurgency fascinated Clausewitz. He studied and lectured on insurgency in Spain during the Napoleonic occupation. Nor did he restrict his definition of war as only occurring between States (although, given his experience of the Napoleonic wars, this is what takes up much of the focus on operational manoeuvres in *On War*). But he found the 'free play of intelligence, which operates in the small wars' to be 'extraordinarily interesting'.[13] Clausewitz's trinity of policy (or politics), 'the play of chance and probability within which the creative spirit is free to roam' and passion or 'primordial hatred' are at their most magnetic during wars of insurgency. Asymmetry – the subversion and opportunism of insurgent forces – increases the likelihood that the Army, government and people will each be affected by different

9 Clausewitz, *On War*, 76.
10 Clausewitz, *On War*, 78.
11 Clausewitz, *On War*, 218.
12 Clausewitz, *On War*, 88.
13 P. Paret, *Clausewitz and the State: The Man, His Theories, and His Times* (Princeton, NJ: Princeton University Press, 2007), 237–239.

components of the trinity.[14] Clausewitz believed that this 'swaying' effect of the trinity, so pronounced during wars of insurgency, made such conflicts fascinating to study.[15] 'Small wars', Clausewitz concluded, occurred more frequently than 'major wars'. He observed that, 'the preferred method of war judging from the frequency of its use, is to wear down the enemy ... Wearing down the enemy in a conflict means using the duration of the war to bring about a gradual exhaustion of his physical and moral resistance'.[16]

Even a cursory glance at the scale of the violence reveals that Northern Ireland during the 1970s more than meets our modern-day definitions of war. Gradually 'wearing down the enemy', particularly his 'moral resistance', would have eloquently served to describe the IRA's war aims in Northern Ireland. The British Army also described the conflict in Northern Ireland as 'a war', privately and later publicly. The Army's own Operation Banner 'end of mission' report acknowledged that soldiers in the 1970s were confronted by a war of insurgency.[17] In 1972, 134 British soldiers were killed (108 regular, 26 part-time Ulster Defence Regiment) – more than in any year during recent operations in Afghanistan. The Army recorded over 3,500 explosions or bomb incidents carried out by paramilitaries in that year alone. In early 1970, 2,500 British soldiers were deployed on operations in Northern Ireland. By 1972, this number had increased to over 22,000, briefly rising to more than 27,000 during Operation Motorman in the summer of that

---

14 Christopher Daase has developed this logic further, arguing that insurgencies see a breakdown in normative political and military structures. Asymmetric conflict leads to political, military and moral confusion:

> States, fighting small wars strategically in the offence, tactically in the defence, are forced to increase pressure constantly. In this process they undermine their own state institutions and normative standards as well as the rules of the international system. Non-state actors in turn, fighting strategically in the defence, but tactically in the offence, have no incentive to wage war according to any rules.

C. Daase, 'Clausewitz and Small Wars', in H. Strachan and A. Herberg-Rothe (eds), *Clausewitz in the 21st Century* (Oxford: Oxford University Press, 2007), 194.

15 Paret, *Clausewitz and the State*, 190.

16 Clausewitz, *On War*, 93.

17 British Army, *Operation Banner: An Analysis of Military Operations in Northern Ireland* (London: Ministry of Defence, 2006), 2.10.

year.[18] It is this book's objective to study the behaviour and motivations of soldiers during the early and most violent period of this static and social war within the UK.

Clausewitz warned that the study of war is incomplete if the scholar focuses only on the plans and thoughts expressed by a commander over time. A true comprehension of the very essence of war meant looking at the 'tremendous friction' that occurred between the formulation of a plan in military headquarters and those at the front doing the actual fighting.

> In theory, it sounds reasonable enough: a battalion commander's duty is to carry out his orders; discipline welds the battalion together, its commander must be a man of tested capacity, and so the great beam turns on its iron pivot with a minimum of friction. In fact, it is different, and every fault and exaggeration of the theory is instantly exposed in war. A battalion is made up of individuals, the least important of whom may chance to delay things or somehow make them go wrong.[19]

By recalling the soldier's capacity for individual autonomy, intense emotion such as hatred and balancing it against the rationalised interests of policy, the weight and power of hierarchical political structures and military institutions, we can come to a better understanding of how wars are fought. Here I examine the behaviour of British soldiers from 1971 to 1972 by applying a 'bottom up' study of the Northern Irish war. By focusing on the conduct of small groups of soldiers in a brief period of time it is possible to capture and examine these soldiers' orientation, loyalties, rationale, confusion, motivation and fears during a period of profound tactical confusion regarding aims and the conduct of operations.

The central argument of this study is that British Army small infantry units enjoyed considerable autonomy during the early years of Operation Banner and could behave in a vengeful, highly aggressive or benign and conciliatory way as their local commanders saw fit. The strain of civil–military relations at a senior level was replicated operationally – as soldiers came to resent the limitations of waging war in the UK. The unwillingness of the Army's senior leadership to investigate and punish

18 The National Archives (hereafter TNA): CJ 4/1764 Shooting Statistics.
19 Clausewitz, *On War*, 119.

serious transgressions of standard operating procedures in Northern Ireland created uncertainty among soldiers over expected behaviour and desired outcomes. Mid-ranking officers and non-commissioned officers (NCOs) often played important roles in restraining soldiers in Northern Ireland. The degree of violence used in Northern Ireland was much less that that seen in the colonial wars fought since the end of the Second World War. But overly aggressive groups of soldiers could also be mistaken for high-functioning units – with negative consequences for the Army's overall strategy in Northern Ireland from 1971, namely the erosion of the IRA's capability and support among the Northern Irish population.[20]

This study aims to make four original contributions to the study of the British Army and the Northern Ireland conflict. First, the literature on the British Army and Northern Ireland is less extensive than the subject deserves, and the existing work (though valuable) does not sufficiently exploit the vast array of first-hand sources currently available for scholarly scrutiny of the topic. This study, through the extensive use of interviews and newly available archive material, goes some way towards addressing that deficit, examining issues such as cohesion, experience of combat and criminality or deviancy among soldiers in Northern Ireland. It also offers fresh insights and analysis of important events during Operation Banner, revealing, for the first time, key information relating to the murders of two men in County Fermanagh, Michael Naan and Andrew Murray, and that of Warrenpoint hotel owner Edmund Woolsey in South Armagh in the autumn of 1972.

In drawing on new material, the study seeks to add to the valuable contributions already made by scholars on counter-insurgency and counter-terrorism in Northern Ireland. Christopher Andrew, Keith Jeffery and Andrew Sanders have all provided accounts of the intelligence and operational environment of Northern Ireland. Andrew has written that both the Security Service (MI5) and, to a lesser degree, the Secret Intelligence Service (SIS or MI6) were under-resourced and poorly informed during the early years of Operation Banner. It took some years

---

20 Report dated October 4, 1971 from General Sir Michael Carver, Chief of the General Staff, to the Secretary of State for Defence, Lord Carrington, entitled 'Northern Ireland – Appreciation of the Security Situation as of 4th October 1971', Inquiry Reference No.: G14B.86.8, evidence reproduced in the *Report of the Bloody Sunday Inquiry*, http://webarchive.nationalarchives.gov.uk/20100401161904/ http://www.bloody-sunday-inquiry.org.uk/ (accessed December 4, 2017).

for the Security Service to gain operational momentum in Northern Ireland.[21] Meanwhile, despite a paucity of literature relative to that on paramilitary groups, there have also been some illuminating studies of the Army in Northern Ireland. Alistair Irwin, Mike Mahoney, Richard Iron and Peter Neumann have examined British strategy, allowing for a better understanding of the decision-making and logic of top British political and military leaders. However, the analysis of military operations is less than comprehensive: Irwin, Mahoney and Iron provide a brief overview of the British Army's campaign over more than thirty years, while Neumann does not delve into operational detail, being more concerned with politics and diplomacy.[22]

Michael Dewar, a former Royal Green Jackets officer, has written a vivid and sympathetic account of the Army's operations in Northern Ireland during the 1970s. Dewar observes that the Army acted with great restraint and probity, albeit taking some time to acquire situational awareness and actionable intelligence.[23] Dewar's work echoes some of the earlier conclusions of Robin Evelegh, who, following his retirement from the Army in 1977, wrote a book castigating the British government for forcing the Army to adhere to peacetime legislation during a time of military emergency.[24]

21 C. Andrew, *Defence of the Realm: The Authorized History of MI5* (London: Allen Lane, 2009), 645; M. Kirk-Smith and J. Dingley, 'Countering Terrorism in Northern Ireland: The Role of Intelligence', *Small Wars and Insurgencies* 20 (3–4) (2009), 551–573; K. Jeffery, 'Security Policy in Northern Ireland: Some Reflections on the Management of Violent Conflict', *Terrorism and Political Violence* 2 (1990), 21–34; A. Sanders, 'Northern Ireland: The Intelligence War 1969–1975', *British Journal of Politics and International Relations* 13 (2) (2011), 230–248.

22 See R. Iron, 'Britain's Longest War: Northern Ireland, 1967–2007', in D. Marston and C. Malkasian (eds), *Counterinsurgency in Modern Warfare* (London: Osprey Publishing, 2008), 167–185; P. Neumann, *Britain's Long War: British Strategy in the Northern Ireland Conflict, 1968–98* (Basingstoke: Palgrave Macmillan, 2003); P. Dixon, 'Hearts and Minds? British Counter-insurgency from Malaya to Iraq', *Journal of Strategic Studies* 32(3) (2009), 353–381; A. Irwin and M. Mahoney, 'The Military Response', in J. Dingley (ed.), *Combating Terrorism in Northern Ireland* (London: Routledge, 2009), 198–226.

23 M. Dewar, *The British Army in Northern Ireland* (London: Arms and Armour, 1985), 60.

24 R. Evelagh, *Peace Keeping in a Democratic Society: The Lessons of Northern Ireland* (London: McGill–Queen's University Press, 1978).

Andrew Sanders and Ian Wood have contributed a highly original historical account of the experiences of British soldiers in the early years of Operation Banner. Dipping into the experiences of individual soldiers across a wide range of different units, they capture the confusion and complexity of operations when violence was at its height in Northern Ireland. Sanders and Wood's work is similar to that of Desmond Hamill, who conducted many interviews of soldiers who served on Operation Banner, collating Army voices and experiences.[25] However, these works do not systematically examine different unit experiences; the chapters follow Northern Irish events rather than the battalions themselves, plucking apt military participant accounts as the narrative progresses.

Much has been made of specific incidents in the British Army's campaign in Northern Ireland, investigations into alleged 'shoot-to-kill' policies and atrocities such as Bloody Sunday.[26] British Army interrogation methods in the early 1970s have been closely examined by scholars: for example, Huw Bennett has provided a rigorous study of allegations of British Army mistreatment of prisoners in the early 1970s, concluding that there were more incidents of soldiers committing criminal acts against the local population than the Army was prepared to admit at the time.[27] Charles Townshend has also written of Britain's 'direct importation' of colonial interrogation methods from Aden, methods which were later indicted as torture by the European Court of Human Rights.[28]

Relatively little scholarly attention has been focused on soldiers' cultural perceptions of Northern Ireland, despite frequent Republican

---

25 D. Hamill, *Pig in the Middle – The Army in Northern Ireland, 1969–1984* (London: Methuen, 1985); A. Sanders and I. Wood, *Times of Troubles: Britain's War in Northern Ireland* (Edinburgh: Edinburgh University Press, 2012).

26 See N. O'Dochartaigh, 'Bloody Sunday: Error or Design?', *Contemporary British History*, 24(1) (2010), 89–108; D. Benest, 'Aden to Northern Ireland, 1966–76', in H. Strachan (ed.), *Big Wars and Small Wars: The British Army and the Lessons of War in the Twentieth Century* (London: Routledge, 2006), 115–145; F. Ní Aoláin, *The Politics of Force: Conflict Management and State Violence in Northern Ireland* (Belfast: Blackstaff Press, 2000), 76–83.

27 H. Bennett, '"Smoke Without Fire"? Allegations against the British Army in Northern Ireland, 1972–5', *Twentieth Century British History* 24(2) (2013), 280.

28 C. Townshend, *Britain's Civil Wars* (London: Faber and Faber, 1986), 70–71.

assertions about Scottish soldiers' inherent 'Orange bias'.[29] More broadly, Graham Walker and Ian Wood, among others, have valuably explored the ties and tensions between Scotland and Ulster during the twentieth century, concluding that Loyalist paramilitary groups had a very modest impact in Britain during the 1970s.[30] By probing into the working lives of Scottish soldiers, drawing on unpublished diaries and other contemporaneous sources, it is possible to test claims of sectarian behaviour among Scottish soldiers. Scottish units have been deliberately selected because of their cultural affinity with Ulster over the centuries – the significant exchange of populations, imagery and ideas – in order to gain an insight into how soldiers coped with carrying out repressive and difficult actions among the population many regarded as 'kith and kin'. The early years of Operation Banner allows for a valuable view of counterinsurgency and counter-terrorism at its most intimate – close to home. Scots made up approximately 13 per cent of the British Army's infantry for much of the latter part of the twentieth century.[31]   Nevertheless, relative to overall numbers, Scottish soldiers frequently played a central role in Operation Banner – at one point in 1975 the Northern Ireland Office pointed out that every battalion deployed in Belfast was Scottish or 'had a strong Scottish element'.[32] During the summer of 1972, Scottish units were responsible for all of South Down, South Armagh (Argyll and Sutherland Highlanders, Royal Scots Dragoon Guards) and East Tyrone (Queen's Own Highlanders) – a 'tartan belt' across the border. Scottish officers also observed that because Irish and Gurkha regiments were not permitted to serve on operations in Northern Ireland during much of Operation Banner – these, like Scottish (particularly Highland) regiments, had significant recent counter-insurgency experience – this placed a greater strain and emphasis on Scottish deployments during Operation Banner.[33]

29 G. Adams, *Before the Dawn: An Autobiography* (London: William Heinemann, 1996), 136–137.

30 See I. Wood (ed.), *Scotland and Ulster* (Edinburgh: Mercat Press, 1993); G. Walker, *Intimate Strangers, Political and Cultural Interaction between Scotland and Ulster in Modern Times* (Edinburgh: John Donald, 1995).

31 'The Myth of the Tartan Army', *Herald*, July 24, 2011.

32 TNA: CJ 4/1290 Army – Northern Ireland Officer, 1975–1976, Letter from SS Bampton to Permanent Under Secretary of State at the Northern Ireland Office, dated August 8, 1975.

33 A. Beevor, *Inside the British Army* (London: Corgi Books, 1991), 308.

This study does not apologise for viewing the British Army through such a Caledonian prism; it does not pretend to be a definitive history of Operation Banner. Others are welcome closely to examine the experience of other nations within the British Army to test the cultural strains of their experience of war within the British Isles.

The second area where this study makes an original contribution is in the analysis of the vital role played by small unit culture during Operation Banner. Eyal Ben-Ari has written of his regret at not being able to contrast the Israeli Defence Forces' small unit culture and experiences of asymmetric warfare with an equivalent study of the British Army in Northern Ireland.[34] Ben-Ari observes that an understanding of formal and informal education in the Army – how group norms and loyalties are inculcated – is central to explaining soldiers' behaviour, including how group norms are inculcated.[35] In a highly influential article published shortly after the end of the Second World War, Edward Shils and Morris Janowitz argued that high levels of social cohesion within the German Army are central to explaining why German soldiers fought so tenaciously until near the end of the war.[36] In recent years, Leonard Wong et al. have reasserted the emphasis of Shils and Janowitz on social cohesion as a determinant of battlefield behaviour.[37] By contrast, Anthony King has emphasised the primacy of professional or task cohesion in all-volunteer forces as a key determinant in battle performance. Soldiers take professional pride in their training and skills; they want to achieve goals in order to demonstrate that capability. Friendship between soldiers was not a decisive factor.[38] It is my contention that, although King is right to stress professional training, pride and combat craft as a key determinant in soldiers' behaviour under fire, soldiers in Ulster were also strongly motivated by their emotions. Feelings of fear, isolation and, above all, a desire to avenge the fallen were also important influences on their operational behaviour.

---

34 E. Ben-Ari, *Mastering Soldiers* (New York: Berghahn, 1998), 2.

35 Ben-Ari, *Mastering Soldiers*, 2.

36 E. Shils and M. Janowitz, 'Cohesion and Disintegration in the Wehrmacht in the Second World War', *Public Opinion Quarterly* 12(2) (1948), 280–315.

37 L. Wong, T.A. Kolditz, R.A. Millen and T.M. Potten, *Why They Fight: Combat Motivation in the Iraq War* (Carlisle, Pa.: US Army War College, 2003).

38 A. King, *The Combat Soldier: Infantry Tactics and Cohesion in the Twentieth and Twenty-First Centuries* (Oxford: Oxford University Press, 2013), 352.

Third, this study also argues that existing literature contains some assumptions or orthodoxies that require correction. Aaron Edwards has recently teased out some of the strategic and operational dilemmas that faced the British Army in a concise and original guide to the main events and players in the Northern Ireland conflict.[39] Edwards contends that, 'Perhaps the biggest stimulant in the Army's lesson-learning process was the decision by senior military commanders to take steps to admit its mistakes.'[40] I come to a different conclusion, namely that Headquarters Northern Ireland (HQNI) and relevant brigade headquarters were often slow to investigate abuses of local civilians by soldiers, which in turn fuelled general hostility towards the Army. Meanwhile, rotating battalions failed to share information about IRA tactics in their areas of operation. The Army's own 'end of mission' report for Operation Banner also concludes that the relationship between brigades and battalions was too 'laissez faire'.[41]

A casual disregard and contempt for the civilian populace at the top was occasionally replicated and exacerbated by soldiers on the ground: instead of correcting prejudices, senior commanders occasionally fuelled them. I conclude that senior officers in HQNI did not quickly learn from its mistakes in 1971 and 1972 – an imperative characteristic of any successful counterinsurgency campaign.[42] It was often up to pivotal civilian leaders such as William Whitelaw, Secretary of State for Northern Ireland, to learn lessons for them, pressing for a more judicious use of force and oversight.

Fionnuala Ní Aoláin uses the terms 'set piece deaths' and 'pre-planned operations' to suggest that the more controversial killings of civilians by British soldiers were rendered unavoidable due to structures of command and training in the British Army. She argues that because elite soldiers are trained to set ambushes and kill people, they will inevitably use maximum, lethal force in a situation where they are

---

39 A. Edwards, *The Northern Ireland Troubles: Operation Banner, 1969–2007* (Oxford: Osprey Publishing, 2011).
40 Edwards, *The Northern Ireland Troubles*, 84.
41 British Army, *Operation Banner: An Analysis of Military Operations in Northern Ireland* (London: Ministry of Defence, 2006), 2.10.
42 J. Nagl, *Learning to Eat Soup with a Knife: Counterinsurgency Lessons from Malaya and Vietnam* (Chicago: University of Chicago, 2005), 6–7.

confronting potentially armed IRA Volunteers.[43] Such an analysis is too simplistic. It removes the autonomy of decision-making from soldiers in particular circumstances.[44] Army units self-evidently have officers and NCOs with different personalities, desires and experiences. They, in turn, operate under different commanders at various times during the conflict; these may demonstrate alternative levels of competence, aggression and oversight. These distinguishing characteristics are critical to understanding why individual units, occasionally even within the same battalion, may interpret an order and execute it differently. It is important to suspend judgement, not to over-generalise but to examine each incident in terms of the protagonists; their command structure, unit culture and recent operational history, local circumstances and specific orders. Such a process is laborious but it is necessary in order to draw accurate, incident-specific conclusions. Moreover, contrary to Ní Aoláin's general conclusions, I argue that soldiers in Northern Ireland found it more difficult to take life in Northern Ireland than in other conflicts. Highly trained soldiers, including those from elite regiments, often froze when confronted with a legitimate opportunity to kill.

Fourth, this study also contends that there are aspects of wider scholarly literatures that can throw more light on our understanding of the British Army. I draw upon literature from sociology, anthropology, psychology and criminology, including on gang culture and gang violence, to help explain the behaviour of soldiers in Northern Ireland. Among the relevant studies cited in this study is that by sociologist Ruth Horowitz on Chicano street gangs in Chicago. Horowitz observed that groups of young men in gangs establish narratives of collective group violence or toughness and strive to maintain that reputation.[45] Narratives of 'mythic violence' – 'the legends and stories shared by gang members about their participation in violence' – increases group cohesion but also leads to expectations that the group will react in a highly aggressive, uncompromising manner if challenged.[46] Psychiatrist Gwen Adshead, in responding to the summary execution of a wounded Taliban prisoner

---

43 Ní Aoláin, *The Politics of Force*, 76–83.

44 Ní Aoláin, *The Politics of Force*, 76–83.

45 R. Horowitz, *Honor and the American Dream: Culture and Identity in a Chicano Community* (New Brunswick, NJ: Rutgers University Press, 1992), 93.

46 S. Decker and B. Van Winkle, *Life in the Gang: Family, Friends and Violence* (Cambridge: Cambridge University Press, 1996), 69.

on September 15, 2011 by Royal Marine Sergeant Alexander Blackman, noted that the incident had 'more in common with gang violence in a way than it does with regular homicide ... knowing that it may be wrong in the eyes of others but from their own perspective, from the code of the gang warfare, there is a type of honour to it'.[47] Meanwhile, the tendency to demonise and dehumanise irregular fighters, who normally seek to avoid sustained, direct confrontation, has been carefully elucidated by Sibylle Scheipers and will be drawn upon here in the case of Northern Ireland.[48]

Other scholars have also observed a pronounced risk of deviancy among small groups of soldier during insurgencies. Pascal Vennesson has defined 'deviant cohesion' as a situation where a military unit's actions are believed, by the perpetrators at least, to support 'operational goals at the tactical and operational level' but which contradict 'the self-identity promoted by the Army as a whole and has negative strategic and political consequences'.[49] Michael Ignatieff has written about the need to study the 'micro ethics' in military groups to understand the actions of soldiers in complex, low-intensity operations. Ignatieff argues that the evolving social interactions of soldiers with a local population, the deconstruction of grievance narratives and justifications for actions, is vital to understand the trajectory of a conflict in key pressure point areas. Ignatieff suggests that 'all conflict is local'. As soldiers in small units came to know a relatively limited geographical area during a counter-insurgency campaign, grievances against the local population may become important triggers for group deviancy with wide-ranging political and military consequences. In other words (and in a nod to Clausewitz), such personalised micro-wars within a wider campaign develop their own local grammar.[50] To analyse these micro-conflicts requires the close study of small units of soldiers deployed to these

---

47 Dr Gwen Adshead, interviewed in the BBC television documentary, 'Marine A: Criminal or Casualty of War', first broadcast on BBC 1, April 9, 2014.

48 S. Scheipers, *Unlawful Combatants: A Genealogy of the Irregular Fighter* (Oxford: Oxford University Press, 2015).

49 P. Vennesson, 'Cohesion and Misconduct: The French Army and the Mahé Affair', in A. King (ed.), *Frontline: Combat and Cohesion in the Twenty-First Century* (Oxford: Oxford University Press, 2015), 236.

50 H. Strachan, *Clausewitz's 'On War': A Biography* (London: Atlantic Books, 2007), 69–70.

areas, including their formal and informal leaders, their desires, past experiences and fears, and not simply the orders they have been given.[51]

Modern military institutions are understandably reluctant to acknowledge that their soldiers can come to hate a civilian population and/or their enemies. Their work is supposed to be that of a science; soldiers should use violence professionally according to cold calculations. Erella Grassiani points out how frequently militaries and governments seek immediately to explain away military atrocities as the result of one or a very few 'rotten apples', thereby refusing to examine the wider group processes at play – effectively isolating a guilty individual from the small, constant group of individuals whom he influences and is, in turn, influenced by.[52] Grassiani, drawing upon Arne Johan Vetlesen's research on concepts of morality, has also argued that 'Physical proximity/distance is not enough to explain immoral behaviour or the avoidance of it; it is also important to look at the way we perceive this person and at our relationship with them.'[53] Rising resentment towards a non-compliant, potentially complicit local population, augmented by sharp bursts of anger following the death or wounding of a popular soldier, can ultimately prompt soldiers to contemplate actions they would previously have regarded as contrary to sound military practice and their own moral values.

Donna Winslow has described 'hyper-investment' in the military, a situation where 'unit pride can become so exaggerated that one only respects the members of one's unit, ignoring and sometimes resenting those outside the group. What is clearly an effective and necessary attitude [small unit cohesion] for the battlefield can then become an exaggerated force which undermines good order and discipline.'[54] These

---

51 M. Ignatieff, 'Handcuffing the Military? Military Judgment, Rules of Engagement and Public Scrutiny', in P. Mileham and L. Willett (eds), *Military Ethics for the Expeditionary Era* (London: Royal Institute of International Affairs, 2001), 25–33.

52 E. Grassiani, *Soldiering under Occupation* (Oxford: Berghahn, 2013), 1.

53 Grassiani, *Soldiering under Occupation*, 24. See also A. Vetlesen, *Evil and Human Agency: Understanding Collective Evildoing* (Cambridge: Cambridge University Press, 2005).

54 D. Winslow, *The Canadian Airborne Regiment in Somalia: A Socio-Cultural Inquiry. A Study Prepared for the Commission of Inquiry into the Deployment of Canadian Forces to Somalia* (Ottawa: Ministry of Public Works, 1997), 263.

same responses or instincts, finely honed in training, can also lead to acts of deviancy if a unit's desire to assert its absolute physical dominance area of operations and/or over rival groups of young men is not contained or tempered by the wider institution, the Army, to which they belong. Fuelled by resentment and consumed by an immediate threat, a group could construct their own 'micro-ethics' or justification for 'hitting back', beyond the role and rules to which they were expected to adhere. In short, the Army seeks to foster cohesion in small units but then may fail to limit its growth to a state of group hyper-investment, resulting in deviant behaviour that works against the military interest.[55]

According to Keith Jeffery, hyper-investment among small groups of counter-insurgents can be further exacerbated where there is an apparent political deadlock and a shortage of actionable intelligence, leading to physical inertia on the part of the security forces. Soldiers, trained according to norms demanding positive action, look for unconventional means to overcome an asymmetric enemy, using methods that are often politically disastrous.[56] David Charters has pointed out that 'special operations by their very nature are conducted in a legal and moral twilight zone; if control or discipline fails, they become merely a guise for counter-terror which reduces the government and the security forces to the status of criminals'.[57] As I will observe later, 'counter-terror' was exactly what soldiers from D Company, 1 Argylls, visited upon County Fermanagh in October 1972.

Charles Moskos and Laura Miller have questioned the suitability of sending soldiers with a hyper-masculine, aggressive, warrior ethos to fulfil complex roles requiring tact and restraint. In the case of US soldiers and marines in Somalia on Operation Restore Hope – initially a humanitarian mission, Moskos and Miller observed how combat troops, under occasional attack from rebel groups, came collectively to view the entire Somali population as their enemies.[58] Meanwhile, the influential French

55 E. Durkheim, 'The Normal and the Pathological', reprinted in E.J. Clarke and D.H. Kelly (eds), *Deviant Behaviour: A Text Reader in the Sociology of Deviance* (New York: Worth, 2003), 80–81.
56 Jeffery, 'Security Policy in Northern Ireland: Some Reflections on the Management of Violent Conflict', 32.
57 D. Charters, 'The Changing Forms of Conflict in Northern Ireland', *Journal of Conflict Studies* 1(2) (1980), 37.
58 L. Miller and C. Moskos, 'Humanitarians or Warriors? Race, Gender and

strategist, David Galula, concluded that soldiers dedicated to mobile warfare (such as Paratroopers) were often unsuited to the more static, often less kinetic, duties of counterinsurgency.[59] Charles Townshend has described such a counter-productive mixture of excessive cohesion and aggression in the case of Northern Ireland, noting that 'the employment of self-conscious elite units such as paratroops in urban policing has had disastrous results.'[60] More recently, Frank Ledwidge has observed a tendency among senior British officers in Afghanistan to reward aggression, when restraint may be the better course of action. (This problem is not new – as we will see, it was also a characteristic of early operations in Northern Ireland.)[61]

Today's officers recall lessons predominantly from the end period of Operation Banner (when they themselves served in the Province). Soldiers very rarely came under fire, if at all, and were acting in support of a capable, informed and motivated police force, the Royal Ulster Constabulary (RUC). According to these soldiers the campaign in Northern Ireland was characterised by battalions measuring success by the absence of fire fights and a lack of positive military action; the aim was not to fire a shot.[62] But this was not a realistic objective during the chaotic and very violent days of 1971–1972 – when 1st Battalion, Scots Guards (1 Scots Guards) suffered 55 casualties (including five dead) and 1st Battalion, Argyll and Sutherland Highlanders (1 Argylls) suffered eight fatalities on a four-month tour (a period when the RUC were mostly unarmed, demotivated and absent from many Catholic urban, and some rural, areas). During this phase of the conflict frequent fire fights were inevitable for any battalion. As we shall see, many soldiers during this period measured success according to aggressive operations. Instead of assuming that 'minimum force' was a constant in Northern Ireland, there are lessons for military command in those occasional incidents of excessive violence that occurred in the early, confused days of Operation Banner, such as the shooting of a number of

Combat Status in Operation Restore Hope', *Armed Forces and Society* 21(4), 613–637.
59 D. Galula, *Counterinsurgency Warfare* (Westport, Conn.: Praeger Security International, 2006), 67.
60 Townshend, *Britain's Civil Wars*, 71.
61 F. Ledwidge, *Losing Small Wars: British Military Failure in Iraq and Afghanistan* (New Haven, Conn.: Yale University Press, 2011), 183–184.
62 Ledwidge, *Losing Small War*, 183–184.

civilians, including an unarmed mother of eight children and a local priest, in Ballymurphy at the beginning of internment (Operation Demetrius) during August 9–11, 1971.[63]

The stabbing to death of two County Fermanagh men, Michael Naan and Andrew Murray, by a group of Argyll NCOs on October 23, 1972 also offers an instructive episode for future officer and NCO training, namely how mid-ranking and junior leaders should manage a desire for vengeance and restrain violence when units start taking casualties. Lessons from Fermanagh, where D Company, 1 Argylls had been briefly deployed, on command, cohesion, interrogation, the proper gathering and use of intelligence could have been learned long before the Iraqi hotel receptionist Baha Musa died after being mistreated by soldiers from the Queen's Lancashire Regiment in Iraq in 2003, an incident that bears some resemblance to the murders of Naan and Murray 31 years earlier. The British Army, to its own detriment, has been highly selective when it comes to the lessons it has learned from its Northern Ireland campaign.[64] Managing soldiers' expectations, including their desire for combat, is complicated in any overseas operation situation. It was even more difficult at home in the UK, under the full glare of public scrutiny.

The Case Studies:
The Scots Guards and the Argyll and Sutherland Highlanders

This study is part micro-history and part ethnography. It seeks to fill a gap in the academic literature of the British Army in Northern Ireland by exploring the motivations, orientation and decision-making of small Army units that experienced relatively high levels of casualties at a uniquely dangerous period in the Army's long campaign in Northern Ireland. In studies such as Sanders and Wood, soldiers are introduced, cited in a single few lines before the authors move on to the next account of a historical event, ranging across the decades of the Northern Irish conflict. Here I take a more in-depth and focused approach; I follow two regiments and their sub-units before, during and after their initial deployment to Northern Ireland. I explore how the death or injury

---

63 M. McCleery, *Operation Demetrius and its Aftermath* (Manchester: Manchester University Press, 2015), 58–59.
64 Ledwidge, *Losing Small Wars*, 29–30.

of soldiers affected these units' outlook and their behaviour towards the local population. This is not to criticise Sanders and Wood or Hamill, whose wide-ranging narratives provide rich source-material and first-hand accounts of key events, but is instead meant to be a complementary extension of their work.

Taking illustrative events that occurred during the exceptionally violent tours of 1st Battalion, Scots Guards (1 Scots Guards, West Belfast, August–December 1971; area of operations: part of the Lower Falls, St James', parts of Beechmount, Ballymurphy, parts of Turf Lodge); 2nd Battalion, Scots Guards (2 Scots Guards, Derry, July–November 1972; area of operations: City/Bogside and Brandywell) and 1st Battalion, Argyll and Sutherland Highlanders (1 Argylls, July–November 1972; area of operations: RUC H Division – South Down and South Armagh; A Company, detached to serve under 1st Battalion, Queen's Own Highlanders throughout – east Tyrone, Dungannon, Cookstown; D Company – South Fermanagh, Lisnaskea, Newtownbutler, Belleek, October 21–27, 1972), I examine the political, social and operational context that informed soldiers' actions and responses. This study is interested primarily in the combat side of military professionalism, as opposed to administrative or support roles. It provides a bottom-up analysis of military life in a hostile environment but also covers what Ben-Ari has described as the 'little-explored areas such as socialisation into military life, the different criteria by which soldiers appraise themselves and their service, or the creation within the armed forces of certain folk images and stereotypes.'[65]

The number of interviews and the amount of archival research required for an in-depth analysis of regimental/battalion and sub-unit culture (a battalion in 1971 was composed of approximately 500 to 700 men) necessitated a narrowing of focus down to two regiments, the Scots Guards and the Argyll and Sutherland Highlanders. There are some similarities between the two. Both are Scottish infantry regiments, infused with pride in their combat readiness, unit cohesion and toughness. They were deployed on active service during the 'End of Empire' counter-insurgency and internal security campaigns from the 1940s to the end of the 1960s. Both regiments were seriously affected by the Labour government's defence cuts at the outset of Operation Banner (2 Scots

65 Ben-Ari, *Mastering Soldiers*, 18.

Guards was effectively mothballed for a period in 1971 – its companies scattered among other units of the Household Division. Meanwhile, the Argylls' single battalion in the Scottish Division was very briefly reduced to a reinforced company in that same year). By 1972, both regiments were largely back to their pre-1969 numbers – the Argylls were back up to full battalion strength and 2 Scots Guards had also been reformed. Both regiments saw regular deployments to Northern Ireland in the early years of Operation Banner, in the most violent areas of the province, and saw some of the heaviest casualties among the battalions deployed to Northern Ireland in the early years of Operation Banner. Eight soldiers serving under 1 Argylls command were killed on one tour of Northern Ireland in 1972 and 12 Scots guardsmen lost their lives in IRA attacks between 1971 and 1974.[66] This study focuses on the three most violent and deadly of the Scots Guards and Argylls' tours of Northern Ireland, all of which occurred between 1971 and 1972.

Both regiments enjoyed strong political connections in the early 1970s: the former commanding officer (CO) of 1 Argylls during its 1967 tour of Aden, Colonel Colin Mitchell, successfully campaigned as a Conservative MP to save his regiment from disbandment. Another former Argyll officer, George Younger, 4th Viscount Younger of Leckie, was an MP for Ayr and would later go on to become Secretary of State for Defence between 1986 and 1989.[67] Major William Whitelaw, the first Secretary of State for Northern Ireland after the suspension of the Northern Irish executive in March 1972, was a decorated Scots Guards officer, winning a military cross as a tank commander during the Normandy campaign.[68] However, there are also clear differences between the two regiments. The Argyll and Sutherland Highlanders was

66 See D. McKittrick, S. Kelters, B. Feeney and C. Thornton, *Lost Lives* (Edinburgh: Mainstream, 1999).

67 C. Mitchell, *Having Been a Soldier* (London: Hamish Hamilton, 1969); W. Whitelaw, *The Whitelaw Memoirs* (London: Aurum Press, 1989); D. Torrance, *George Younger: A Life Well Lived* (Edinburgh: Berlinn, 2008).

68 Major Whitelaw felt a profound guilt over the casualties suffered by his 3rd Battalion, Scots Guards tank squadron at the Battle of Caumont Ridge on July 30, 1944, a day that 'profoundly influenced my character and thus my reactions to different events for the rest of my life'. Whitelaw was awarded the Military Cross for his actions at Caumont where the British Army was outgunned by the new German JAGD Panther tanks. W. Whitelaw, *The Whitelaw Memoirs*, 18–24.

the most junior (most recently founded) highland regiment and recruited from a counties base that comprised the counties to the immediate west and east of Glasgow (but notably did not recruit from Glasgow itself).[69] By contrast, the Scots Guards was a regiment of the Foot Guards and Household Division – officered by a close-knit social elite, including senior members of the Scottish aristocracy. Scots Guards officers were socially upper class – almost all public school educated and many with English rather than Scottish backgrounds. One prospective candidate for the Scots Guards in the early 1960s recalled that he was deeply concerned about the prohibitive costs of being a Guards officer, not least the tailoring bills.[70] Many Scots Guards officers would have been educated at Eton, Wellington or Winchester. A number of Argyll officers were also educated at elite public schools, including Harrow, Eton and Marlborough but also from some of the Scottish public schools such as Dollar and Glenalmond. In the early 1970s, prompted by a shortage of officers due to disbandment, the Argyll and Sutherland Highlanders began to recruit additional officers from these prestigious Scottish schools.[71] In sum, the Scots Guards and the Argyll Sutherland Highlanders were selected because of *both* their cultural and operational similarities and divergences. They share sufficient commonalities – Scottish, combat effective, politically influential, they both took significant casualties in Northern Ireland and were involved in frequent fire fights – but also clear differences – the Argylls as a relatively new, more county-based, junior regiment, were slightly less socially elite than the Scots Guards, with a greater reputation for aggression, bordering on insubordination, that had been honed under Colonel Colin Mitchell; they also served in a rural area of operations in Northern Ireland unlike the Scots Guards – to make for an interesting comparison within the context of Operation Banner in 1971 and 1972.

---

69 The Argyll traditional recruiting areas are Argyllshire, Stirlingshire, Clackmannanshire, Dunbartonshire, Renfrewshire and Kinross-shire.

70 Interview with Scots Guards Soldier 8 (Officer), March 2013. The historian Antony Beevor, a former cavalry officer, provides an excellent account of the social backgrounds of many British Army Regiments; Beevor, *Inside the British Army*.

71 Interview with Scots Guards Soldier 8 (Officer), March 2013; Interview with Argyll Soldier 10 (Officer), December 2013; Interview with Argyll Soldier 5 (Officer), May 2014; Interview with Argyll Soldier 30 (Officer), December 2016.

Introduction

The Challenge of Source Material

In his account of the war in Vietnam, the historian Bernd Greiner observed the limitations of only studying military history through the use of archives. Such files, he noted, 'contain painstaking entries about supposedly stolen bags of rice or the numbers of chickens requisitioned, but where little is to be found about the "command climate", apart from stereotypical records of successes'.[72] These relatively pristine reports written in a spare military lexicon did not reflect the true experience of soldiers at the front but rather 'the professional fears of their authors'.[73] In the same vein, an Argyll officer warned that, when it came to compiling battalion reports or regimental histories, 'You put into it what you are going to admit to.'[74] Shouting matches between a battalion commanding officer and his company commanders are unlikely to be recorded in any official records. However, the careful scrutiny of battalion log books, commanders' war diaries, adjutants' reports and soldiers' journals does occasionally hint at challenges or events not later recorded in official regimental histories. So too does the trawling of local material, including, newspapers, court documents, police reports and memoirs. Then the best course of action is simply to ask key individuals, military and civilian, about what happened and compare accounts, using extant information from other witnesses to the events in question. Here I have tried not to rely upon single interview sources but have examined other evidence to corroborate or refute interviewee testimony. In the case of allegations of misconduct made by civilians against soldiers or by soldiers against other soldiers that are uncorroborated by court proceedings, I have been careful to cite them as such, and have left out material that could not be confirmed by more than one participant/witness or by material available in archival sources.

Fortunately, in the case of the Scots Guards and Argyll and Sutherland Highlanders, the significant majority of participants and witnesses to operations in Northern Ireland in 1971 and 1972 are alive and many are willing to speak about their experiences. Such interviews are central to the following discussion about formal and informal leadership structures,

---

72 B. Greiner, *War without Fronts: The USA in Vietnam* (London: Random House, 2009), 90.
73 Greiner, *War without Fronts,* 89.
74 Interview with Argyll Soldier 15 (Officer), December 2013.

attitudes towards the local population, intelligence, cohesion, definitions of success and combat experiences. Almost all of those interviewed had not been consulted before about their experiences. Soldiers described six-hour gun battles in West Belfast, cross-border operations into the Republic of Ireland, and the murder of Michael Naan and Andrew Murray in County Fermanagh in 1972. They also talked about more mundane but significant interactions such as the hardening of attitudes towards the local populace, boredom and the long-term effects of serving in Northern Ireland. Thirty-six former British military personnel were interviewed in total, many on more than one occasion. Fifteen former Argylls were interviewed (all ranks) and 18 former Scots Guards (all ranks) were interviewed between 2013 and 2015. I also interviewed a full-time Ulster Defence Regiment (the largely part-time, local Army unit in Northern Ireland) officer attached to 4th Battalion (Fermanagh), UDR, a former Military Intelligence officer (attached to HQNI in Lisburn), a former Royal Scots Dragoon Guards officer and two senior RUC officers. A number of soldiers also sent personal correspondence or permitted access to personal diaries, photographs and other material relating to their military service. I also interviewed, by phone and email, two US Navy sailors who in 1972 were based at the United States Naval Communications Station (NAVCOMMSTA) in Derry. It was more straightforward to contact former officers and senior NCOs than ordinary private soldiers or guardsmen – many of whom only spent a relatively short time in the Army. Officers and NCOs make up the bulk of interviewees – which obviously impacts upon the research results. Much of the discussion in the study is focused on senior and junior leaders' experiences within a battalion, but wherever possible I have tried to contrast such views with those of private soldiers/guardsmen interviewed. A number of key police and civilian witnesses were also consulted; eight granted interviews – Bishop Edward Daly, Roman Catholic Bishop Emeritus of Derry, Henry Crichton, 6th Earl of Erne KCVO (both now deceased), Frank McManus, independent Republican MP for Fermanagh and South Tyrone (1970–1974), two former RUC officers, three legal professionals involved in the trial of Argyll soldiers for murder, Fergus McQuillan, a former Social Democratic and Labour Party representative in County Fermanagh, and a former representative of Official Sinn Féin from South Down, who preferred not to be named. I also conducted an interview with James Naan, the nephew of Michael Naan, who was murdered by soldiers from 13 Platoon, D Company, 1 Argylls.

It became clear early in this research that, for a variety of reasons, including personal security, military interviewees did not wish to be quoted by name and granted interviews only on the condition that their identities would not be made readily available. Instead of using pseudonyms I have simply employed interview reference numbers and rank identification – for example, 'Interview with Argyll Soldier 2 (officer), November 2013'. To obscure further a soldier's true identity, I have occasionally given a soldier more than one number. I have also been deliberately vague about the place and dates of interviews. The ranks given here correspond to those which interviewees held while serving in Northern Ireland between 1971 and 1972. Sanders and Wood have employed a similar approach in their work on the Army in Northern Ireland.[75] All the soldiers interviewed are now retired, but here I continue to refer to them as soldiers (not ex-soldiers).

All interviews were semi-structured, designed to allow sufficient flexibility to observe group dynamics or to explore themes that appear to be of particular focus or interest to the interviewee, itself an insight into experience.[76] Highly structured interviews risk formulaic or generic responses and can obscure valuable clues to group values and individual experience and character.[77] Interviews were mostly conducted with individual soldiers, with the exception of one group interview (in which five guardsmen took part), and normally lasted between two and four hours. Most interviews were conducted in soldiers' homes, where interviewees appeared to be most comfortable. During individual and particularly group interviews, I was conscious of the dangers of prompting memories through leading questions or overwhelming interviewees with details of events they had taken part in but might have mostly forgotten. During a general conversation about the nature of soldiering in Northern Ireland, I would ask soldiers for examples from their experiences. The results were often highly illuminating and unprompted. During a group interview with five Scots Guardsmen, I was surprised that individual soldiers generally stuck to original accounts, even when challenged by other members of the group. They related events according to their own

75 Sanders and Wood, *Times of Troubles*.
76 A. Bryman, *Social Research Methods* (Oxford: Oxford University Press, 2004), 30.
77 F. Bechofer and L. Paterson, *Principles of Research and Design in the Social Sciences* (London: Routledge, 2000), 62–63.

perceptions, and were less susceptible to group narrative pressures than I had expected from a reading of literature on social sciences' interview techniques.[78] Former rank structures did resurface to an extent: some interviewees in the group session were occasionally interrupted and corrected by the most senior former NCO in the room – but individuals did not change their version of events.

I have remained conscious of the limitations of interviews conducted more than 40 years after events; hence my emphasis on using extensive archival sources to corroborate accounts. Soldiers interviewed could generally recall the details of specific operations in Northern Ireland, particularly significant, searing events, such as fire fights, that occurred during their tours there, but often could not remember local detail such as the names of RUC officers and civilians they encountered during their separate tours. Interviewees' abilities to recollect also differed: some interviewees could recall remarkably vivid details that proved to be accurate upon corroboration by contemporaneous written sources. At the other end of the scale there were two interviewees who could only offer generalities. Some interviewees were simply better communicators; several were published writers. For every wordsmith, there was a plain soldier; the latter's insights could be told with a laconic candour, also highly revealing in its unadorned simplicity and bluntness. Nevertheless, the very subjective nature of perception and memory, the capacity for exaggeration and invention, mean that I have treated single source interviewee accounts of incidents with a lot of caution and have looked for corroboration in every instance.

I have made extensive use of government, museum, military and newspaper archives from across the UK and Ireland. On several occasions, the public record office of Northern Ireland (PRONI) kindly acceded to freedom of information requests. The crown office and procurator fiscal service (COPFS) of Scotland refused my request for partial access to records pertaining to the investigation into accounts of murder and other atrocities made by former soldiers of the Argyll and Sutherland Highlanders who served in Aden, South Yemen during 1967.[79] My efforts to access parts of military files relating to HQNI and respective

---

78 Bechofer and Paterson, *Principles of Research and Design*, 62–63.
79 National Archives of Scotland (NAS), AD 23/58 Linlithgow Procurator Fiscal Records, Precognitions and Productions, 1981–1983.

brigade headquarters held by the National Archives (TNA) at Kew and closed for at least another 50 years were also unsuccessful (I was able to access one open 39 Brigade file for July 1971, one for 3 Brigade for May 1972 but none for 8 Brigade). Consequently, my conclusions dwell more heavily on the battalions' view of the relations with brigade and HQNI than vice versa. But there is sufficient evidence available from open PRONI/TNA files on HQNI, other government departments in London, through the Conservative Party archive in the Bodleian Library at Oxford University and interviewees who worked in HQNI/respective brigade headquarters to gain some insights on the thoughts and plans of senior Army commanders in Northern Ireland in 1971 and 1972. In the case of the court documents relating to the murders of Michael Naan and Andrew Murray near Newtownbutler, on October 23, 1972 and the Coroner's inquest into the death of Edmund Woolsey on September 18, 1972 (all held by PRONI), I agreed not to use the real names of any of the persons identified in the files who are not already in the public record (via newspaper reports or other publications). This was overcome by my gaining access to the same files (plus additional court documents) through the assistance of a former lawyer involved in the trial.

All the battalion war diaries for 2 Scots Guards from the Londonderry 1972 tour have been released by the National Archives in recent years (with a few redacted names). These files are highly illuminating, providing contemporaneous minute-by-minute accounts through battalion watchkeepers' log books, intelligence summaries, situation reports, commanding officer's diaries, adjutant reports, communications with Scots Guards HQ, 8 Brigade HQ and HQNI on the security situation in the Bogside, Creggan and other areas of Londonderry from July to November 1972, a hint of the rich material that lies in wait for future historians once other files are released (the bulk of the UK National Archives WO 305 series for Operation Banner remains closed). Other files, including official war diaries for 1 Scots Guards and 1 Argylls do not appear to be held by the National Archives and could not be traced in the respective regimental museums and archives. Thankfully, both regimental associations made available a wealth of material including battalion diaries and correspondence relating to Operational Banner deployments. Moreover, material held by other regiments that served alongside the Scots Guards and Argylls also proved very useful – including battalion war diaries and other material from the 16th/5th The Queen's Royal Lancers, Royal Scots Dragoon

Guards and a number of Royal Artillery regiments. Such files provided helpful timelines, intelligence and operational reports. I also refer to archival sources dealing with other British Army post-Second World War counterinsurgency campaigns, particularly in Borneo and Aden during the 1960s. These experiences shaped the Army and its regiments and it would be a mistake not to study their features and effects so as to understand the similarities and deviations between Army operations in the colonies and those in Northern Ireland at the outset of Operation Banner. Although regiments are generally careful not to record internal disputes in such documents, one could occasionally read between the lines and ask a pertinent question of an interviewee. For example, the regimental diaries of 1 Scots Guards in Northern Ireland during 1971 recorded an unusual number of incidents of soldiers shooting themselves in the foot.[80]

Personal accounts such as the unpublished memoirs of Private Scott Strichen of the Royal Regiment of Fusiliers held at the National Army Museum and the diary of a young Royal Scots Dragoon Guards intelligence officer, Lieutenant Colin Mitchell (not to be confused with the 1 Argylls' commanding officer, Colonel Colin Mitchell), also offer insights into the frustrations of individual soldiers, even if contemporaneous diaries are prone to exaggeration borne out of a desire to vent frustrations, often at the end of a long, sleep-deprived day. Strichen is intelligent and eloquent but clearly holds a sceptical view of the Army's record in Northern Ireland. Mitchell kept a diary throughout his 1971–1972 tour of Northern Ireland. He comes across as young, outspoken and impatient; his views are politically conservative and he strongly criticises his superiors in the Army for not taking a stronger line against the IRA. He is also critical of those soldiers who seek to punish the wider populace for the crimes of a small number of terrorists. Finally, I also made extensive use of the primary sources, including contemporary Republican and Loyalist pamphlets/newspapers, available in the political collection at the Linen Hall Library in Belfast and at the British Library in London.

---

80 Adjutant's Diary, 1st Battalion, Scots Guards, 1970–1971, Scots Guards Regimental Headquarters, Wellington Barracks, London.

Introduction

Overview

The following text – minus this Introduction and the Conclusion – is divided into four chapters. The first chapter looks at the legacy of empire. It suggests that although the Army emphasised a hyper-masculine group identity, and employed a training programme that had not changed its aims for many years, its values and prejudices were at least partially reflected in wider British society. I also examine the assimilation of new recruits into Army life and the inculcation of automatism and status honour. I argue that the degree of violence that was employed in Malaya, Kenya, Cyprus and Aden was generally much greater than that seen in Northern Ireland, even if the language and tactics employed could occasionally sound similar to the colonial experience. I then analyse the different motivations and leaders that sustained soldiers in combat in Aden, Borneo and elsewhere. I contend that the precise details of regimental histories or symbols matter little and can be easily reinvented. The function is the same; what is important is that these collective myths, memories and symbols represent a compact between individuals who are asserting primacy over other groups that may seek to challenge them.

In the first chapter, I also explore the experiences of the Scots Guards and the Argyll and Sutherland Highlanders in Borneo and Aden during the 1960s. Both Scots Guards battalions had relatively scant combat experience compared with that of 1 Argylls. The Argylls prided themselves on their combat effectiveness – and could act decisively to get rid of 'dead wood': officers or NCOs who were not performing to an expected standard. The Argylls' experiences of insurgency varied considerably: Argyll soldiers showed little animosity towards the local population in Borneo. However, the minority ethnic Chinese population, from whom the Borneo insurgents principally drew their support, was forcibly moved from certain areas, self-evidently reducing the requirement of the Argylls to operate among this populace. In Cyprus and again in Aden, the Argylls came deeply to resent the local population, whom they suspected of harbouring or supporting insurgents. Revenge became an increasingly powerful and occasionally dangerous motivation [modus operandi].

The second chapter provides the wider political, operational and social contexts that set the conditions for the regiments and the three operational tours of duty that are the focus of this study (1 Scots Guards,

West Belfast, August–December 1971; 2 Scots Guards, Londonderry, July–November 1972; and 1 Argyll and Sutherland Highlanders, South Down, South Armagh, East Tyrone and South Fermanagh, July–November 1972). In reviewing the military and political environment of Northern Ireland from 1969 to 1972, I will also build upon the work of such scholars as William Beattie-Smith,[81] Thomas Hennessey,[82] Aaron Edwards,[83] Martin McCleery,[84] Ian Wood and Andrew Sanders,[85] Richard English[86] and Henry Patterson[87] by making use of new archival sources in addition to interviews with protagonists and witnesses to the events described. I offer examples of where military leaders put the blame on their civilian counterparts for failing to capitalise on alleged military gains; I argue that many of these gains were in fact illusory and that the detrimental effects of measures such as the Falls Road curfew, internment, the over-indulgence of Loyalist paramilitary organisations, including the still-legal Ulster Defence Association (UDA) and the methods occasionally employed by the Army in the early years of Operation Banner, adversely hardened relations between the Army and civilians. I also describe the Army's lack of actionable intelligence, the defensiveness, inability or unwillingness of the military to police itself effectively and the lack of a civilian corrective or alternative to address this institutional defect.

After Operation Motorman (Carcan[88] in Londonderry), the military operation to retake urban 'no go areas' from the IRA, the Army's increasing ascendancy in urban areas in late 1972 came at a time of rising insurgency in the rural, border regions. Nevertheless, 1973 saw

---

81 W. Beattie-Smith, *The British State and the Northern Ireland Crisis* (Washington, DC: US Institute for Peace, 2011).

82 T. Hennessey, *Northern Ireland: The Origins of the Northern Ireland Troubles* (Dublin: Gill and Macmillan, 2005).

83 Edwards, *The Northern Ireland Troubles*.

84 McCleery, *Operation Demetrius and its Aftermath*.

85 Sanders and Wood, *Times of Troubles*.

86 English, *Armed Struggle*.

87 H. Patterson, *Violent Frontier* (Basingstoke: Palgrave Macmillan, 2013).

88 The title 'Carcan' was an unfortunate choice. A carcan is 'an iron ring used for a form of public humiliation by exposition at a pole', suggesting a punitive operation rather than one of liberation. J. Bentham, *The Works of Jeremy Bentham* (London: William Tait, 1838), 46.

considerable progress: although the number of house searches remained very high, the Army was more selective in its operations and intelligence was beginning to improve. Moreover, a change in government south of the border in the Republic of Ireland saw better security cooperation between London and Dublin. The Secretary of State for Northern Ireland, William Whitelaw, was the key architect of London's more sophisticated approach to Northern Ireland; Whitelaw believed the Army was too optimistic, short-termist and prone to an overly punitive approach that would squander any political momentum.

Chapter 2 also offers a social or cultural benchmark or prism, through which it is possible to examine the behaviour and attitudes of soldiers in their respective infantry units. I go on to analyse soldiers' interactions with the local population, including allegations of wrongdoing, during the early period of Operation Banner. As well as making reference to the Army in Northern Ireland, I place soldiers' attitudes within the wider social context of Britain in the early 1970s. I demonstrate that senior officers such as General Officer Commanding Northern Ireland (GOCNI), Lieutenant General Harry Tuzo, could draw on crude, contemporary stereotypes to denigrate 'the Irish race'. Nevertheless, despite the currency of such stereotypes in Britain, I argue that, on operations, soldiers used derogatory descriptions of the Irish not necessarily out of long-held prejudice but primarily as a transient means of 'getting at' the local population. Sectarian abuse towards outsiders did not significantly affect relations between Catholic and Protestant soldiers. I show that the use of racial and/or sectarian taunts escalated commensurately as units took casualties. Unable to locate an individual enemy, soldiers started to blame the population as a whole. Finally, I conclude that group cohesion was primarily conditioned by internal norms focused on military competency. All ranks of leadership were important in Northern Ireland, but particularly the role of company commanders and section commanders; these were the two ranks that had the most constant and decisive influence over the planning and execution of operations.

Chapter 3 is a deep analysis of the operational experiences of the Scots Guards and the Argyll and Sutherland Highlanders in order to test and highlight the themes and features of the conflict in Northern Ireland discussed in previous chapters. I focus particularly on questions of leadership, victimhood or grievance, retribution, intelligence/situational awareness and experiences of combat. In doing so, I frequently draw on the experiences of other units that deployed to the same area of operations in the early 1970s (for example, the Royal Scots Dragoon Guards, who served alongside 1 Argylls in RUC H Division). I examine the autonomy, or agency, enjoyed by battalion and sub-unit commanders in the case of 1 Scots Guard, 2 Scots Guards and 1 Argylls. Both regiments enjoyed considerable autonomy; the behaviour of sub-units such as companies could also be strikingly different, depending on the respective company commander in charge. The commander of 39 Brigade had relatively more direct control over his battalions than was the case for 8 Brigade and 3 Brigade. The remote, disparate location of 3 brigade units, spread across the Southern border, meant that 3 Brigade HQ in Lurgan, County Armagh, had the least direct influence of the three long-standing brigades that were deployed to Northern Ireland.

Chapter 3 investigates the roles of junior officers and NCOs on operations, including responses under fire. Fatigue, fear and a raw desire to identify an enemy led to occasional indiscipline, including the firing at large targets such as St Eugene's Cathedral in Derry and the taking of enemy 'trophies'. I discuss self-inflicted wounds and 'skiving', or deviation from duty, and evidence of a descent into 'gang behaviour' by some units. Group enmities could easily be re-made, even within a battalion during training exercises, if a group felt that its superiority or survival was being threatened. I illustrate the internal rivalries within 1 Argylls and between 2 Scots Guards and the US Navy in Londonderry. I describe the hardening of attitudes towards the IRA and the local population in some areas. Soldiers found IRA actions repugnant; they also frequently did not want to put the lives of potentially friendly locals in danger by socialising with them, leading to a corrosive distancing of soldiers from the local population. (Soldiers were less likely to sympathise with people with whom they had little contact, except to inflict punitive or precautionary measures.) Finally, I also look at instances where soldiers engaged in acts of collective punishment against the local population and examine evidence of respect for, and opinions of, the military capability of the IRA.

Chapter 4 analyses how a County Fermanagh farmer, Michael Naan, went from being a suspect, to a *known* IRA operative (there is no evidence to suggest that he was), to murder victim (along with his employee Andrew Murray) at the hands of a patrol of 1 Argylls soldiers. Drawing upon the work of Stathis Kalyvas on selective violence during civil wars, Winslow and Vennesson's work on military deviancy, and extensive primary research, I conclude that Naan and Murray died as a result of local denunciation relating to a sectarian land dispute, a breakdown in command and intelligence structures, a botched interrogation in the aftermath of the disappearance of an Argyll soldier and a desire by an aggressive unit to go on the offensive, to exact revenge for previous casualties.[89] I argue that a number of key weaknesses in the Army's operations in Northern Ireland, particularly inconsistencies regarding command and control, contributed to the deaths of Michael Naan and Andrew Murray. I also examine how local atrocities committed by the IRA in South Fermanagh created an additional pressure on the Army to take a more aggressive approach. Finally, the chapter considers soldiers' narratives that continue to justify, at least indirectly, the murders.

Where the word 'terrorism' is used, it refers to the nomenclature employed by the British Army during the early years of Operation Banner. This is not an attempt to diminish IRA responsibility for their crimes but is simply to avoid an ongoing, hotly contested debate about definitions of terrorism that is not central to the aims of this study.[90] 'The IRA' refers to the Provisional IRA as opposed to the Marxist Official IRA. I use the term 'Volunteer' to describe a member of the IRA, since this was the nomenclature used by that organisation. 'The Army' refers to the British Army. I have used Londonderry/Derry interchangeably to describe the city, similarly for County Derry/Londonderry and Roslea/Rosslea in County Fermanagh.

---

89 S. Kalyvas, *The Logic of Violence in Civil War* (Cambridge: Cambridge University Press, 2006); Winslow, *The Canadian Airborne Regiment in Somalia*; Vennesson, 'Cohesion and Misconduct'.

90 For example, Alex Schmid has analysed more than 100 individual definitions of terrorism – and has produced his own. See A.P. Schmid and A.J. Jongman, *Political Terrorism* (New Brunswick, NJ: Transaction Publishers, 2012).

1

The British Army Before 1971

Many of us who grew up used to seeing the map painted red and thinking a quarter of the globe as 'our Empire' find it hard to adjust ourselves to Britain's loss of material power and diminished status ... We shudder at references to 'mini' Britain, and are appalled at the apathy which has grown as our power has waned.[1]

An Imperial Institution in a Domestic Setting:
Purpose and Identity

In the 1960s, the British Army came home. After the withdrawal from Malaya, Borneo, Aden, Uganda, Sudan, Nigeria etc. there was precious little to garrison in Asia and Africa and an escalating threat to Europe from the Soviet Union. Britain was experiencing major cultural and social changes, including rapid rates of immigration and the growth of pacifist movements linked to demands for gender equality. The Army had deployed on 64 different campaigns, of varying duration and scale, between 1945 and 1970 – more than 1,800 soldiers were killed and 5,200 wounded during this period. But the 'successes' of Malaya and Kenya were generally uninteresting to the general public since the result was the same – withdrawal, albeit a better ordered one.[2] The empire was all but finished; overseas career opportunities were greatly reduced and the Army struggled to recruit enough young officers to fill vacancies. The years of peacetime conscription or National Service (1949–1963) meant

1 A.J. Barker, 'British Prestige', *Army Quarterly and Defence Journal* 98(1), 69.
2 C. Downes, *Special Trust and Confidence: The Making of an Officer* (London: Frank Cass, 1991), 18; C. Blacker and H. Woods, *The Story of the 5th Royal Inniskilling Dragoon Guards, 1928–1978* (London: Spottiswoode Press, 1978), 174–175.

that many in Britain came to view the Army as something to be avoided, or endured, instead of a desirable career choice or a public institution accorded a high level of social prestige. For a period, many regiments became increasingly reliant for officer recruits on those military and/ or aristocratic families that traditionally valued military service (such as the Leasks or Erskine-Crums for the Scots Guards and the Youngers or Grahams for the Argylls). The Army became isolated from wider British society to a degree unprecedented for many decades.[3]

The implosion of Northern Ireland from 1969 to 1971 focused military minds – and gave them an immediate task. A declining empire and the end of conscription meant a significantly smaller military; the total number of personnel in the armed forces had been reduced by more than a third in just over a decade (down from 703,900 in 1957 to 383,000 in 1969. The Army had been whittled down to 50 British and five Gurkha battalions).[4] The conflict in Northern Ireland also fed a sense of post-imperial insecurity among senior officers. To some senior officers, such as Major General Robert Goldsmith, Northern Ireland was just another Cold War theatre. International communism was gaining momentum and, by extension, the Soviet Union:

> Their hand is observable behind the programmes of terrorism followed by the I.R.A. Provisionals in Northern Ireland. It is for present and future British governments to ensure that similar accidents do not produce equally favourable conditions anywhere else in these islands, as they might do, for example, if the populations of our big cities come to be segregated on racial lines.[5]

In hindsight, such views appear to be a simplistic way of looking at the Provisional IRA (here referred to as the IRA), many of whose leading members had split from what became the Official IRA leadership in 1969 because of the intense international socialist sympathies of some of its

3 Downes, *Special Trust and Confidence*, 18; Blacker and Woods, *The Story of the 5th Royal Inniskilling Dragoon* Guards, 174–175.
4 'Army Cuts: How Have UK Armed Forces Personnel Numbers Changed Over Time', *Guardian*, July 5, 2012.
5 R.F.K. Goldsmith, 'Editorial', *Army Quarterly and Defence Journal* 103(1) (1971), 2.

leaders.[6] But they do reflect the sense of decline, suspicion and social tension that affected Britain during the late 1960s and 1970s.

The British Army, with its long history of garrisoning multi-ethnic colonies, was particularly prone to reproducing racial stereotypes. Phrases like 'the British race' was commonly used in military journals in the 1960s and 1970s. There was also an enduring belief in, and respect for, 'martial races' including Scottish Highlanders and Gurkhas. According to Antony Beevor, Scottish regiments 'had a reputation for loathing blacks'.[7] The Gurkhas were the exception to an informal 2 per cent 'colour bar' on blacks and Asians that operated in many regiments until the 1980s.[8] The Irish were also occasionally included in the 'martial race' category. Indeed, the Army was an exceptionally welcoming place for Irishmen, including from the Republic of Ireland. Forty out of every 100 recruits to Irish regiments were from the Republic of Ireland; the majority of Irish soldiers recruited from the whole island of Ireland were catholic. A widespread view of Ireland in the British Army was of 'an island with a centuries-old tradition of producing fine soldiers'.[9] Catholic Irishmen, from the North and South, also made up a sizeable number of non-officer recruits to the Scots Guards and the Argyll and Sutherland Highlanders.[10]

The Foot Guards, particularly the Irish and Scots Guards, recruited a high number of Catholic officers in the early and mid-twentieth century; the Lieutenant Colonel Commanding the Scots Guards in 1970, Colonel Archie Fletcher, was a devout Catholic.[11] In the Scots Guards there was very little evidence of anti-Catholic discrimination. By contrast, the Argylls had an informal, but persistently effective, ban on recruiting Catholic

6 See R. English, *Armed Struggle: The History of the IRA* (London: Pan Macmillan, 2004), 101–120.

7 Beevor, *Inside the British Army*, 308.

8 See S. Crawford, 'Race Relations in the Army', in H. Strachan (ed.), *The British Army, Manpower and Society into the Twenty-First Century* (London: Frank Cass, 2000).

9 H.E.D. Harris, 'The New Irish Rangers', *Army Quarterly and Defence Journal* 98(2) (1969), 195–197.

10 Interviews with Scots Guards Soldier 8 (Officer), March 2013 and Argyll Soldier 15 (Officer), December 2013.

11 M. Naylor, *Among Friends: The Scots Guards, 1956–1993* (Barnsley: Pen and Sword, 1995), 21.

officers that endured until 1973. The reason for the ban dated back to the Anglo-Irish War of 1919–1921, when 2 Argylls had been stationed in County Mayo in the west of Ireland; the CO of 2 Argylls, a Catholic, had court-martialled a fellow Argyll officer for using excessive violence against the local population.[12] The position of Regimental Sergeant Major was also out of bounds for a Catholic, but there were some, more junior Catholic NCOs in the regiment.[13] However, the ban did not endure simply because of a casual dislike of Catholics, although some sectarian tensions in a predominantly Presbyterian, Church of Scotland, regiment may have endured, but rather a belief that an informal military covenant of absolute loyalty between officers in the regiment had been broken.

Officership and the British Army: A Hereditary Profession

The military of the late 1960s and early 1970s was, to a degree, a hereditary profession, its senior ranks officered by Britain's social elite. C.B. Otley's investigation of the social origins of Army officers in the 1970s observed that although there had been a notable decline in propertied backgrounds, 39 per cent of officers were the sons of soldiers (almost all of whom were also officers).[14] Meanwhile, 84 per cent of generals were educated at public schools; of which 24.4 per cent went to three schools: Eton, Harrow and Winchester.[15] In the 1960s, even officers who were not from a propertied background or did not go to a public school, tended to adopt the characteristics of those that did. Max Weber has described such pressures as being linked to 'status honour ... a *style of life* can be expected from all those who wish to belong to the circle. Linked with this expectation are

---

12 A group of Argyll officers vowed to 'ban' the recruitment of Catholic officers in the future, a practice especially insisted upon by the Argylls' Colonel of the Regiment, Major General Freddie Graham, in the years leading up until 1972. The appointment of Brigadier Sandy Boswell as Colonel of the Regiment in 1972 effectively ended the informal policy of non-recruitment of Catholic officers to 1st Battalion, Argyll and Sutherland Highlanders.

13 Interviews with Argyll Soldier 15 (Officer), December 2013 and with Argyll Soldier 11 (Officer), May 2014. Interview with Argyll Soldier 10 (Officer), December 2013.

14 C.B. Otley, 'The Social Origins of British Army Officers', *Sociological Review* 18(2) (1970), 213–219.

15 H. Strachan, *The Politics of the British Army* (Oxford: Clarendon Press, 1997), 16.

restrictions on "social intercourse".[16] Officers had to meet not only *professional* (combat proficiency) but also *social* criteria – formal and informal rules about how they should conduct themselves.

Colonel Colin Mitchell – 'Mad Mitch', the CO of 1 Argylls in Aden during 1967, provides a useful example of this 'chameleon effect' on young officers. Mitchell became famous for his sometime brutal remarks about how to deal with insurgents in the British colony of Aden in 1967: 'It was like shooting grouse, a brace here and a brace there.'[17] Mitchell appeared to be the epitome of an upper-class military caste that enjoyed its shooting, both for sport and on operations. But Mitchell was not born to grouse shooting; he even served as a private soldier for a period. Rather, he was taught to shoot grouse by officers of his regiment, being slowly 'introduced to the mysteries of ornithology and shotgun shooting'. Another officer instructed him on what clothes to wear when not in uniform and other social etiquette expected of officers.[18] Such conditioning or conformity is a hallmark of the military, both on and off duty; Beevor relates how officers and soldiers could be easily spotted in civilian clothes coming through Belfast's Aldergrove airport.[19] Officers and soldiers were fitting in with the Weberian status honour of their groups and the social expectations that came with membership. Soldiering was a job, but it was also a way of life.

The British Army in the 1960s and 1970s perpetuated a strict divide between officers, NCOs and other ranks. NCOs (particularly those who had been promoted to sergeant) maintained a distinct sense of pride – frequently describing themselves as being in the 'engine room' of a battalion. To some outsiders, the Army, and especially the socially elite Household Division (of which the Foot Guards are part), appeared to be a feudal relic, or 'a semi-feudal Squirearchy which somehow worked'; Scots Guards officers indeed often took on a 'lairdly' bearing, seldom seen when not on operations or exercise.[20] But there was (and is) an underlying

---

16 M. Weber, *Essays in Sociology* (London: Routledge, 1970), 262.

17 BBC News, 'Return to Aden – without Mad Mitch', December 1, 2007, http://news.bbc.co.uk/1/hi/programmes/from_our_own_correspondent/7120629.stm (accessed February 18, 2015).

18 Mitchell, *Having Been a Soldier*, 55.

19 Beevor, *Inside the British Army*, xxii.

20 D. Barker, *Soldiering On: An Unofficial Portrait of the British Army* (London: Andre Deutsch, 1981), 150–151.

professional motive for rigid rank separation; regiments did not merely reflect an archaic feudal system out of habit alone. Combat required social division: an officer, and/or a senior NCO, may have to send men to their deaths. He cannot be their friend; soldiers are not supposed to question superiors as they might their friends.[21]

The British Army and Counterinsurgency before Northern Ireland

In 1969, the British Army was an institution confident in its ability to confront insurgents. Aden had been a disaster, at least in many Army officers' minds, but only because Britain's political leaders had got cold feet and unilaterally ripped up mutual defence agreements with the sultanates of South Arabia.[22] Malaya, under the 'dual-hatted' civilian–military leadership of General Sir Gerald Templer (who was in charge of both civil government and military operations), and the similar arrangement in Borneo in the mid-1960s established under General Sir Walter Walker, were regarded as outstanding successes. However, critical to victory in Malaya in the 1950s and again in Borneo in the 1960s had been the ability to isolate the 'Chinese squatter population', from whom the communist insurgency drew much of its support. As one Army officer noted: 'This ethnic division helped the large-scale resettlement plans which contributed so much to the success of British efforts to isolate their enemy. Chinese squatters had little traditional claim to the land they occupied'.[23] Repeating this successful, highly coercive approach in Northern Ireland was not possible. Political leaders baulked at the idea of a military 'supremo' operating within the UK's borders, while the forced resettlement of populations in a British context was simply unthinkable.[24] General Walker would later admonish the 'flabby way' in which the government countered a threat in Northern Ireland that, in his mind, clearly emanated from the Soviet Union.[25] The British Army's concepts of counterinsurgency and internal security operations would have to be rewritten for a domestic context.

21 Winslow, *The Canadian Airborne Regiment*, 20.
22 BBC News, 'Return to Aden – without Mad Mitch'.
23 C.A.H. Bushell, 'Insurgency and the Numbers Game', *Army Quarterly and Defence Journal* 84(1) (1969), 62.
24 W. Walker, 'Borneo', *British Army Review* 32 (1969), 15.
25 Strachan, *The Politics of the British Army*, 181.

The Regimental System in the British Army

Soldiers (excluding officers) in the late 1960s and early 1970s joined the Army for a variety of reasons: a few were attracted to romance of a military career and wanted to join up from an early age. However, the most pressing motivation was disillusionment with prospects in their civilian lives. A large proportion came from working-class backgrounds in areas experiencing significant unemployment. One Argyll private soldier recalled walking about the Clydeside town of Paisley looking for a job, when he came upon a recruiting parade of 1st Battalion, Argyll and Sutherland Highlanders, his local regiment:

> The martial atmosphere that they had about them … They looked like tough guys and you wanted to be a part of that. The sergeant said, 'Look, you look like a fit young man. You want to get into the Argylls, I can put a word in for ye', which is a recruiting sergeant's job anyway. A couple of the boys [Argyll soldiers] … were all round about me giving me encouragement saying, 'Come in', and so I went and did it. I was unemployed, had been for three weeks about this point. And it was getting me down.[26]

Soldiering may have offered some sense of 'family' in the 1960s and 1970s, but soldiers for the most part remained poor, even after joining the Army. Problems with alcohol abuse and domestic violence were common. In some areas, infant mortality remained twice as high in Army families as in the rest of society. Army salaries rarely kept up with inflation; in the late 1970s, more than 8,000 families of serving soldiers were receiving social welfare benefits. Officers enjoyed much better wages; a strict social hierarchy prevailed. The wives of NCOs and other ranks were often expected formally to address officers' wives as Ma'am.[27]

The trainee or junior soldier is taught to view his regiment in quasi-religious terms; its symbols – the flags that make up its 'colours', for example – are sacred. Frank Richardson, in his study on morale in the military, describes the regimental colours as 'the ark of their [the soldiers'] covenant … Kings and Queens must come and go; the Regiment lives for

---

26 Interview with Argyll Soldier 8 (Private Soldier), November 2013.
27 Beevor, *Inside the British Army*, 71.

ever'.[28] In the trooping of the colour by the Foot Guards, for example, it is the regimental colour, not the sovereign's, that is the focus of the soldiers' loyalty.[29] By making the regiment appear so powerful, so reverential, it seems impossible for the individual to countenance going against it; the regiment becomes a living Leviathan.[30]

Regimental Traditions and Loyalties

Regiments were, for the most part, still a very regional affair in the late 1960s and early 1970s. The Household Division, regiments with a specific, technical or mechanical role (Royal Artillery, Royal Signals etc.) and some larger, newly amalgamated regiments such as the Royal Regiment of Fusiliers were the exceptions. The Foot Guards Regiments were also spread out over large regions: the Coldstream Guards generally recruited from the north and middle of England, the Grenadiers from London and the south, and the Scots, Irish and Welsh Guards from each of these nations, with a good sprinkling of others who were 'taught' how to be sufficiently Scottish, Irish and Welsh. Their lack of specifically local roots, i.e. from a county, meant their identity was more clearly vested in being 'Guards' to the monarch (belonging as they did to the Household Division).[31] Household Division NCOs were widely regarded as among the best in the British Army and they tended to occupy the most important NCO training positions, at Royal Military Academy Sandhurst and elsewhere. The pride or prestige of being a Foot Guards sergeant was uniquely high; moreover, a full Corporal in a Guards Regiment is known as a Lance Sergeant, and is a member of the Sergeants' Mess, where he quickly learns the strict and rigorous expectations of dress and discipline, formal and informal, from more senior NCOs.[32]

---

28 F. Richardson, *Fighting Spirit: A Study of Psychological Factors in War* (London: Leo Cooper, 1978), 15.

29 Richardson, *Fighting Spirit*, 15.

30 'For by Art is created that great Leviathan called a Commonwealth, or State, which is but an artificial man; though of greater stature and strength than the Natural, for whose protection and defence it was intended; and in which, the Sovereignty is an artificial soul, as giving life and motion to the whole body.' T. Hobbes, *Leviathan* (Cambridge: Cambridge University Press, 1996), 1.

31 Beevor, *Inside the British Army*, 320–321.

32 Interview with Scots Guards Soldier 14 (Officer), May 2014.

The Argyll and Sutherland Highlanders were a local regiment – recruiting from Argyllshire, Dunbartonshire, Renfrewshire, Stirlingshire, Clackmannanshire and Kinross-shire (Sutherland itself was 'lost' in the Cardwell reforms of the late nineteenth century and constituted part of the recruiting area of the Queen's Own Highlander).[33] The Argylls continued to be very much a 'Clan Campbell Regiment'; Princess Louise, the daughter of Queen Victoria and wife of John Campbell, the 9th Duke of Argyll, designed the regimental logo (the Campbell boar's head and the Sutherland wild cat linked together by the Princess's cyphers).[34] Although much of the Argyll recruiting area was outside the Highlands, the regiment nevertheless followed a looser approach to discipline typical to many Highland regiments. Communications between the ranks were generally less rigid and more fluent than was the case in the Scots Guards.[35]

Initial promotion was almost invariably the hardest jump for a young infantryman, as a freshly minted junior officer or as a junior NCO. It was perhaps hardest for a lance-corporal, promoted from among other private soldiers: 'lance-corporal is the most difficult rank in the Army. There is no break. One day you were promoted over your buddies but you stayed in the same section. And when you are asked to pull rank it is very hard. They are as likely to tell you to "fuck off" if they don't like the order.'[36] An officer who had served through the era of national service recalled that the emergence of the professional, career NCO saw a huge improvement in standards. These men were 'proud of their trade, handling their weapons and specialised skills'.[37]

Soldiers were often obsessively loyal to their regiments, to the point where rivalry could get in the way of function. One officer recalled that the programming of soldiers to believe in the tribal loyalty to their regiment meant that regimental amalgamations were extremely difficult. The best way to unite such a fractured regiment, busy fighting over contested

---

33 The old recruiting ground of Sutherland was not retained when the 91st Princess Louise's Argyll Regiment joined with the 93rd Sutherland Regiment under the Caldwell Reforms in 1881.

34 See P. Mileham, *Fighting Highlanders: The History of the Argyll and Sutherland Highlanders* (London: Arms and Armour, 1993) for an account of the early history of the Argyll and Sutherland Highlanders.

35 L.C. Archer, 'Discipline and Drill', *Scots Guards Magazine* (1964), 68.

36 Interview with Argyll Soldier 6 (Private Soldier), May 2014.

37 Interview with Argyll Soldier 31 (Officer), May 2014.

symbols, reputations and music, was to 'stick them into a conflict where then they have to forget all about their differences and get on with it. And then suddenly they realise, actually, everybody is pretty damn good'.[38] Combat, as King observes, is a great leveller; soldiers who had been through combat together soon forged new group loyalties based on those experiences.[39] Regimental symbols were the totems of investment in the primacy of one group over outsiders and security of the individual within the group was the reward of such unconditional loyalty. But, as will be seen in subsequent chapters, the company was the key unit when it came to giving soldiers day-to-day operational orientation and guidance.

Training and Preparing for War Before Operation Banner

The Army is a 'total institution'. Erving Gottman has defined total institutions as places 'of residence and work where a large number of like-situated individuals, cut off from the wider society for an appreciable period of time, together lead an enclosed, formally administered round of life'.[40] Entrants must adapt their behaviour in radical ways upon entering total institutions such as a monastery, a prison or, in this case, the British Army. Most British soldiers in the 1960s and 1970s joined the Army when they were very young; the average age was 17½, young enough still to absorb strong impressions similar to those experienced in childhood. Firm, almost humiliating, control is immediately exerted over recruits. Recruits were given demeaning names – 'red-arses', 'trogs' or 'crows' at the Guards depot at Caterham (adult recruits) or Waterloo and Pirbright (junior guardsmen). Recruit training is designed, 'to break down the system of supports and values that the recruit had before entry, and to replace them with those of the institution.'[41] To survive, an entrant must learn to obey immediately. Upon being accepted into the regiment, however, the soldier learns that there is usually some room for divergence away from nominal rank structures. Depending on the rank,

---

38 Interview with Argyll Soldier 5 (Officer), May 2014.

39 Barker, *Soldiering On*, 151; King, *The Combat Soldier*, 352.

40 G. Harries-Jenkins, 'Role Images, Military Attitudes, and the Enlisted Culture in Great Britain', in D.R. Segal and H.W. Sinaiko (eds), *Life in the Rank and File: Enlisted Men and Women in the Armed Forces of the United States, Australia, Canada, and the United Kingdom* (Washington, DC: Pergamon-Brasseys, 1986), 254.

41 Edmonds, *Armed Services and Society*, 108.

circumstance and/or the personalities of those in positions of group power, the balance of importance between formal and informal rules can shift.[42] An aggressive attitude is carefully cultivated – but one that accepts the immediate discipline of superiors. This also applied to their general behaviour off duty: 'The collective goal of their R & R was to outdrink, out-fuck, and if necessary out-fight all those with whom they came into contact.'[43] Homosexuals were routinely mocked and despised. Officers often approved of such conduct: 'You expect them [recruits] to behave like soldiers, to get involved in fights and to get drunk and so on. In a way you are disappointed if some of them don't, but of course you can't acknowledge it, or inform them.'[44]

Many NCOs interviewed – from both the Scots Guards and the Argylls – frowned upon their peers who had to resort to formal discipline, imposed by the commanding officer of the battalion, except in the most serious of offences. Argyll NCOs, less so in the case of the Scots Guards, were known for administering 'a few thumps' in place of formal charges; the offending soldier could choose between the two.[45] Hockey also wrote of the informal threat of violence against a soldier violating group norms. The worst offence, according to one senior NCO, was to 'steal off your mates ... If we catch you it's gaol for sure. And when you get out, well you can see blokes walking around their fingers in plaster. Where they've caught them in doors, if you get my meaning?'[46] Soldiers would get even with those who broke with the code of loyalty, even if the latter had left the Army.

Few soldiers enjoyed drill practice; marching around a square or endlessly performing synchronised motions with rifles did not seem like 'real soldiering'. However, there was a clear operational logic to drill, as explained by one senior Scots Guards NCO:

> Drill and discipline form the basis on which success of all other training depends. The object being to make you physically and mentally alert at all times and under all circumstances. Your

42 J. Shay, *Achilles in Vietnam* (New York: Touchstone, 1995), 150.

43 J. Hockey, *Squaddies: Portrait of a Sub-culture* (Exeter: Exeter University Publications, 1986), 117.

44 Hockey, *Squaddies*, 117.

45 Interview with Argyll Soldier 2 (Officer), November 2014.

46 Hockey, *Squaddies*, 37.

brain, receiving messages from the eyes and ears, immediately transmits its signals to the muscles and limbs. The response of these being instantaneous by reason of exercise and training.[47]

The aim, in short, was automatism under stress. Marching around a barrack square established the introduction to a process aimed at inculcating collective, automatic battlefield responses.

The Strengths and Risks of Group Cohesion

Anthony King has questioned the true value of 'mateship' or dying for the 'family' values of the regiment. King argues that a common ethnic, social and cultural background is not important, as was put forward in the classic paper on unit cohesion in the German Wehrmacht by Morris Janowitz and Edward Shils.[48] Instead, King puts much more weight on professionalism and task cohesion than the social network of the regiment as the underlying motivational force behind soldiering in dangerous environments:

> Friendship follows function, comradeship performance. Although it potentially disturbs Western notions of friendship as authentic lasting relationships, the evidence seems to suggest that, in the all-volunteer force, comradeship is not some everlasting union of souls but, on the contrary, a contingent product of institutional assignment and function. The better the training and the higher the levels of performance, the more intense this feeling of solidarity becomes.[49]

In other words, bonds have been formed through the job, the task and a sense of professional pride, rather than through social empathy or cohesion. Friendship follows competence rather than the other way around.[50] In the next chapter, I will examine professionalism and other motivations in the case of the Scots Guards and the Argyll and Sutherland Highlanders.

47 Archer, 'Discipline and Drill', 68.
48 E. Shils and M. Janowitz, 'Cohesion and Disintegration in the Wehrmacht in the Second World War', *Public Opinion Quarterly* 12(2) (1948), 280–315.
49 King, *The Combat Soldier*, 352.
50 King, *The Combat Soldier*, 352.

As will also be seen in subsequent chapters, the perception of 'who was the enemy' could be rapidly redefined if a group of soldiers felt they were under threat. They were not trained to back down in the face of violence but quickly to close ranks and repel or go on the offensive – even if faced by people they knew in a training exercise. According to the Israeli psychologist Ben Shalit: 'All that is needed is for the opposing troops to be seen as upsetting the soldier's personal equilibrium, either by direct threat to himself or to his peers.'[51] Army trainers carefully construct 'a common account of orders', rehearsing again and again what soldiers are to do when they come under fire. A common understanding of expected behaviour leads to increased cohesion and social pressure; as long as everybody does what is expected of them in an operation, they will survive and even prosper.[52] A common understanding of group expectations, *combined* with 'routinised charisma' and an emphasis on aggressive dominance, can lead to the blocking out of external voices. The craving for certainty or positive action in complex environments also can overwhelm legitimate doubts over a course of action. Excessive or deviant cohesion must be constantly guarded against lest it establish group norms that are not shared by the wider Army and the State to which soldiers owe their service.[53]

Breaking with a group, even if an individual soldier has his doubts about the morality of a course of action, is far from straightforward. The soldier has been thoroughly imbued with a sense of loyalty to the soldiers in his section, platoon and battalion. He is bound to an implicit compact with his unit. According to Winslow, 'the soldier's natural fear of loneliness and death, as well as his disinclination to take life, is less than his fear of losing those who provide him safety, security, a firm sense of belonging, affection status and prestige, order, system and structure.'[54] A very young soldier may literally owe his life to his section commander or platoon sergeant, a man often initially perceived by younger soldiers as a 'God' and later as a father figure. Ostracism from such a group is a painful, possibly dangerous, betrayal of bonds that many soldiers simply cannot contemplate.

---

51 B. Shalit, *The Psychology of Conflict and Combat* (New York: Praeger, 1988), 24.
52 King, *The Combat Soldier*, 302.
53 Winslow, *The Canadian Airborne*, 263.
54 Winslow, *The Canadian Airborne*, 74.

Soldiers, especially young soldiers, need a frame of reference, or what Emile Durkheim called 'a skeleton of thought', in which they can make sense of a complex area of operations, such as operating in a low-intensity environment against a largely invisible enemy.[55] A frame of reference requires a basic knowledge and orientation. Moreover, soldiers need to understand 'what consequences a decision can have'.[56] Who gives soldiers such frames of reference? There are many different contributors to a soldier's frame of reference, before and during operations. First, training plays a role – soldiers are taught to rely upon their nearest superiors, non-commissioned officers, including a lance-corporal, corporal and their platoon sergeant, for almost absolute guidance. Winslow, in her study of a Canadian paratroop regiment that murdered a Somali prisoner, argues that soldiers can become so enthralled to NCOs that they will usually emulate their behaviour even if they sense that it is wrong or do not agree. Winslow cites the account of a Canadian paratrooper:

> We're so connected physically and mentally, that if there's one person that we admire ... if he incites his group to racist behaviour, they'll follow, even if they don't agree, because they won't distinguish themselves from the group. Because the group's all you've got. If you're in battle, no one else is looking out for you.[57]

In a recent study, Anthony King has drawn attention to the importance of the pre-operation briefing or 'rehearsal of concept', that each group of soldiers goes through prior to going on patrol. Above all, King describes a 'moral commitment', a common understanding of the situation and a pact to see through the operation that will take place.[58] Professional competence and adherence to the common plan of action are everything. Soldiers do not think of deviating from a shared understanding of their mission and will look to key charismatic individuals to provide a lead in putting plans into action: 'Each soldier is under constant and mutual

55 E. Durkheim, *The Elementary Forms of Religious Life* (New York: The Free Press, 1995), 424.
56 S. Neitzel and H. Welzer, *Soldaten* (London: Simon and Schuster, 2012), 8.
57 Winslow, *The Canadian Airborne*, 80.
58 King, *The Combat Soldier*, 301.

surveillance to ensure that everyone fulfils their duties competently.'[59] Once the soldier commits to a course of action, it is extremely difficult to go against the group and its leaders, for a soldier to admit that he did not know what was expected of him.

The Scots Guards, 1963–1970

Scots Guards units have always had to strike an uneasy balance between the competing commitments of public duties and operational tours. The Guards, together with other regiments of the Foot Guards (Grenadier Guards, Coldstream Guards, Irish and Welsh Guards) and the Household Cavalry (the Life Guards, the Blues and Royals), make up the Household Division, the Queen's own personal bodyguard. The Foot Guards were instrumental in the forming of both the Parachute Regiment and the Special Air Service (SAS) and a sizeable proportion of guardsmen, particularly NCOs, spent periods with both during the 1950s and 1960s. The Scots Guards could expect regularly to form one of the five public service battalions operating out of Wellington Barracks, Chelsea, Hounslow, Pirbright and Caterham under the command of a Major General, General-Officer-Commanding (GOC) for London District and the Household Division. Operationally the Scots Guards would often fall under a brigade made up of Foot Guards battalions, but, increasingly during the 1950s, 1960s and into the 1970s, served in a diverse range of brigades and divisions.[60]

Borneo

In October 1964, 1 Scots Guards moved to South-east Asia as part of a Commonwealth brigade, with their headquarters in Terendak Camp outside Malacca in peninsular Malaysia. The battalion deployed twice on active operations in Borneo: beginning in January 1965 when 1 Scots Guards was based for four months in Semengo Camp, outside Kuching in Sarawak, Malaysian Borneo, taking charge of Western Sector, Western Brigade. From September 1965 to January 1966, the battalion served for almost five months in the eastern part of Malaysian Borneo,

59 King, *The Combat Soldier*, 350.
60 Naylor, *Among Friends: The Scots Guards*, 1–3.

operating out of Kalabakan Camp, Tawau, Sabah. From 1962 to 1966, 'a confrontation' was taking place between British-supported Malaysia and a volatile Indonesia under the leadership of President Sukarno who rejected Kuala Lumpur's partial control of the island of Borneo.[61] Police intelligence reports in Borneo confirmed that the insurgent Borneo Chinese Clandestine Organisation (CCO), with alleged communist and pro-Sukarno sympathies, drew its principal support from the Chinese rural population and had infiltrated a number of villages.[62] However, the Scots Guards were soon to discover that police intelligence was not as reliable as they had hoped; interrogators were using harsh methods 'to get the results they wanted', but such information led to wasted patrols and arrests on the part of the military, a mature judgement by a perceptive group of officers.[63]

The overwhelming task of British Army units in Borneo was to keep their area of operations clear of the enemy – both regular Indonesian troops and local insurgents – and to gather intelligence that would make that job easier. The interior of Borneo is mountainous, with outcrops of limestone rock rising up to 4,000 feet, with sheer cliffs on both sides. Patrols encountered both primary and secondary rainforest; the former, with its towering trees, was easier to penetrate than the 'impenetrable scrub' of the latter. Patrols often followed streams as easily navigational tools, although many still became lost and resorted to calling in Howitzer fire to identify their location.[64] Radio communications were also notoriously difficult; sometimes patrols could not communicate with their own company HQ even though they could pick up US military radio chatter emanating from Vietnam. Leeches and scorpions were a constant risk, as were water-borne diseases; the CO of 1 Scots Guards, Lieutenant Colonel Archie Fletcher, very nearly

---

61 TNA: WO 305/2105 Army Unit Historical Records and Reports, 1 Battalion Scots Guards, Semengo Camp, December 1965: Weekly Intelligence Summary, No. 13, dated December 17, 1965.

62 TNA: WO 305/2007 Army Unit Historical Records and Reports, 1 Battalion Scots Guards, Semengo Camp, January 1965: Operational Instructions No. 1/65, signed by Major Sir Gregor Macgregor of Macgregor on behalf of the commanding officer, dated January 2, 1965.

63 TNA: WO 305/2105 1 Battalion Scots Guards, Semengo Camp, December 1965.

64 Naylor, *Among Friends*, 43.

died after swimming in a river and was invalided back to Singapore in March 1965.[65]

The first tour of 1 Scots Guards was uneventful, with almost no contacts with insurgents. The second tour provided a few incidents to test junior patrol commanders. They were occasionally expected to operate across the border inside the Indonesian part of Borneo, sometimes up to five miles across as part of Operation Claret, a series of cross-border raids targeting Indonesian regulars and insurgents. On November 25, 1965, one such patrol, led by Lieutenant Michael Nurton, surprised a large encampment of Indonesian regular and irregular forces, inflicting multiple casualties before escaping back across the border.[66] It was the singular event of another relatively quiet operational tour. The tedium of constant jungle patrolling took its toll on 1 Scots Guards. A number of courts martial were held during the tour in Borneo: in November 1965, one guardsman was convicted to 84 days' detention for striking an officer and another was sentenced to nine months' detention for sleeping while on sentry duty. Striking an officer was one offence, but letting down basic, professional standards of soldiering was altogether more serious.[67] Meanwhile, the CO, Colonel Fletcher, was increasingly concerned about poor fire discipline on the part of his troops, warning that frequent accidental discharges would eventually result in the accidental death of British soldiers or local civilians.[68]

From 1961 to 1964, 2 Scots Guards were deployed to East Africa and witnessed the end of British imperial rule in Zanzibar and Kenya. They did so with some nostalgia and a lot of goodwill towards those newborn countries. Many of the officers in the new armies of East African had served as NCOs in the King's African Rifles, including under Scots Guards officers on detachment. In 1964, 2 Scots Guards helped the

65 Interview with Scots Guards Soldier 13 (Officer), December 2014.
66 Nurton would go on to win a Military Cross as a Company Commander in Ballymurphy in West Belfast in 1971. Naylor, *Among* Friends, 49.
67 TNA: WO 305/2104 Army Unit Historical Records and Reports, 1 Battalion Scots Guards, Kalabakan Camp, November 1965 Commander's Diary, November 10, 1965.
68 TNA: WO 305/2103 Army Unit Historical Records and Reports, 1 Battalion Scots Guards, Kalabakan Camp, October 1965: Operational Instruction headed 'Safety', signed by Colonel Archie Fletcher, Lieutenant Colonel Commanding, 1st Battalion, Scots Guards, dated October 20, 1965.

Ugandan government put down a mutiny, surrounding a military camp of mutineers at Jinja, but despite the potential for violence in Kenya, Uganda and Zanzibar, 2 Scots Guards saw no significant action during their more than two years in East Africa.[69]

At the beginning of 1970, 1 Scots Guards deployed to Sharjah for a nine-month tour in what was then part of the Trucial States British Protectorate. Sharjah, along with six other Emirates, later formed the United Arab Emirates in 1971/1972. The battalion's new commander, former SAS squadron commander, Lieutenant Colonel Murray de Klee, imposed a tough regime of long desert marches and exercises in the sand dunes of the Rub' al Khali. De Klee's Adjutant and Quartermaster were also former members of the SAS: 'fitness and more fitness' became the mantra of the battalion. According to one officer, the battalion left the Arabian desert 'with its tail up and at a peak of efficiency'.[70] However, 1 Scots Guards' extensive desert training was very different from the skills that would be required on the streets of West Belfast less than a year later. The Scots Guards were training for jungle and desert warfare; nobody predicted that the overwhelming number of operational tours for the next decade would be in the United Kingdom.

The Argyll and Sutherland Highlanders, 1963–1970

In 1967, 2nd Lieutenant Dick Parata, 1st Battalion, the Black Watch, was temporarily attached to the Argyll and Sutherland Highlanders and deployed to Aden. *The Thin Red Line*, the regimental magazine of the Argylls, asked Lieutenant Parata to write an article on the differences between the two regiments. In a strikingly honest article, that may not have endeared him to other Black Watch officers, Parata wrote that the principal difference between the two regiments was 'active service'; the Argylls had been on almost constant active service since the Second World War. By contrast, the Black Watch had deployed overseas on only a handful of occasions.[71] Active service had given the Argylls a keener sense of professional soldiering. It had also loosened formal discipline between the ranks. In a nod to the Argylls' reputation for aggression, Parata noted

---

69 Naylor, *Among Friends*, 34.
70 Naylor, *Among Friends*, 82.
71 D. Parata, 'Reflections of a Black Watch Officer', *Thin Red Line*, September 1967.

that the Argylls' formal training structures had been complemented by the use of methods 'not entirely in the book'.[72] Lieutenant Parata was also impressed by the rather brutal fashion in which

> the Argylls have been able to prune out the old lags at each level of seniority who have proved of no use on active service. Many soldiers, a nuisance in barracks, have risen to considerable heights in Borneo and Aden. It is apparent that the good, well-behaved barrack room soldier may be quite useless in the field while the reverse also applies.

Combat, 'the surprising jolt of bullets passing very close ... quickly induces a professional outlook' and makes the soldier value his training.[73] Parata concluded that the great divide between regiments was not ancient customs or inherited NCO culture: it was which had had the most opportunity to learn from operating under fire. The Argylls, although notoriously unbending when it came to punishing 'shirking', the dereliction of duty, permitted a certain amount of 'banter' between the ranks. Indeed, officers were gently mocked in regimental publications.[74]

Borneo

The Argylls deployed to Borneo on three operational tours: April–September 1964, February–May 1965 and November 1965–April 1966. Many of the 'infiltrated' Chinese villages had been relocated; the Argylls showed little or no animosity towards the remaining inhabitants. Instead, their officers thought that the local indigenous population were on the whole generally cooperative. Comparisons were drawn with Cyprus where the Argylls had faced a profoundly hostile reception in 1958 and responded in kind.[75] But soldiers needed to endure almost unbearable heat. Temperatures frequently reached close to 40 degrees Celsius. Extreme humidity was the norm; each Argyll carried at least 70–80 pounds on their backs. On the second tour, in 1965, the soldiers had been issued with

---

72 Parata, 'Reflections of a Black Watch Officer'.
73 Parata, 'Reflections of a Black Watch Officer'.
74 'Signal Platoon Notes', *Thin Red Line*, September 1964.
75 Interview with an Argyll officer who served in Cyprus. Interview with Argyll Soldier 31 (Officer), May 2014.

American carbine .223 inch 'Armalite' rifles, weapons the Argylls would later face in Northern Ireland, instead of the heavier 7.62 mm self-loading rifle (SLR).[76] The Argylls were also given lighter uniforms. But better equipment came with consequences. Longer patrols became the norm; soldiers would frequently walk for 8–10 hours a day. A platoon commander would normally establish a base camp in his patrol area so that they could dump some equipment and return to it at night; this position would be changed at least every 48 hours to avoid detection.[77]

The first major contact of 1 Argylls' tour in Borneo occurred on the night of August 2, 1964 when a patrol led by Lieutenant David Thomson was mortared at their border base in Pa Lungan in Sarawak. A quick follow-up, including the use of helicopters, enabled a party led by Lieutenant Thomson and Sergeant Brian Baty to ambush the Indonesian-led group, resulting in the death of six insurgents.[78] Sergeant Brian Baty was awarded the military medal for his actions. The then second-in-command of the battalion, Major Colin Mitchell, wrote, 'NCOs did the work of officers and platoon commanders were given wide geographical areas which in any other campaign would have fallen to the lot of a battalion commander. It bred self-sufficiency and confidence to an astonishing degree.'[79] Sergeant Baty would later go on to be commissioned, command an SAS Squadron and face trial in Dublin in 1977 for an incursion into the Republic of Ireland.[80]

Discipline began to fray on the second and third tours; in April 1965, two soldiers (Lance Corporal Grant and Private Allan) were court-martialled; in the same month, the commanding officer, Colonel Malcolm Wallace, had to apologise to the civilian authorities in Lundu for an accidental shooting incident at Kuala Brunei involving his soldiers.[81]

76 The Argylls would come to miss their lighter Armalites when they were covering long distances by foot in the border areas during their 1972 tour of Northern Ireland.
77 J. MacMillan, Officer Commanding, Delta Company, 1st Battalion, Argyll and Sutherland Highlanders, 'Borneo Patrol', *Thin Red Line*, May 1966.
78 D. Thomson, 'The Combat Tracker Teams', *Thin Red Line*, September 1967.
79 Mitchell, *Having Been a Soldier*, 120.
80 Interview with Argyll Soldier 10 (Officer), December 2013.
81 TNA: WO 305/2199 Army Unit Historical Reports, 1 Argyll and Sutherland Highlanders, April 1965, Minutes of the Meeting of the Divisional Executive Committee held at HQ Miri on May 7, 1964.

On December 8, 1965, during the third and final tour, when the Argylls were based in the area around Serian in Sarawak, a soldier refused to go on patrol.[82] The most significant fire fight of the Argylls' Borneo tours took place in June 1965. Again, Lieutenant Thomson was in command, winning the Military Cross during an encounter in which his platoon ambushed and killed 11 insurgents.[83] Thomson's well-set ambush against superior enemy numbers and his subsequent extraction of his platoon by 'fire and manoeuvre' became a textbook example of platoon commander leadership for future Sandhurst students.[84] Borneo made Thomson's reputation and he was a widely respected combat officer when he arrived to command a company in Newry in July 1972.

Aden

In 1967, *The Thin Red Line* reflected on its wealth of operational experiences over two decades: 'Not only can we claim to be the "most travelled Regiment in the British Army" ... but it would also be very fair to say that "where there is trouble you will find the Argylls ... HAVE GUN ... STILL TRAVELLING".'[85] However, if the Argylls are recalled today, it is often for their tour of Aden in 1967 and particularly their outspoken commanding officer, Lieutenant Colonel Colin Mitchell, whose blunt interviews to the world's press earned him the sobriquet of 'Mad Mitch'. Sinn Féin leader Gerry Adams would later try to draw a direct continuum between operations in Aden and Northern Ireland, part of a concerted attempt by Irish Republicans to portray Operation Banner as simply another rear-guard 'colonial' war.[86]

Colonel Colin Mitchell took over command of 1 Argylls on January 12, 1967. Major Paddy Palmer, who would later command 1st Battalion

---

82 TNA: WO 305/2208 Army Unit Historical Reports, 1 Argyll and Sutherland Highlanders, December 1965.

83 TNA: WO 373/140/16 Recommendation for Award for Thomson, David Philip. Rank: Lieutenant. Regiment: 1st Battalion, Argyll and Sutherland Highlanders. Theatre: Borneo.

84 Interview with Argyll Soldier 10 (Officer), December 2013.

85 'Aden', *Thin Red Line*, September 1967.

86 Gerry Adams, 'Britain's Dirty War in Ireland Exposed', *Guardian*, November 21, 2013 http://www.theguardian.com/commentisfree/2013/nov/21/britain-dirty-war-ireland-bbc-panorama (accessed May 3, 2015).

in Northern Ireland in 1972, was appointed as OC of B Company.[87] Mitchell was a proven soldier – not only had he seen action in the Second World War but he had also commanded B Company in Korea and taken part in some hard fighting. His headstrong reputation and dislike of compromise were well known.[88] The tour in Yemen initially appeared to be straightforward, if somewhat inglorious: Aden Crown Colony was due to be handed over to a new South Yemeni government at the end of 1967. The only task that was left was for the British Army to try to contain violence in the Colony and to a lesser degree in the outlying Protectorates in advance of the final withdrawal, to leave as much as possible to a new, politically and militarily inchoate South Yemeni government. Mitchell meticulously trained his battalion for its Aden deployment; he turned Seaton Barracks in Cornwall, where the Argylls were based, into an innovative training ground for the type of colonial internal security operations he expected to face in Aden. But just a week before the Argylls were due to arrive en masse in Aden to take over security duties from the 5th Royal Northumberland Fusiliers in the Crater district of the city, the situation in Aden took a dramatic turn for the worse. The Aden Armed Police, long suspected of being infiltrated by the Yemeni socialist group, the National Liberation Front (NLF) and the Front for the Liberation of South Yemen (FLOSY), mutinied. On June 20, 1967, the mutineers ambushed a convoy led by Major John Moncur, OC of Y Company, 5th Battalion, Royal Northumberland Fusiliers. Moncur had decided to drive into the centre of the Crater district to assess the extent of the mutiny for himself and was accompanied by Major Bryan Malcolm and two private soldiers who were part of the Argyll advance party. All three Argylls were killed; in total 22 British soldiers lost their lives in a carefully planned ambush of Moncur's convoy.[89]

The Argylls had a deep sense of foreboding upon arriving in Aden at the end of June 1967, a feeling of being alone and exposed: 'the first impressions gained are of choking humidity, barbed wire, watchfulness,

---

87 'Aden', *Thin Red Line*, September 1967; BBC News, 'Return to Aden – without Mad Mitch'.

88 Interview with Argyll Soldier 10 (Officer), December 2014.

89 For an excellent account of the political dynamics at play in South Yemen before the Aden withdrawal, see A. Edwards, *Mad Mitch's Tribal Law: Aden and the End of Empire* (Edinburgh: Mainstream Publishing, 2014).

and a rather sinister deserted air about the buildings'.[90] Soldiers voiced their dislike of the Adeni women who they found to be covered in unattractive *abayas* and did not seem to enjoy the occasional encounters they had with them: 'Some of the women try out their few English words on the Jocks at the roadblocks, cackling shrilly at their own cleverness and temerity'.[91] Unattractive, 'cackling' women; a dislike or disdain for local women was also to feature as a theme of the Argylls' experience of Northern Ireland.

Colonel Mitchell was not the type of commanding officer to sit back and leave provocation and attacks upon his men go unpunished. An assault into the centre of Crater district was called for:

> The plan was … to enter by Marine Drive and establish ourselves by phases in the Business and Banking sector, then exploit to the Crater police station and form up in the central and southern parts of the town with a view to move northwards towards the armed police barracks [the effective command post of the mutiny].[92]

Mitchell addressed the battalion before they went into Aden: 'If you have no ammunition you are to go in with the bayonet. It is better the whole Battalion dies in Crater to rescue one Jock than any one of us come out alive.'[93] Whether Mitchell exceeded his orders during the operation to retake Crater district has become a topic of persistent debate; his immediate superiors clearly felt that he had done so.[94] What is not in doubt is that Mitchell achieved what he wanted to achieve on July 3, 1967: he took Crater and he got revenge for the death of Major Malcolm. Wielding Bryan Malcolm's *Cromach*,[95] Mitchell ordered Pipe Major Robson to play the Argylls' regimental charge, the regimental marches 'and Glendaruel Highlanders', the B Company march past. A lot of bloodshed was avoided by two factors: first, the rapidity of the Argyll advance into Crater, and second, and perhaps more importantly, the Arabic skills of Mitchell's

---

90 'Aden', *Thin Red Line*, September 1967.
91 'Aden', *Thin Red Line*, September 1967.
92 'Aden', *Thin Red Line*, September 1967.
93 Mitchell, *Having Been a Soldier*, 193.
94 See Walker, *Aden Insurgency: The Savage War in Yemen*.
95 An Argyllshire shepherd's crook or stick – ceremonially carried by officers of the Argyll and Sutherland Highlanders.

second in command, Major Nigel Crowe, who persuaded several units of the mutinying police to stand down and cooperate with the Argylls. Mitchell applied his own personal touch, telling the commander of the mutinous Aden Armed Police:

> [T]hat if, when we advanced again, there was any trouble, I was prepared to wipe out the Armed Police to a man. I told him that my soldiers were fresh from the Indonesian War and we were 'hillmen' like many of his armed policemen, who believed in deeds rather than words. He got the point![96]

The following days saw the consolidation of the Argylls control over the Crater district. Mitchell imposed what he called 'Argyll law':

> [I]f an act of terrorism were committed I would give the order, 'Portcullis!' 'Portcullis' was a code-word I chose with care. It implied strength and security. This one word was an order that brought down the full weight of the Argyll and Sutherland Highlanders. With a crash like the descent of a portcullis at the gates of a castle Crater was sealed … The Jocks spread out in the streets rounding up all terrorist suspects – usually males between the ages of 15 and 35 – herding them into the compound we had erected for their reception.[97]

There was nothing very complex about such an approach: the Argylls simply chased after and captured all the men of military age they could find in area, detaining them until they felt they could be safely released. The Argylls were out for revenge against the population writ large: 'We didn't like the Arabs. To us Jocks they were just smelly, dirty people. And we treated them like smelly, dirty people.'[98]

In a BBC documentary broadcast in 2004, soldiers from both the Royal Northumberland Fusiliers and the Argyll and Sutherland Highlanders described acts of 'murder' and 'war crimes' perpetrated by British soldiers

96 Mitchell, *Having Been a Soldier*, 85.
97 Mitchell, *Having Been a Soldier*, 195–196.
98 Jimmy Lynn, ex-Argyll and Sutherland Highlanders, interviewed in BBC television documentary, 'Mad Mitch and his Tribal Law', released as part of a DVD collection, 'Empire Warriors' (London: BBC, 2004).

in Aden.[99] These allegations echoed accounts given by several former Argylls to the (Glasgow) *Sunday Herald* of the indiscriminate firing on civilians including local Adenis queuing for water and men who were sitting at a café, the summary execution of a taxi driver by an Argyll officer who wanted to 'try out his pistol' and the bayoneting of an unarmed Arab teenager.[100] Private Brian Roy of the Royal Northumberland Fusiliers described to the BBC how soldiers in Aden 'shot innocent people to gain glory'.[101] An Argyll account described escalating inter-platoon rivalry over 'kill-counts' and that, to encourage his men, one officer awarded a 'Golliwog' sticker, taken from Robertson jam jars, for each 'kill' during the Argylls' 'Gollyhunt'.[102] Such allegations have refused to go away over the decades and have been made by a succession of Argyll soldiers who served in Aden.

Interrogation by the Army in Aden often meant torture, using methods far more brutal than would be seen in Northern Ireland. Major Joe Starling, second-in-command of 1st Battalion, Parachute Regiment (1 PARA) and later a Brigadier and Deputy Commander of 3rd Infantry Brigade in Northern Ireland in 1972, was also deployed with his battalion to Aden in 1967. He described 'Player' battalions in Aden – units that were tough, knew how to get the job done and did not care for legal niceties. Starling recalled that when prisoners were interrogated in Aden, frequently in the basement of the Chartered Bank building, they were often tortured and occasionally summarily executed. According to Starling, Aden Brigade HQ was determined to clamp down this behaviour by 'Player' battalions, including 1 PARA: 'It was made quite clear that if any more prisoners were shot "trying to escape" or damaged by "accidentally falling downstairs" a full investigation would be initiated, from which, it was hinted, dire consequences would follow.' Eventually, Starling's battalion resorted to simulating torture, threatening prisoners with medical sterilisation, a process that Starling believed yielded excellent results.[103]

99 Jimmy Lynn, 'Mad Mitch and his Tribal Law'.

100 'More ex-Soldiers Speak out about Aden', *Sunday Mail*, May 3, 1981.

101 Brian Roy, ex-Royal Northumberland Fusiliers, interviewed in BBC television documentary, 'Mad Mitch and his Tribal Law'.

102 'They Killed for More Golliwog Labels: Aden File', *Sunday Mail*, May 17, 1981.

103 J. Starling, *Soldier On! The Testament of a Tom* (Tunbridge Wells: Spellmount, 1992), 52.

The Argylls were to suffer a total of 29 casualties (5 dead and 24 wounded) during their four-month Aden tour. Mitchell was particularly disgusted with the Labour government's acceptance of the NLF as the de facto rulers of Aden, and their willingness to negotiate the colony's handover to them. Mitchell's disdain for the British political and military hierarchy trickled down the ranks: one Argyll ended a poem to the five Argylls killed in Aden with, 'In this fight there is no glory, and death comes by the rules. The lives of Highland soldiers in the hands of senseless fools.'[104] However, the experience of Aden and Mitchell's leadership divided the Argylls. One Argylls officer was concerned that the Argylls in Aden had earned a reputation as a 'slightly rogue' battalion in the British Army. Another officer from the Queen's Dragoon Guards recalled his experience of deploying alongside the Argylls in Aden: 'They were accused of robbing people. They did. I saw it! I was told mind my own business. All the accusations against the Argyll and Sutherland Highlanders were always pooh-poohed by Colonel Mitchell as "They're trying to blacken our name". And that's all he put it down to. They were extremely violent.'[105] The future editor of *The Times*, Charles Douglas-Home, met with senior officials at the Ministry of Defence to express his concern over abuses perpetrated by Argyll soldiers in Aden. Some brief enquiries were made, but no Argyll soldier was interviewed. The Ministry of Defence findings were inconclusive; the Under-Secretary of State for the Army, James Boyden MP, was at pains to keep such enquiries secret from the Argylls and especially from Colonel Mitchell, who was popular with much of the Conservative Party and the media.[106]

Events during an exercise in Cyprus in the summer of 1968 did nothing to dispel suspicions about Argyll misconduct in Aden. Four Argylls were convicted of looting watches from a shop owned (unfortunately for them) by a retired Major from the Cameron Highlanders. The Argylls were already mistrusted in Cyprus over a series of alleged atrocities committed in or near the village of Kathykas on September 13–14, 1958. These included allegations of rape, the mistreatment of an orthodox priest and the shooting of a local man who, according to

104 Aden', *Thin Red Line*, September 1967.
105 'Mad Mitch and his Tribal Law'.
106 TNA: DEFE 24/1854 Allegations of Misconduct in Aden, dated 1968.

the Argylls, failed to stop at a checkpoint, all of which occurred within 24 hours of an insurgent (EOKA) ambush in which one Argyll was killed and several were wounded.[107] Before going to Cyprus, the Argylls had also drawn more negative attention to themselves in the spring of that year when a number of Chinese residents of Plymouth (where the Argylls were based at Seaton Barracks) ended up in hospital after 'a violent encounter' with off-duty Argyll soldiers.[108]

Disbandment and Rebirth

The threatened disbandment of the Argyll and Sutherland Highlanders prompted a massive public relations campaign to save the regiment. The 'Save the Argylls' campaign became a badge of mutually reinforcing Scottish national pride and British patriotism. The campaign gathered more than a million signatures and a compromise was reached whereby a single company was retained, Balaklava Company. Most Argylls were sent to join other Highland regiments, including the Gordon Highlanders and the Royal Highland Fusiliers. Then, in response to public pressure, Conservative attempts to shore up their vote in Scotland for the 1970 election and a sudden increase in operational requirements in Northern Ireland, Prime Minister Edward Heath reversed the decision to disband the Argylls. The regiment's single battalion was reconstituted on January 17, 1972, a few months before its first tour to Northern Ireland.[109]

In the late 1960s, 2nd Battalion, Scots Guards, was also threatened with disbandment – the Scots Guards were to be reduced to one regular battalion. However, Scots Guards officers played a very different hand to the confrontational approach of the Argylls. Lieutenant Colonel John Swinton, the Scots Guards' Lieutenant Colonel Commanding, knew his way around Whitehall considerably better than Colonel Mitchell. From his contacts in the Conservative Party, Swinton understood that 2nd Battalion would most likely be re-established if there was a change of government. He succeeded in persuading the Ministry of Defence to place 2 Scots Guards in 'suspended animation', meaning that its soldiers

---

107 C. Foley, *Legacy of Strife: Cyprus from Rebellion to Civil War* (Harmondsworth: Penguin, 1962), 136–137.

108 TNA: DEFE 24/1854 Misconduct in Aden.

109 Interview with Argyll Soldier 31 (Officer), May 2014.

would be sent to other Guards Battalions on a temporary basis. The Labour government did not object.[110] The Scots Guards approach was to work the corridors of power, not to seek mass public support.

Conclusion

Senior officers of the British Army in the 1960s and early 1970s retained a faith in old training standards and attitudes, not only because these reflected their instinctive preference in preserving the rituals and instruction they had gone through as young men, but also because they believed that such methods were indispensable to combat effectiveness. The Army was convinced that drills and rank structures, many of which were inherited from the nineteenth century, still had operational merit. These encouraged automatism; other tactics could be learned later, whether for jungle warfare in Borneo or laying ambushes in the ditches and hedgerows of South Armagh. Rehearsing training concepts was also a ritual, one in which each soldier would commit his professional skills as a soldier to further the interests of the group. If he failed, he risked exclusion and/or contempt from his peers; his sense of professional and social worth was at stake. Both in training and on operations, a young private soldier would look to a 'reality constructor', often a junior NCO, to set the professional and social norms that he should emulate.

Although public school officers dominated the higher ranks of the Army, the institution also exhibited a 'chameleon effect' on the sons of the lower-middle and middle classes. All soldiers, but particularly NCOs and lower ranks, were expected to conform to a hyper-masculine norm. The Argylls had more recent combat experience than most British Army regiments before their deployment to Northern Ireland, including the Scots Guards. In Aden, the Argylls appear to have treated the local Arab population with considerable contempt and brutality. As will be observed in subsequent chapters, the Argylls did not behave in such a generally cruel and violent manner towards the Northern Irish population. Colonel Palmer, as a company commander in Aden (B Company, 1 Argylls), was reported by another Argyll officer to have had several bitter arguments with Colonel Colin Mitchell, his battalion commanding officer, over what he perceived to be an overly aggressive approach to operations in the

110 Naylor, *Among Friends*, 84.

Crater district of the city. As 1 Argylls CO, Palmer knew that the use of such tactics in the UK would be disastrous.[111]

The Scots Guards exhibited a more rigid separation of rank than the Argylls; Scots Guards NCOs were well known, if not notorious, for their strict enforcement of discipline and standards. Guards' officers delegated considerable authority to NCOs for the day-to-day running of battalions. However, each Guards officer in the early 1970s was expected to go through the same basic recruit training at Pirbright prior to going on to officer training at Sandhurst, a humbling experience for the more privileged recruits.[112] The Argylls were extremely proud of the leadership calibre of their NCOs, reporting that they occasionally fulfilled the tasks of officers when called upon. The exceptionally talented NCOs were made full, operational officers, a rare occurrence but more possible in the Argylls, partly due to a shortage of officer recruits, than the Scots Guards, where late commission entries (former senior NCOs) were often expected to fill administrative rather than combat roles.[113] Combat proved to be a great leveller: officers such as Lieutenant David Thomson enjoyed a special 'honour status' due to his professional combat success in Borneo; in Northern Ireland he could relax rank structures and occasionally demand that his soldiers 'throttle back' without a fear of losing respect. Until professional accomplishment had been attained, however, it was better for junior officers to keep some social distance from the rest of his Platoon and the gap should never be closed completely.

Both the Scots Guards and the Argylls were severely affected by the Labour government's decision to cut the number of infantry regiments in 1968; in the Argylls' case the decision marked the demise of their regiment. The Argylls retained a single company, while 2 Scots Guards was put into 'suspended animation'. Interviewees would later recall the detrimental effect this would have upon operational readiness in 1972 as both regiments re-assembled two battalions weeks before deploying to Northern Ireland. The Argylls harboured a particularly acute sense of wounded betrayal.[114] Moreover, in 1971, upon its return from desert

---

111 Interview with Argyll Soldier 17 (Officer), May 2014.
112 Interview with Scots Guards Soldier 15 (Officer), December 2013.
113 Interview with Argyll Soldier 11 (Officer), May 2014.
114 Interview with Scots Guards Soldier 13 (Officer), December 2013.

training, 1 Scots Guards lost precious weeks of training for their West Belfast deployment due to the insistence of the Duke of Edinburgh that they take part in the re-enactment of a Napoleonic battle, to the immense frustration of their CO, Lieutenant Colonel Murray de Klee.[115]

115 Adjutant's Diary, 1st Battalion, Scots Guards, 1970–1971, Scots Guards Regimental Headquarters, Wellington Barracks, London.

2

The Political and Operational Environment in Northern Ireland, 1969–1972

Soldiers are frustrated by the politicians' failure to combat the terrorists with strength. What can you say to one of your men when he asks, 'Which side are the politicians on sir?'[1]

Civil-Military Relations, Political Aims and Operational Tensions in Northern Ireland, 1971–1972

In 1969, Defence Secretary Denis Healey looked back with satisfaction upon his part in reforming the military for a new, post-imperial era. Healey had cut defence spending by a third since 1964, making savings in the defence budget of £5 billion over five years. He had also brought the Army home; more than half of the UK's 59 infantry battalions now served in the UK, including ten in Northern Ireland on the newly constituted Operation Banner, the essential aim of which was to prevent sectarian rioting during a period of wider political reform in the province. Britain now had a military 'fit for a different era'.[2] But, within the senior ranks of the Army, a change in location did not mean a shift in values and tactics. In 1969, a police officer who worked closely with the Army, described the military ethos as he knew it:

1 Lord Richard Cecil, a Captain in the Grenadier Guards and son of the 6th Marquess of Salisbury, quoted in A. Turner, *Crisis? What Crisis?* (London: Aurum Press, 2008), 67. See also Strachan, *Politics*, 6.
2 D. Healey, 'British Defence Policy', *RUSI Journal* 114(656) (1969), 1.

The basic duty of an infantry soldier is to seek out the enemy and destroy him. From the day he joins he has the offensive spirit drummed into him. 'Law', as far as he is concerned, is a matter of army regulations. He is a fighter, and when he strikes he does so with devastating force and preferably without warning ... The most narrow-minded type of soldier thinks of guerrillas as a purely military force, and measures success in terms of the 'bag' recorded in the Battalion game book.[3]

This chapter contends that it took key senior officers a considerable time to adjust to the operational limitations of war at home in the UK. In Northern Ireland, 'the offensive spirit' had to be contained. The enemy was not to be shot on sight, unless he or she was imminently preparing an attack; he or she was to be arrested and tried by civilian courts. Discord between military and civilian leaders and dissent within battalions over the *right* type of tactics to pursue led to an inconsistent approach by the Army in Northern Ireland. Soldiers also found that military operations in Northern Ireland were open to unprecedented levels of public scrutiny and criticism. It was left to political leaders, including the Secretary of State for Northern Ireland, William Whitelaw, to help focus and limit the Army's approach in Ulster so that it conformed to the policies, laws and values of the UK.

The Origins of the Troubles

In the aftermath of the devastating border explosions near Narrow Water, County Down that killed 18 British soldiers on August 27, 1979, Prime Minister Margaret Thatcher commissioned a review of counter-terrorism operations in South Armagh, headed up by the former head of SIS (MI6), Sir Maurice Oldfield. In a joint submission to the review, senior RUC and Army representatives reported that the origin of the IRA's campaign in South Armagh in 1972 was the culmination of a number of factors which eventually ignited an insurgent campaign:

> [T]he 1960s civil rights Campaign, the exodus of displaced Belfast Catholics across the border arising out of the street disorders in

3 S. Hutchinson, 'The Police Role in Counterinsurgency', *RUSI Journal* 114(4) (1969), 53.

1969, internment, terrorists on the 'run' North and South of the border; the closing of border roads and the accidental shooting dead in 1971 by the army in Belfast of a local Crossmaglen man, Henry Thornton, shaped and hardened attitudes not seen to the same extent during the last IRA campaign, 1956–1962, during which the police coped alone with just 3 losses in the area and an indifferent attitude on the part of the local community.[4]

The death of Henry Thornton was the moment when rising resentment mutated into violent and persistent insurgency. The people of South Armagh had long been aggrieved by sectarian violence in Belfast and Derry and their long-standing political isolation from the rest of Ireland. But it took a local event, the fatal wounding of a local man, to precipitate what would endure for decades as the most enduring micro-conflict within Northern Ireland. According to an IRA Volunteer interviewed by journalist Toby Harnden, 'That night Mickey McVerry [a future leading member of the Provisional IRA] and a group of other fellows almost took Crossmaglen [police] barracks over with their bare hands and a couple of nail bombs.' There was a surge in the number of recruits to the IRA.[5]

Remarkably, 11 years after the start of Operation Banner, and despite the presence of 734 soldiers (six companies and one close observation platoon), a security review of South Armagh reported that, 'we have no forward intelligence whatsoever. We react to PIRA's activities and our planned offensive operations are to a greater or lesser degree speculative'.[6] The material gathered by Oldfield clearly demonstrated an almost total lack of cooperation between the local population and the Army/RUC in South Armagh. However, Oldfield also argued that there was nothing inevitable about support for the IRA, even in an area with a long history of antipathy to the Union like South Armagh. A hardening

4 TNA: CJ 4/3090 South Armagh: South Armagh Security Review, Joint Police/Army Submission to the Security Coordinator Sir Maurice Oldfield and his Staff by Assistant Chief Constable (South) and Brigade Commander 3 Infantry Brigade, Armagh Monday, January 21, 1980.
5 T. Harnden, *Bandit Country: The IRA and South Armagh* (London: Hodder and Stoughton, 2000), 40.
6 TNA: CJ 4/3090 South Armagh, South Armagh Security Review, Joint Police/Army Submission.

of attitudes had taken place in response to the perceived brutality of the security forces, brought home with deadly effect by the killing of a local Crossmaglen man.[7]

Reading the reports of the 1980 security review helps contextualise and magnify the challenges faced by units in the earlier, much more violent days of Operation Banner in 1972, when just over 100 soldiers from B Company, 1 Argylls, took on responsibility for countering the IRA in South Armagh. The small geographical area of South Armagh was affected by wider events in Northern Ireland, but local ones tended to be decisive. Soldiers played their part in fostering an escalation of conflict as well as reducing it, depending on the tactics employed at the time. As Richard English has observed, 'The actions of the British Army at times stimulated precisely that subversion against which they were often clumsily and lethally deployed. Each of these actions made internal sense to their practitioners; each contributed to the emergent war; and between them they led to the birth of the Provisional IRA.'[8]

Army Doctrine and Military Aid to the Civil Power

Once basic training – physical fitness, discipline, familiarisation with rifle drills – had been completed, soldiers could expect to receive instruction, mostly within their battalions, for specific operations. Internal security operations, or military aid to the civil power (MACP), was one such contingency. MACP training in the late 1960s and early 1970s, until the development of the Northern Ireland Training and Advisory Teams (NITATs), leaned heavily on the British colonial experience. Indeed, there is a discernible continuation of principles espoused by the influential Major General Sir Charles Gwynn in *Imperial Policing*, written during the 1930s, and internal security and MACP doctrine published by the Army in 1969. Army doctrine continued to emphasise 'minimum force' but also 'firm and timely action' to arrest or shoot 'ring-leaders' and mutual understanding between the security forces (including the police).[9] An Argyll officer who served with Balaklava Company in Gibraltar in 1971, recalled that, a year before deploying on Operation Banner, the Argylls

---

7 TNA: CJ 4/3090 South Armagh.
8 English, *Armed Struggle*, 146–147.
9 C. Gwynn, *Imperial Policing* (London: Macmillan, 1934).

were still training for 'internal security operations' according to colonial 'disperse or we fire' loudhailer tactics.[10]

British Army MACP doctrine firmly underlined that operations in the UK must adhere to the limitations imposed by British civil law.[11] Training was recommended in small convoy movements, urban patrols, counter-improvised explosive devices techniques, covert observation posts, setting and evading ambushes and manning road-blocks and vehicle checkpoints. Special training was also suggested in intelligence, psychological operations and community relations. Army doctrine carefully expounded the various options available to commanders to disperse hostile crowds or illegal demonstrations, including verbal persuasion, a 'show of force' and more positive actions such as water cannon and baton rounds. Hong Kong crowd control techniques were seen as a useful model: soldiers were drawn up in four lines of eight, beginning with the arrest section, followed by eight men armed with CS gas, who were in turn succeeded by eight other soldiers with baton rounds and finally by a firearms section. A soldier was detailed to take pictures of the crowd for later use in identifying potential criminals. Soldiers were also taught tactics such as 'assaults from an unexpected direction'. Soldiers were only to open fire when 'the situation is so dangerous that other means … are ineffective and that it is necessary and reasonable to do so'. Fire was only to be aimed against those instigating the most serious and potentially deadly violence against soldiers. Wherever possible, police force was recommended instead of military force.[12]

Soldiers deployed to Northern Ireland were also instructed on 'Yellow Card' restrictions, a short document issued to each soldier offering guidance on when to open fire. The Yellow Card succeeded the more permissive 'Blue Card' that had been used in Aden and other colonial conflicts during the 1960s. Yellow Card restrictions were continuously revised during the early years of Operation Banner. In 1972, they stressed that soldiers should use all other means first before opening fire. No ammunition was to be carried in the breech of a rifle. Only company commanders and above could order weapons to be cocked

10 Interview with Argyll Soldier 5 (Officer), May 2014; Interview with Argyll Soldier 30 (Officer), December 2016.

11 Ministry of Defence, *Land Operations*, vol. 3, *Counter Revolutionary Operations: Part 1 – Principles and General Aspects* (London: Ministry of Defence, 1969), 85–86.

12 Ministry of Defence, *Land Operations*, vol. 3, 65–70.

and automatic fire used. The Yellow Card went on to say that, 'Wherever possible a warning should be given before you open fire.' A warning could be dispensed with only in circumstances where soldiers first came under direct fire and against a person carrying a weapon about to be used for offensive purposes. The same guidance applied to individuals who appeared to be about to throw a bomb at soldiers and, more vaguely, on occasions where, 'There is no other way to protect yourself or those whom it is your duty to protect from the danger of being killed.'[13] In every instance, soldiers were expected to follow clear orders and drills. Operationally, in 'a blackened, burning city filled with gas and smoke', baited, bewildered and exhausted soldiers struggled to implement such guidelines.[14]

The Trouble with Northern Ireland

Senior Army officers had some grasp of the historical trajectory and narratives of the Ulster conflict, tracing its modern manifestation back to the tumultuous seventeenth century when the Stuart monarchs of Britain and Ireland had seized large amounts of land from the native Catholic Irish aristocracy and given it to Protestant 'planted' settlers from Britain. A Protestant ascendancy was later confirmed during the 'glorious revolution' of 1688 and the triumph of Protestant William III of Orange over Catholic James II (who had briefly tried to reverse many of the policies that discriminated in favour of Protestants). In discussing the origin of 'the Troubles', senior Army officers understood, and often sympathised with, the enduring grievances of the large Catholic minority in Northern Ireland since the partition of Ireland in the early 1920s. The gerrymandering of electoral boundaries, unfair allocation of housing and discriminatory employment practices by local authorities, particularly west of the River Bann, fostered alienation among many Catholics.[15] The overwhelmingly Protestant Ulster Unionist party (UUP) had dominated the government of Northern Ireland since its creation; there was never any prospect of the political parties supported by most Catholics entering

13 Liddell-Hart Centre for Military Archives: Rt. Hon. Sir Frank Cooper Papers GB0099 KCLMA Cooper, F.: 'Instructions by the Director of Operations for Opening Fire in Northern Ireland', dated November 1972.
14 Interview with Scots Guards Soldier 1 (Officer), May 2014.
15 Dewar, The British Army, 15–21.

government at any stage over the five preceding decades of devolved rule in Belfast.[16]

Prior to the 1960s, Catholics were disaffected but poorly mobilised. Most Catholics wanted to retain a British connection; for many, the quarrel was primarily with local Unionist misgovernment and a reformed UK was a potentially attractive place for Catholics. Catholics identified with being 'Irish' (as opposed to 'Northern Irish' or simply 'British'), but this did not automatically translate into allegiance to a government in Dublin.[17] Indeed, the tentative reforms of Northern Irish Prime Minister Terence O'Neill in the mid-1960s, including a curtailment of sectarian bias in the allocation of public services and promises to end gerrymandering, hinted that Catholic grievances in Northern Ireland might be resolved peacefully. It took the violent response to the civil rights movement for communal tensions to erupt.[18] The civil rights movement was a broad coalition, from conservative Nationalist Party leaders, to left-wing students, to members of the IRA, that was energised by the example of political protest movements elsewhere during the 1960s and willing to pit itself against the Northern Irish government during a period of significant political reform and change in the UK as a whole. The banning and severe police crackdown on marches and the failure by the RUC to prevent Loyalist violence against peaceful demonstrators served as tinder to the civil rights flame.[19]

Rioting on the streets of Belfast and Derry in response to the civil rights movement's campaign significantly worsened during the summer of 1969. The RUC and the part-time Ulster Special Constabulary's reputation among Catholics for sectarian bias and excessive violence had steadily worsened since the preceding year. On August 15, 1969, Prime Minister Harold Wilson acceded to a request by the Northern Irish government to deploy troops on the streets of Belfast and Londonderry to assist in dealing with the sectarian riots. Reinforcements were deployed to bolster the 2,500 soldiers already stationed in Northern Ireland.

---

16 TNA: CJ 4/1290 Army – Northern Ireland Office 1975–1976, Discussion Paper written by Mr Gowdy, Northern Ireland Office, November 24, 1976.
17 Beattie-Smith, *The British State*, 35.
18 TNA: CJ 4/1290 Discussion Paper written by Mr Gowdy.
19 See S. Prince and G. Warner, *Belfast and Derry in Revolt* (Dublin: Irish Academic Press, 2012), 103–132 for an insightful account of the emergence and make-up of the civil rights movement.

Soldiers fixed bayonets and formed squares, as was standard practice for dealing with riots in the colonies.[20]

The Beginning of Operation Banner

The arrival of troops on the streets of Belfast was already too late for the hundreds of people, mainly Catholics, who had been burned out of their homes in Belfast. Downing Street issued a communiqué on August 19, 1969 stating that the new GOC Northern Ireland, Lieutenant General Ian Freeland, would have overall command for 'security operations' (but not more conventional crime prevention and investigation – the line between the two was hard to draw), including authority over 3,200 RUC personnel, and would be accountable to the Ministry of Defence rather than the Northern Irish government. The GOC would also assume full command over the almost exclusively Protestant Ulster Special Constabulary. In subsequent months, the RUC would be disarmed and the USC disbanded. Plans for a new Ulster Defence Regiment (UDR), a part-time local defence force led by regular British Army officers and NCOs, were also announced. The decision to disband the USC caused serious rioting in Protestant areas of Belfast in October 1969, the firing of approximately 1,000 rounds by Loyalist paramilitaries at the Army and the wounding of 22 soldiers. In response, the Army shot a number of Loyalists, killing two.[21]

Northern Ireland Army Headquarters (HQNI) in Lisburn during the early days of Operation Banner was a small, increasingly crowded and rather chaotic place. One former officer recalled that, 'Everybody was struggling because nobody knew their way around the Province. There would be an incident in the Kashmir Road and we would all be pouring over the map to find Kashmir Road. It was a steep learning curve.'[22] The Catholic Bishop of Derry, Edward Daly, recalled a very 'colonial' attitude during his occasional visits to 8 Infantry Brigade Headquarters in Ebrington, Londonderry, with officers playing croquet over drinks beside the helipad. Some of the officers, he observed, knew more about India than Ireland. Later, a very different, savvy and 'modern' officer would emerge, but the years between 1969 and 1972 were a time of

20 Sanders and Wood, *Times of Trouble*, 3–4.
21 Dewar, *The British Army*, 39.
22 Interview with a former Military Intelligence Officer, May 2014.

flux.[23] Operation Banner's first GOC, Lieutenant General Ian Freeland, had apparently come to Northern Ireland as an end-of-career 'sinecure'; nobody predicted the outbreak of such levels of violence.[24]

In February 1971, Lieutenant General Vernon Erskine-Crum was appointed to take over as GOC Northern Ireland from General Freeland. Erskine-Crum, a Scots Guards officer who had served as a trusted adviser to Lord Mountbatten during negotiations over Indian independence in 1948, was regarded as one of the most outstanding officers of his generation, exceptionally intelligent and well briefed; he died of heart failure just weeks after assuming command in February 1971. To the surprise of many, Erskine-Crum was replaced by Lieutenant General Harry Tuzo, who had not been expected to rise above his post as director of artillery at the Ministry of Defence. Tuzo, according to one officer who served in HQNI, was 'not in the same class' as Erskine-Crum. His views on counter-insurgency operations had been cemented in Borneo, where he served as a brigadier under General Sir Walter Walker. Tuzo was sceptical of the efficacy of civilian authority during an 'emergency' such as that in Northern Ireland, preferring the 'military supremo' approach adopted by Templer in Malaya and Walker in Borneo. He found it difficult to adapt to operations in the UK.[25]

From Peacekeeping to Counter-Insurgency

Writing in an Army journal a young Grenadier Guards company commander captured the confusion and shock of these initial days of Operation Banner. His unit was deployed on the night of September 13, 1969 to prevent rioting between Catholics and Protestants at the interface of Tiger's Bay in North Belfast.

> As I set up company TAC [Tactical] headquarters, innumerable lawyers, clergymen, local leaders, vigilantes and drunks in turn clutched my elbow explaining how the incident had started. As

23 Interview with Edward Daly, Lord Bishop Emeritus of Derry, Londonderry, May 16, 2014.
24 Interview with a former Military Intelligence Officer, May 2014; 'Obituary: Harry Tuzo', *Independent*, August 19, 1998.
25 Interview with a former Military Intelligence Officer, May 2014; 'Obituary: Harry Tuzo'.

all explanations inevitably differed in most respects, they merely added to the confusion. Soon reports came in that schools and churches in the mixed areas were being threatened. Sections were redeployed accordingly. We stood there. The crowd stood there. Everyone glowered at everyone. The sky gradually lightened. The stars gently faded. Another day dawned. As I thinned out the company I was too tired to sense any relief or elation that bloodshed had been avoided. (In any event it hadn't been. That night, within the brigade, one soldier had taken his life and another had accidentally shot dead his friend in a telephone box.)[26]

Constant dialogue with 'citizens groups' and regular community relations projects were daily fare for many officers in late 1969 and early 1970. Some responded better to this requirement than others: in Belfast, artillery regiments often appeared to be more comfortable in liaising with local Republicans than the Infantry. Patrolling by foot through the streets of Belfast was not a familiar activity for the average gunner. Because they had neither a history of infantry soldering nor fixed preconceptions about their own 'toughness' in previously counter-insurgency campaigns, gunners were often more adaptive to local conditions and less sneering about activities considered 'unsoldierly' by others. For example, in early 1970, 1st Regiment, Royal Horse Artillery (RHA) recorded its close working relationships with local defence committees, and deliberately discreet patrolling, in its area of operations in West Belfast (the Falls/Springfield Road):

Maximum contact with the militants on both sides: Officers talked, talked and talked long into the night with spokesmen of either side. This effectively de-escalated the situation and took the steam out of events, which would otherwise have exploded. It enabled us, too, to be able to predict what would happen next. Maximum patrols with minimum showing. We soon learnt where and when to have patrols, some showing, some discreetly hidden. These patrols gave constant reports on every possible event.[27]

26 O. Linsday, 'Do Not Pass "GO" – Ulster 69', *British Army Review* 34 (1969), 42–48.
27 M. Farndale, 'To Belfast as Infantry', *Journal of the Royal Artillery* 97(2) (1970), 127–128.

Artillery soldiers also put their technical skills to good use, doing odd jobs in people's homes on 'a daily basis'.[28] However, 1st Battalion, Royal Scots, the unit that took over from 1st Regiment, RHA, welcomed a chance to take on both wings of the Republican movement (a split had occurred in the IRA at the end of 1969, leading to the emergence of the Marxist Official IRA [OIRA] and the Provisionals [IRA]; the latter steadily increased its support, partly due to its more fervent commitment to escalating the armed campaign, outstripping the Officials by late 1971, early 1972).[29]

The Royals Scots found the RHA's negotiating over barricades and other deal-making with local 'defence committees' too much to bear, an offence to UK sovereignty and to the hard-won reputation of the regiment.[30] Upon arrival in West Belfast in March 1970, the commanding officer of 1st Battalion, Royal Scots, Lieutenant Colonel Bob Richardson, recalled meeting Jim Sullivan, an Official IRA member and leader of the Central Citizens' Defence Committee (CDCC) on the Lower Falls Road that had put up barricades in response to Loyalist incursions in the area and to keep the RUC out. Sullivan claimed he wanted to avoid confrontation with the Army.

> [Sullivan] came up the road to see me in Springfield Road RUC station, where we had set up our battalion HQ. He sat down and told me of an agreement that had been operating with our predecessors, the Royal Horse Artillery. They, he said, when on street patrols either on foot or in their vehicles, moved in and out of the area and past barricades at times agreed with him and his committee. My reply to him was 'I'm sorry. We don't work that way. You take the barricades down or we will. We're the Royal Scots. Our job is to see that the Queen's writ runs here.' He wasn't very happy with that reply, I'm afraid.[31]

Colonel Richardson's views are understandable – only the State should provide protection for its citizens, the monopoly on the use of violence was under threat – but insensitive given the recent failures of the RUC

---

28 Farndale, 'To Belfast as Infantry', 127–128.
29 English, *Armed Struggle*, 146–147.
30 Sanders and Wood, *Times of Troubles*, 10.
31 Sanders and Wood, *Times of Trouble*, 3–4.

to act impartially and the Army's inability to prevent the sectarian burning of houses. Jim Sullivan was later suspected of killing a number of soldiers, including Scots Guardsmen during 1971 and 1972.[32]

The labour government in London was desperate to avoid getting 'sucked into the Irish bog'.[33] Labour also had a natural mistrust of the UUP, which was politically close to the Conservative party. A joint security committee (JSC) had been created in Belfast to coordinate operations between the police and the Army. However, the power of veto over new, tougher security operations resided with London. Home Secretary Jim Callaghan showed a keen interest in the workings of the JSC. There was a lull in the violence in the first months of 1970, which followed the announcement by the Northern Irish government of a package of local government reforms and an economic stimulus from London. But worse was yet to come: another round of sectarian rioting was triggered by contested Orange Order marches in Belfast, an early challenge for the new Conservative government in London under Prime Minister Edward Heath that took office in June 1970. A prolonged gun battle on June 27, 1970 in the Catholic Short Strand enclave of predominantly Protestant East Belfast saw IRA Volunteers defending St Matthew's church and the surrounding area from a Loyalist mob. Irish diplomats reported that this was a critical watershed – for the IRA and the British Army. The IRA had now emerged as the principal defenders of beleaguered Catholic areas from Loyalist violence, after months of sectarian riots in which Catholics had suffered most.[34]

Instead of focusing on why the Army had failed to protect working-class Catholic areas from Loyalist violence, a decision was taken by military leaders to go on the offensive against those who were now newly seen as those areas' defenders. The IRA was a readily recognisable 'enemy', with secessionist and subversive aims; militant Loyalism was a different tiger, one with a complex relationship with mainstream Unionism, including latent (and even overt) support from Northern Irish government ministers. Some accommodation had to be found with

32 Interview with Scots Guards Soldier 4 (NCO), November 2013.
33 J. Callaghan, *A House Divided: The Dilemma of Northern Ireland* (London: Collins, 1973), 15.
34 The National Archives of Ireland (hereafter NAI): 2000/5/33, British Troops in the North, 1969–October 1971, Paper entitled, 'British Army Policy in the North', undated.

the latter, albeit an uneasy one, but the former was growing in strength. HQNI concluded that the Republican boil had to be lanced; a curfew and search of the Falls Road in early July was the first significant step in this departure from more conciliatory Army tactics when it came to engaging with Republican groups. It was a disaster: the Army found 106 weapons and 250 lb of explosives, but the rough tactics of the Army – 'the destruction of homes and sacred objects, and acts of abuse and intimidation' – had a devastating effect on local attitudes. Many residents were angry at the weapons' seizures, claiming that these were necessary to defend vulnerable Catholic areas that the Army had proved incapable of protecting. Although a number of British journalists witnessed and wrote about the lead unit's (1st Battalion, Black Watch) apparently brutal behaviour on the Falls Road, the regiment itself rejected any criticism.[35] The CO of 1st Battalion, Black Watch, Lieutenant Colonel Andrew Watson, wrote that, 'When we came to compare notes between companies afterwards there was not one responsible person who had not been extremely impressed by the restraint, sense of compassion and general conduct of the Jocks throughout the operation.'[36] The Army and locals' accounts of the 'Curfew' remained diametrically opposed. Both versions were fiercely defended and restated without compromise.

Prime Minister Edward Heath was concerned by the Catholic and international reaction to the Falls Road Curfew, and insisted that the Army seek cabinet approval for such operations in the future.[37] Generally, however, the new Conservative Home Secretary, Reginald Maudling, and the Defence Secretary, Lord Carrington, allowed the Northern Irish government greater discretion over security policy than had been the case under the previous Labour government. Senior Army officers became more responsive to Northern Irish Prime Minister Brian Faulkner, who had replaced James Chichester Clark in March 1971 (the latter had replaced a beleaguered, exhausted Terence O'Neill in 1969 before resigning in protest at London's 'half-hearted' attempts to counter a growing IRA threat).[38] Faulkner was under pressure from those on the right of his UUP who demanded much harsher security measures,

35 Beattie-Smith, *The British State*, 151.
36 'First Battalion Notes', *Red Hackle*, December 1970, 12.
37 Beattie-Smith, *The British State*, 152.
38 Beattie-Smith, *The British State*, 153.

including the return of the USC and the imposition of 'martial law' in areas seen as sympathetic to Republicans.[39]

Operation Demetrius

In August 1971, Prime Minister Brian Faulkner's increasingly urgent appeals to the British government to put internment without trial into effect finally paid off. Operation Demetrius began on August 9, 1971; the overwhelming majority of internees were suspected Catholic members of paramilitary groups. In early 1971, there were only seven soldiers (including three officers) working in the Military Intelligence unit in HQNI. One officer recalled a chaotic scene in military intelligence at HQNI on the eve of Operation Demetrius:

> 7 o clock in the morning, [a] telephone call comes into the officer and they told me, 'Internment starts tomorrow.' The RUC have asked if you can produce pictures of all the people we want to pick up. But what they had were pictures of maybe 20 people – and trying to blow up the pictures in that limited time ... We lacked technical capabilities and so did the RUC. Between us we did what we could but it really wasn't sufficient. I was given 48 hours in which to produce a whole pile of photographs. I didn't even know who the people were. There was nothing more. To try to collate intelligence and cross-reference everything was a real labour.[40]

By March 1972, 2,989 people had been arrested under the Internment Act, of whom 732 were eventually interned. According to a later Northern Ireland Office report, internment, and the manner in which people were arrested (often in the middle of the night, doors smashed in and homes upended), severely ruptured relations between the Catholic community and the Army. Interrogation techniques could be violent, involving

39 Future UUP leader, Harry West MP, quoted in 'Talented Needed for a New Cabinet – West', *Belfast Telegraph*, March 20, 1971.
40 Interview with a former Military Intelligence Officer May 2014. Nevertheless, Martin McCleery has also demonstrated that RUC/army intelligence was relatively sound – the considerable majority of those arrested were active in Republican militant groups. See McCleery, *Operation Demetrius*.

'stress positions', later condemned as 'inhumane' by the UK courts. Although valuable intelligence was undoubtedly gained from questioning suspects, some mistaken arrests were also made (those arrested in error were generally released within a day or two but this also added to a widespread, albeit simplistic, public perception of a bungled operation).[41]

Sectarian attacks also escalated during this time and more than 2,000 families abandoned their houses as a direct result of violence and intimidation in the six weeks after August 9, 1971. A campaign of civil disobedience began on August 16, 1971 and approximately 200 Catholics resigned from the already overwhelmingly Protestant UDR. Internment and 'Bloody Sunday', the fatal shooting of 14 unarmed civilians on January 30, 1972, had a catastrophic effect on the public image of the Army among Northern Ireland's Catholic population. Despite the errors of the IRA and the excessive violence and intimidation of local communities, the British Army increasingly became the focus of Catholic grievances, particularly from August 1971 to January 1972.[42] Tommy Gorman, an IRA Volunteer in Andersonstown, West Belfast in the early 1970s, later recalled that

> We were creating this idea that the British state is not your friend ... and at every twist in the road they were compounding what we were saying, they were doing what we were saying, fulfilling all the propaganda ... The British Army, the British government, were our best recruiting agents.[43]

The IRA was benefitting from the occasionally clumsy actions of soldiers who were more accustomed to employing 'exemplary counterinsurgency' tactics in the colonies. The Army was struggling to adapt to the rigours of internal security operations in the UK.

The IRA's Tactics Against the British Army in 1971 and 1972

On October 4, 1971, General Carver sent a memorandum to Edward Heath updating him on military strategy in Northern Ireland. In it he explained that the IRA were conducting an effective campaign, spreading

---

41 TNA: CJ 4/1290 Paper written by Mr Gowdy.
42 English, *Armed Struggle*, 141.
43 English, *Armed Struggle*, 122.

fear through its bombing campaign and inflicting damage on the security forces through its active service unit raids and ambushes. 'In short,' Carver wrote, 'the IRA has the initiative and is causing disruption out of all proportion to the relatively small numbers engaged.'[44] According to Carver, the IRA knew it could not win a military victory; its primary target was public opinion in Britain. The more British soldiers it killed, the more the British public would demand a withdrawal from Northern Ireland.[45]

The summer of 1971 saw a major escalation in IRA attacks on the Army. Army officers were concerned by the IRA's rapidly escalating rate of success in targeting mostly vehicle and foot patrols (70 per cent of all attacks) or bases and sangars (25 per cent). IRA attacks were normally launched by one or two gunmen and had a one in nine 'partial success rate' (wounding a soldier) and a one in 40 'kill rate'. Most firing points were in the open, albeit with some cover (80 per cent), while for other attacks mostly occupied houses were chosen. IRA shooting was reasonably accurate for an irregular force made up of mostly very young and inexperienced recruits; over 50 per cent of attacks on the Army were at ranges greater than 300 metres; relatively few were initiated at ranges under 200 metres. According to the Army, the IRA knew that it was difficult to respond with highly accurate fire with a standard SLR beyond 300 metres. 'Fire fights at this distance would be generally ineffective without the deployment of heavier weapons such as machine guns.' The IRA would take a carefully planned single shot or two and then withdraw before accurate fire could be brought to bear against the sniper.[46]

Some 60 per cent of IRA shooting incidents occurred in Belfast, compared with 30 per cent in rural areas and 10 per cent in Londonderry. Attacks normally occurred in the afternoon or the late evening (the Army observed that 17.00 to 19.00 seemed to be an IRA tea break, of sorts).[47] The vast majority of IRA weapons were of Second World War (and occasionally First World War) origin. Common among these were the .30 Garand and .303 Lee Enfield rifles; some versions of the Garand rifle acquired by the IRA could fire armour-piercing rounds, a deeply

44 Report dated October 4, 1971 from General Sir Michael Carver.
45 'Belfast at War', *An Phoblacht*, February 1971.
46 TNA CJ 4/1764 Shooting Statistics, 1977, Report on IRA Attacks, signed by Martin J. Sands, Division 1 (B), December 20, 1976.
47 TNA CJ 4/1764 Shooting Statistics, 1977, Report on IRA Attacks.

unnerving weapon for soldiers expecting to be ambushed. The principal modern weapons recovered by the Army in late 1971 were Armalites (237) and M1 Carbines (309); most had been imported from the USA during 1970 and 1971. Eighty Thompson sub-machine guns (SMGs) and 140 9 mm SMGs (Sterling or Sten type) were also seized by the Army from 1970 to 1971. The IRA possessed a variety of handguns: 70 .357 Magnums, 163 Lugers and 78 Browning pistols (sourced from a range of countries including within the UK, the USA and Eastern Europe) were recovered by the Army from 1970 to 1971. However, despite regular 'finds' of these weapons, senior officers reported that IRA resupply was easily outstripping any losses.[48]

By late autumn 1971, the security situation in Ulster was rapidly deteriorating: on October 6, 1971, Brian Faulkner announced, with prior approval from London, the sending of three more battalions to Northern Ireland, bringing the total number of British military forces to 13,600. The majority of battalions were on four-month tours, looking after a designated 'patch'. According to the Army, whole areas of Belfast were now under the effective control of the IRA. This was particularly the case in Andersonstown in West Belfast, 'where the IRA almost completely control the movement of people. In certain roads they decide who shall live in which house and who shall go to work and who shall not.'[49] Meanwhile, the Army reported, any major operation in the Divis Flats (high-rise local authority flats where approximately 2,500 Catholics lived and from were IRA snipers operated) would require two and a half battalions. Even though Army estimates for total IRA membership was between 2,000 and 3,000 men, the hostility of Catholic areas to any Army incursion was at an all-time high. In Derry, 200 'extremists' were now in control of the Bogside and Creggan areas. IRA Volunteers were generally very young; it was estimated that of the 48 active IRA Volunteers in the North Belfast area of Ardoyne only 10 were over the age of 20.[50]

In his October 1971 report on combating the IRA, General Carver presented three future options to Edward Heath. The first was to keep operations at a low intensity, not seeking to go on the offensive against

---

48 TNA CJ 4/1764 Shooting Statistics, 1977, Report on IRA Attacks.
49 Report dated October 4, 1971 from General Sir Michael Carver.
50 Report dated October 4, 1971 from General Sir Michael Carver.

the IRA in 'hard' areas. The danger inherent to this option was Protestant opposition, which could 'find practical expression in the formation of a third force and which might make the imposition of direct rule inevitable'.[51] The second option was to cease political engagement with the minority population and clamp down hard and unrelentingly on Catholic areas – a coercive option against the population at large with echoes of colonial campaigns. The third option was to remain politically engaged with Catholic leaders but increase the tempo of military operations against the IRA, satisfying Protestant concerns about excessive Army passivity. This third option, which Heath adopted, meant 'the intensification of border operations, including the humping and cratering of roads, and an operation in Londonderry [the much delayed Operation Carcan or Motorman].'[52]

Cooperation and Discord: The Army, the RUC and the UDR

Although the RUC's strength reached 4,193 (plus 2,190 reservists) by late 1972, the Army viewed the police as disarmed, demoralised and incapable of dealing with the terrorist threat. In a scathing assessment of police capabilities at the end of 1971, General Carver concluded that the RUC's attitude was 'passive and its contribution to the security situation minimal'.[53] According to Carver, only Special Branch offered any meaningful assistance to the Army's operations.[54] Personal dislike and recrimination at the highest levels of military command and policing in Northern Ireland festered throughout 1971 and continued into 1972.[55]

---

51 Report dated October 4, 1971 from General Sir Michael Carver.

52 Report dated October 4, 1971 from General Sir Michael Carver.

53 TNA: CJ 4/668 Matters Concerning the Security Forces, June 1, 1973–January 31, 1974, Report entitled, 'Strength of Security Forces in Northern Ireland', dated July 1973; Report dated October 4, 1971 from General Sir Michael Carver.

54 TNA: CJ 4/668 Matters Concerning the Security Forces; Report dated October 4, 1971 from General Sir Michael Carver.

55 The level of mutual resentment between the army and police leadership was clearly in evidence during a 'study day', which had been organised as a means of 'clearing the air' on October 8, 1970. During the GOC's presentation, the Chief Constable, Graham Shillington, objected to the proposed use of the RUC in future riot control operations, pointing out that his force was not armed and therefore incapable of dealing with the current, very violent levels of rioting in Northern

A lack of communication and trust had a negative effect upon intelligence: a senior Security Service (MI5) officer in Northern Ireland recalled that, 'The scene was chaotic. With mutual distrust between the police and the Army, the home office was responsible but not in effective political control.'[56] Moreover, as Keith Jeffery has observed, the police intelligence required to secure convictions under UK civil law was often of greater quality than the information used by military intelligence officers for operational purposes. Military officers often thought they 'knew' who was guilty of terrorism; a perceived lack of subsequent positive police action and judicial convictions created a significant strain on the police–Army relationship.[57]

The UDR was created in the early 1970s as a means of channelling local Unionists' desire to protect the integrity of the UK from an IRA threat into a legal and constructive part-time force. UDR recruitment numbers were set at approximately 9,000; the regiment would operate mainly in rural areas, guarding key installations, establishing checkpoints and roadblocks and patrolling. It was not supposed to deal with riots/crowd control or engage in complex intelligence operations or analysis due to the risk of sectarian confrontation or bias.[58] Most of its senior ranks were made up of officers and NCOs from regular British Army units. However, Army officers were concerned that the UDR would simply be regarded as the same as the USC in all but name; it was vital to recruit from the minority community. 'Unless there was Catholic support for the UDR it would in due course come to be seen as sectarian.'[59] Writing

---

Ireland. The GOC, General Freeland, was furious and directly contradicted the Chief Constable: 'Despite his remarks the Chief Constable will, and I repeat will, increase RUC participation in anti-riot duties, both the Chief Constable's end and my political bosses have said so.' Chief Constable Shillington was outraged that Freeland, with the support of Chichester-Clark, wished to use the old Northern Irish Special Powers Act to intern suspects without trial, calling it 'an embarrassment to the police and an affront to the rule of law'. TNA: CJ 3/85 Military Assistance and Police, 1970–1971, Memorandum from the RUC Chief Constable to the Home Office (undated).

56 Andrew, *Defence of the Realm*, 618.

57 Jeffery, 'Security Policy in Northern Ireland', 24.

58 TNA: CJ 4/1784 Paper entitled, 'The Future Role and Organisation of the UDR'.

59 PRONI: D/3687/26/1 Meeting between G.B. Newe, Minister of State, and Senior Officers from the Ulster Defence Regiment, November 17, 1971.

in 1986, Charles Townshend later reflected on the problematic legacy of the USC: too many UDR recruits had previously served as 'B Specials'. 'Officially, there was no continuity between the two organisations, and the new one looks on the face of it like a "third force". But its undoubted vigilante origins and extreme ethnic divisiveness throw grave doubts over its social effectiveness.'[60]

Negative perceptions of the UDR among the Catholic population of Northern Ireland did become a persistent problem.[61] Of the few Catholics that joined (Catholics made up less than 10 per cent of the force in 1971, despite Catholics numbering more than a third of the population), many of these resigned from the UDR upon the introduction of internment and in response to other events such as the shooting dead of civilians in Londonderry on Bloody Sunday in January 1972. A former sergeant in 7th Battalion, UDR left the regiment to set up the Catholic Ex-Servicemen's Association (CESA), an organisation whose aim was to police working-class Catholic areas, providing an alternative to both the security forces and the IRA.[62] Meanwhile, a fear of a Protestant backlash prevented the Northern Irish and UK governments from banning the Loyalist paramilitary group, the Ulster Defence Association (UDA), despite the involvement of its members in a number of sectarian murders. In late 1972, the Commander of the UDR, Brigadier Denis Ormerod, acknowledged that he could do little to prevent members of Loyalist paramilitary groups from joining the UDR. There was a particular tolerance of the still-legal UDA, whose checkpoints, patrols, recruiting and fundraising activities were rarely challenged by the security forces in the early 1970s.[63] John Potter, in his history of the UDR, concluded that the reasons for paramilitaries joining the regiment were self-evident, namely 'free training, plus access to weapons, ammunition and intelligence'.[64] Loyalist paramilitary recruiting numbers dwindled as the 1970s went on and IRA violence subsided; meanwhile, regular British officers and NCOs began to weed out

60 Townshend, *Britain's Civil Wars*, 70.
61 TNA: CJ 4/1784 'The Future Role and Organisation of the UDR'.
62 TNA CJ 4/1784 Working Group on Security Force Capability, 1977, Paper entitled, 'The Future Role and Organisation of the UDR', signed by Lieutenant Colonel R.M. McLarney on behalf of GOCNI, HQNI, dated September 22, 1977; J. Potter, *The UDR* (London: Pen and Sword, 2001), 78.
63 Wood, *Crimes of Loyalty*, 107.
64 Potter, *The UDR*, 82.

'undesirable elements' of the UDR. But there were occasional instances of UDR soldiers' involvement in sectarian, paramilitary murders, which in turn exacerbated Catholic suspicion of the regiment and the wider Army. 2nd Battalion (Armagh), UDR gained a particularly negative reputation for involvement with paramilitary organisations in the 1970s.[65] Indeed, on one occasion (January 15, 1972), Lieutenant Colin Mitchell recalled the CO of 2 UDR, Lieutenant Colonel Robin Chappell, discussing the possibility of bombing a pub situated along the border near Killeen, County Armagh.[66]

Border Operations

The patrolling of the border between the UK and the Republic of Ireland was a constant operational and logistical problem for the Army, one that would occupy 1 Argylls during their 1972 tour. The border is 303 miles long; a Northern Ireland Office (NIO) paper warned that in addition to the difficulty of sealing off roads, 'there are 30 miles of water, numerous lanes and smugglers' pads, and border lands which are easily negotiable on foot.'[67] On January 19, 1972, the Army received an intelligence briefing from RUC Special Branch warning that the IRA was going to intensify operations along the border in 1972. ASUs made up of 'on the run' IRA fugitives based themselves in Southern counties along with local units, moving across the border for brief periods in order to attack the security forces and intimidate the local population.[68] The harassment, killing or wounding of Protestant farmers along the border, many of whom were members of the UDR and RUC reserve, prompted some to abandon

65 Interview with a former UDR officer (4th Battalion), June 2014.

66 Royal Scots Dragoon Guards Association (hereafter RSDGA): R12, RB09 Lieutenant Colin Mitchell, 'An Officer's Diary: Scots Dragoon Guards, Northern Ireland, 1971–1972'.

67 TNA: CJ 4/317 Secretary of State (William Whitelaw) Private Office, Correspondence and Minuting about Matters Concerning Advisory Council and Army 1972–1973. Report entitled 'Control of the Border' by the Government Security Unit, Stormont Castle, dated March 20, 1972.

68 RUC Special Branch Memorandum, dated January 19, 1972, evidence reproduced in the *Report of the Bloody Sunday Inquiry*, http://webarchive.national archives.gov.uk/20100401161904/http://www.bloody-sunday-inquiry.org.uk/ (accessed December 4, 2017).

their farms and move closer to the main towns. By early 1973, 101 border crossings had been blocked or 'cratered' by the Army.[69]

In the wake of mounting cross-border attacks in late 1972, MPs and other public representatives demanded that the border be 'sealed'. In response, an exasperated NIO official wrote a report 'to bring home to Members of Parliament and the public what "sealing" of the Border really implies'.[70] Twenty-nine battalions would be required along the border to monitor all traffic. Although conceding that border checks were made on only 1 in 33 vehicles entering Northern Ireland, a total closure of the border would be 'enormously costly in time, money, manpower and Britain's standing in the EEC'.[71] The Army wanted to continue to focus its existing resources on securing the more populated cities and towns. Meanwhile, the government wanted to avoid significantly increasing troop levels: 'sealing the border' was simply not an option.[72] Existing efforts to restrict movements across the border were already having a very adverse effect on public opinion in those counties in the South that bordered Northern Ireland.[73]

The Southern Dimension: Anglo-Irish Security Cooperation and the Border

In the early 1970s, the Army and the Northern Ireland Office were frustrated by a perceived passivity or even tacit acquiescence by the Irish government in failing to prevent cross-border attacks. Matters were not helped by a personal dislike between some senior Irish and UK officials; the senior diplomat in the Republic of Ireland Department in the FCO, Kelvin White, was not trusted by the Irish Embassy in London and in the Department of Foreign Affairs in Dublin. White, for his part, boasted to Irish diplomats of his previous counter-insurgency experiences in the colonies and could be insensitive in his approach to Irish officials.[74] White argued that 'Rubbing Irish noses in particular cases seems to be

---

69 Patterson, *Ireland's Violent Frontier*, 43.

70 TNA: CJ 4/317 Report entitled 'Control of the Border'.

71 TNA: CJ 4/317 Report entitled 'Control of the Border'.

72 TNA: CJ 4/317 Report entitled 'Control of the Border'.

73 PRONI: D/3687/26/1 Meeting between Dr Newe and a deputation from Co. Monaghan [led by Billy Fox TD] on Friday, December 3, 1971, which came to make representations about the cratering of Border roads.

74 NAI: DFA 2001/43/1407 Correspondence of Irish Embassy in London

the best approach. The Irish may not prove very effective, and Dublin's authority may not amount to much, but it is worth a try.'[75] Meanwhile, the discovery in 1972 of a British mole in the Garda's Special Branch, Patrick Crinion, who had passed on lists of suspected IRA Volunteers to his British handler John Wyman, saw a further deterioration in relations. In his work on Anglo-Irish relations during this period, Anthony Craig has noted that a clear divergence existed between Britain's ambassador in Dublin, Sir John Peck, and those, including Kelvin White, who were less sympathetic to Jack Lynch's political predicament when it came to responding to increased security measures along the border and strongly advocated the increased closure of border roads whose reopening would be dependent on increased security measures and cooperation emanating from Dublin. Peck thought the cratering of roads along the border to be politically counter-productive.[76] This assessment echoed the concerns of moderates on both side of the border. Billy Fox, a Fine Gael TD from County Monaghan who, as a Protestant, was infamously slandered as 'a B Special' [a member of the USC] during an exchange in the Irish parliament (and was later murdered by the IRA in 1974), warned of the devastating, radicalising effects of 'cratering' on the economy of the border region. Farmers were cut off from fields and markets; towns such as Clones in County Monaghan had been completely crippled, with access denied to their natural business hinterland across the border. Fox warned that 'Attitudes on both sides of the Border have hardened because of the policy ... supporters [of Mr Fox] are being converted into extremists ... Many people who would normally have ignored the "gunmen" are now willing to shelter these men and even keep their guns for them.'[77]

Across the border in County Fermanagh, SDLP councillor Fergus McQuillan recalled that the cratering of roads was the single most important catalyst for sympathy and recruitment for the IRA in the

1970–1971. Account of a lunch on March 19, 1970 between Kevin Rush, Irish Embassy and Kelvin White, First Secretary, FCO.

75 TNA: FCO 87/120 Border, Letter to A.W. Stephens, Minstry of Defence from W.K.K. White, Republic of Ireland Department, FCO, dated June 13, 1972.

76 A. Craig, Crisis of Confidence: Anglo-Irish Relations in the Early Troubles, 1966–1974 (Dublin: Irish Academic Press, 2010), 130.

77 PRONI: D/3687/26/1 Meeting between Dr Newe and a deputation from Co. Monaghan, December 3, 1971.

border region.[78] The government in London was either unable or unwilling to respond to such concerns; the views of Kelvin White were in the ascendant.[79]

Unionists were outraged at Dublin's half-hearted approach towards countering IRA activities on the border. On September 29, 1972 UUP leader Brian Faulkner telegrammed Edward Heath:

> Security situation on our border intolerable. On behalf of the people of Northern Ireland I ask that you demand from Mr. Lynch immediate action to prevent the Republic from being used as a harbour for gunmen. I ask that the full strength of Her Majesty's government be put behind such a demand forthwith.[80]

What exactly Faulkner meant by 'full strength' is unclear.

Passions were running high in the South; many people were outraged at what they saw as the brutal and highly partial behaviour of the British Army and the RUC. The Irish State had never renounced its constitutional claim over Northern Ireland's 'six counties'; its rhetorical ambition for the unification of Ireland was now sorely tested by the actions of the IRA who claimed to be defending Catholics under attack by the British Army and the RUC. In 1970 at least three senior government ministers from the ruling Fianna Fáil party, with some support from officers in the Irish Army, had attempted to provide arms for Catholic paramilitaries in the North (they were later sacked and tried for their involvement in this 'arms plot'; all of the accused were acquitted).[81] In another court case a Newry civil rights activist, caught carrying gelignite and firearms south of the border, successfully had his case overturned on the basis that the items in his possession had been provided by the Irish government.[82]

In April 1972, Irish Military Intelligence (G2) concluded that public opinion in the southern border counties was shifting dangerously in

---

78 Interview with Fergus McQuillan, former SDLP Councillor, Newtownbutler, November 28, 2016.

79 Craig, *Crisis of Confidence*, 155.

80 TNA: FCO 87/120 Border, telegram from Brian Faulkner to Edward Heath, September 29, 1972.

81 Patterson, *Ireland's Violent Frontier*, 33.

82 Patterson, *Ireland's Violent Frontier*, 33.

favour of the IRA. An Irish Army intelligence officer, writing from the border town of Letterkenny, offered a bleak assessment of the situation along the border near Londonderry:

> The leadership in Derry Provos and Official IRA are mainly young men in their early twenties and teens. They are in the sanctuary of the Bogside and can operate freely from there. They have fairly free access to the Republic ... In spite of what is said otherwise the main portion of the RCs [Roman Catholics] on the Donegal side of Lough Foyle still support the IRA.[83]

The chief of staff of the Irish Defence Forces, Lieutenant General Thomas O'Carroll, could not convince his political masters to reinforce the border area. On December 6, 1972, General O'Carroll sent a stark warning to the Minister for Defence in Dublin, Jerry Cronin; he went on to make an uncompromising case for reinforcing the border area. O'Carroll pointed out that, since the Second World War, no permanent posts of battalion size or more had operated north of the town of the midlands town of Mullingar, a very long way from the border. Tellingly, O'Carroll's request for major reinforcements on the border was denied.[84] The Fianna Fáil government of Taoiseach (Prime Minister) Jack Lynch did not want to be too helpful to the British security forces along the border; limited cooperation was mostly confined to cross-border personal contacts between police officers. General O'Carroll issued a directive to his soldiers outlining the 'rules of engagement' with respect to the IRA. IRA Volunteers suspected of involvement in attacks on British security personnel were to be 'energetically pursued' but only fired upon if they directly attacked Irish soldiers or members of An Garda Síochána, the Irish police force.[85] Military to military contacts were further complicated by a refusal by the Irish government to allow a direct dialogue between senior British officers and their

83 Military Archives of Ireland (hereafter MAI): SCS/29/71/1 Message from 'Poplar' to 'Intel Section', forwarded to Irish Defence Forces Headquarters by Colonel Quinlivan, April 14, 1972.
84 MAI: SCS/29/71/1 Message from 'Poplar', April 14, 1972.
85 MAI: SCS/29/71/1 Border Operations – Memorandum from Chief of Staff, Lieutenant General Thomas O'Carroll on actions to be taken on encountering British Army personnel, dated June 27, 1972.

Irish counterparts; the Irish claimed that the Minister for Justice was solely responsible for the direction of all internal security matters. Nevertheless, the Garda Síochána had neither the numbers nor the equipment to mount operations of a similar efficiency to those on the UK side of the border.[86] Indeed, Eunan O'Halpin has noted that the early 1970s was a time of 'great strain' for the Garda, including internal friction of how to concentrate resources in a rapidly urbanising country and a general rise in armed crime and violence (much of which was unrelated to the conflict in Northern Ireland).[87]

Political reluctance on the Irish side to seriously disrupt IRA operations from south of the border focused minds in London on the need for better equipment for the British Army and the RUC to detect arms and explosives smuggling. More radar kits, night observation devices, weapons sights, vehicle search devices and hand-held metal detector devices were purchased at the end of 1971.[88] 1 Argylls were to discover the severe limitations of Irish police and military assistance in the latter part of 1972.

Senior British Army officers were careful to emphasise that soldiers should not, under any circumstances, cross the border. However, during 1971 and 1972, the Irish government believed that certain units of the British Army were deliberately ignoring the border as it suited them. One former UDR officer readily acknowledged that Army units crossed the border for 'a few hundred yards or so' to gain either advantage of terrain or to avoid a long trek around a particular corner of border (such as the hated, incongruous Drummully salient near Wattlebridge in County Fermanagh), but such border crossings were relatively rare nonetheless.[89] During 1972, the Irish government complained of the increasing number of raids conducted by British soldiers on the houses of suspected Republicans living south of the border: for example, on May 7, 1972, the Irish government alleged that British soldiers crossed into

---

86 NAI: 2010/19/1618 Border Security; Contacts with British for Matters other than control of Explosives: Confidential Report from the Chief Superintendent, Dundalk Garda Station on VCP checkpoints; Conservative Party Archive (hereafter CPA): CRD 3/18/1 Minutes of a Meeting of the Conservative Party Northern Ireland Backbench Committee, January 31, 1973.
87 E. O'Halpin, *Defending Ireland: The Irish State and its Enemies since 1922* (Oxford: Oxford University Press, 1999), 328.
88 TNA: CJ 4/317 Report entitled 'Control of the Border'.
89 Interview with a former UDR Officer (4th Battalion), June 2014.

the South to search the house of Philip McDonald in Derrybeg, in the north-east corner of the 'Drummully salient' between Newtownbutler and Clones. McDonald was a prominent member of the IRA; according to Sinn Féin, his house was later burnt by 'pro-British elements' while he was 'on the run'.[90] Some border incidents were particularly embarrassing and difficult to explain for the government in London: on May 25, 1973, six soldiers from a Royal Artillery regiment were arrested near the centre of the town of Clones in County Monaghan, approximately one mile from the border. Two were dressed in civilian clothes, all were armed and had travelled from Lisnaskea RUC station (although they initially claimed they were based in Belfast). The British government at first told the Irish government that the incident was a map-reading error but later were forced to admit that the information they had received from HQNI was inaccurate and that the local unit commander in Lisnaskea had exceeded his orders in conducting operations south of the border.[91] The names of IRA suspects living in the southern border counties were secured by a British intelligence source working in a sensitive position in Garda Headquarters in Dublin.[92] As will be explored in the next chapter, frustrated units of 1 Argylls were to embark on 'visits' south of the border as pressure mounted in their area of operations.

Loyalists also launched cross-border bombing attacks south of the border, as revenge for alleged Irish government collaboration with the IRA and to sabotage IRA arms and explosive materials. On December 28, 1972, the UVF planted bombs in the border towns of Clones (County Donegal), Belturbet, Swanlinbar (County Cavan) and Pettigo (County Donegal), killing two people in Belturbet. However, the UDA also launched border raids during 1972: on October 6, the UDA claimed to have seized four Armalite rifles and 'churns of explosives' in County Monaghan, and on October 16, attempted to blow up a fertiliser store near Carrigans in County Donegal. Senior Garda officers suspected that these attacks were assisted, or even carried out, by members of the UDR.[93]

90 TNA: WO 305/4209 3rd Infantry Brigade, Log Sheet, May 9, 1972; 'Fógraí Bháis', *An Phoblacht*, March 30, 2006.
91 Patterson, *Ireland's Violent Frontier*, 56.
92 Committee on Finance – Adjournment Debate: British Army Border Infringement. See also Patterson, *Ireland's Violent Frontier*, 44–45.
93 TNA: FCO 87/120 Border, Letter from K.C. Thom to W.K.K. White, Republic of Ireland Department, dated October 6, 1972 for a timeline and discussion of UDA

Direct Rule: Heath's Gamble

In early March 1972, after much speculation and the further decline of the security situation in the wake of the Bloody Sunday shootings, Prime Minister Edward Heath informed Brian Faulkner that London would pass a bill to cede powers over law and order to London. Faulkner 'made clear his view that a transfer of law-and-order powers would leave no credible basis of viable government' for his cabinet at Stormont.[94] At the end of March 1972, Heath introduced direct rule, dissolved Northern Ireland's government and appointed William Whitelaw as Secretary of State for Northern Ireland. Heath, a naturally suspicious and prickly man, trusted Whitelaw, calling him 'one of the most skilful and dependable men in politics'.[95] Many Unionists, not least Faulkner, were appalled that Heath had stripped Stormont of its powers. Others were more optimistic, believing that Major Whitelaw, an ex-Scots Guards officer, who had won a Military Cross in Normandy during the Second World War and served on counter-insurgency operations in Palestine in the late 1940s, would now introduce a similar type of internal security campaign such as that employed in the colonies. David Lowry Cole, the 6th Earl of Enniskillen, an influential peer who had been a senior officer in the Kenya Police Reserve during the Mau Mau rebellion and helped negotiate Kenyan independence before returning to County Fermanagh where he served as a Major in 4th Battalion (County Fermanagh), UDR (4 UDR), wrote a memorandum for Whitelaw. In it he congratulated the new Secretary of State for Northern Ireland on his appointment, before urging him to look to colonial tactics, including allowing the RUC to take their place in 'the total war machine … a system of integration such as we had abroad and which proved very efficient and effective'.[96]

and UVF bombings in the Republic. See also 'Final Report of the Commission of Investigation into the Dublin and Monaghan Bombings', published April 4, 2007, available at www.taoiseach.ie (accessed February 26, 2015).

94 K. Bloomfield, *A Memoir: Stormont in Crisis* (Belfast: Blackstaff Press, 1994), 166.

95 Edward Heath, *The Course of My Life* (London: Hodder and Stoughton, 1999), 436.

96 PRONI: D1702/12/69/1–9 Earl of Enniskillen Papers, Letter from the 6th Earl of Enniskillen to the Secretary of State for Northern Ireland, William Whitelaw, dated April 6, 1972.

The IRA believed that the introduction of direct rule was a clear indication that they had the Army on the back foot. Encouraged, the IRA's campaign of violence escalated further. Northern Ireland pitched into a maelstrom of violence: in the four months after March 1972, 600 bombs were detonated in Northern Ireland, 2,057 people were injured and 192 killed. In the month of March, security forces recorded 399 shooting incidents; by July, this figure had risen to 2,718.[97] Despite the rising violence and the intense pressure from Unionists, and many conservatives, to mount a forceful response, Whitelaw, ex-Scots Guards and 'booming with bonhomie', adopted a more low-key approach. He began releasing large numbers of internees over the protests of senior Army officers. He opened negotiations with both the Official IRA and the Provisional IRA, the former announcing a ceasefire that effectively ended their military operations.[98]

Negotiations with the Provisional IRA fared badly. During a short ceasefire in late June/early July 1972, key leaders including Seán MacStiofáin, Ivor Bell, Gerry Adams and Martin McGuinness were flown to London on an RAF plane to meet with Minister of State for Northern Ireland Paul Channon at his house in Bayswater in London. The Provisional leadership tried to negotiate the terms of British withdrawal from Northern Ireland, when no such break up of the UK was seriously being considered on the British side. Provisional over-reach and the political damage of such fruitless negotiations convinced Whitelaw that a tougher approach would have to be taken. The events of Bloody Friday on July 21, a series of IRA bombs in the city centre of Belfast that killed nine and seriously injured 130, also had a profound effect on Whitelaw, as Ken Bloomfield, a senior Northern Irish civil servant recalled:

> That evening, after Whitelaw flew back to Belfast, I sat in on an emergency meeting at Stormont Castle where he was joined by Lord Carrington, the Secretary of State for Defence. A man of equable temperament, Carrington was at first inclined to argue the line 'steady as she goes', but Whitelaw had had enough and was incandescent with rage. From that moment debate

97 TNA: CJ 4/1764 Report on IRA Attacks, December 20, 1976.
98 Bloomfield, *A Memoir*, 173–174.

about alternative methods to restore no-go areas to ordinary authority ceased: a military strike it would be and as soon as possible.[99]

Whitelaw was deeply angry but he also saw a political opportunity. 'It was important to achieve as much as possible by military action while the feelings of revulsion caused by Friday's explosions remained.'[100] The Army believed that such action was long overdue.[101] But Whitelaw, the politician, understood that timing is everything.

Operation Motorman

Operation Motorman (Operation Carcan in Derry) began on July 24, 1972 in Belfast and on the morning of July 31, 1972 in Londonderry. Motorman was the largest single operation by the British Army in Northern Ireland and successfully brought to an end the IRA 'no-go' areas, inserting an Army presence into Republican areas that allowed for the better collection of intelligence and monitoring of terrorist suspects. The operation saw Army force levels rise to over 28,000. Infantry soldiers were supported by armour including Armoured Fighting Vehicles and a troop of AVREs to dismantle the barricades in Londonderry and elsewhere. The *Derry Journal* described how local residents in Moville, County Donegal (across the border) gathered to watch the operation: 'On Sunday night hundreds of people watched as launching barges carrying equipment including the Centurion tanks [AVREs] sped up the [Lough] Foyle towards Derry, taking their cargo through Irish territorial waters to launch an assault on Irish people.'[102] All areas were secured within hours of the commencement of operations. The IRA had decided not to fight; however, two Volunteers in Londonderry were shot in disputed circumstances during Operation Carcan (Edward Heath had been prepared to accept 100 deaths, including significant military casualties, if necessary).[103]

99 Bloomfield, *A Memoir*, 177.
100 PRONI: CAB/9G/27/6/5 Conclusions of Morning Meeting at Stormont Castle on Sunday, July 23, 1972, at 10.00 a.m.
101 PRONI: CAB/9G/27/6/5 Conclusions of Morning Meeting at Stormont Castle on Wednesday, July 12, 1972, at 10.00 a.m.
102 'Prague-like Invasion of Bogside and Creggan', *Derry Journal*, August 3, 1972.
103 Beattie-Smith, *The British State*, 161.

At a minimum, Motorman gave the impression that the British government was willing to stay the course against the IRA. According to the Derry political activist, Eamonn McCann, Operation Motorman (Carcan) was successful, in part, due to a wave of revulsion over IRA attacks and because the Stormont government was gone: 'Had the Army moved in before direct rule it is certain that thousands of people would have come out to face them, guns or no guns. Now, however, the detested Stormont was gone.'[104] In its official 2006 'end of mission' report on Operation Banner, the Army concluded that Motorman had removed the IRA's safe havens and could be seen as 'a turning point in the campaign, changing it from a counter insurgency to a counter terrorist operation'.[105] Such a conclusion is neat, but inaccurate. Violence was significantly reduced but would remain considerable during the successive months of 1972 and would escalate in the border region. Nevertheless, by 1973, the security situation had significantly improved: the daily average of shooting incidents showed a drop from 92 in July 1972 to just nine, 12 months later.[106]

Fixing the Intelligence Deficit

In the two months after Motorman, 85 people were charged with offences under the Firearms Act, 53 under the Explosives Act, 1 person was charged with murder and 11 with attempted murder. This was a relatively limited number given that the Army made 1,410 arrests (the RUC also made 913) on suspicion of terrorism-related offences during this same period. Sixty-five 'known' IRA men were arrested. However, arms finds were significant: 24 machine guns and 217 rifles were seized during raids in Catholic areas, while 4 machine guns and 44 rifles were found during searches of Protestant homes. Soldiers poured into areas like the Creggan and the Bogside and began building platoon bases and observation posts. In the weeks after Motorman, troop levels were maintained at 21,000 before settling closer to 16,000 in mid-1973. Searches increased to unprecedented levels. During the week of October 5–11, 1972, 147,345 vehicles and more than 1,100 houses were searched

---

104 E. McCann, *War and an Irish Town* (Harmondsworth: Penguin, 1974), 114.
105 British Army, *Operation Banner*, 2.10.
106 TNA: CJ 4/1764 Shooting Statistics: Report compiled by HQNI, 1970–1977.

by the Army, but only one machine gun and 11 rifles were found. The sheer weight of the Army presence was having an effect; but a lack of intelligence was still a problem.[107]

Intelligence gathering in the early days of Operation Banner could be a clumsy affair: homes were turned upside down; whole neighbourhoods sealed off. The interrogation of suspects was often violent and local people were generally outraged by the aggressive approach of the soldiers involved. The relationship with the RUC was difficult; the intelligence product that the RUC chose to share with the Army failed to impress. Steps were taken to bolster Army intelligence capabilities in late 1971, particularly in Belfast where the energetic commander of 39 Brigade, Brigadier Frank Kitson, began to forensically 'map' hard Republican areas to discover who the new young leading figures of the IRA were and how the organisation worked.[108] Kitson already had a public reputation for some of his more controversial writings on colonial counter-insurgency operations (Gerry Adams and other Republican leaders would later assert that he employed such tactics in Northern Ireland).[109]

Kitson's approach was relatively simple: getting in a position to watch and listen (through signals intelligence). Communication was in writing or by word of mouth; the IRA was listening in on their relatively insecure radio communications. Whereas the approach of other senior officers was immediately to break down the door of any suspected IRA terrorist, Kitson preferred to watch and wait.[110] Soldiers watched for patterns and opportunities: locals who were fed up with IRA intimidation, had money problems or extra-marital affairs. A trickle of information eventually became a flow; the saturation of Republican areas began to pay dividends. A Scots Guards company commander later recalled, 'In the early days they watched us and had the initiative. They knew all the territory and knew our movements. Later on we watched them. We would cover every street and knew every house.'[111]

---

107 TNA: CJ 4/317 Secretary of State (William Whitelaw) Private Office, Correspondence and Minuting about Matters Concerning Advisory Council and Army 1972–1973.
108 Interview with Scots Guards Soldier 8 (Officer), March 2013; Interview with a former Military Intelligence Officer, May 2014.
109 G. Adams, 'A Compensation Double Standard', *Guardian*, September 8, 2009.
110 Interview with a former Military Intelligence Officer, May 2014.
111 Interview with Scots Guards Soldier 1 (Officer), May 2014.

However, improvements in intelligence were uneven: in late 1971, HQNI in Lisburn concluded that accurate intelligence outside of Belfast was 'virtually non-existent'.[112] Army 'kill' statistics for Northern Ireland also remained notoriously unclear: 'Troops tended to assume that when they fired their weapons, and saw targets move that they had hit them. When no evidence emerged of a body, they assume that they had hit the person and that the body had been spirited away across the border.'[113] Soldiers were exaggerating reports of their engagements with the IRA.

Civil–Military Tensions after Motorman

Leading Conservative Party and UUP representatives applauded Operation Motorman. Within the Army, Motorman came as a welcome relief, an opportunity to get on the front foot after months of military inertia against the IRA, due to political considerations many could not fathom or agree with. But what was to come next? British political representatives and an older generation of soldiers, such as General Harry Tuzo, who had served in 'internal security' operations in the colonies now wanted a return to 'tried and tested tactics' such as had been seen in the colonies. The Army had proposed introducing some form of 'martial law' in early July 1972.[114] At a meeting on August 29, 1972, there was a terse discussion between the GOC, General Tuzo, and the Secretary of State for Northern Ireland, William Whitelaw:

> [T]he GOC said that the Army was suffering casualties which compared unfavourably with other internal security operations such as those in Borneo and Kenya but without the special processes of law which had enabled effective action to be taken against terrorists in those theatres. Accurate sniper fire was particularly worrying as his troops felt that they were presenting

---

112 Interview with Scots Guards Soldier 1 (Officer), May 2014.
113 Military Intelligence Captain, Bloody Sunday Inquiry Witness – Reference No.: INQ 2225, evidence reproduced in the *Report of the Bloody Sunday Inquiry*, http://webarchive.nationalarchives.gov.uk/20100401161904/http://www.bloody-sunday-inquiry.org.uk/ (accessed December 4, 2017).
114 PRONI: CAB/9G/27/6/5 SOSNI Daily Meetings, Conclusions of Morning Meeting at Stormont Castle on Wednesday, July 12, 1972, at 10.00 a.m.

sitting targets without the will on the part of the authorities to retaliate against the known enemy.[115]

Tuzo accused Whitelaw of putting his troops in danger by winding down internment too quickly. According to the GOC, at least 64 former internees released by Whitelaw had returned to active service with the IRA whose ranks now contained between 800 to 1,000 active members. Post-Motorman, he should reverse this policy. Army morale would deteriorate sharply if new legal powers were not granted the Army to arrest and detain suspected terrorists. He concluded by saying 'that it was essential for a soldier to have faith in the organisation which he served and the time had come to cease acting in a civilised way against an uncivilised enemy'.[116] This was near mutinous talk from a senior British general to a cabinet minister.

Instead of using Motorman as a springboard to a more aggressive military approach, Whitelaw insisted on 'throttling back'.[117] The former Scots Guards officer infuriated military leaders by telling them not to arrest any Provisional IRA members on sight during the months after Motorman, with the exception of suspected IRA battalion commanders and above; any other 'special cases' had to be cleared by him personally before action could be taken.[118] Tuzo's deputy and CLFNI, Major General Robert Ford, pushed back:

115 PRONI: CAB/9G/27/6/5 SOSNI Daily Meetings, Conclusions of Meeting held at Stormont Castle on Tuesday, August 29, 1972, at 2.45 p.m.

116 PRONI: CAB/9G/27/6/5 SOSNI Daily Meetings, Conclusions of Meeting, August 29, 1972, at 2.45 p.m.

117 Prime Minister Edward Heath came under pressure from MPs in his own party and peers in the House of Lords to replace Whitelaw in 1972. The 5th Duke of Westminster, Robert Grosvenor, a resident at Ely Lodge near Enniskillen, former Royal Artillery officer, and a former Unionist MP for Fermanagh and South Tyrone, wrote to Heath to inform him that Whitelaw, the Secretary of State for Northern Ireland, had 'lost all credibility in Ulster'. Some Conservative MPs, such as Peter Tapsell, called for the introduction of 'martial law'. CPA: CRD 3/18/1 Minutes of a Meeting of the Conservative Party Northern Ireland Backbench Committee, July 12, 1972; Letter from the 5th Duke of Westminster to Edward Heath, dated July 13, 1972, available at www.thebrokenelbow.com/2014/03/25/ (accessed March 12, 2015).

118 PRONI: CAB/9G/27/6/5 SOSNI Daily Meetings, Conclusions of Meeting, August 29, 1972, at 2.45 p.m.

The army was used to known and active IRA volunteers being able to do this [avoid arrest], but IRA officers were in quite a different category. They included adjutants who planned the bombing and shooting; explosives officers who prepared bombs; quartermasters who alone knew the sites of all company arms and ammunition; and training officers responsible for recruitment ...
If the IRA was ever to be neutralised, these key men had to be removed from the scene.[119]

Eventually, Whitelaw relented and did allow a greater number of suspected IRA officers to be arrested on sight by the Army. Meanwhile, he actively sought out solutions to the problem of jury and witness intimidation, which eventually led to the introduction of the Diplock courts – where hearings were held out of public view and without juries – in 1973.[120] But the Secretary of State's message was clear – no arrests of IRA members unless they were actively and demonstrably engaged in plotting an attack or they were known to be at the top levels of the organisation. Under Whitelaw, Army discretion over arrests was considerably circumscribed. To the chagrin of the Army, Whitelaw also continued his policy of releasing the vast majority of internees.[121]

Some in the Army agreed with Whitelaw that the days of colonial tactics were over. Writing in 1973, a Royal Military Police Special Investigations Branch (RMP SIB) officer concluded that, 'Tactics learnt in other theatres further afield, when imported by the Army into Northern Ireland, have often proved of acute political embarrassment and left a long trail of litigation, for every military operation and incident is subjected to close political scrutiny.'[122] Whitelaw realised that a

119 PRONI: CAB/9G/27/6/5 SOSNI Daily Meetings, Conclusions of Morning Meeting held at Stormont Castle, August 23, 1972, at 10.00 a.m.
120 'RMP and Legal Consequences of the Army's Involvement in Northern Ireland: Lecture by DAPM (Legal Affairs) for Army's Study Period, November 6, 1973', reproduced in *Report of the Bloody Sunday Inquiry*, http://webarchive.nationalarchives.gov.uk/20100401161904/http://www.bloody-sunday-inquiry.org.uk/ (accessed December 4, 2017).
121 'RMP and Legal Consequences of the Army's Involvement in Northern Ireland'.
122 'RMP and Legal Consequences of the Army's Involvement in Northern Ireland'.

military response to IRA violence was not the primary means of victory but it was the main route to defeat if implemented incorrectly. Political power sharing and agreement over policing were the main solutions. In the absence of such an accord between Northern Ireland's main political parties, careful monitoring, clever intelligence work and selective arrests were the best approach. Whitelaw was increasingly critical of the Army in late 1972, complaining to Conservative Party colleagues that the Army was 'over-optimistic' in seeking short-term military fixes to a long-term political problem. The Defence Secretary, Lord Carrington, and the Home Secretary, Reginald Maudling, were also concerned about 'over-optimism' on the part of the GOC that he could 'finish off' the IRA in a matter of months. Both men, like Whitelaw, thought violence would continue to fester in Northern Ireland for many years, even at reduced levels. They were embarked on a long and painful project.[123]

Confused about policy and strategy, the Army became obsessed about coordination. In the 'end of mission' report for Operation Banner published in 2006, the Army complained that during the 1970s:

> There was no single authority in overall charge of the direction of the campaign, but rather three agencies, often poorly coordinated: Stormont followed by the NIO; the MOD; and the RUC. From a military perspective, for most of the campaign there was little coherence and synergy. There was little evidence of a strategic vision and no long-term plan ... It was not important that the 'supremo' should be military; but rather there be a single figure of authority.[124]

Such criticism is misplaced. The introduction of direct rule saw much better coordination among UK security agencies and ministries in London. William Whitelaw wrested control of policy in Northern Ireland from a confusing conglomerate of Northern Irish politicians, military leaders and Westminster civil servants. He appointed a director for intelligence and a better system of liaison between the Army and local government. Home Secretary Reginald Maudling was relieved to hand over cabinet responsibility for Northern Ireland to Whitelaw. General

---

123 CPA: CRD 3/18/1 Minutes of a Meeting of the Conservative Party Northern Ireland Backbench Committee, November 2, 1972.
124 British Army, *Operation Banner*, 8.4.

Blacker, the Vice-Chief of the General Staff, recalled the 'cumbersome ritual' in the days before direct rule of trying to reach to the Secretary of State for Defence, and then the Home Secretary, in order to get the government in London 'to remonstrate with [Northern Ireland Prime Minister] Chichester-Clark for insisting on operations the Army did not want to implement'. William Whitelaw, by contrast, was 'a powerful Minister', one who 'took all such decisions by himself'.[125]

Northern Ireland had 'a Supremo' – but the Army did not always like the decisions that he made.[126] Whitelaw preferred to err on the side of exposing the Army to more danger, a form of 'courageous restraint', at least until the Diplock courts could be introduced and the 1973 Sunningdale power-sharing agreement between Ulster's political parties could be negotiated, rather than continuing the politically damaging policy of internment without trial. For a conservative, and a former Scots Guards officer, that took courage. But, as will become clear in subsequent chapters, Whitelaw's approach would cause deep resentment among many soldiers who could not understand why many terrorists and their supporters were not being interned or given lengthy prison sentences.

The Social Environment:
Soldiers' Interactions with the Local Population

Group Solidary, Leadership and Micro-Conflicts

Even in peacetime, military units turn inwards when confronted by an external threat – and will use language to demonise those perceived to be the enemy or the community from which the enemy draws its support. Although regular Irish regiments in the British Army did not serve in Northern Ireland in the early days of the Troubles, an account of a 1980 riot in England by soldiers of 2nd Battalion, the Royal Irish Rangers provides an example of this phenomenon (with a particularly Ulster flavour). On this occasion, 60 Rangers went on a drunken rampage after an altercation at a Chinese restaurant in the town of Tidworth in Wiltshire. After getting the upper hand against the Military Police, reinforcements were called from both the Wiltshire and Hampshire Constabularies. During the fighting, the Rangers, most of whom were

---

125 Blacker, *Monkey Business*, 173.
126 Beattie-Smith, *The British State*, 303–304.

Protestant Ulstermen, began to sing Irish rebel songs as a means of taunting, or 'getting at', the police. When confronted by baton-wielding English policemen, loyal sons of Ulster became Fenian rebels.[127]

The only side to be on was that of other soldiers. The fear of being killed in Northern Ireland set a soldier's priorities; urgency brought the unit even closer together:

> It was no longer the spectre of superior authority but the fear of being mined, sniped, rocketed, mortared and booby-trapped that was the private's main concern. In the face of this threat, the company and all who comprised it, regardless of rank, were resources which aided privates in surviving.[128]

Soldiers were predominantly focused on their respective 'patch' during their four-month tours of Northern Ireland. A major in charge of a company's area of operations would occasionally refer up to the commanding officer of the battalion for guidance or logistical support. But because there were few offensives and scarcely any battalion-sized operations, commanding officers usually let their company commanders get on with their tasks – searches, cordons, surveillance or sniper operations etc. The major would principally look downwards, at his 'patch', and was too busy to consider the wider strategic or operational picture. A narrowing of view or focus ran ever downwards to the private soldier who would never consider much more than his immediate surroundings (often just a small neighbourhood in West Belfast) and what/who would best keep him safe in it.[129] Local Republican or IRA units were also consumed by their small 'patches', waging their own micro-wars in their respective areas. Future Sinn Féin president Gerry Adams recalled that during his initial years as a Republican the wider context of the IRA's campaign 'went over my head. To a large extent, my political world was Ballymurphy. I was busy enough there without worrying about the rest of the struggle.'[130] The micro-conflict, fought over a small 'patch' of streets or fields, was all-consuming.

---

127 'Rampaging Rangers – 11 Court Martialled', *Belfast Telegraph*, January 13, 1981.
128 Hockey, *Squaddies*, 131.
129 Interview with Scots Guards Soldier 15 (Officer), May 2014.
130 Adams, *Before the Dawn*, 122.

Unnecessary risks or self-initiative were not welcome: according to Hockey, 'hero' became a term of abuse in dangerous areas for an officer or NCO who recklessly exposed themselves and other soldiers to danger without any obvious benefit.[131] Private soldiers looked most frequently to a lance-corporal, corporal (half-section or section commander) for professional and emotional support. But the company commander set the operational tempo and tone in both urban and rural operations. The company was the largest unit that made sense to a private soldier on operations in Northern Ireland – 'the Major' was constantly on the ground every day, visiting each of his platoons and sub-units. He was not caught up in as much burdensome administrative work as the battalion CO or negotiating with brigade HQ. Battalions were often broken up – units of 1 Argylls were sent to Dungannon, Newry and South Armagh (all quite different operating environments; A Company, 1 Argylls [east Tyrone] were under the operational command of 1st Battalion, Queen's Own Highlanders) – whereas companies tended to stay together.[132] Chapter 3 will explore this concept further through case studies as well as the role of informal and formal rank structures that helped or obstructed soldiers to adjust to their tasks and environment.

Isolation, Retribution and Denial

As casualties mounted, so did soldiers' desire for retribution. In late 1971, a journalist from *Soldier* magazine visiting 1 Scots Guards captured the contradiction between the 'warrior' self-image of soldiers and the extreme frustrations of soldiering in a domestic, low-intensity conflict:

> The implicit threat in the proud motto of the Scots Guards – Nemo me impune lacessit (nobody provokes me with impunity) – has been quietly shelved by the 1st Battalion during its four month stint in Belfast, where the provocation is constant and considerable ... This attitude is particularly marked towards local children – in a city where a friendly word to a child may

---

131 Hockey, *Squaddies*, 167.
132 Interview with Scots Guards Soldier 15 (Officer), May 2014; Interview with Argyll Soldier 10 (Officer), December 2013; Interview with Argyll Soldier 18 (Officer), May 2014.

be rewarded with a torrent of abuse, a brick in the face or even a burst of fire from an automatic weapon.[133]

Mounting losses on the part of the Army, vengeful or extreme acts of violence such as Bloody Sunday, combined with violent retribution by the IRA on those who 'collaborated' with the Army, meant that acts of kindness between soldiers and the local population became increasingly rare between the beginning of 1971 and the end of 1972. Those in Catholic areas who were overtly friendly to soldiers risked 'tarring and feathering', torture and possibly death at the hands of the IRA. Soldiers were to be treated like 'lepers of old':

> How do you deal with informers, touts and those who break the law and to escape prison become RUC informers? When the IRA warn, they warn only once. Tar and feathers is as old as the Black and Tan days, and others beware lest the tar spills again.[134]

Upon returning for yet another tour in Londonderry in April 1974, Major Hugh Lockhart, an officer in 1st Battalion, Grenadier Guards, wrote to Bishop Edward Daly, the recently appointed Catholic Bishop of Derry. Lockhart confided that it was difficult to get his soldiers even to think about trying to win over the local population. 'Hearts and minds' was fine rhetoric but a hard sell to his soldiers in the Creggan and Bogside because of their previous experiences there in 1972 and 1973:

> One of the main problems of changing patrolling policy is the bitterness that exists. As you said, the people have no confidence in the army after four years, but our soldiers are equally bitter after several years of stoning, shootings, and constant rebuffs, and it will be a hard task to convince and inspire them to put into practice on the ground a policy which we at command level agree is correct.[135]

133 'Patience under Provocation', *Soldier* 28(2) (1972).
134 'Tar and Feathers', *An Phoblacht*, February 1971.
135 Derry Roman Catholic Diocesan Archives, St Columb's College, Derry: Bishop Edward Daly Papers, Letter from Major Hugh Lockhart, 1 Grenadier Guards, to Bishop Edward Daly, regarding introduction from Bishop of Glasgow, dated April 2, 1974.

Bishop Edward Daly was convinced that the Grenadier Guards were meting out collective, retributive punishment to the general population in Derry, behaviour that went directly against the nominal values and procedures of the Army. He wrote an angry letter to the GOC, Lieutenant General Frank King. Daly pointed out that other Army units had behaved well prior to the Grenadier Guards arrival; support for the IRA had diminished due to the diligent work of soldiers and community leaders. Now months of work was being undone in a few days, or, as he put it to Major Lockhart: 'Your men are antagonizing a whole population, and you are playing right into the hands of the Provos.'[136] Daly had an ally in Taoiseach Liam Cosgrave, whose new Fine Gael-led government had significantly improved Anglo-Irish security cooperation. Cosgrave raised the issue of the 'overly-zealous' behaviour of the Grenadier Guards in Derry. The Secretary of State for Northern Ireland, Francis Pym, and General King were outraged:

> SSNI said how annoyed he had been by complaints to the Taoiseach about the 1 GREN GDS behaviour and attitude in Londonderry. GOC explained how well 1 GREN GDS had done in the area and that violence had in fact decreased. He drew comparisons to the smear campaign against 3 PARA in the Ardoyne in 1973.[137]

A piqued General King subsequently wrote a letter to Bishop Edward Daly, putting the blame on the people of the Creggan: 'I cannot think of such a difficult community as the Creggan in terms of self-discipline and self-behaviour anywhere in Northern Ireland ... as you and I know, the remedy is really in their hands and in the hands of their elected leaders. They can throw out the evil men.'[138] The reactions of both Pym

---

136 Derry Roman Catholic Diocesan Archive, St Columb's College, Derry: Bishop Edward Daly Papers, Letter from Bishop Edward Daly, Bishop of Derry, to Major Hugh Lockhart, 1 Grenadier Guards, May 14, 1972.
137 TNA: CJ 4/834 Intelligence Army and RUC – Role of the Army in Northern Ireland, 1974–1975, Note for the Record – Discussions Held at HQNI on Monday, July 22, 1974 between SOSNI and GOC.
138 Derry Roman Catholic Diocesan Archives, St Columb's College, Derry: Bishop Edward Daly Papers, Letter from General Officer Commanding Northern Ireland, Lieutenant General Frank King, to Bishop Edward Daly, dated May 25, 1974.

and King were instinctively defensive and dismissive, despite Bishop Daly's praise for other Army units that had pursued a different approach to 1 Grenadier Guards. Senior Catholic clergymen and political leaders were convinced that some regiments were worse than others. Gerry Fitt, the Nationalist MP for West Belfast, complained of British Army unit operational inconsistency in the same areas, warning that the return of some units would guarantee an increase in harassment of the local Catholic population and a surge in support for the IRA.[139]

Sectarianism and the Attempted Co-Option of Scottish Regiments

Republican literature often stressed that Scottish regiments could not be trusted due to the inherent bias of Scottish 'Orange' soldiers[140] and the general prevalence of sectarianism in Scotland: 'little enough had changed, with bigoted Scotsmen simply replacing the hated RUC as the primary aggressors'.[141] Some Scottish soldiers were indeed in the Orange Order; a quartermaster of the Scots Guards was a senior member of a lodge in Glasgow.[142] Gerry Adams wrote that, 'The use of Scottish soldiers, amongst whom support for Orange bigotry was strong, guaranteed that provocation and abuse would be directed against residents.'[143] Scottish soldiers were the 'quislings' of England, or so the Republican argument went:

> Are things so perfect in Scotland that men are prepared to force the imperialistic policies of England down the throats of Irish people? Don't members of the Scotch regiments of the British Army serving now realize that when Scotch pride of race reasserts itself once more, as it will under the present conditions to which they are being subjected to, then quislings of the British army will be sent to their country to carry out the dirty work that they have been doing here.[144]

139 TNA: CJ 4/1657 Powers of Search Houses – Army 1976–1977, 'Army Harassment', dated March 31, 1976.
140 *Lower Falls Street Bulletin* (1971) (no specific date).
141 K. Conway, *Southside Provisional* (Dublin: Orpen Press, 2014), 24.
142 Interview with Scots Guards Soldier 10 (Officer), May 2014.
143 Adams, *Before the Dawn*, 136–137.
144 Untitled article published in *Saoirse*, the newspaper of the St James's and District Sinn Féin, Robert Emmet/Francis Ligett Cumman, 1974.

Attempts to stir up Scottish Nationalism failed to have much of an impact on Scottish soldiers.

Occasionally, provocative incidents did take place: one Scots Guardsman recalled an incident when 1 Scots Guards came under attack before they even left Britain. Waiting to board a troop ship on Merseyside bound for Northern Ireland, a piper decided to play 'the Wearing of the Sash', the emblematic song of the Orange Order. Guardsmen quickly found themselves dodging nuts and rivets thrown by outraged Liverpool-Irish dockers working nearby.[145]

Nevertheless, most Guards officers, NCOs and guardsmen interviewed were adamant that sectarian tensions did not arise between soldiers; Catholic guardsmen did not break with Protestant guardsmen as a result of the conflict. In a group interview, a former officer described how upon joining the Scots Guards as a young platoon commander, 'one of my Lance Sergeants had a fairly swift word in my ear, explaining why there should be no Roman Catholics in his section, which is something I had never even thought about, you know'.[146] A former senior (Catholic) NCO sitting next to him during the interview was outraged, 'I would have sacked him. If somebody said to me, "don't have any Catholics in your thing mate", I would have put him so far inside the jail he would have need fed by a pole.'[147] The relatively large number of Catholic officers and NCOs in the Scots Guards meant that overt sectarian bullying or tension within the regiment was usually swiftly dealt with. Guardsmen with 'King Billy' or other Orange Order emblems tattooed on their arms were told to wear their sleeves rolled down.[148] But most soldiers interviewed also accepted that sectarian opinions were sometimes voiced in Northern Ireland: for example, a 2 Scots Guards officer was deeply suspicious of the Commander of 8 Brigade, Brigadier David Mostyn, partly because he was a Catholic.[149]

Less than a week after his arrival in Derry, the CO of 2 Scots Guards, Colonel Tony Boam, wrote that some of his area of operations was 'rabid Catholic and contains some fairly barbery fellows'.[150] The

145 Interview with Scots Guards Soldier 3 (Guardsman), November 2013.
146 Interview with Scots Guards Soldier 5 (Officer), November 2013.
147 Interview with Scots Guards Soldier 4 (NCO), November 2013.
148 Interview with Scots Guards Soldier 12 (Officer), December 2014.
149 Interview with Scots Guards Soldier 18 (Officer), June 2013.
150 TNA: WO 305/4271 Commander's Diary of 2nd Battalion, Scots Guards, July

phrasing is unfortunate, especially for a man of Colonel Boam's evident intelligence. However, Boam was expressing his shock at the level of hatred that his troops encountered, one that he viewed as inherently sectarian and local in its origin. He also could not fathom the sheer absurdity and inhumanity of internecine violence in a small place like Northern Ireland.[151] Although Britain in the 1970s had its own racist and sectarian problems, many Scots Guards and Argyll soldiers were taken aback at the ferocity of feeling they encountered in Northern Ireland. This distaste could quickly turn to outright repugnance. In condemning what he saw as 'hatred masquerading as virtue', one officer described meeting a local Unionist dignitary in Lurgan, County Armagh:

> I went to take tea with him – it was no more than tea because he was strictly teetotal and extremely religious. The second or third time he was describing how they would put Catholics down man-holes and then plant a truck on top of a man hole cover. This was done all the while when we were sitting very pleasantly having tea. I kept my mouth shut because I needed the contact with him. But an awful lot of my time was spent talking to evil.[152]

Efforts by Loyalists to co-opt Scottish regiments were generally unsuccessful. Although there was a degree of fraternisation between some Argylls and Loyalist paramilitaries during the early 1970s, relations soon soured. Sergeant George Spence, an uncompromising 'bruiser' of an Argyll, 'used to go drinking with Gusty Spence [UVF leader] – until they fell out. George thought he was the tougher Spence.'[153] Both the Scots Guards and the Argylls were wary of being 'captured' by Loyalists for political purposes; officers particularly were repulsed at the extreme sectarian language used by some Loyalists to

29, 1972–August 31, 1972; Letter dated August 5, 1972 from Lieutenant Colonel Tony Boam to Colonel Sir Gregor Macgregor of MacGregor Battalion, Lieutenant Colonel Commanding, Scots Guards.
151 TNA: WO 305/4275 2nd Battalion, Scots Guards, Operational record of battalion net communications, December 1973.
152 Interview with Scots Guards Soldier 10 (Officer), May 2014.
153 Interview with Argyll Soldier 3 (NCO), September 2014.

describe Catholics. Argyll officers were enraged by Loyalist support for an A Company soldier, Private John Brown, who was fined by his regiment for swearing at a child. Ulster Loyalists raised thousands of pounds for the soldier 'to pay his fine', condemning the 'animal-like behaviour' of the Catholic child who they believed abused the soldier.[154] The truth was very different:

> A soldier in A Company, Private Brown, was fined for swearing at somebody, but it wasn't an Irishman, it was the son of an RAF [Royal Air Force] Corporal. The mother was shopping in Dungannon and this young guy, who on every patrol he had been out on had behaved badly, said something he shouldn't have to the young boy. The mother of the young boy was right to complain. Private Brown came sauntering into Ian Purves-Hume's office [A Company's Commander] and Ian blew a fuse and sent him marching about pretty quickly.[155]

Argyll officers believed that Private Brown made approximately £5,000 from the incident. They were disgusted at 'the stupidity' of Private Brown's Loyalist supporters.[156]

When Loyalist paramilitaries sought to challenge the Argylls on the Shankill Road in Belfast in 1976, the response was an all-out escalation by the Argyll soldiers. Loyalist paramilitaries were beaten up, UDA clubs were raided and money 'confiscated'. A Loyalist leader, Hughie Smyth, later called the regiment 'a highly organized criminal syndicate' after several soldiers were convicted of stealing from Loyalist-controlled businesses and committing other robberies including on Royal Avenue in the centre of Belfast.[157] The Argylls in turn generally had a very low opinion of Loyalist paramilitary groups – especially their mimicry of military organisation.[158] A handful of soldiers did declare sympathy for

---

154 Loyalist pamphlet cutting held at the Argyll and Sutherland Highlanders Museum, Stirling Castle (no reference number; undated).

155 Interview with Argyll Soldier 2 (Officer), November 2013.

156 'Sympathy £s to Soldier Annoys Army', *Belfast Newsletter*, August 28, 1972.

157 'Soldiers Raiding UVF Safe Left Names List, Judge Told', *The Times*, October 9, 1981; Sanders and Wood, *Times of Troubles*, 183.

158 TNA: WO 305/4407 The Argyll and Sutherland Highlanders Battalion Diary, April 1969–March 1974.

one side or another; one former Argyll started fund-raising for the UDA in Scotland.[159] Another ex-Argyll collected money for the IRA.[160]

Considering the strong Presbyterian (Church of Scotland) make-up of the Argyll and Sutherland Highlanders and the familiarity or even identification of some of the soldiers with the Orange Order in Scotland, the regiment would have been an obvious candidate to harbour stronger Loyalist sympathies, with the potential to cause problems for the Army. Scottish Protestant extremists did try to incite soldiers, including the Argylls. After one protest at the opening of the General Synod of the Church of Scotland in 1973 – where the guard of honour was provided by the Argylls, the *Scottish Protestant View* reported that, 'The Argylls gave Pastor Glass the thumbs up as they left in their coaches after the parade. They obviously appreciated the protest against the IRA Catholic extremists.'[161] In the month (July 1972) that the Argylls deployed to Ulster, over 6,000 Orangemen marched through the North Ayrshire coastal town of Saltcoats and pledged their support to William Craig, the former Minister for Home Affairs of Northern Ireland and leader of the 'Ulster Vanguard' paramilitary movement, who also attended a number of other rallies in 1 Argylls' recruiting area.[162] Thousands of Orangemen travelled from Northern Ireland to the Glasgow and Clydeside areas in the same month to march with their Scottish brethren and the Grand Orange Lodge of Scotland promised recruits to Loyalist paramilitary organisations if they were needed.[163]

Republicans drew their own conclusions; the Argylls must be more sympathetic to, or even in collusion with, Loyalists. The reality was much more complex: for example, most of the Argyll soldiers came from, or near, 'Red Clydeside', an area saturated with ideas about working-class (non-sectarian) solidarity. Socialism was much more of a Clydeside creed than any adherence to the Orange Order and soldiers were influenced by the overwhelming left-wing sentiment in their local areas. The *Greenock Telegraph* (the port town of Greenock was an important Argyll recruiting area) was quick to condemn William Craig and his Vanguard movement, claiming that they were 'to all intents and purpose Fascist in their

159 Wood and Sanders, *Times of Troubles*, 172.
160 Interview with Argyll Soldier 2 (Officer), November 2013.
161 Interview with Argyll Soldier 2 (Officer), November 2013.
162 'Orange March Ban Defied at Saltcoats', *Greenock Telegraph*, July 1, 1972.
163 'Scots on Standby to Fight Terror', *Sunday Mail*, October 10, 1971.

outlook'.[164] Moreover, the Argylls seemed to clash with any other group of young men, including Loyalists, who sought to establish dominance over what the Argylls thought to be their 'patch'. Contrary to the view of inherent Argyll 'Orange bigotry', so frequently expounded by Republicans, the Argylls' loyalties lay within, to the group. Any rival group of young men, Loyalist or Republican, that sought to challenge the Argylls' supremacy on the latter's 'patch' would not be tolerated. Despite a strong Church of Scotland identity within the regiment, the Argylls also contained a large Catholic minority; a third of all Argyll soldiers in 1972 were Catholics.[165] Anti-Irish rhetoric was more typical than sectarian abuse; soldiers generally did not want to offend their mates. Catholic and Protestant soldiers would also unquestioningly work together against all such challengers, who would occasionally be mocked and ridiculed using whatever lexicon hurt most, in the same way as 'rampaging' Royal Irish Rangers would sing Irish rebel songs to irritate English policemen.[166]

Misconduct and Military Justice

Other regiments, including the Parachute Regiment, also had a difficult relationship with Loyalist Belfast. Following a series of clashes between the UDA and the Army, UDA leaders Tommy Herron and Jim Anderson met with the GOC on October 18, 1972 to demand that 1 PARA (the unit responsible for the Bloody Sunday shootings in Londonderry) be withdrawn from Loyalist areas. Herron and Anderson complained that soldiers from 1 PARA had 'executed' Robert Johnston. On the night of September 7, 1972, Robert Johnston was drunk, wandering up Berlin Street, when he encountered a group of soldiers. One witness described what happened:

> I went out to see what was happening. I saw the man shouting down at the troops at the bottom of Berlin Street on the Shankill Road. The words I heard him say were, 'I run about in my bare

---

164 '"Green Paper" is Ulster's Hope for the Future', *Greenock Telegraph*, November 8, 1972.
165 'IRA Fears Eagle Eyes in the Sky', *Greenock Telegraph*, October 26, 1972.
166 Interview with Argyll Soldier 3 (NCO), September 2014; Interview with Argyll Soldier 20 (Private Soldier), April 2014.

feet thirty years ago ... The weak shall inherit the earth.' Then he was shot.[167]

Another witness in the Shankill Road recalled soldiers driving around the area shouting: 'Come out and fight like men you Orange bastards, we fucked your wives and daughters and now we will kill you, take down your Union Jacks. You're nothing but a lot of Irish bastards.'[168] Shankill residents were outraged and afraid.

Loyalists were not alone in questioning the negative relations that had built up between individual regiments and the local populace. In 1975, the Northern Ireland Office asked the Ministry of Defence to consider the 'habits and traditions of individual battalions' in order to see whether they were suitable for service in Northern Ireland. Another official was concerned that too many battalions in Belfast 'are Scottish or have a strong Scottish element and that there might be scope for discussing with MOD the deployment of particular units to Northern Ireland and within the Province'.[169]

Senior Army officers often instinctively dismissed allegations of abuse as lies peddled by terrorists through gullible (or deliberately malicious) mainstream political, religious or other community representatives. The Commander of 39 Brigade, Brigadier Frank Kitson, later recalled the tendency of terrorist groups to try deliberately to target 'successful' commanders with false allegations of abuse or atrocity:

> Sometimes the pressure comes from apparently uncommitted members of the community who suggest that a particularly successful commander is being abrasive and destroying hopes of a better relationship with the people: such an approach is likely to be instigated by the insurgents. Resisting these pressures is one of the most difficult tasks facing commanders in countering insurgency.[170]

---

167 'The Shankill Disturbances: A Series of Eyewitness Accounts Compiled by an Ulster Defence Team' (Belfast: Ulster Defence Association, 1972).
168 'The Shankill Disturbances'.
169 TNA: CJ 4/1290 Army – Northern Ireland Officer, 1975–1976, Letter from SS Bampton to Permanent Under Secretary of State at the Northern Ireland Office, dated August 8, 1975.
170 Kitson, *Directing Operations*, 60.

Kitson warned that any 'outcry [against the Army] is not usually a spontaneous reaction originating from the public, but is carefully orchestrated by sympathisers of the insurgents'.[171] He concluded by warning military commanders of the gullibility of the civil authorities in believing such allegations of military abuse; officers should work assiduously to persuade the government of the complex nature of subversive 'dirty tricks'.[172]

Edward Heath needed little persuading; he refused to countenance the idea that some units in Northern Ireland had behaved particularly badly. He responded testily to Taoiseach Liam Cosgrave's criticisms of the Parachute Regiment. Cosgrave had contrasted the Parachute Regiment unfavourably with the good work of other Army units:

> It is not in fact correct that the Parachute Regiment is the only unit to be criticised. Scottish Regiments are frequent targets. Any effective unit, deployed in a notable trouble spot, must expect the propaganda treatment ... the Protestant extremists certainly wanted the Parachute Regiment removed. Parachute Battalions are extremely effective units, but no different from any other in their rules and methods. They are noted for their excellent NCOs, who ensure tight discipline.[173]

Nevertheless, despite having the confidence of the Prime Minister, General Harry Tuzo worried about the increasing number of incidents where commanding officers covered up the misdeeds of their soldiers, a misplaced loyalty of 'My soldiers right or wrong'. But he did little to act upon his concerns.[174] Even in an incident where wrongdoing had, according to Tuzo, undeniably taken place – the abduction and severe beating of two Legion of Mary workers, Raymond Muldoon and Francis Creagh, by soldiers from 1 PARA on February 3, 1972 – Tuzo's wrath focused on the victims, Muldoon and Creagh, because they did not seek Army or RUC assistance to investigate their allegations. 'One is

171 Kitson, *Directing Operations*, 56.
172 Kitson, *Directing Operations*, 56.
173 TNA: CJ 4/668 Matters Concerning the Security Forces, June 1973–January 1974, Message from the Prime Minister to Mr Cosgrave, April 18, 1973.
174 Dixon, 'Hearts and Minds: British Counterinsurgency Strategy in Northern Ireland', 280.

forced', Tuzo wrote, 'to the conclusion that they are more interested in propaganda than in the redress of grievance'.[175]

A more considered reflection on why Muldoon and Creagh and other alleged victims of Army mistreatment did not liaise directly with the Army and the police might have considered the following prevailing factors: first, the dangers for residents of areas with a significant Republican presence of cooperating with the Security Forces lest they be intimidated, assaulted or murdered by the IRA; second, locals may not have had confidence in the desire of the security forces to investigate such abuses. Both were legitimate concerns. During the early years of Operation Banner there were a number of barriers towards uncovering the truth behind allegations of bad behaviour on the part of soldiers. There was a somewhat pejorative view within the Army when it came to the Northern Irish population writ large, an underlying assumption that local people inevitably made things up or grossly exaggerated incidents and were not to be believed. In short, there was something 'wrong' with the Irish. The GOC, Harry Tuzo, approvingly quoted the writer Honor Tracy to describe the Irish:

> 'If anyone lays a finger on them [the Irish] the world must hear of it with embellishment. And like children they believe in their fantasies ... Furthermore, nothing that happens, no action of troops or police, relates in any way to anything done by themselves. Nothing is ever their fault, nor do they ever do wrong.' Because the world at large is unaccustomed to this style of behaviour, complaints and allegations by Irishmen against the Army are apt to shock and disturb.[176]

Very few soldiers were prosecuted for offences committed in Northern Ireland between 1969 and late 1972. In 1970, the then GOC, General Freeland, concluded an agreement with the chief constable of the RUC on the investigative process that should be followed if allegations of misconduct were made against the Army: The Army alone would

---

175 PRONI: D/3687/26/1 Letter from General Officer Commanding to Dr Newe, February 27, 1972.
176 PRONI: CAB/9G/27/6/5 Campaign to discredit the Army. Paper by GOC Northern Ireland, November 25, 1972.

interview military witnesses, and the RUC would speak to civilians. Only a handful of cases ever made it to court; according to an RMP SIB major, this was a 'honeymoon period' for the Army:

> With both RMP and RUC sympathetic towards the soldier, who after all was doing an incredibly difficult job, he was highly unlikely to make a statement incriminating himself, for the RMP investigator was out for information for managerial, not criminal purposes, and, using their powers of discretion, it was equally unlikely that the RUC would prefer charges against soldiers except in this most extreme of circumstances.[177]

Direct rule brought this 'gentleman's agreement' between the RUC and the Army to an end. In March 1972, the British government appointed a Director of Public Prosecutions (DPP) for Northern Ireland, Sir Barry Shaw, who reviewed procedures for the investigation/referral of allegations against the Army and found them 'far from satisfactory'.[178] At the end of 1972, Shaw revoked RUC discretionary powers, ordering all allegations against the Army to be passed to him for examination.[179]

Shaw was not alone in believing that due process was not being correctly followed: in 1974, during the trial of Corporal Francis Foxford from the Royal Hampshire Regiment accused of the manslaughter of 13-year-old Kevin Heatley, the Lord Chief Justice of Northern Ireland, Sir Robert Lowry, condemned 'the curtailment of the function of the police' during investigation of allegations of Army criminality in previous years. Lowry also questioned the truthfulness of a number of soldiers' accounts of the circumstances surrounding the death of Kevin Heatley, who was shot by Corporal Foxford in Newry's Derrybeg estate on February 28, 1972.[180] Lowry had good reason to worry; some years

177 'RMP and Legal Consequences of the Army's Involvement in Northern Ireland'. 'Managerial' was defined as 'the provision of information for management purposes, counter-propaganda, meeting and defending claims and civil actions, etc., MOD and other government agencies'.
178 'RMP and Legal Consequences of the Army's Involvement in Northern Ireland'.
179 'RMP and Legal Consequences of the Army's Involvement in Northern Ireland'.
180 Sanders and Wood, *Times of Troubles*, 178.

later, Roger Coleman, regimental sergeant major of 1st Battalion, Royal Hampshire Regiment, recalled the killing of Heatley:

> Corporal Foxford believed that there was a shot fired at his patrol. And he turned around, shot and killed Kevin Heatley. Kevin Heatley was taken to the Daisy Hill hospital and before anybody from the RUC or from any form of outside medical support [arrived], Kevin Heatley's body had been wiped down, it was told to me, with a paraffin rag and of course using a paraffin rag will of course remove all traces of burnt propellant from ammunition.[181]

Corporal Foxford was initially convicted, before being acquitted on appeal.[182] By January 1975, the Ministry of Defence had made out of court settlements in 410 cases of alleged abuse, out of an approximate total of 6,000 claims.[183] And, under scrutiny from the DPP, the RMP SIB were forced to conduct more thorough, 'normal SIB standard' inquiries into alleged abuses.[184] Soldiers were outraged: 'Who the hell were SIB working for anyway? Whose side were they on? RMP investigators in Belfast, who hitherto had been regarded as the soldiers' friend, suddenly began to encounter all sorts of difficulties with the units on the ground.'[185] The GOC, General Frank King, complained to the Attorney General on January 8, 1974 that there had been a large increase in soldiers charged with manslaughter or attempted murder (the first such charges were brought in 1973). He admitted that, 'looked at in isolation, each individual case is, I suppose, supported by some evidence against the soldier which in strictly legal terms justifies the prosecution'. But these soldiers were making 'lightning decisions' on the use of violence. For the State to then prosecute them was 'nothing short of monstrous'. General King was more than defensive; he was deeply angry. His soldiers were

---

181 Imperial War Museum, London (hereafter IWM): 13915 Audio Recording – Roger Coleman, Hampshires, Service in Northern Ireland.
182 Christine Keighrey, 'Historical Enquiries Team to Investigate Murder of Kevin Heatley', *Crossmaglen Examiner*, October 30, 2012.
183 Bennett, '"Smoke Without Fire"?', 292.
184 Bennett, '"Smoke Without Fire"?', 292.
185 RMP and Legal Consequences of the Army's Involvement in Northern Ireland.

constantly in danger yet both communities in Northern Ireland were 'hovering in the wings ready to pounce on him and prosecute him in the courts while many of the real lawbreakers remain free'. King rejected any insinuation that the Army was failing properly to investigate itself.[186]

Some officers may have also mistrusted the ability or desire of their superiors to take firm measures against other units that used excessive force. The Army would deny any serious misconduct on Bloody Sunday, even though it was later revealed that the CO of 1 PARA, Lieutenant Colonel Derek Wilford, disobeyed orders from his immediate superior, Brigadier Pat MacLellan. Both men were subsequently rewarded for their operational tours in Northern Ireland during 1972. Nothing was wrong, or so it appeared: Wilford received an OBE and MacLellan was promoted to the rank of Major General.[187] However, despite the non-recognition of any problem on the part of HQNI, there are examples of officers taking measures to mitigate the behaviour of officers or units that were believed to be too violent. For example, Major Tony Wilson, a Light Infantry company commander who was deployed to Newry during late 1971, was awarded a Military Cross for his service in Northern Ireland and put on a track to promotion as lieutenant colonel. He returned to the 3 Brigade area of operations for an emergency tour in early 1972; the Intelligence Officer of the Royal Scots Dragoon Guards recalled his arrival: 'Major Tony Wilson of A Coy 2LI – "the Beast of Newry" – reappeared having flown out from UK for an emergency tour. He was promptly told by brigade on no account to show his face in Newry.'[188] Officially there was no problem, but operationally 3 Brigade knew that Wilson's return would incite the local population, who believed that 2 Light Infantry had behaved in a wilfully violent manner. Brigadier Tony Wilson later refused to cooperate with the Police Service of Northern Ireland Historical Enquiries Team (PSNI HET) in relation to the killings of three men in Newry in October 1971.[189]

---

186 TNA: CJ 4/668 Matters Concerning the Security Forces, June 1973–January 1974, GOC's Briefing Notes on Soldier Prosecutions.

187 See *Report of the Bloody Sunday Inquiry*, vol. 1, para. 3.19 (p. 60), http://webarchive.nationalarchives.gov.uk/20100401161904/http://www.bloody-sunday-inquiry.org.uk/ (accessed December 4, 2017).

188 RSDGA: R12, RB09 Lieutenant Colin Mitchell, 'An Officer's Diary: Scots Dragoon Guards, Northern Ireland, 1971–1972'.

189 See a summary of the PSNI HET, 'Report into the Death of John Francis

Such behaviour was profoundly contradictory; the Army was rewarding soldiers who had arguably made the situation worse through their actions. One Argyll officer in Newry later reflected that to win back the population's trust, operating very selectively and avoiding unnecessary confrontations, he had to forego any thought of medals; the Army incentive system was self-evidently tilted towards aggression.[190] A Scots Guards company commander in Belfast in 1971 reflected that offensive operations should have been the last of many priorities for the Army in Northern Ireland: 'The most important thing was public relations, second was intelligence and quite a long way last was the military operation. Not everybody necessarily grasped that order of things straight away. Different regiments, battalions took varying amounts of time to adjust.'[191] Two very different approaches, the aggressive Colonel Derek Wilford and Major Tony Wilson, and the more cautious instincts of battalion commanders such as 2 Scots Guards CO Tony Boam and company commanders such as Major David Thomson, were both being praised and rewarded simultaneously.

The shift to the Diplock court system was generally welcomed by the Army. Diplock got rid of 'the Belfast juries that would never convict a soldier or a policeman, nor the Londonderry juries who would never convict an IRA man, and the outcome of a case now depends solely upon the evidence presented before the court'.[192] The Diplock system made results far more consistent, but Army officers still felt that the burden of proof and procedures insisted upon by Northern Irish judges remained too high. Senior Army officers compared the swift and successful prosecutions of the perpetrators of the Birmingham bombings with what they regarded as the excessively pedantic approach of the Northern Irish judiciary in the trial of alleged terrorists (the 'Birmingham Six' convictions were later found to be unsafe and overturned sixteen years later).[193]

Ruddy on October 23, 1971', published by the Pat Finucane Centre, copy in the author's possession.
190 Interview with Argyll Soldier 15 (Officer), December 2013.
191 Interview with Scots Guards Soldier 10 (Officer), December 2013.
192 'RMP and Legal Consequences of the Army's Involvement in Northern Ireland'.
193 TNA: CJ 4/1290 Note of Two Meetings Held by the Secretary of State with Senior Army Officers and with Senior RUC Officers at HQNI and RUC HQ on Friday, August 15, 1975.

During the early years of Operation Banner there were a number of barriers towards uncovering the truth behind allegations of misbehaviour on the part of soldiers. First, there was a somewhat pejorative view of the Army towards the population – an underlying assumption that local people inevitably made things up or grossly exaggerated incidents and were not to be believed. Overwhelmed by complaints about behaviour, denied by officers he respected, senior officers such as General Tuzo may simply have become what Bruna Seu has described as a 'desensitized subject'.[194] But 'switching off', or blaming the victim or the community the victim belongs to, is still a conscious choice.[195] Inexcusable behaviour was excused on the basis that the victims were somehow at fault. Another example of such a reflexive defensiveness and denial was the attitude of the commanding officer of 3rd Battalion, Parachute Regiment (3 PARA), Colonel Peter Morton, who robustly defended a soldier in his battalion, Private Michael Williams, who shot and killed a 12-year-old girl Majella O'Hare in South Armagh on August 14, 1976. Colonel Morton even went so far as to insinuate that Majella O'Hare's father may have been (or at least knew who was) the IRA gunman who was alleged by Private Williams to have been in the area: 'As Majella lay mortally wounded in the road her father appeared from the churchyard where he had been cutting the grass in approximately the area where the GPMG gunner had seen his gunman.'[196] Majella O'Hare's father was the caretaker at the local school and held his daughter while she was dying.[197] The PSNI HET later concluded that no IRA gunman had been in the area and that 3 PARA's account of the incident was not credible.[198]

194 B. Seu, '"Your Stomach Makes You Feel that You Don't Want to Know Anything about it": Desensitization, Defence Mechanisms and Rhetoric in Response to Human Rights Abuses', *Journal of Human Rights* 2(2) (2010), 183–196.

195 S. Cohen, *States of Denial: Knowing About Atrocities and Suffering* (Oxford: Blackwell Publishers, 2001), 59.

196 P. Morton, *Emergency Tour: 3 Para in South Armagh* (Northampton: William Kimber, 1989), 95.

197 'Majella had her hand in her long hair. I could see her moving her hand, trying to ease herself, she was hurting. Eventually she took her hand up along my chest to near my right shoulder and said: "Daddy, Daddy," in a very faint voice. A second later she fell between me and Nurse Campbell and just died.' McKittrick et al., *Lost Lives*, 671.

198 'Ministry of Defence Says Sorry for Killing of Majella O'Hare', *Guardian*,

Local people did make frequent complaints, which increased soldiers' scepticism; senior Republican (the future Lord Mayor of Belfast) Alex Maskey's father called up 39 Brigade HQ to ask why soldiers were observing his house and 'harassing' his family by asking them questions – behaviour which soldiers saw as acceptable since his son was an active Republican.[199] But, particularly in 1971 and 1972, the Army did not show due diligence or conduct SIB investigations of a 'normal standard'. The military instinct, practised at every level in Northern Ireland, was to turn inward and defend itself against all outsiders.

Conclusion

In the initial years of its deployment to Northern Ireland after 1969 the Army found waging war against the IRA extremely disorientating. It could no longer employ tactics that it used in all of its wars (with the exception of Suez) over the last two decades. A senior officer in the UDR recalled the difference between the campaign in Yemen and the campaign in Northern Ireland. In Yemen in the early 1960s, people were 'driven from their homes and villages, their crops burned, their houses levelled, their livestock scattered and their grain stores destroyed'.[200] Such options were unthinkable in the case of Northern Ireland. In his account of the Army's experiences in Ulster, Colonel Dewar also underlined the divergence between colonial and domestic operations: 'In a colonial situation it was acceptable to impose curfews, to issue identity cards, to control food supplies and even to move the entire population of a village to a fortified government location to protect it from terrorist intimidation.'[201] The legal powers of the Army in a domestic, UK context, such as arresting or shooting a British citizen, as opposed to a colonial subject, were uncertain at the beginning of the Army's deployment and a degree of caution was required. Indeed, the longer Operation Banner continued, the more the use of force was officially restricted.[202]

Different scholars have concluded that there was a direct, unbroken

---

March 28, 2011.
199 TNA: WO 305/4248 Army Unit Historical Records and Reports, 39 Infantry Brigade Headquarters, July 1971.
200 Sanders and Wood, *Times of Troubles*, 204.
201 Dewar, *The British Army in Northern Ireland*, 219.
202 Dewar, *The British Army in Northern Ireland*, 219.

continuum between military practice in the colonies and in Northern Ireland. Aaron Edwards has argued that minimum force characterised Britain's counterinsurgency (COIN) approach before and during Northern Ireland.[203] Coming to a starkly different conclusion, Niall O' Dochartaigh and David Benest have claimed that the excessive use of force and the collective punishment of populations through 'exemplary violence' by the Army in the early days of Operation Banner was symptomatic of a direct continuation of colonial operations.[204] Britain's counterinsurgency approach in its colonies may not have been of the scale and intensity of violence perpetrated by the French military in Algeria,[205] but 'minimum force' creates a misleading impression of the surgical, precise punishment of terrorists. Moreover, as Huw Bennett has succinctly argued, 'the concept is virtually meaningless in analytical terms, because it lacks clear criteria for judging when it applies and when not'.[206] The Army did not behave according to a strict colonial template in Northern Ireland – there was never any question of the forcible movement of people or destruction of villages in places such as Fermanagh or South Armagh. As John Newsinger has observed, 'the Army fell between two stools: it was not brutal and oppressive enough effectively to intimidate the Catholic working class, but it was brutal and oppressive enough to successfully alienate it.'[207] The Army neither employed a successful

203 'Minimum use of force was a constant feature of the British approach to COIN and had its genesis in the dialectical relationship between Christianity and Victorian sensibilities, on the one hand, and in the practical necessity of imperial policing on the other. It became the essential bedrock for the Army's rules of engagement in Northern Ireland, calling upon even the most junior of commanders to exercise tight control over their subordinates in the face of provocation.' A. Edwards, 'Misapplying Lessons Learned? Analysing the Utility of British Counterinsurgency Strategy in Northern Ireland, 1971–1976', *Small Wars and Insurgencies* 21(2) (2010), 305.

204 N. O'Dochartaigh, *From Civil Rights to Armalites: Derry and the Birth of the Irish Troubles* (Cork: Cork University Press, 1997); Benest, 'Aden to Northern Ireland, 1966–76', 115–145.

205 See A. Horne, *A Savage War of Peace* (New York: New York Review of Books Publications, 2006).

206 H. Bennett, 'The Other Side of the COIN: Minimum and Exemplary Force in British Army Counterinsurgency in Kenya', *Small Wars and Insurgencies* 18(4) (2007), 640.

207 J. Newsinger, 'British Security Policy in Northern Ireland', *Race and Class*

'hearts and minds' approach nor did it clamp down as it had done in the colonies. Much harsher measures may have been introduced in Northern Ireland if the Secretary of State for Northern Ireland, William Whitelaw, had bowed to military pressure and persuaded the cabinet to introduce some form of 'martial law' in areas of Northern Ireland in the autumn of 1972. If he had done so it may have been more plausible to draw direct analogies with colonial counter-insurgency campaigns.

The relatively small geographical area of Northern Ireland did not prevent the development of highly localised and self-contained areas of operations. In the same way that the South Armagh IRA operated relatively autonomously from the rest of the IRA organisation, so did the local British Army units sent to combat them. Because the war was often stagnant and reactive, at least for the Army, soldiers found themselves continuously observing and interacting with the same area and its inhabitants, sometimes over several operational tours. Attitudes between soldiers and locals could harden very quickly as a result of a single incident such as a deadly IRA attack or the retribution meted out to the general populace by soldiers after taking casualties; changing soldiers' and civilians' attitudes after such an event was very difficult. Brigade and battalion HQ set operational priorities. But company commanders, usually of major rank, were critical in setting the tactical tone, tempo and morale for soldiers on Operation Banner. Soldiers came under relentless scrutiny from both communities in Northern Ireland; however, government oversight was initially limited by disbelief, defensiveness and deference to the Army.

Senior commanders in the Army displayed a disbelieving attitude to allegations made against soldiers but they also lacked compliance from more junior commanders who sometimes preferred to keep disciplinary matters 'in house'. Unit cohesion was vital for soldiers to survive and make sense of their duties. However, if improperly managed, cohesion also risked undermining good discipline, frustrating attempts to apply a consistent operational approach and investigations into military misconduct. Even senior military commanders occasionally found it difficult to get to the bottom of allegations of abuse as units closed ranks. The IRA used every such incident of abuse or excessive violence to its advantage, also pointing out the lack of official punishment for such

37(1) (1995), 86.

incidents. In my reading of contemporaneous IRA and other Republican publications, the only time that a normally bullish, defiant organisation seems to be truly unnerved by British Army tactics was when a Welsh regiment[208] arrived in Ardoyne in 1972 and adopted a friendly, restrained attitude towards the local population, despite provocation. The local Republican newspaper, the *Ardoyne Freedom Fighter*, took on a somewhat panicked, even pleading tone to local residents:

> The soldiers stationed in Ardoyne are nice for one reason and that is to win the people over so that if any of this regiment are wounded or killed by the Ardoyne Unit, this will automatically turn the people against the Irish Republican Army. This regiment has been sent in to soft soap the people and it looks as if they are succeeding. Don't forget you once depended on the Ardoyne Freedom Fighters … So now help those who in the past have helped you.[209]

The deep animosity that set in between the Grenadier Guards and the people of the Creggan was much more to the IRA's liking.

The UK government's introduction of direct rule restricted the Army's ability to prioritise a military solution to the conflict. The Secretary of State for Northern Ireland, William Whitelaw, became the unequivocal political authority. Whitelaw also quickly appointed an energetic and capable Director of Public Prosecutions. The Northern Irish courts system also played its role in ensuring that, in future, allegations against the Army would be investigated with more vigour. The operational and social landscape in Northern Ireland from 1971 to 1972 was in flux. The Army was evolving, seizing back 'no-go areas' but making mistakes based on poor intelligence, the occasional employment of tactics unsuited to the UK (such as the disastrous 'Falls curfew', a type of measure introduced as standard in colonial 'emergencies' but quickly abandoned in the case of Northern Ireland). Increasingly constrained by the civil authority, pursuing a policy of intense micro-surveillance or saturation of urban Republican areas, the Army's performance was slowly improving.

---

208 Probably the Royal Regiment of Wales (24th/41st Foot).
209 *The Ardoyne Freedom Fighter*, 1973.

3

The Scots Guards and Argyll and Sutherland Highlanders Regiments in Northern Ireland, 1971–1972

To understand the conditions under which we made decisions you have to put yourself in the position of a young officer wearing a gas mask, which in those days greatly restricted your line of vision, trying to see shapes moving through a blackened, burning city filled with gas and smoke. Those were the conditions.[1]

Who's in Charge?
Levels of Authority and Charisma in the Battalion

Chain of Command: The Relationship between Brigade and Battalion

Battalion commanding officers in Northern Ireland were mostly left to get on with their core task, dominating their area of operations and trying to win the support of the local population. The role of brigade commanders often seemed distant, while the GOC and his deputy, Commander Land

---

[1] Interview with Scots Guards Soldier 1 (Officer), May 2014. The future leader of the Liberal Democrat Party in the UK, Paddy Ashdown, then a young Royal Marine Captain, recalled a similar oppressive environment: 'A great pall of black smoke hung over us, and the cacophony of noise and shouting threatened to drive all rational thought out of the brain.' P. Ashdown, *A Fortunate Life* (London: Aurum Press, 2009), 143.

Forces Northern Ireland (CLF), were rarely seen. One Argyll company commander recalled that:

> Battalions by and large did what they wanted to do. You were very seldom told what to do by Brigade Headquarters. Brigade Headquarters liaised quite closely with the police, passed information down, took information back up and looked over it with the police. Most of them were there for two years. They were a different outfit; they had a nine to five culture. Not far away you had a 24-hour a day Battalion operating according to its own way of doing things. And each Battalion liked coming in and doing their own thing. This is what happened to the Argylls. They came in – didn't like what they saw. And got stuck in.[2]

The battalion commanding officer and his headquarters staff dealt with demands from Brigade. Most Brigade Commanders, particularly Brigadier David Mostyn (Commander, 8 Brigade – 2 Scots Guards) and Brigadier Peter Bush (Commander, 3 Brigade – 1 Argylls) left their units to manage the details of their daily operations, albeit while providing some intelligence and occasionally coordinating a larger multi-battalion operation.[3] In West Belfast in late 1971, 1 Scots Guards saw a lot more of 39 Brigade Commander, Brigadier Frank Kitson than was the norm (a company commander, Major Michael Nurton of Left Flank, recalled once waking up to find Kitson sitting at the end of his bed waiting for a debrief after a night operation).[4] But even Kitson, known for his restless nature, recognised that battalions and companies should be left to plan and execute their own operations without much interference from brigade headquarters:

> The job of the senior commander in this process is to select the right size of the force to cover a particular area and then to ensure its commander is left in peace for long enough to build up his operations, because the process takes weeks or months to come to fruition and every time the local commander is changed,

---

2 Interview with Argyll Soldier 5 (Officer), May 2014.
3 Interview with Argyll Soldier 13 (Officer), December 2014.
4 Naylor, *Among Friends*, 95.

or the troops moved, the process has to start again from the beginning.[5]

Some battalion officers saw brigade HQ as being completely out of touch with reality. Lieutenant Colin Mitchell was an Intelligence Officer with the Royal Scots Dragoon Guards, a cavalry regiment that served alongside the Argylls in 1972. Mitchell could not hide his contempt for the leadership of 3 Brigade (and HQNI), which boiled over when the Royal Scots Dragoon Guards were questioned on why they had used so much ammunition in a three-hour fire fight with an IRA unit led by Martin Meehan on the border near Forkhill, County Armagh on January 27, 1972:

> Brigade acted like a lot of hysterical old women and couldn't believe it when we told them that we had fired 5,209 rounds ... Then they pulled the final treachery and with the crack of umbrellas going up, issued a directive. I strongly suspect on the order of the old maids of Lisburn [HQNI] that major border confrontations are to be avoided at all costs and only minimum fire returned, 'Sufficient to disengage from enemy'. I don't know whether it is ignorance, a complete lack of understanding or concern for the morale of the soldiers, or sheer moral cowardice to political pressure that prompted this infamous signal.[6]

The OC of the unit involved, C Squadron, Royal Scots Dragoon Guards, was also furious with Brigade Headquarters over its attempts to limit the firepower available to soldiers along the border. Major Charles Ramsay stressed that the fire fight on January 27 was, 'a welcome opportunity to avenge the previous attack in this area ... Terrorists who fire on our forces from the sanctuary of the Republic with intent to kill must expect a very full dose'.[7]

A Scots Guards company commander expressed a similar resentment of Brigade Headquarters. Brigade were living behind a desk, issuing

---

5 F. Kitson, *Directing Operations* (London: Faber and Faber, 1989), 59.

6 RSDGA: Mitchell, 'An Officer's Diary'.

7 RSDGA: 'Operational Report 7/72 Narrow Water Incident 1 February', C Squadron, Royal Scots Dragoon Guards, signed by Major C.A. Ramsay, Officer Commanding C Squadron, dated February 7, 1972.

directives and warnings about minimum force that meant nothing to the soldier being sniped and 'bricked' on the streets of Londonderry. The company commander described how, as orders filtered down the chain of command, there was a hardening of approach by the commanders on the ground.[8] Soldiers, including 1 Scots Guards in 1971, would sometimes shoot out the street-lights in their areas so as to avoid being targeted by snipers; such a decision was understandable, but local residents were angered that their streets were now plunged into darkness.[9] The health of the relationship between brigade and battalion depended on utility – the predominantly rural 3 Brigade was badly resourced compared with 8 Brigade (headquartered in Derry) and even more so when it came to 39 Brigade, which was centred on Belfast. For much of 1972, 3 Brigade and 8 Brigade were very short of actionable intelligence. Arriving in the streets of Londonderry and the hills of South Armagh just before Operation Motorman, 2 Scots Guards and 1 Argylls had, comparatively, far less information on which to plan operations and counter threats than units in Belfast.

Colonel Paddy Palmer, the CO of 1 Argylls, was an experienced and intelligent officer who had commanded a company in Aden under Colonel Colin Mitchell. Unlike Mitchell he was not particularly charismatic and he could not supervise or direct the daily operations of his companies along the border. Nor did he want to: even getting to B Company, headquartered in the RUC Station at Crossmaglen, required a time-consuming improvised explosive device (IED) route-clearing operation or the use of helicopters. He largely let his company commanders 'get on with it', facilitating what he could in terms of occasional advice, intelligence, other police/community liaison and dealing with a stream of requests from Brigade. Such delegation took its toll on Palmer who was a good field officer. An Argyll officer recalled the atmosphere at Battalion Headquarters in Bessbrook Mill:

> The Ops Room was a long narrow thing, a couple of chairs and some tables for the CO and 2IC. Paddy Palmer used to pace up and down breaking paper clips. Meanwhile, the 2IC [Major]

8 Interview with Scots Guards Soldier 18 (Officer), June 2013.
9 Interview with Scots Guards Soldier 9 (NCO), December 2013; O. Lindsay, *Once a Grenadier* (London: Pen and Sword, 1996), 134.

Alastair Scott-Elliot needed specs but couldn't get to an optician. He had this big magnifying glass, which he was pouring over documents with.[10]

The commanding officers of 1 Scots Guards (Lieutenant Colonel Murray de Klee and Lieutenant Colonel Richard Mayfield) and 2 Scots Guards (Lieutenant Colonel Tony Boam), deployed to urban areas, were able to exercise more supervision over operations. The officers of 2 Scots Guards saw their CO, Tony Boam, as a competent, tough commanding officer who emphasised attention to detail and discipline, but was not particularly charismatic.[11] Colonel Boam stopped short of telling company commanders how to deploy their patrols on a daily basis but he constantly visited company locations to gauge performance for himself.[12] Boam was meticulous but he could also leave out some material from battalion reports that might upset 8 Brigade HQ, particularly when it came to engagements that pushed the boundaries of the Yellow Card (the Army's rules of engagement). In a letter to the regiment's lieutenant-colonel commanding, Colonel Gregor MacGregor of MacGregor, Boam described how in the immediate aftermath of Operation Carcan, 2 Scots Guards:

> Continued the role of controlling the city and dominating it for about 2 days during which we got two gunmen from the G Company area. One was on the top of the Rossville Flats and the other was down in the Bogside. The OPs [Observation Posts] on the city walls have the most marvellous observation and opportunities for good shots. The only casualty we had was a minor flesh wound to a sniper left behind in G Company area by 3RRF [3rd Battalion, Royal Regiment of Fusiliers].[13]

---

10 Interview with Argyll Soldier 11 (Officer), May 2014.
11 Interview with Scots Guards Soldier 11 (Officer), December 2013.
12 Interview with Scots Guards Soldier 14 (Officer), May 2014; Interview with Scots Guards Soldier 15 (Officer), May 2014.
13 TNA, WO 305/4271 Commander's Diary of 2nd Battalion, Scots Guards, July 29, 1972–August, 31 1972, Letter dated August 5, 1972 from Lieutenant Colonel Tony Boam to Colonel Sir Gregor Macgregor of Macgregor Battalion, Lieutenant Colonel Commanding, Scots Guards.

Another officer also later recalled that snipers from Recce Platoon shot suspected IRA Volunteers who were preparing for an attack in the gasworks in Derry's Bogside/Brandywell area.[14] 'Snipers on the city walls' was not something for the battalion records, and indeed there is no mention of Scots Guards snipers shooting gunmen in the aftermath of Operation Carcan (Motorman) in the log books, incident reports or intelligence summaries of the period. Ten shooting incidents were recorded in the battalion watchkeeper's log at 04.00 on August 31st, the time scheduled for the start of Operation Carcan (Motorman) in Londonderry, but, unusually, there is no description of what occurred.[15] Corporal Nimmo, a sniper attached to 3 RRF in the Bogside, received 'a minor flesh wound' to the shoulder (although Piper McQuarry was later cited as the battalion's first Ulster casualty, shot in the left shoulder on September 6, 1972).[16]

A third 2 Scots Guards officer also recounted that in the days after Operation Carcan (Motorman), snipers shot some IRA Volunteers carrying Thomson sub-machine guns near the Bogside Inn from almost a kilometre away.[17] These incidents figure prominently in the memories of a number of interviewees. Later, the 2 Scots Guards operational magazine hinted that officers knew they were teetering on the verge (if not falling off) of the Yellow Card rules of engagement on such occasions. In a spoof article, the services of one of the battalion's 'troubleshooters' was advertised: 'Out of work film star, aged 26 seeks employment, preferably as a sniper, but anything illegal considered. Ring G Company and ask for Sgt. Hughes, N.'[18]

Company Commanders: Decisive Leadership

Almost all interviewees, of every rank, agreed that the company commander was the officer who 'stamped his personality' over operations in Northern Ireland. A commanding officer might not visit a company

---

14 Interview with Scots Guards Soldier 11 (Officer), December 2013.

15 TNA, WO 305/4271 Commander's Diary of 2nd Battalion, Scots Guards, July 29, 1972–August 31, 1972.

16 Adjutant's Diary, 2nd Battalion, Scots Guards, 1971–1972, Regimental Headquarters, Wellington Barracks, London.

17 Interview with Scots Guards Soldier 18 (Officer), June 2013.

18 'Classified Ads', *Rose and Thistle*, Second Battalion Scots Guards, November 1, 1972.

for a few days but a company commander 'would see every man in his company every day'.[19] A senior officer in 1 Argylls' Battalion HQ observed that company commanders 'were very much in their own little worlds'.[20] Proximity was everything to soldiers; they could usually only see as far as the company commander and consequently much of the strain of operational leadership fell on him. And soldiers could be exacting; the relationship was built on two-way respect. Lieutenant Mitchell recalled in his diary how an uncaring company commander could destroy morale very quickly:

> Charles seems to be doing his level best to wreck C Sqn [Squadron]. Not only is he completely impersonal to the soldiers, leading to their dislike and distrust, to the point where last week when Chas got two bullets through his Land Rover at Newcastle the soldiers drank to the next time, that it might go through his head.[21]

Interviewees often talked about wanting a company commander they could look up to, a man of action but also consideration. Company commanders could exert a unique authority over their respective 'patches' in the early years of Operation Banner. Local people knew it; the British Army was by far the most visible arm of the UK government and many requests and complaints would be put 'to the major'.[22] Major Martin Smith of the 2nd Battalion, Grenadier Guards, the unit that preceded the Argylls' tour of Ardoyne in RUC C Division, in late 1973/early 1974, described his 'tough but fair' approach to his 'patch' in North Belfast:

> When we took over from the Parachute battalion it was too dangerous to drive down the Old Park Road in Belfast; we could only patrol on foot. I never allowed more than four Irishmen to group together. At night I switched off all street lights with the master key so the IRA couldn't see us. But they had a key too, so switched them on to set up ambushes for us. I twice shot out the

19 Interview with Scots Guards Soldier 15 (Officer), May 2014.
20 Interview with Argyll Soldier 13 (Officer), December 2014.
21 RSDGA: Mitchell, 'An Officer's Diary'.
22 Interview with Argyll Soldier 10 (Officer), December 2013.

lights, just as we shot at petrol bombers ... I was known as the Reverend Bastard.[23]

Smith used systematically to 'tear up' a house if the IRA used it as sniping position. Walls were knocked in, floor-boards removed and the garden dug up using Royal Engineer mechanical diggers. Technically all this might be dressed up merely as a legitimate search, but, according to Smith, 'The locals soon got the message'.[24] Major Smith's rather punitive approach to Ardoyne/the Old Park road area was by no means government policy or Army strategy. But he was very much in charge.

Major Johnny Clavering, OC, Right Flank, 2 Scots Guards, was the most charismatic and aggressive of 2 Scots Guards' company commanders in Londonderry. A big, 'rugby player' type, Clavering was brave to a flaw.[25] On October 5, 1972, he personally searched a garage for a bomb that was supposed to go off at any second.[26] When a soldier, Lance Sergeant Thomas McKay, was killed by a sniper who fired on the last vehicle (an armoured Land Rover) in a mobile patrol, Clavering insisted on going out almost every day on patrol as 'tail-end Charlie' or gunner in the last vehicle of a mobile patrol.[27] He was later awarded the Military Cross for his bravery during this tour of Derry.[28] Clavering was a man who liked to get even: IRA snipers killed 5 guardsmen in Londonderry during the 1972 tour (including three from Right Flank); more were wounded. The *Rose and Thistle* recorded how Major Clavering became a 'resident expert' on pub searches, enjoying a chance to get 'stuck in' against Republicans in pubs such as the Brandywell Inn.[29] A number of Right Flank officers appear to have deliberately cultivated a 'no nonsense' reputation in the Brandywell and the Bogside. One officer described how he became concerned that snipers were operating with impunity from the walls of a convent near to his Bridge Camp. He

23 O. Lindsay, *Once a Grenadier* (London: Pen and Sword, 1996), 134.

24 O. Lindsay, *Once a Grenadier* (London: Pen and Sword, 1996), 134.

25 Interview with Scots Guards Soldier 13 (Officer), December 2014.

26 'Life at the New Bridge Corral', *Rose and Thistle*, 2nd Battalion Scots Guards, November 1, 1972.

27 Interview with Scots Guards Soldier 13 (Officer), December 2014.

28 2nd Battalion Notes, *Scots Guards Magazine*, September 1973.

29 Life at the New Bridge Corral', *Rose and Thistle*, 2nd Battalion Scots Guards, November 1, 1972; Interview with Scots Guards Soldier 18 (Officer), June 2013.

ordered his men to give the convent walls 'a barrage of fire'. It was not Yellow Card rules but it was believed to be effective.[30]

Another 2 Scots Guards company commander, Major Robin Buchanan-Dunlop was regarded as 'utterly dependable' but very deliberate and cautious. Meanwhile, Major Richard Jenner-Fust, the OC of G Company, was regarded as the least energetic company commander, if still relatively competent. According to another officer, Jenner-Fust was 'a very nervy individual. He was very musical, really a very talented, other-than military person. You would never have thought he was a soldier to meet him'.[31]

A highly instructive example of very different company commanders within the same battalion – all with divergent views on how operations should be carried out – was offered by 1 Argylls.[32] D Company's OC is worth discussing in depth, since D Company is also the focus of a subsequent chapter. Major Jeremy Mackenzie was the 1 Argylls company commander who would rise highest, finishing his career as a four-star general and NATO's Deputy Supreme Allied Commander Europe (DSACEUR). According to another Argyll officer, 'He [Mackenzie] was one of the most outstanding young officers of his generation: he was just better at everything. He is not necessarily a popular man around the Army. I think that is mainly jealously. He was a great soldier, a great artist, a great sportsman, an incredible shot – a really good man.'[33] Mackenzie was of Scottish, colonial stock, the son of an officer in the Seaforth Highlanders, Colonel J.W.E. Mackenzie. Colonel Mackenzie had served with the King's African Rifles and later commanded 3rd Battalion, North Rhodesian Regiment in Burma where, in early 1945, 'overcoming by sheer tenacity the difficulties imposed by disease and country reduced to a morass by the monsoon', Mackenzie 'successfully led his battalion through trackless and precipitous country of the Arakan to cut the enemy's line of withdrawal'.[34] Colonel Mackenzie's determi-

---

30 Interview with Scots Guards Soldier 18 (Officer), June 2013.
31 Interview with Scots Guards Soldier 19 (Officer), December 2014.
32 A Company, commanded by Major Ian Purves-Hume, served under the command of the Queen's Own Highlanders in East Tyrone and will not be examined closely here.
33 Interview with Argyll Soldier 15 (Officer), December 2013.
34 TNA: WO 373/43/11 Recommendation for Award for Mackenzie, John William Elliot Rank: Temporary Lieutenant Colonel, Major.

nation and fearlessness impressed all who met him (attributes also ascribed to his son). After the war, he became a senior superintendent of the Tanganyika Police Force.[35] His son Jeremy later recalled that in East Africa his father 'would shoot two large bull elephants. The sale of the tusks of these paid fully the school fees of both my sister and me'.[36]

Jeremy Mackenzie had spent much of his childhood in Kenya, boarding at the Duke of York School outside Nairobi. He shone at sport and seemed to be a natural soldier; he was senior under officer at Sandhurst and his company won the Sovereign company competition. He intended upon following his father into the Seaforths, but in 1961 his father's regiment was amalgamated with the Cameron Highlanders to form the Queen's Own Highlanders (QOH). Mackenzie was one of the first new officers to join the amalgamated regiment.[37] He was assigned to command 3 Platoon, A Company, 1st Battalion, QOH. The battalion was soon deployed to south-east Asia where Mackenzie excelled as a platoon commander during the Borneo Confrontation with Indonesia. In November and December 1962, 3 Platoon moved twelve times in eight weeks, putting down a coup in Brunei and engaging in a fire fight in Seria, north-west Sarawak, Borneo. Mackenzie's platoon also stayed in Labi in the interior of Borneo where they were lodged in a longhouse during the local harvest festival.[38] Throughout his military career Mackenzie pushed every unit he commanded. From Africa he knew 'bushcraft'; in Borneo and later on training exercises in the desert near Sharjah, the United Arab Emirates, he would shoot the local wildlife to supplement his men's rations. There is also a trace of the exhibitionist, a leader who prided himself in unorthodoxy and toughness. One Argyll officer recalled that Mackenzie and former Special Air Service (SAS) officer, Major Rod Liddon, both then serving in the Argylls, won a boat race by picking up the boat and running with it between stages – they later maintained that the rules did not disqualify such 'innovation'.[39] In Sarawak, on patrol along the thick jungle of the banks of the Baram

35 TNA: WO 373/43/11 Recommendation for Award for Mackenzie, John William Elliot.
36 'Obituaries', *Queen's Own Highlander* 30(80) (1991), 18.
37 'Newly Gazetted Officers', *Queen's Own Highlander* 1(4) (1961), 4.
38 '3 Platoon Notes', *Queen's Own Highlander* 3(2) (1963).
39 Interview with Argyll Soldier 5 (Officer), May 2014.

River, Mackenzie tied a head to his pack, which was given to him by local Iban tribesmen. A 3 Platoon soldier later recalled the Baram operation:

> This patrol was notable in that the Platoon walked 30,000 yards in 3 days and that Lt. Mackenzie was presented with a head from one of the headhunting Iban longhouses. This was duly christened 'Charlie', killed in 1849 during the rebellion quashed by James Brooke, and spent the remainder of the trip grinning from the back of Lt. Mackenzie's pack.[40]

Mackenzie was in his element. He later worked for 'E Group', a special paramilitary unit reporting to the Secret Intelligence Service (SIS or MI6), and was sent to live among the tribes of Borneo for two years to counter Indonesian influence during the early and mid-1960s. Mackenzie's time in Borneo coincided with that of a distinguished Queen's Own Highlander, Major General Peter Hunt, General Officer Commanding Land Forces Borneo, and later Chief of the General Staff in 1973 at a critical period in the Northern Ireland campaign. Another key officer in Borneo during the Operation Claret raids was Brigadier Harry Tuzo.[41] Tuzo's 51st Gurkha Brigade and Mackenzie's E Group (or Branch) frequently conducted operations with the SAS and Special Boat Service (SBS) in Borneo from 1963 to 1965. Tempted by the opportunity to become an Acting Major at the relatively young age of 31, he temporarily transferred to the Argylls from the Queen's Own Highlanders in the spring of 1972.[42]

Mackenzie's soldiers in D Company were impressed by their company commander's professionalism and charisma: 'He was a fit, fit man. He could bollock you with a smile.'[43] They also respected D Company's Sergeant Major, John Higgins: 'We called him "Hig the Pig", but he was a great teacher. If you misbehaved in such a way and you could be charged he would give you a cuff and tell you, "Come on, you should know better", and he would make you feel ashamed of yourself rather than putting you in front of the Company Commander.'[44] Mackenzie soon had

---

40 '3 Platoon Notes', *Queen's Own Highlander*, 3(3) (1963).
41 Interview with Argyll Soldier 5 (Officer), May 2014.
42 Interview with Argyll Soldier 5 (Officer), May 2014.
43 Interview with Argyll Soldier 8 (Private Soldier), November 2013.
44 Interview with Argyll Soldier 8 (Private Soldier), November 2013.

D Company 'humming'. In the summer of 1972, 14 Platoon, D Company, and 15 Platoon, D Company, came first and second in the Argylls' inter-platoon march and shoot competition (13 Platoon also did well).[45] When the Argylls deployed to the Stanford training range in Norfolk in the weeks prior to their deployment to Northern Ireland, Major Mackenzie insisted that D Company, unlike the rest of the battalion, would camp out, forage and kill its own food.[46]

D Company's officers were disappointed not to be given a bigger 'patch' on arrival in Bessbrook, South Armagh in July 1972.[47] Nevertheless, the company threw itself into its operations in Northern Ireland: one D Company platoon guarded the Battalion Headquarters camp at Bessbrook, the airfield and the RUC Station as well as providing escorts. Meanwhile, the patrols and intelligence platoon went on patrol throughout the immediate area around Bessbrook during the day and at night 'sneaked around villages on a peculiar form of patrol called "blackface".' The final platoon manned the main Dublin road vehicle checkpoint (VCP), searching cars and clearing roads for improvised explosive devices (IEDs). This platoon was also responsible for helicopter patrols, 'swooping down on unsuspecting cars anywhere in the area'.[48] Mackenzie trusted his key NCOs; he expected results and wanted his platoons to use their initiative.[49] The Argylls were impressed, exhausted and occasionally amused by Mackenzie's operational zeal. At the end of the 1972 tour, 15 Platoon, D Company, in a humorous article in *The Thin Red Line* wrote that the only remaining question on Major Mackenzie's mind post-Armagh was, 'When can he take over everything else in Ireland?'[50]

In total, D Company searched 25,611 vehicles during its four-month tour of South Armagh and South Down.[51] The soldiers of D Company were frustrated not to make more significant arms finds, although their haul did include 600 lb of explosives, including one remote-controlled 200 lb and a 300 lb car bomb.[52] Major Mackenzie became known for his

45 'D Company Notes', *Thin Red Line*, September 1972.
46 *Thin Red Line*, September 1972.
47 *Thin Red Line*, September 1972.
48 *Thin Red Line*, September 1972.
49 Interview with Argyll Soldier 23 (NCO), March 2015.
50 'D Company Notes', *Glengarry Tales*, August 1972.
51 'D Company Notes', *Glengarry Tales*, August 1972.
52 D Company finds and arrests were as follows: 'Finds – 184 rounds. One

unceasing demands for better intelligence from Battalion and Brigade Headquarters.[53] Mackenzie also revelled in the element of surprise, particularly 'eagle patrols' – using the Army's helicopters to move soldiers quickly into ambush or search positions. One Argyll officer also remembered that D Company maintained an 'illicit stock of PE [plastic explosives], for use in the event that a suitable requirement was found'.[54]

Major David Thomson, the commanding officer of Support Company, headquartered at the UDR Centre in Newry, was known for his intellect. He was evidently brave, having won an MC in Borneo, as described in Chapter 1. Like Colonel Palmer, Thomson was also quick to realise that the relatively brutal, collectively punitive way of counter-insurgency in the colonies had no place in the UK, including in Northern Ireland. As an officer in the Argylls' Balaclava Company in Gibraltar in 1971, Thomson had written an after-exercise summary under the heading in capital letters, 'WE MUST ERADICATE ADEN TENDENCIES'. Thomson wished to move on from the 'Argyll Law' punitive, colonial operations of the Colonel Colin Mitchell era. But shifting operational culture took time.[55]

Support Company was responsible for security in much of Newry, including the town centre and the docks. Thomson was fortunate to have an extremely capable second-in-command, Captain Rod Liddon, formerly of the Parachute Regiment and the SAS (and a future candidate for the Scottish National Party).[56] Support Company was a good fit for Newry. Its soldiers tended to be older, wiser, less likely to take things personally. Made up of anti-tank and mortar platoons as well as more eclectic units such as the pipes and drums, Support Company quietly rebuilt relations in Newry between the Army and the local populace.[57] One of the first challenges Thomson faced in August 1972 was a potentially violent protest

shotgun, three .303 rifles, one M1 rifle, one Garand, one Mauser, 17 and a half pounds of gelignite, six detonators, 30 ft. of detonator cord, 7 ft. of safety fuse, one 20 lb. bomb in a five gallon container, six 15 lb. bombs, one radio controlled bomb of 200 lb. and one 300 lb. car bomb. Arrested 7 men of whom 3 are awaiting trial.' 'D Company Notes', *Thin Red Line*, September 1972.

53 Interview with Argyll Soldier 14 (Officer), May 2014.
54 Interview with Argyll Soldier 30 (Officer), November 2016.
55 Interview with Argyll Soldier 10 (Officer), December 2013.
56 'S Company Notes', *Thin Red Line*, September 1972.
57 Interview with Argyll Soldier 13 (Officer), December 2014.

on the first anniversary marking the introduction of internment. An angry crowd gathered outside the UDR centre. Instead of deploying water cannon, Thomson used the bagpipes instead. The *Newry Reporter*, not known for its overt British Army sympathies, reported on what took place:

> At the UDR Centre, slogans were shouted at the Army personnel. A piper inside began to play 'Amazing Grace' and some of the younger members of the demonstration could not resist joining in and singing this popular hymn. But they were silenced by their leaders who reminded them they were playing with the Army.[58]

According to another reporter from the *Oban Times*, among the other tunes played was the 'Minstrel Boy': 'Before long the whole incident turned into a sing-song, much to the annoyance of the Provo organisers of the demonstration.'[59]

A gentler approach was relatively typical of Support Company. Catholic Argyll soldiers started attending mass at Newry Cathedral. Thomson even went so far as to salute the funeral cortège of an IRA Volunteer (although he also positioned a sniper nearby in case armed IRA Volunteers made an appearance).[60] Whereas D Company went in on foot into the Derrybeg estate during Operation Motorman – Major Mackenzie wanted his soldiers physically to dominate the estate and 'stick it up' to local Republicans – Support Company moved into Derrybeg in armoured vehicles, de-bussing when necessary to make an arrest; Major Thomson was keen to avoid unnecessary riots and provocation.[61] Newry was much quieter than predicted, in part due to the death of five local IRA Volunteers in August when two bombs prematurely exploded during separate attacks, but also due to the decision of Major Thomson to 'throttle back'. During Support Company's four-month tour presence in Newry, only 30 shots were fired at the Argylls and eight bombs exploded (three more were defused). Unlike in South Armagh, local IRA Volunteers proved to be poor shots; Argyll patrols were missed at relatively short-range by IRA snipers.

58 'Protests Mark First Year of Internment', *Newry Reporter*, August 10, 1972.
59 'Argylls Come under Fire', *Oban Times*, August 17, 1972.
60 Interview with Argylls Soldier 10 (Officer), December 2013.
61 Interview with Argyll Soldier 30 (Officer), November 2016.

Local people became increasingly likely to pass information to the Army in the wake of IRA atrocities. When John Ruddy, a popular Newry man who was a part-time soldier in the UDR, was murdered, the Argylls received valuable intelligence:

> About 48 hours later I walked into my office and the telephone rang in the Ops [Operations] Room. This Irish guy on the other line; he said he would give me the suspect within 24 hours. We had a phone call to say that this guy was in McAlinden's bar. The MIO [Military Intelligence Officer] didn't want us to do anything about it. I said we only have one chance ... The MIO [Military Intelligence Officer] relented and said go for it. I rolled down the road with two land rovers, eight or ten Jocks. It was only after I got in I realised I was entirely on my own. I looked about the bar. There was nobody that met the description, wearing a blue blazer with a brown parcel. And then the door to the loos opened and that exact guy walked through the door. About this time some of the Jocks came to help their Boss. We spent the next hour going over the place to make it look like we had just arrested this guy by chance.[62]

Good detective work by the appropriately named Colour Sergeant Noel Lightfoot, who followed his nose – the rudimentary explosives used by the IRA left a distinctive smell of marzipan – and located an IRA bombmaking factory, led to charges being brought against a Newry Republican, Hugh Treanor.[63] Weapons finds were more disappointing: 2 × .30 M1 carbines, 1 × Thomson SMG, 1 × .30 SAKO rifle, 1 × .303 rifle and 1 × 9 mm pistol. Also recovered was 295 lb of explosives. But Newry was certainly more secure at the end of the Argylls' tour even if a lack of operational intelligence remained a problem.[64]

B Company was given what would arguably prove to be the most difficult area of operations for the British Army during Operation Banner – South Armagh. B Company's OC was Major Robin Buchanan, who was considerably older than Mackenzie and Thomson. A true regimental

---

62 Interview with Argyll Soldier 10 (Officer), December 2013.

63 'Newryman for Trial Charged with Possessing Explosive Substance', *Newry Reporter*, January 18, 1972.

64 'S Company Notes', *Thin Red Line*, January 1973.

officer, he loved the music and the other traditions of the Argylls, who probably knew he was not going to progress beyond the rank of major.[65] In the late 1970s, a full battalion would be tasked with patrolling South Armagh, and many more assets including air, special forces and fixed OPs would be made available to units there. D Company could occasionally be called upon to reinforce B Company, but this happened only occasionally. D Company was needed for Bessbrook security duties and to control the Dublin Road VCPs.[66]

The Strain of Command: B Company in South Armagh

Buchanan's second-in-command, Captain Bill Watson, and two successive Commanders of 6 Platoon, B Company (2nd Lieutenant Stewart Gardiner and Colour Sergeant Jimmy Struthers) were to die in South Armagh and B Company suffered a steady flow of other casualties. Nobody had predicted the ferocity of the IRA onslaught on the border in late 1972. The strain began to show; some officers began to question if Major Robin Buchanan had suffered a mental breakdown. He appeared never to sleep and, if he did lie down for a brief time, he did not take off his combat gear. Buchanan was also not a charismatic leader; some men in B Company began to blame him for a lack of initiative in responding to their mounting casualties.[67] This was despite some limited successes such as the arrest of two suspected, and armed, IRA Volunteers at a roadblock on September 14, 1972.[68] Tensions in B Company cracked open during the fire fight on September 23, 1972 that claimed the life of 2nd Lieutenant Stewart Gardiner, OC of 6 Platoon, who had recently joined the British Army after serving with the Australian Army in Vietnam. Lieutenant Gardiner was shot at Drumuckavall, right on the border and approximately a mile and a half from the Argyll base in Crossmaglen RUC Station. Gardiner had been fatally wounded and radio operator Private Jimmy Taylor badly hurt in the initial burst of fire; 6 Platoon had been sent to the area to check out reports of an IED. Private Jimmy Chestnut had been collecting part of a command wire on a road along the border, set by the IRA so as to be ready to be fitted

---

65 Interview with Argyll Soldier 5 (Officer), May 2014.
66 Interview with Argyll Soldier 5 (Officer), May 2014.
67 Interview with Argyll Soldier 3 (NCO), September 2014.
68 'Two for Trial on Gun and IRA Charges', *Newry Reporter*, November 23, 1972.

with explosives at a later point. Hearing a burst of fire, he jumped to the ground and began to crawl towards the rest of the patrol. In a subsequent written account, Chestnut described what happened next:

> Our platoon commander was lying on his back with blood spurting out of a hole in his side. We put a bandage on the hole and blood came through; another bandage and it still came through. We used about four altogether although we knew more than two and it was pointless. He was in deep shock, not registering anything. His face was draining of colour and it was as if he was clenching his teeth, breathing hard through them, so we gave him morphine, which didn't really help.[69]

Chestnut, trained as a radio operator, took the A41 set from the wounded Private Jimmy Taylor, called in a report of two casualties and requested support from company HQ. The request was denied by Major Buchanan – the patrol must first get out of the 'kill zone' before help could arrive. Led by Colour Sergeant Jimmy Struthers, the patrol picked up the dying Gardiner and the wounded Taylor and moved a few hundred metres up the road towards Crossmaglen, where they again radioed for help. Once more, 6 Platoon's request for reinforcements was denied. Another soldier recalled Chestnut cursing company HQ on the radio. Meanwhile, back at Crossmaglen, soldiers were 'crying with frustration'.[70] They could hear the sounds of firing and the increasingly desperate calls for back-up being radioed in by Private Jimmy Chestnut. Some troopers from B Squadron, the Royal Scots Dragoon Guards, volunteered to go down in an Alvis FV601 Saladin armoured car to extricate Gardiner's patrol. Buchanan refused, fearing that any attempt to relieve the men at Drumuckavall could lead to a further ambush and more casualties. This was what the IRA expected them to do, he said. According to Chestnut's account, B Company HQ began to fall apart:

> One of tankies [RSDG], a big guy from Aberdeen, got the company commander by the throat against a wall and threatened

---

69 RMASH: N-J.I.CHE – 'Memories of Pte James Chestnut, 22 Bravo, Crossmaglen, South Armagh, 1972', unpublished manuscript.
70 Interview with Argyll Soldier 1 (Private Soldier), April 2014.

to kill him ... Our CSM Danny the Chin, who was a hard man, grabbed this guy and led him off, talking quietly to him.[71]

Only the firm actions of Danny 'the Chin' Mullen, B Company's highly respected Company Sergeant Major, pulled the men of B Company, 1 Argylls, and B Squadron, the Royal Scots Dragoon Guards, back from near mutiny. Meanwhile, back near the ambush site, Lieutenant Gardiner's platoon sergeant, Jimmy Struthers, bundled some local people out of two passing cars and got the patrol (Gardiner and Taylor included) out of the ambush area. Two RUC officers were later shot and badly wounded trying to recover an Argyll SLR that had been left at the ambush, reportedly by the same weapon they were trying to locate. A highly distressed mother of one of the RUC officers (Constable Sam Malcolmson) later suffered a suspected heart attack at her son's bedside, dying before he regained consciousness.[72]

A month later, on Hallowe'en night, the Argylls filled up a basin for 'ducking for apples' and invited Major Buchanan to have a go. As he bowed his head, 'a gang of Jocks descended on him and gave him a good baptizing ... Morale was very good that night.'[73] The Argylls' commanding officer, Colonel Paddy Palmer, noting the exhaustion of his company commander, considered replacing Buchanan. He consulted with some other officers but concluded that he simply could not humiliate Major Buchanan by sacking him from command. One of these officers reminded Colonel Palmer that Buchanan had a challenging job trying to get on top of his area of operations with such few resources.[74] The regiment was fond of Buchanan and tried to look out for him; officers in the regiment knew that relieving him of command would be a devastating personal blow.[75] Such an approach was quite different from the ruthlessness displayed by the commanding officer of 1 Scots Guards, Colonel Murray de Klee, who unceremoniously sacked officers he did not believe were up to standard including

---

71 RMASH: 'Memories of Pte James Chestnut'.
72 RMASH: 'Memories of Pte James Chestnut'.
73 'B Company Notes', *Thin Red Line*, January 1973.
74 Interview with Argyll Soldier 10 (Officer), December 2013.
75 Interview with Argyll Soldier 21 (Officer), November 2014; Interview with Argyll Soldier 31 (Officer), May 2014.

just prior to deployment in the summer of 1971.[76] It was a difficult decision; but Buchanan stayed.

After the death of Buchanan's second-in-command, Captain Bill Watson, Colonel Palmer did switch Captain Rod Liddon from Support Company to B Company. Morale had plummeted, particularly in 6 Platoon, B Company, after the death of Colour Sergeant Jimmy Struthers, the 'father figure' of the platoon, the one who would somehow get them through unscathed. Liddon expected very high standards from his men, and usually got what he wanted. He made a point of exposing himself to danger, although he always seemed in control of any situation.[77] When, on the last morning of the Argylls' time in Crossmaglen, the RUC Station was hit with rocket propelled grenades (RPGs) and small arms fire, Liddon ordered his soldiers to go out and find the firing point, even though they had already handed in some of their weapons and kit prior to departing for Scotland. The soldiers did what they were ordered; Liddon was not a man to say no to.[78]

Major Buchanan was desperately short of men: within a few years, the British Army would deploy more than 800 soldiers to South Armagh. B Company's Commander also saved lives by obsessively sandbagging and reinforcing the RUC Station at Crossmaglen, which proved vital when the RUC Station was attacked with RPGs on the morning of November 28, 1972.[79] Moreover, his hunch that the IRA were preparing a follow-up ambush near the site of the initial contact with Gardiner's patrol was correct. But Buchanan's lack of charisma and the failure to project an image of controlled aggression made him unpopular with his men. Buchanan was also an older type of soldier, one whose formative years as a young officer had been in the 1950s, the era of conscription. A new, younger generation, including Thomson and Mackenzie, loved their craft, their profession at arms more than they did the trappings of regimental tradition. The soldiers of B Company could tell the difference.[80]

76 Interview with Scots Guards Soldier 2 (Officer), June 2014.
77 Interview with Argyll Soldier 3 (NCO), September 2014.
78 Interview with Argyll Soldier 3 (NCO), September 2014.
79 'B Company Notes', *Thin Red Line*, October 1972.
80 Interview with Argyll Soldier 3 (NCO), September 2014.

NCOs, Leadership and 'Switching On'

Patrols in 1971 and 1972 were normally carried out in sections or half-sections. Section patrols were more common in the early days of Operation Banner, before the concept of 'working in multiples' or half-sections became standard procedure.[81] Corporals would often lead section patrols, and a lance corporal would take charge of a half-section. A Scots Guards NCO described the routine, and weakness, of section patrols in the early years of Operation Banner:

> When you were out on patrol there was none of this working even two half sections together. You went out and you patrolled and you were out on the ground for eight hours. You only came in for your meals and when you came in they sent out another one of the sections of the patrol platoon and they drove around your area. Given the size and saturation of the areas the IRA could usually predict that you would pass almost all the streets once in eight hours and that reinforcements would not be immediate. That certainly helped them set up ambushes.[82]

In Derry, 2 Scots Guards did a lot of 'hard targeting', 'Each patrol that went out was eight-strong, divided into two, and loosely working together. You didn't walk from A to B. You ran from a far fire position to a far fire position with three other people covering you. And the children would laugh and sing "run rabbit run" and throw stones.'[83] In the case of 1 Scots Guards, sections would patrol for three days, then were assigned standby or quick reaction force (QRF) duties for another three days and then did three days guard or other camp tasks.[84] Other, more senior NCOs would pass on instructions but section and even half-section commanders had significant autonomy in deciding how they carried out their patrols. One senior Scots Guards NCO recalled that:

> I could give out a set of orders to a Lance Sergeant or a Lance Corporal. I would say, 'You're doing this, you're doing that. And

81 Interview with Scots Guards Soldier 9 (NCO), December 2013.
82 Interview with Scots Guards Soldier 9 (NCO), December 2013.
83 Interview with Scots Guards Soldier 14 (Officer), May 2014.
84 Interview with Scots Guards Soldier 16 (NCO), January 2014.

I would be quite exact.' There would be timings etc. But they would still put their own interpretation on the orders you gave. It would never, ever exactly work as the way you gave the orders for. Unless you rehearsed it endlessly and you rarely had time to do that. You had too many patrols, operations … you would always get some divergence.[85]

In 1971 and 1972, NCOs often gave out the orders or the plan for a given day's operations. By the end of the decade junior officers increasingly took on this role, an important switch in emphasis. As Anthony King has noted, the giving out of orders, the making of a plan or a rehearsal of concept, is a crucial means of giving soldiers both situational awareness but also binding the group to shared expectations of outcome for any operation.[86] The balance of power and relationship between junior officers and NCOs has occasionally fluctuated in the British Army. The early 1970s was a period where NCOs enjoyed more power than the late 1970s. According to a number of senior NCOs interviewed, by the end of the decade a more assertive junior officer had emerged within the British Army: 'There had been a massive change in attitude from officers. The platoon commanders became much more professional, less bowler hat, more visor and riot gear. They are not figure-heads as much as they used to be. They are now soldiers as much as the rest.'[87] Among Argyll soldiers in the early 1970s, there was some resentment among NCOs for officers sometimes known as 'the lairds', those officers from traditional, sometimes aristocratic families who would stay in the Army for three years to keep up a family tradition and wear the regimental tartan, but who neither wished to make the Army their profession nor took sufficient pride in their combat skills.[88]

NCOs played a vital role in keeping soldiers 'switched on'. One Argyll Private soldier recalled, 'You actually want somebody to kick your arse to keep you switched on. If nothing happens to you for a few weeks,

85 Interview with Scots Guards Soldier 16 (NCO), January 2014.
86 King, *The Combat Soldier*, 301.
87 Interview with Scots Guards Soldiers 9 (NCO), October 2013; Interview with Scots Guards Soldier 16 (NCO), January 2014; Interview with Argyll Soldier 3 (NCO), September 2014.
88 Interview with Argyll Soldier 23 (NCO), March 2015.

you can easily get complacent and then you get hit.'[89] The same soldier went on to describe the seemingly endless drills the soldiers had to do after operations in Northern Ireland: cleaning kit, foot inspections for blisters etc. and how his section commander would insist that they all went to the dining facility together when most of his section just wanted to sleep.[90] Drill helped soldiers ritually to 'switch on' and 'switch off';[91] the soldier's mind relaxed, his focus tightened accordingly.[92] Sometimes, NCOs would deliberately increase the ante even though no immediate threat was not present, just to ward off complacency. Arriving for the first time in Crossmaglen, after landing in Sioux helicopters on the local football pitch, a private soldier recalled 6 Platoon's NCOs, 'screaming at us ... "Get on the Ground, Get on the fucking ground" ... Throwing ammo at you. I thought we were under fire. But it was just [6 Platoon, B Company, Colour Sergeant] Jimmy Struthers' way of waking you up.'[93]

A guardsman from 1 Scots Guards recalled his Section Commander as, 'a God. A hard cookie and for an urban tour in Northern Ireland he was very, very streetwise. He was a Glaswegian. He was also respected because he was a boxer.'[94] The Lance Sergeant in question kept him safe, and the guardsmen were also afraid to make a mistake. An Argyll private soldier also recalled how the fear of mild physical punishment also taught him to stay alert: 'The radio was too heavy to be lying down and getting up all the time. Once I stayed standing when I was supposed to lie down. [The NCO – Platoon Sergeant] whacked me on the head with the butt of his rifle. That taught me a lesson.'[95] However, as well as keeping soldiers 'switched on', operational experience brought an unusual level of familiarity and a blurring of formal rank distinctions. In some cases, Argyll privates began to call their platoon sergeants by their first names.[96] NCOs also played a vital role in generating and containing anger. An NCO who served in 1 Scots Guards recalled that the most effective way to stop soldiers lashing out after provocation or abuse from the local population

89 Interview with Argyll Soldier 8 (Private Soldier), November 2013.
90 Interview with Argyll Soldier 8 (Private Soldier), November 2013.
91 Hockey, *Squaddies*, 142.
92 Interview with Argyll Soldier 8 (Private Soldier), November 2013.
93 Interview with Argyll Soldier 1 (Private Soldier), April 2014.
94 Interview with Scots Guards Soldier 9 (NCO), December 2013.
95 Interview with Argyll Soldier 1 (Private Soldier), April 2014.
96 Interview with Argyll Soldier 8 (Private Soldier), November 2013.

was to point out that they were putting other soldiers' lives at risk by escalating the situation unnecessarily: 'Don't use us as a shield. He is now walking away laughing because you lost your cool. So keep it.'[97] A Scots Guards officer reflected that a bad platoon sergeant could completely ruin what was previously an effective platoon. He described how a sergeant in Left Flank during the 1971, 1 Scots Guards tour of West Belfast, 'used to gripe constantly and he very badly affected his guardsmen who began to emulate him. He was just a poor operational sergeant'.[98] Emulation could work positively or negatively: guardsmen were still likely to seek to follow the older man, unless it was clearly obvious that he lacked good professional soldiering skills. Platoon commanders and sergeants were important for general morale and situational awareness. Nevertheless, most interviewees, officers, NCOs and other ranks, concluded that the most important operational units for command and control in Northern Ireland were the company and section/half-section.

Crossing the Border: Small Unit Autonomy

Border incursions into the Republic of Ireland provide a good example of the degree of autonomy enjoyed by local units. The 303 miles of international boundary between the UK and the Republic of Ireland was occasionally difficult to locate, since it followed no natural boundary such as a river. Increasingly, the British and Irish governments took to marking clearly all 'approved' and even some 'unapproved' border road crossings. In the case of the Scots Guards and the Argylls, accidental crossings of the border certainly did happen: on one occasion, a group of soldiers from 2 Scots Guards were dropped ten miles into County Donegal across the Irish border, instead of near Creggan, west of the River Foyle in County Londonderry. The pilot somehow mistook Lough Swilly for Lough Foyle. The guardsmen walked back to Derry, not encountering any Gardaí or Irish soldiers along the way.[99]

But there were also instances of deliberate border crossings, most particularly by the Argylls whose area of operations in South Down/South Armagh (and briefly Fermanagh) ran along the border. The Irish

---

97 Interview with Scots Guards Soldier 4 (NCO), May 2014.
98 Interview with Scots Guards Soldier 2 (Officer), June 2014.
99 Interview with Scots Guards Soldier 11 (Officer), December 2013.

authorities south of the border noted a change in the tempo of British Army operations along the border in the Argylls' area of operations during the autumn of 1972. According to the Garda Síochána and the Irish Army, the Argylls were persistently (and illegally) crossing the border. The Argylls in turn had no confidence in the Garda ability or willingness to pursue IRA units that attacked British patrols along the border.[100] On August 14, 1972, Commandant Fogarty of the Irish Army reported that seven or eight Argyll soldiers were deployed by an Army helicopter to the border, which they crossed before taking up position 100 yards south of the Irish Customs Post at Drumbilla. Irish customs officials reported that the Argylls stayed in the South for 45 minutes despite repeated requests to leave; they conducted a search of a vehicle in the South during their 'visit' south.[101]

On September 7, 1972, a 14 Platoon, D Company, 1 Argylls patrol led by Corporal McCulloch was fired on at the border at Ballybinaby in County Louth. The Argylls believed they had stumbled upon an IRA unit planting a roadside bomb. Six rounds were fired at the patrol and Corporal McCulloch was shot in the thigh. The Argyll patrol returned fire, called for reinforcements, including from 6 Platoon, B Company at Crossmaglen, and managed briefly to pin down at least one IRA Volunteer at a farm on the southern side of the border.[102] Meanwhile, a patrol led by 14 Platoon's Commander, Colour Sergeant Arthur Cairns, commandeered a local civilian truck to get to the fire fight as quickly as possibly, an action which, to the Argylls' disgust, they would have later to justify to 3 Brigade HQ.[103] Medic Jackie Stilley managed to reach Corporal McCulloch and he was evacuated soon after.[104] An Irish Army incident report on the incident, dated September 14, 1972, describes what happened next.

[The Argylls] believed that the man [a suspected IRA volunteer] had taken cover in a cattle truck … parked near the house, and

---

100 Interview with Argyll Soldier 14 (Officer), May 2014.

101 MAI: 2003/15/94-G2/C/1872 Pt 2. Border crossings and border incidents by British Army: Increp 14/8/1972 signed by Commandant M. Fogarty, 1st Infantry Company Group, Eastern Brigade, Dundalk.

102 TNA: WO 305/4407 The Argyll and Sutherland Highlanders Battalion Diary, April 1969–March 1974.

103 Interview with Argyll Soldier 24 (NCO), March 2015.

104 Interview with Argyll Soldier 3 (NCO), September 2014.

they fired at it. There were 5 to 7 bullet holes in the cab and evidence that other rounds had struck the vehicle just under the cab. It is thought a total of 12 rounds hit the vehicle. The subversive fled southwards. British personnel crossed the border and pursued him in to the Republic for a distance of about half a mile.[105]

Half a mile was a considerable distance.[106] The Argylls pursued the IRA gunman onto a farm apparently owned by the Murphy family (one of the three Murphy brothers, Thomas 'Slab' Murphy, would later become among the most feared leaders of the South Armagh Republican movement).[107] The Argylls expended a lot of ammunition; at one point a general-purpose machine gun (GPMG) was brought into action. After initially ignoring protests from local Gardaí, an Argyll officer, 2nd Lieutenant Stewart Gardiner, OC of 6 Platoon, B Company – who was fatally shot a week later – eventually spoke to a Garda inspector. The inspector noted that Gardiner had taken a weapon from a firing point south of the border.[108] One soldier recalled that the Gardaí tried to arrest some of the Argylls but were firmly told to 'fuck off'.[109]

The Argylls were frustrated by their inability to seize IRA firing points and weapons south of the border. They also wanted to even the scores with the IRA after taking a casualty. A poem about the incident was later written by 14 Platoon:

> Our man we did find
> Behind a wall he hid
> Surprise, Surprise when he saw us
> Because the line was North of us.

---

105 MAI: 2003/15/94-G2/C/1872 Pt 2. Border crossings and border incidents by British Army, Letter marked SCS 29 RONG P70 14/9/72 'Colonel P. O'Diomsaigh to Runaí'.

106 Interview with Argyll Soldier 3 (NCO), September 2014; Interview with Argyll Soldier 24 (NCO), March 2015.

107 'Attempted Murder of a Soldier', *Newry Reporter*, May 17, 1973.

108 According to a Garda report, 'This officer [Lieutenant Gardiner] had a Lee Enfield Mk II .303 rifle. No. 0910, bearing the date 1918, and four rounds of ammunition (in a magazine).' MAI: 2003/15/94-G2/C/1872 Pt 2. Colonel P. O'Diomsaigh to Runaí.

109 Interview with Argyll Soldier 3 (NCO), September 2014.

But triumph was ours to be
His Hide, his Lair for all to see
Guns and bullets, Explosives too
Were there by you know who
His life preserved was all his thought
For fighting spirit he had nought.[110]

In order to gather intelligence about a suspicious vehicle, 14 Platoon, D Company, 1 Argylls would also cross the border near Belleek in Fermanagh.[111] Many of the Argylls, including officers, had a very negative attitude towards the Gardaí. According to an Argyll private soldier, 'We absolutely hated the Gardaí as a result of our encounters with them … Our section treated them like the enemy. They never showed us any favour or any willingness to do something when they had an opportunity to do it, especially when a soldier was being killed.'[112] An Argyll officer observed that:

The border was a free area from the IRA's point of view. The more noise you made the further back the Garda went. There was no cross-border liaison at all. We regarded them, the other side of the border as hostile – you could be shot at any time and indeed you were. The IRA brought in a Garand .50 calibre sniper rifle. A .50 calibre sniper rifle is a big brute and you can shoot somebody from up to 2 kilometres with that thing.[113]

The Argyll relationship with the Gardaí was not helped by an incident early in their tour when a Garda near the border at Flurrybridge in south-east Armagh permitted the Army to send an ammunition technical officer (ATO) twenty metres over the border to defuse a bomb in an abandoned shop. HQNI promptly released a press statement praising a new spirit of border cooperation. The Gardaí, fearful of the political response in the south, were less than amused by this perceived breach of trust.[114]

110 '14 Platoon Notes', *Thin Red Line*, October 1972.
111 Interview with Argyll Soldier 23 (NCO), March 2015.
112 Interview with Argyll Soldier 8 (Private Soldier), November 2013.
113 Interview with Argyll Soldier 5 (Officer), May 2014.
114 Interview with Argyll Soldier 12 (Officer), May 2014.

The Argylls' very negative, if not occasionally hostile, assessment of the performance of the Garda Síochána is understandable but it is also incomplete. Although the Irish government pursued a politically cautious approach to border security, not wishing to be seen to be too helpful to the British Army, a number of important arrests were made in 1972, including along the border. Three South Armagh IRA Volunteers, Frank Rooney, Kevin and Martin McAllister, were convicted in Dublin in 1973 by the Irish Special Criminal Court. Having located an IRA unit on a border farm near Ballybinaby, an unarmed Garda tackled Frank Rooney to the ground and disarmed him; another pursued the McAllister brothers before arresting them both. The testifying Gardaí were abused with shouts of 'traitors' by the accused, and from the public gallery, during the trial.[115]

Deliberate Argyll border incursions into the Republic of Ireland were not Brigade-sanctioned operations. But, within the Argylls, it was accepted, as explained by one Argyll officer. 'We were a self-contained unit. We were more or less on our own and we had to get on with it ... Although not encouraged or frequent, crossing the border was not forbidden if it was in "hot pursuit" to kill or capture a terrorist.'[116] 'Visits to the south'[117] were dictated by local events; junior officers and NCOs on the scene took the key decisions. Occasionally, 3 Brigade HQ did chastise the Argylls for 'visits to the South'.[118] But there was little prospect of formal charges or disciplinary measures being taken against any officer or patrol commander who made such a deliberate encroachment into the Republic of Ireland. As Henry Patterson has concluded, such incidents were considered in London to be relatively 'harmless': 'British politicians and officials, while ready to point out that the IRA was a threat to both states, found it difficult to acknowledge that incursions in to the Republic by its troops might also be considered a violation of Irish sovereignty.'[119]

115 'Three Crossmaglen Men Gaoled in Dublin', *Newry Reporter*, January 25, 1973.
116 Interview with Argyll Soldier 23 (NCO), March 2015.
117 RMASH: File Reference D71, 'Historical Record 1 ASH', 1972–1973.
118 Interview with Argyll Soldier 23 (NCO), March 2015.
119 Patterson, *Violent Frontier*, 57.

Soldiers as Victims

Soldiers' Responses to Coming under Attack

An IRA attack on soldiers usually involved a single gunman, firing one shot from a concealed position.[120] An account by a soldier in Right Flank, 2 Scots Guards of the shooting of Guardsman Fee in Derry on September 22, 1972, highlights the disorientation and frustration in responding to such an attack:

> It took ages to identify where the shot came from. We went haring off to the right. We found the weapon and there was a man painting who claimed he did not see anything. I don't know why the painter wasn't picked up. He probably got on the ladder after having done the shooting ... Chair and a skylight and wait for a patrol to come by, which was very likely, given the frequency of how many times we had to patrol those streets.[121]

The temptation for soldiers to blame the painter is obvious – the soldiers clearly suspected that he was either involved in the ambush or knew who was involved. Meanwhile, one member of the patrol is lying on the roadside fighting for his life.

The IRA had developed a rudimentary but effective way of planting roadside IEDs, particularly along the border. At approximately 14.00 on August 24, 1972, Trooper Ian Caie, a 19-year-old Royal Scots Dragoon Guards driver of a Ferret Scout armoured car, was killed in an explosion near Moybane in South Armagh, the area of operations of B Company, 1 Argylls. The blast occurred on the driver's side of the vehicle, propelling it off the road into a nearby field. The Ferret Scout commander, Trooper Kieran, was hurled ten feet from the vehicle; the turret in which he was standing was found thirty feet away. The overturned remains of the Ferret Scout car caught fire; the patrol commander and two other troopers who had been travelling in the lead Saladin vehicle tried to retrieve Trooper Caie's body from the vehicle, 'but the fire and explosions from ammunition that was contained on board made these

---

120 TNA: CJ 4/1764 Shooting Statistics, 1977.
121 Interview with Scots Guards Soldier 12 (Officer), December 2014.

efforts impossible until support arrived'.[122] The Argylls' medical officer, Captain Charles Boyle and a patrol from 6 Platoon, B Company, 1 Argylls, were on the scene minutes after the explosion. Captain Boyle reported that Trooper Caie was dead upon his arrival at the scene at 14.25; later, he had to prevent the badly wounded Trooper Kieran, who had suffered a brain injury and was thrashing about, from accidentally throwing himself out of a Scout helicopter when accompanying him to hospital in Belfast.[123]

Trooper Caie was killed instantly; the State Pathologist later found that, 'No fumes had been inhaled and there was no sign of carbon monoxide after death.'[124] But some of the Argylls and an RUC officer at the scene believed that he had burned to death. RUC police Constable Sam Malcolmson told journalist Toby Harnden that he had seen Trooper Caie's hand move while trapped under the burning vehicle. Malcolmson and the Argylls also recalled that a hostile crowd gathered at a road cordon nearby and began mocking the soldiers.[125] An Argyll soldier who arrived at the scene minutes after the explosion remembered feeling a burning sense of anger. The Argylls had worked closely with B Squadron, Royal Scots Dragoon Guards; 'Scotland's Cavalry' were respected and liked by the Argylls.[126] The same Argyll soldier thought briefly about shooting the people shouting abuse at him at a road cordon he was guarding, but then calmed himself down. The horrific prospect of Trooper Caie burning to death and the jeering crowd accelerated mounting Argyll ill-feeling towards the local populace. Constable Sam Malcolmson only found out the truth, that Trooper Caie had died instantly, forty years later, following a PSNI HET investigation into the incident. The Argylls, as with the deaths of so many other soldiers, were also upset that nobody was charged with the murder of Trooper Caie. A fingerprint taken from a cup retrieved from the firing point, on a hillside 600 metres away, was later misplaced by the RUC.[127]

---

122 RSDGA: Police Service of Northern Ireland Historical Enquiries Team, 'Report on Tpr Ian Caie, Killed by IRA Bomb Northern Ireland, August 24, 1972', File Reference R301:00, RB 42, Entry No. 648.

123 Interview with Argyll Soldier 2 (Officer), November 2014.

124 RSDGA: 'Report on Tpr Ian Caie'.

125 Harnden, *Bandit Country*, 45–47.

126 Interview with Argyll Soldier 3 (NCO), September 2014.

127 RSDGA: 'Report on Tpr Ian Caie'.

A common theme raised among soldiers who served in Northern Ireland during the early years of Operation Banner is the difficulty of seeing *known* IRA men released without charge soon after being arrested by the Army for suspected terrorist activities, contributing to acts of retribution against the local population.[128] The operational magazine of 2 Scots Guards in Derry acknowledged the strain this placed on morale and, in an attempt to reassure guardsmen, presented statistics relating to convictions for terrorism offences.[129] This was not enough for many guardsmen. Eight years after serving as OC of Left Flank, 2 Scots Guards in Londonderry, Major Robin Buchanan-Dunlop, now the CO of 8 Battalion (County Tyrone), UDR, met with Sir Maurice Oldfield, security coordinator for Northern Ireland and former director of MI6:

> [Oldfield] put the following question to the meeting: 'Are we winning?' There was a short silence after which I replied, 'No, we are not winning, and the members of my battalion will not be convinced that we are winning while they can meet people in the streets who they know have committed murder or have aided and abetted in murder, and yet are untouchable by the law.' I was told later that this comment made a distinct impression on him.[130]

Soldiers were understandably frustrated that Republican activists were able openly to taunt and threaten them. For example, after Operation Carcan in Derry, local Republican leader Barney McFadden addressed a meeting along with local left-wing activists Eamonn McCann and Bernadette Devlin MP (later McAliskey): 'We will strike [back] when the time comes and we will take a larger toll of death than before'.[131] Under Whitelaw's 'go softly' approach, soldiers believed that Republicans like

---

128 This theme was also raised by American soldiers who served in Iraq, 'We couldn't rely on Army intelligence to put these guys in jail, so we had to let that town know we were in charge.' J. Frederick, *Black Hearts* (London: Pan, 2010), 244.
129 'A Bad Month for the IRA', *Rose and Thistle*, Second Battalion Scots Guards, November 1, 1972.
130 Colonel Robin Buchanan-Dunlop, quoted in T.A. Ferguson, *8th Battalion (Co. Tyrone), Ulster Defence Regiment* (Dungannon: Dungannon Branch of the Ulster Defence Regiment Association, 1995).
131 'Treat Troops like Lepers – McCann', *Derry Journal*, August 1, 1972.

McFadden were able openly to threaten the Army and organise armed attacks with impunity.[132]

But despite the conviction that the law was not on their side, the Scots Guards and the Argylls were involved in multiple court cases to do with attacks or threats made against soldiers. A forestry worker in Newtownhamilton in South Armagh was fined in court for using 'bad language' in protesting at being searched for a second time by a B Company, 1 Argylls' patrol.[133] On September 10, 1972, a D Company, 1 Argylls patrol led by 2nd Lieutenant Andrew Snowball was fortunate to escape a remote-controlled IED explosion at a crossroads in Dromintee village, South Armagh.[134] On this occasion, thanks to a quick follow-up by an Army helicopter pilot and the foolhardiness of two 18-year-old IRA Volunteers, Thomas McCoy and John McCormick, who were followed from the scene to a nearby pub, charges were brought for the attempted murder of Lieutenant Snowball and other members of his patrol.[135] Both were convicted of being members of the Provisional IRA.

D Company, 1 Argylls, may have had a lucky escape on the morning of September 10, 1972, but their comrades in A Company in East Tyrone were not so fortunate. Later that day, between 22.00 and 22.30, an A Company Saracen vehicle was blown up by a huge roadside bomb at Saranaghanroe, on the Dungannon to Benburb Road. The explosion was heard for several miles; the force of the blast hurled the Saracen twenty yards from the road, landing upside-down in a field. The explosion left a 30-foot-wide, 20-foot-deep crater in the road that a local woman later

---

132 'Barney McFadden: Father of Derry Republicanism Laid to Rest', *An Phoblacht*, January 10, 2002.

133 'Abuse to Soldiers – Fined', *Newry Reporter*, November 9, 1972.

134 'Ambushed', *Falkirk Herald*, September 16, 1972.

135 Sergeant George Spence was accused by one of the suspected IRA men, John McCormick, of heavy-handedness: 'McCormick to Witness: "Did you not kick us round to the van?" [Sgt. Spence:] "I never made any bodily contact with any of them." The Three Steps Inn was owned by the McCreesh family and was the same pub where Captain Robert Nairac, a Grenadier Guards officer who also worked for a time as a Military Intelligence officer at 39 Brigade and 3 Brigade during successive tours, was abducted, prior to being tortured and executed by the IRA. South Armagh men for trial – charged with attempted murder of 6 soldiers.' *Newry Reporter*, December 7, 1972; 'Gaol for Being in the IRA', *Newry Reporter*, February 1, 1973; McKittrick et al., *Lost Lives*, 722–724.

drove into (she was treated for shock).[136] Three Argylls were killed, two instantly – Privates Douglas Richmond and Duncan McPhee, both 21 years old. Lance Corporal Billy McIntyre lingered on, mortally wounded, dying in a Belfast hospital at 06.45 the next morning. The other soldiers in the Saracen were also badly hurt; Private George Collins suffered a serious brain injury and was not expected to survive. He later made a remarkable, if partial, recovery – and still suffers from some neurological disability.[137] The other soldiers suffered multiple fractures, including broken arms, jaws and skull fractures. Only one soldier from the section, its commander, Corporal John Mackay, escaped unscathed, but the deaths and injuries to so many men effectively wiped out a whole section. Lance Corporal McIntyre had recently transferred to the Argylls from 1 QOH in Germany so that he could be nearer to his baby son in Scotland, who suffered from a kidney defect. Private Richmond's elderly parents both suffered from serious speech and hearing impediments; he was their only child.[138]

An A Company patrol went back to the scene of the explosion on September 11, 1972, to set up a cordon for the REME recovery section that were removing the wreckage of the Saracen:

[The Saracen] had landed nose down in a field, two of the three wheels on one side had been completed ripped off. We had to make sure that all the equipment that was left inside was secure or, if it wasn't, then we had to remove it. The rifles were all bent nearly double by being wrapped round the bodies of the crew. The Section 2IC's brains were spread across the inside of the turret and the whole back of the crew compartment was inches deep in blood, which was spilling over the doorsill. There were no seat belts in those vehicles and the soldiers in the back had more or less all ended up in a compacted mass in the front of the vehicle when it landed in the field.[139]

---

136 'Three Soldiers Die in Eglish Blast', *Fermanagh News*, September 23, 1972.
137 TNA: WO 305/4407 The Argyll and Sutherland Highlanders Battalion Diary, April 1969–March 1974.
138 'A Company Notes', *Thin Red Line*, January 1973.
139 Email correspondence between the author and a former A Company soldier of 1st Battalion, Argyll and Sutherland Highlanders, May 2014.

According to A Company, several passing vehicles had refused to help the survivors of the explosion. Lieutenant Donald Ross told the *Falkirk Herald* that the lack of concern or assistance made the Argylls 'sick': 'We realize that some civilians dare not be seen talking to security personnel but the least they could have done was telephone the police or the military. As it was none of the wounded men was able to get medical attention until we sent out a carrier to look for them.'[140] The incident changed the atmosphere in A Company and had a knock-on effect throughout the battalion. One Argyll interviewee described the shift in attitudes towards the local population, 'On days like that, if people spat at you, you spat back. You begin to think, "This is for keeps. They really hate you." After a while you start taking it personal.'[141]

Fatigue and Stress

The threat of ambush from snipers or IEDs took its toll on soldiers. Struggling to stay alert during an incessant routine of patrolling and guard duties, some began to see things that weren't there. For the Argylls, on night patrols in isolated, rural parts of the border, the problem was particularly acute. Soldiers would fire their weapons thinking they had seen a gunman creeping up on their position. Occasionally, another section would then hear the round and also start firing.[142] The night before Operation Carcan (Motorman), soldiers from 2 Scots Guards on duty in an OP on top of the Embassy building in Derry city were convinced they saw a gunman crawling along a ridge, and fired. The effect was dangerously contagious:

> We had another patrol down below, probably slightly sleepy. Suddenly there was a bullet winging over their heads [the Embassy OP] and they fired back. Then about a mile down was a UDR section commanding a checkpoint up towards Donegal and they were convinced that they were being fired at – God knows how. They decided to shoot out all the remaining street lights in the area as a result. There was now a major fire-fight

---

140 'Ambushed', *Falkirk Herald*, September 16, 1972.
141 Interview with Argyll Soldier 8 (Private Soldier), November 2013.
142 Interview with Argyll Soldier 8 (Private Soldier), November 2013.

going on! You can stare at something long enough in the night and be persuaded it was moving. I don't believe it was an IRA sniper.[143]

As the 2 Scots Guards 1972 Londonderry tour went on, guardsmen from Left Flank became more and more obsessed about the threat from snipers operating from the spire of St Eugene's Cathedral, on the edge of the Bogside. Shot reports flooded into battalion HQ. In response, guardsmen fired at the cathedral spire on several occasions.[144] On August 6, 1972, a patrol reported that they had seen the glow of a sniper's cigarette. An officer from Left Flank decided to investigate the 'sniper's nest' in the cathedral:

> Eventually I managed to persuade a very senior policeman called 'Paddy Mary' to go and search the cathedral. We went together. Obviously I couldn't be armed. We went into the cathedral. We looked into one or two confessional boxes. I'm not very good on heights. You had to climb ladders to get up onto the bell tower. And sure enough you could see the whole of Derry down below you. I looked for things like cigarette butts. There were some expended bullets there that had pinged off the bells, not from my guys but from other soldiers.[145]

The officer was convinced that his guardsmen were 'seeing things': 'Patrols were constantly sniped at, usually missed, but it is very difficult to know where a shot has come from. You look around at umpteen open windows and then up there, towering above you, is the cathedral.'[146] Soldiers also believed that a number of Catholic priests in Derry were actively helping the IRA.[147] According to Bishop Daly, 2 Scots Guards

---

143 Interview with Scots Guards Soldier 14 (Officer), May 2014.
144 TNA: WO 305/4272 2nd Battalion Scots Guards, Operational record of battalion net communications, August 1972.
145 Interview with Scots Guards Soldier 14 (Officer), May 2014.
146 Interview with Scots Guards Soldier 14 (Officer), May 2014.
147 Derry Roman Catholic Diocesan Archives, St Columb's College, Derry: Bishop Edward Daly Papers, Recorded Telephone Conversation between Major Lockhart/Father Irwin/Bishop Daly – Evening of 14th May 1974.

were not the only unit to target St Eugene's; eventually the roof was replaced in 1989, partly because 'it had been shot so many times'.[148]

Fatigue may also have played a role in the death of Captain Bill Watson, second-in-command, B Company, 1 Argylls, and Colour Sergeant Jimmy Struthers, 6 Platoon, B Company, in a booby-trap explosion near the village of Cullyhanna, South Armagh on November 20, 1972. An Argyll private soldier recalled their deaths:

> We had been called out to a farmhouse north of our base [near Cullyhanna]. One of the other platoons had discovered what they thought was a rifle but felt it was booby-trapped. A dog handler had confirmed this and advised that no one enter the building. We were on call in case it was a hoax and the building needed to be searched. When we arrived our search commander and another officer wanted to go into the building … After they went in there was an explosion and the farmhouse disappeared. Soldiers quickly began digging in the rubble but it was a waste of time.[149]

An Argyll officer believed that Watson and Struthers were impatient at having to wait for an ATO and decided to have a closer look inside the house. Tiredness after more than three months of patrolling Northern Ireland's most deadly rural area of operations may also have impacted upon their decision. According to the Argyll officer, the farmhouse was most likely being watched; the explosion remotely detonated when Watson and Struthers entered.[150]

The threat of imminent death and injury had a very obvious, debilitating effect on some soldiers; one wounded soldier in 6 Platoon, B Company, Lance Corporal Jimmy Boag (an experienced soldier who had served in Aden), had premonitions of his death in Northern Ireland before he was shot.[151] Several 1 Scots Guards soldiers were treated for 'shock' after being near to explosions.[152] A guardsman in 2 Scots Guards was

148 Interview with Bishop Edward Daly, Derry, May 14, 2014.
149 Interview with Argyll Soldier 1 (Private Soldier), March 2014.
150 Interview with Argyll Soldier 15 (Officer), December 2013.
151 'Shot Soldier Had Premonition of Death in Ulster', *Alloa Advertiser*, August 25, 1972.
152 Interview with Scots Guards Soldier 3 (Guardsman), November 2013.

admitted to hospital in Londonderry on October 16, 1972 suffering from hysteria and hyperventilation.[153] Some soldiers also allegedly resorted to self-inflicted wounds:

> One guy was lying on top of his bunk and put his SLR between his toe like that, pulled his trigger and the bullet went between his big toe and the next toe. They actually found the bullet in the pocket of a combat jacket in the end. It went through his locker at the end of the bed. He got charged. It [such behaviour] was actually surprisingly common.[154]

During 1 Scots Guards tour of West Belfast, strikingly, three guardsmen shot themselves in the foot in 'accidental discharges'.[155] However, the reasons for deliberate, self-inflicted wounds are more complex than they first might appear. Many young soldiers had married equally youthful wives; allegations of infidelity or other domestic problems could cause significant strain while soldiers were on operations.[156] It is also important to note that the vast majority of soldiers simply 'cracked on' and did not exhibit any obvious sign of debilitating mental disorders while on operations.[157]

Mental health problems undoubtedly carried a great stigma in the Army during the early 1970s. Cases of mental trauma can also take some years to present themselves. Nevertheless, Army psychiatrists in the 1970s observed fewer, not more, instances of psychiatric problems during times of operational intensity. As one Army psychiatrist put it during the early 1970s, 'The incidence of psychiatric illness amongst troops in Northern Ireland remains low and it is noticeable that as tension heightened and operational activity increased in 1971, so the rate of psychiatric referral fell.'[158] One 6 Platoon, 1 Argylls, soldier recalled

153 Adjutant's Diary, 2nd Battalion, Scots Guards, 1971–1972, Regimental Headquarters, Wellington Barracks, London.
154 Interview with Argyll Soldier 6 (Private Soldier), May 2014.
155 Adjutant's Diary, 1st Battalion, Scots Guards, 1970–1971.
156 Interview with Argyll Soldier 6 (Private Soldier), May 2014.
157 Interview with Argyll Soldier 5 (Officer), May 2014.
158 Army psychiatrist quoted in S. Wessely, 'Psychiatric Disorders, Psychiatric Injury and the Royal Ulster Constabulary', dated December 1, 2004 (unpublished report in author's possession).

that returning to Northern Ireland was the only thing that mattered – it kept him sober and focused:

> Continuity was the important thing. I volunteered for everything in Northern Ireland. I wanted to be there. I wanted more tours, the more the better. When I wasn't there I didn't know what to be doing with myself. It gave me somewhere to focus my anger. I hoped I would get even.[159]

Getting even became the overwhelming desire for many soldiers. Managing such desires or expectations for revenge was challenging, even for experienced officers and NCOs.

Discipline and Shifting Attitudes Towards the Local Population

'Skiving' and 'Glory Hunting'

Formal discipline and informal regimental traditions were sometimes in conflict in Northern Ireland. According to the testimony of former Argylls and other soldiers, the Argylls had been involved in looting in Aden.[160] In Northern Ireland, D Company soldiers referred to looting as 'glory hunting'; 15 Platoon wrote that:

> Our two 'Super Heroes', Major MacKenzie (Batman) [sic] and his right-hand man CSM Higgins (alias Robin) have tried to thwart all our efforts at glory hunting. One of our moments of glory was thwarted when the owner of a house we were searching came back from America after having been there for two years. If only he had come back an hour earlier. It really was tough luck.[161]

A certain 'Clydeside cheekiness' was a common trait of the Argylls; keeping such habits in check was difficult. The Argylls would also poke fun at the fact that many of its soldiers had joined the Army after being in

---

159 Interview with Argyll Soldier 1 (Private Soldier), April 2014.
160 Nigel Stephens, ex-officer, 1st Queen's Dragoon Guards, interviewed in BBC television documentary, 'Mad Mitch and his Tribal Law'.
161 'D Company Notes', *Thin Red Line*, September 1972.

trouble with the police. Describing B Company's position in Crossmaglen, one Argyll wrote, 'The camp itself is like Barlinnie Prison ... with its high fences and guard posts at each corner, but that is why the Jocks settled down quite quickly.'[162] However, a lot of the talk about 'glory hunting' was just that; the scale of looting or theft in Northern Ireland was greatly diminished from the 'glory' days of Aden.

One Argyll officer drew a distinction between looting, which he regarded as unacceptable, and 'spoils of war', the taking of a flag or a small pistol as a memento of service, which he permitted during his time in Northern Ireland.[163] The Argylls of D Company became obsessed with a tricolour, the flag of the Republic of Ireland, flying above the Derrybeg estate in Newry. The disorientating effect of low-intensity counter-insurgency warfare, with so few fixed physical objectives and unending, routine tasks, was temporarily alleviated by the desire to seize the flag over Derrybeg. 'For us it was the command post of the enemy ... Eventually we got it down. It was something to focus on when you were in there. "That tricolour is coming down. It is going to be ours."'[164] The unit that took over from the Argylls in RUC H Division, 1st Battalion, the Royal Hampshire Regiment, were also keen trophy hunters: 'In Crossmaglen the town hall actually flew the Irish tricolour and it was one of the ambitions; and I think it was pulled down by a guy called Alan Withers who was the 2IC [second-in-command] in the rifle company and had also been in the SAS.'[165] Soldiers also kept souvenirs or trophies that

162 'B Company Notes', *Glengarry Tales*, August 1972.

163 Interview with Argyll Soldier 5 (Officer), May 2014.

164 Interview with Argyll Soldier 8 (Private Soldier), November 2013. Bernd Greiner has written of the strain of not being able to make physical gains in a counter-insurgency operation, in this case in Vietnam. 'It's really tough to catch them with a weapon. After a fire fight, they take away all weapons and bodies – there's nothing to show, seems we never accomplished anything. All that was left after a fire fight was my friends' missing arms, legs, and dead bodies.' It was not just a war against an invisible opponent but also a war in which one could leave no trace behind – no symbols of victory visible for miles around like conquered territory or large prisoner-of-war camps, liberated towns or destroyed armaments factories.' Marine Lance Corporal Denizil R. Allen, A Company, 1st Battalion, 27th Regiment, 1st Marine Division, quoted in Greiner, *War without Fronts*, 139.

165 IWM: 13915 Audio Recording – Roger Coleman, Hampshires, Service in Northern Ireland.

reminded them of a near miss – an Argyll soldier kept part of the device that nearly killed him in an explosion at Dromintee in South Armagh.[166]

The habit of 'skiving', a mild defiance of military authority by eluding mundane tasks, was also in evidence in Northern Ireland.[167] A group of soldiers in A Company, 1 Argylls, fed up with the strain and boredom of constant patrols of East Tyrone, would 'find a relatively safe lane where they could park up. They would bring sleeping bags with them. They would park up in the back lane. One guy would send duff radio reports.' Unfortunately, on one occasion the patrol sent a grid reference that identified him as being in the middle of Lough Neagh.[168] Guardsmen could also occasionally fail to meet the standards of discipline expected in Guards regiments. During 2 Scots Guards tour of Londonderry, Lance Sergeant Iley in Right Flank in 2 Scots Guards was caught 'skiving'; his night-patrol routine often consisted of handing over to his section second-in-command and then going to spend the night with a young Protestant woman who lived on the Abercorn Road.[169]

Soldiers' Encounters with Local Women

Most Scots Guardsmen and Argylls were in their late teens or early twenties. The commanding officer, a man usually in his early 40s, seemed quite ancient by comparison. Women were a constant obsession for these young men; pornography was a valuable commodity. Some soldiers, especially the youngest, were given female names, such as 'Sexy Sue' or 'Sweetheart', out of sheer boredom.[170] Local men were convinced that soldiers were spying on their women for personal enjoyment. A John Doherty of Limewood Street in Derry once rang up 2 Scots Guards Battalion Headquarters to let them know that, 'I don't mind enquiries at the front door. But I don't want Fuckin' Peeping Tom at the back window. Next time it happens I will get an axe to them.'[171]

166 Interview with Argyll Soldier 25 (Officer), November 2013.
167 Hockey, *Squaddies*, 142.
168 Interview with Argyll Soldier 6 (Private Soldier), May 2014.
169 Interview with Scots Guards Soldier 12 (Officer), December 2014.
170 'B Company Notes', *Thin Red Line*, January 1973; Interview with Scots Guards Soldier 12 (Officer), December 2014.
171 TNA: WO 305/4273 Commander's Diary, 2nd Battalion, Scots Guards, August 31, 1972–September 30, 1972.

An employee of the Londonderry Development Commission, James Doherty, refused to tell soldiers the names and addresses of his sisters. The head of the Commission had to intervene to prevent his arrest.[172]

As the conflict in Northern Ireland escalated, social interactions between soldiers and local Catholic girls became almost impossible, if not very dangerous for the women involved. Guardsman McKay of Right Flank, 2 Scots Guards, began a relationship with a girl from Newtownstewart in County Tyrone. On August 25, 1972, he went absent without leave; searching his possessions his platoon sergeant found a letter from his girlfriend saying she had been tarred and feathered. McKay was later picked up near the town of Strabane in County Tyrone by the RUC and sent back to Londonderry.[173] A week later two sisters from the Coyle family, who lived in Melmore Gardens, were shot and wounded by the IRA. Both had come to battalion HQ the day before (September 1, 1972) to make a complaint about the behaviour of the Scots Guards.[174] Such actions had a deep effect on 2 Scots Guards and left them in no doubt as to the brutality of the IRA.

The Argylls had a similar experience of IRA actions against local women suspected of 'collaborating' with the Army. One D Company soldier told of how, in the early days of their deployment to South Armagh, they used to stop at a farmhouse near the border.

> This family always gave us a tea and a sandwich at night. But we would always go late at night. We would put a half-section on sentry and half a section would go and get their tea and sandwiches and we would swap over. They were a Catholic family. The question was never asked but you could tell by the pictures on the walls and the cross, crucifix and that. They were the nicest people in the world. We were very close to the family.[175]

The family had a daughter, Nancy McCumiskey, 19 years old and

---

172 TNA: WO 305/4274 2nd Battalion Scots Guards, Operational record of battalion net communications, November 1972.

173 TNA: WO 305/4272 2nd Battalion Scots Guards, Operational record of battalion net communications, August 1972.

174 TNA: WO 305/4273 Weekly Intsum, August 28–September 4, 1972, 2nd Battalion, Scots Guards.

175 Interview with Argyll Soldier 9 (Private Soldier), November 2013.

apparently very pretty. 'She was like an island, a little paradise island in the middle of a rough sea. She was always there.'[176] Nancy McCumiskey's family was relatively well-disposed to the Army; her brother was believed to be serving in the military. Her worst mistake, however, was to talk to Lance Corporal Boag of D Company during the afternoon of August 13 shortly before he was shot by an IRA sniper in the hip.[177] A few days later, when arriving for mass at St Brigid's church in Glassdrumman, she was dragged from her family's car and tied to a pole beside the church where tar and feathers were poured over her.[178]

The assault on Nancy McCumiskey was a watershed moment for D Company; 'It cut us off from the population. No more tea stops, no more regular visits to anybody. We were only putting them and us to danger.'[179] Such 'tarring and feathering' attacks dehumanised the victims but also the soldiers themselves; by association they had become somehow unclean or hateful, like 'lepers of old'. Insulted, shocked and deeply angry, they sought ways to get revenge.[180]

Soldiers found that verbal and physical abuse from women was particularly hard to take. One 2 Scots Guards officer recalled that:

> The women would stir it up. Once I caught this little bugger who was throwing bricks. I marched him over to the nearest woman and said, 'Who are the parents of this child?' And before I knew what was happening my glasses were torn off and stamped on. I had a rifle but I couldn't do anything with it.[181]

Soldiers also could not search women and, in the early days, there were not enough female military or police personnel around to do the job for them. They were convinced that the IRA used women to move weapons and small amounts of explosives, which fuelled greater resentment of the local population.[182] The IRA organised patrols of

176 Interview with Argyll Soldier 9 (Private Soldier), November 2013.
177 TNA: WO 305/4407 The Argyll and Sutherland Highlanders Battalion Diary, April 1969–March 1974.
178 'Tarred Girl', *Newry Reporter*, August 26, 1972.
179 Interview with Argyll Soldier 8 (Private Soldier), November 2013.
180 Interview with Argyll Soldier 8 (Private Soldier), November 2013.
181 Interview with Scots Guards Soldier 14 (Officer), May 2014.
182 Interview with Scots Guards Soldier 16 (NCO), January 2014.

women to harass soldiers and warn any IRA units of their movements: During 1 Scots Guards tour of Ballymurphy in 1971, 'Big Alice Franklin ... made the air blue with the names she called the Brits.'[183] A rumour circulated in 2 Scots Guards that local women were putting ground glass in cups of tea and offering it to guardsmen.[184]

Moral Distancing: The Primacy of the Group

Soldiers, particularly junior officers from more sheltered, privileged backgrounds, recoiled from the poverty they encountered in Northern Ireland, particularly in Catholic areas. But even tough NCOs from relatively deprived areas of Scotland were deeply affected. An NCO from 2 Scots Guards recalled scenes of 'horror' – dirty houses, screaming women, dogs that were encouraged to attack soldiers.[185] The historian and former Army officer Antony Beevor also reported a similar resentment of house searches among British soldiers.[186] Initial shock and even sympathy at the conditions in which some Catholics lived in Northern Ireland gave way to contempt on the part of some soldiers as both regiments suffered mounting casualties on operations in 1971 and 1972. The constant verbal abuse of soldiers took its toll: any perceived weakness (physical appearance, a stutter etc.) would be exploited. A black soldier was called 'Banana muncher' by the Derry IRA newspaper, *Volunteer*, and advised to 'find a tree to hide in'.[187]

In response, some soldiers began to demonise the Catholic poor as inherently 'dirty' or savage, indirectly emphasising a moral or social distance between themselves and the local inhabitants.[188] Locals were either helping the IRA, or knew who they were, but did nothing to prevent soldiers being killed. Pictures drawn by soldiers showed primitive looking, drunken Irishmen, lurking behind corners with barely concealed guns and bombs along with captions such as, 'An innocent Irish bystander

---

183 C. de Baróid, *Ballymurphy and the Irish War* (London: Pluto, 2000). 78.

184 'Bogopoly', *Rose and Thistle*, Second Battalion Scots Guards, November 1, 1972.

185 Interview with Scots Guards Soldier 16 (NCO), January 2014.

186 Beevor, *Inside the British Army*, 264.

187 '3 for the Pot', *Volunteer – The Voice of Republican Derry*, September 1972.

188 'Donegal Despatch', *Rose and Thistle*, Second Battalion Scots Guards, November 1, 1972.

about to do an honest day's work'.[189] An article written in the Argyll Regimental magazine, *The Thin Red Line*, offered a prize for a picture of an, 'intelligent Irishman'.[190] Others now saw the Irish as somehow culturally inferior. A soldier vented his feelings about the 'backwardness' of Ireland in a poem:

> In Ireland they call themselves heroes
> But women there still dress in black
> Oh tell me please tell me why heroes
> Must always shoot in the back.[191]

A joke battalion log-book of the 'good old days', the first Scots Guards deployment to Ireland in 1642, was produced by 2 Scots Guards: 'Event: we have stopped at a road check barrier a potato cart with 6 arrows hidden. Action: peasant's ears cut off and sent on his way.'[192] The Scots Guards also reached back to Pirbright training camp for labels for the local population. Brand new trainee guardsmen were called 'crows', the lowest specimen on the Guards' food chain. Now, guardsmen called the Derry children 'crows'.[193] In the eyes of the soldier in Derry or South Armagh, the ranks of the 'innocent' looked increasingly thin.

Soldiers began to refer to their 'patches' of Northern Ireland, particularly its rural areas, as 'Apache country'; East Tyrone was called 'Ponderosa' by A Company, 1 Argylls, the RUC Station in Crossmaglen was 'High Chaparral'.[194] Argyll soldiers particularly loved holding

---

189 British Army Cartoonists, 'By'eeee the right … Laugh' (undated).

190 'S Company Notes', *Thin Red Line*, January 1973.

191 Driver McCreadie (RCT), 'Poem', *Glengarry Tales*, August 1972.

192 'Battalion Log – 1642', *Rose and Thistle*, Second Battalion Scots Guards, November 1, 1972. The same edition also has a game called 'Bogopoly': 'Seen by Martin McGuinness putting ground glass in soldiers' tea – groomed for stardom – Move on 5.' 'School of Infantry – Donegal' – Knights of Malta – Meenan Square, 'Wait a turn while bullet is removed.' Winner is the first Player who gets to Buncana and is appointed OC Derry Command.

193 'Recce Platoon Notes', *Rose and Thistle*, Second Battalion Scots Guards, November 1, 1972.

194 'Ponderosa' and 'High Chaparral' are references to popular American television 'Westerns' that were broadcast during the 1960s and 1970s. 'A Company Notes', *Thin Red Line*, January 1973. Interview with Argyll Soldier 6 (Private Soldier), May 2014.

their self-loading rifles up 'cowboy-style' for posed photographs.[195] On pre-Northern Ireland training in Lydd and Hythe, Sergeant Kilcullen of 6 Platoon, B Company, somehow acquired a local horse, 'put his Glengarry sloped to the side, his rifle up like the Magnificent Seven and rode up the road'.[196] The locals were 'the Indians'.[197] Much of this was harmless fun; the Argylls had grown up in an era marked by cowboy films. But the 'Indian country' comparison, also present in the US war in Vietnam, reinforced the division between the soldiers and the local population.[198]

Service in Republican or Loyalist areas was often called 'paddybashing'. An officer in the Royal Scots Dragoon Guards used to refer to 'paddy drives' (as opposed to a pheasant drive) southwards from Gosford Castle, near Markethill, towards the border.[199] Such labelling could reinforce an attitude of contempt, with negative consequences for the soldiers' treatment of the local population. An Argyll soldier, Lance Corporal Iain Chestnut of D Company, was particularly known for his verbal abuse of the local population.[200] Unchecked, he went on stuff bolts into a gun and fire them at local people and was later involved in the murder of two men in Fermanagh.[201] Mounting casualties for 1 and 2 Scots Guards and 1 Argylls saw a marked escalation in racial abuse against the local population. But so did the desire to 'do something physical', described by Bernd Greiner as the desire 'to prove that they themselves could seize the initiative and free themselves of the stigma of a loser secretly mocked by the enemy or a plaything in the games of anonymous powers'.[202] Many soldiers enjoyed opportunities for violence. A 2 Scots Guards officer recalled that firing rubber bullets at a riotous crowd was like 'grouse shooting on the 12th' and, in another game analogy, referred to shooting 'a brace' of terrorists. The same officer also began to put notches

---

195 'The Bogside Where Snipers Lurk in Darkened Streets', *Oban Times*, November 9, 1972.

196 Interview with Argyll Soldier 1 (Private Soldier), April 2014.

197 *Oban Times*, November 9, 1972.

198 Greiner, *War without Fronts*, 132.

199 RSDGA: Mitchell, 'An Officer's Diary'.

200 '14 Platoon Notes', *Glengarry Tales*, August 1972.

201 'Republican Clubs Allege Terror Campaign', *Newry Reporter*, October 5, 1972; PRONI: CRCT/3/2/2/159A Court file of Stanley Hathaway, John Byrne, Iain Chestnut and Andrew Snowball.

202 Greiner, *War without Fronts* (London: Random House, 2009), 139.

on his table for every alleged IRA Volunteer he shot.[203] On September 29, in a follow-up operation following the shooting of Guardsman Hoodless, Guardsman Logie 'was at long last able to fire his "Secret Weapon" [possibly an improvised weapon]. He scored a possible and now has two notches on his barrel!'[204] For some soldiers, violence became a game, an opportunity to collect 'notches', souvenirs etc. – a mechanism by which they made sense of conflict.

The ease with which new group identities and enmities can be created may be gleaned from the pre-Northern Ireland training exercises at Lydd and Hythe in 1972. Companies formed up in the square of the mock Ulster village, with one playing the 'enemy', namely rioting civilians. An Argyll soldier recalled:

> After days, never mind weeks, of this training, you would forget that it was your mates opposing you and injuries would occur. I remember a guy being hit in the chest with a rubber bullet, whilst other people had fingers broken with rifle butts. 'Civvies' were instructed to throw only empty beer cans at troops, but not only were stones thrown, but we had one memorable night where petrol bombs were thrown.[205]

When D Company, 1 Argylls took the turn of playing the 'enemy', things began to escalate still further, 'Half way through they started filling the tins up with gravel and started lobbing big rocks at us. One guy was hit by a plastic bullet. A serious riot broke. One guy had a bite mark on his leg. Quite a few fingers were broken, a lot of cuts and bruises.'[206] After the riot was officially over, 'a jealous "enemy" managed to split the skulls of two 6 Platoon heavies.'[207] According to a senior

---

203 Interview with Scots Guards Soldier 20 (Officer), June 2013. A major operation called 'Beat Group' – another game shooting reference – was also conducted in West Belfast by 1 Scots Guards in November 1971 – Adjutant's Diary, 1st Battalion, Scots Guards, 1970–1971, Scots Guards Regimental Headquarters, Wellington Barracks, London.
204 'News from Left Flank', *Rose and Thistle*, Second Battalion Scots Guards, November 1, 1972.
205 RMASH: Chestnut.
206 Interview with Argyll Soldier 1 (Private Soldier), April 2014.
207 'D Company Notes', *Thin Red Line*, September 1972.

Argyll NCO, the rivalry between A Company and D Company was particularly fierce – sometimes things went too far: 'D Company really hated A Company. We called them the bullshitters. A Coy and D Coy simply never got on, all through the 1960s and 1970s.'[208]

Extreme rivalry and violence between soldiers and those playing 'civilians' in simulation training was not uncommon; other units, including the Scots Guards, would describe the same phenomenon.[209] The training was almost too realistic.[210] NITAT trainers had taken events that might only happen once or twice, or indeed never at all, during a battalion tour and made the soldiers think that these were commonplace. The effects used to simulate combat were highly realistic; pigs' bodies were dressed up in uniform and blown up (the smell from burnt human flesh is remarkably similar).[211] The soldiers were certainly revved up: 13 Platoon, D Company, later described how, 'On our arrival there was a bomb under every bush and a mad Irishman behind every tree, but they have now realised that this unfortunately is not so.'[212] Initially, NITAT training provided a 'one size fits all' military guide to soldiering in Northern Ireland. Soldiers could find themselves in environments (South Armagh or Fermanagh) that were very different from the predominantly urban ranges they had trained on, a situation that was exacerbated by the frequent switching of battalion deployment location at the last moment.[213]

The Scots Guards versus the US Navy

The soldier's first loyalty was to his immediate group, most importantly his section and his company. Anybody who challenged that group's security and ascendency would be self-evidently hated and targeted: 'On

208 Interview with Argyll Soldier 23 (NCO), March 2015.

209 Interview with Scots Guards Soldier 6 (Guardsman), November 2013.

210 Interview with Argyll Soldier 1 (Private Soldier), April 2014.

211 RMASH: Chestnut.

212 'D Company Notes', *Thin Red Line*, September 1972.

213 Sam Sarkesian observes a similar problem for US troops preparing to deploy to Vietnam, pointing out the very different operational terrain and tasks in the different regions of South Vietnam. The specific challenges of each region were not reflected in pre-deployment training in the USA. S. Sarkesian, *Unconventional Conflicts in a New Security Era* (Westport, Conn.: Greenwood Press, 1993), 106.

the streets the Jock didn't care who the hell you were. You got a rap over the knuckles, followed by a rap over the head if you didn't push off.'[214] Hatred of rival groups in Londonderry by 2 Scots Guards included the US Navy; a US Naval Communications Station (NAVCOMMSTA) operated in Derry until 1977. Many US sailors evidently sympathised with the negative attitude expressed by the city's inhabitants towards the British Army. A US Navy seaman recalled that he and a number of other American sailors had married local girls; he described visiting his wife's relations and friends in the Rossville flats in the Bogside area of Derry during the shootings of Bloody Sunday.[215] The same sailor claimed to have been beaten up by the Army when walking in the Brandywell in 1971.[216] After Bloody Sunday he and another US Navy sailor decided that they wanted to do something to help the IRA. After a few weeks, the men were brought by an IRA contact to a meeting in a house in the Bogside, where they were met by a group of IRA men, led by Martin McGuinness. According to the American sailor, McGuinness 'thanked us for offering to help, that he appreciated our sympathy but that the best thing we could do is stay out of it.'[217] Local Protestants were aware of the close ties between some of the US sailors and Republican families in the city. Consequently, a US sailor recalled being sent with another group of naval personnel, armed with rifles, to protect Dungiven US Navy Transmitter site, following information that it might be attacked by Loyalist paramilitaries.[218] Bomb threats were also made against the US naval base in Derry including during a command handover ceremony on July 28, 1972.[219]

When American sailors verbally abused Scots Guardsmen, the gloves were off; 2 Scots Guards not only reported such incidents but also alleged

---

214 Interview with Argyll Soldier 5 (Officer), May 2014.

215 Interview with US Navy Sailor 1, February 2015.

216 'We were on our way up to the Creggan, going up the hill. This big four-wheeler pulled up and asked us what we were doing. They wanted to know why we were going up to Creggan. Then they reached out, grabbed us and beat us with their rifles. I eventually managed to get out my ID Card and shout that I was an American sailor. They then stopped beating us.' Interview with US Navy Sailor 1, February 25, 2015.

217 Interview with US Navy Sailor 1, February 2015.

218 Interview with US Navy Sailor 1, February 2015.

219 'Bomb Scare during USN Base Ceremony', *Londonderry Sentinel*, August 2, 1972.

that one sailor was guilty of a homosexual assault against a local man, having paid him to keep quiet. According to an intelligence report, a US sailor, J.L. Smith, may have acted as a driver for the IRA.[220] A 2 Scots Guards officer recalled that he discovered US sailors moving weapons on behalf of the IRA. Relations continued to worsen right up to the departure of 2 Scots Guards from Londonderry.[221] A US Navy yeoman based in Londonderry during 1972 also remembered occasional brawls between a group of 'anti-British' US Navy personnel and various British Army units during 1971 and 1972: 'I would say their sentiments most likely derived from their anti-British Army girlfriends from the largely Nationalist "Derry" side of the river. These guys treated the [British] Army with the sort of hostility that they would show the police in the United States. They tended to view things in black and white.'[222] One out of every three single American sailors married local girls when stationed in Northern Ireland.[223] A mixture of American sailors' genuine Irish Republican sympathies and a dislike of other groups of young men with some training in violence is probably behind the occasionally confrontational attitudes between US Navy sailors and their British Army adversaries during 1971 and 1972.

It is very striking that all the respective groups of young men in Londonderry at this time believed that they were responding to aggression. As the Derry political activist Eamonn McCann observed, 'After Bloody Sunday the most powerful feeling in the area was the desire for revenge.' According to McCann, if a bomb in Aldershot, which killed six innocent people, had killed soldiers, 'there would have been dancing in the streets of Derry'.[224] The many recruits to the IRA in early 1972 wanted revenge for Bloody Sunday and earlier killings by British soldiers, the Scots Guards looked for retribution for their casualties on the streets of Londonderry and US Navy sailors were out to avenge the mistreatment of them and their in-laws by overly aggressive soldiers. Each group hit back, for very local reasons, and each group saw itself as the victim.

220 TNA: WO 305/4273 Annex B to Intsum for week October 2–October 8, 1972 of 2nd Battalion, Scots Guards, dated October 9, 1972.

221 Interview with Scots Guards Soldier 20 (Officer), June 2013.

222 Email correspondence between the author and US Navy Sailor 2, February 2015.

223 'Bomb Scare during USN Base Ceremony', *Londonderry Sentinel*, August 2, 1972.

224 McCann, *War and an Irish Town*, 102.

Soldiers' Opinions of the IRA as a Military Force

Scots Guards' interviewees' opinions of the IRA's military capability tended to be derisive. All ranks of the Scots Guards voiced a strong sense of anger at their losses, but this rarely, if ever, translated into demonstrating professional respect for the IRA's capabilities. The urban IRA in Belfast, Derry (and indeed in Newry) were seen as relatively amateurish – mostly teenagers who were bad shots. A Scots Guards' NCO described his encounter with such a gunman in Belfast in 1971:

> A wee laddie, 16 years old, stupid wee boy, on the Springfield road stood up – he's only 40 metres from me – with a Thomson machine gun. But as luck would have it, he's only a young guy, and the Thomson goes up and to the right. And I had made it to the other side of the pavement by then. A poor taxi driver came down the road and he was shot in the leg ... The young laddie about three days later blew himself and his girlfriend up. They were making a bomb.[225]

The IRA lacked sufficient numbers of skilled bomb-makers. The log books of the Argylls in Newry and 2 Scots Guards in Londonderry are full of details of failed bomb attempts and there are several incidents where the bomb-makers indeed did blow themselves up.[226] However, as discussed in Chapter 2, although the IRA was in the very early stages of developing its bomb-making capabilities including making a number of very fatal errors, its shooting accuracy was reasonably good, considering the very young age and recent recruitment of many IRA Volunteers.

Argyll interviewees had a more complex opinion of the IRA. Some had changed their opinions after years of reflection. 'At the time, I had no respect for the IRA. Just hatred. Later, I knew that all that stuff about "dumb Paddy" was far from the truth. But at the time I had this real hatred for all Catholics, all Republicans and all their women.'[227] An Argyll officer thought that the IRA in South Armagh were 'amongst the best insurgents

---

225 Interview with Scots Guards Soldier 4 (NCO), November 2013.
226 TNA: WO 305/4274 2nd Battalion Scots Guards, Intsum No.7, November 20–26, 1972; TNA: WO 305/4407 The Argyll and Sutherland Highlanders Battalion Diary, April 1969–March 1974.
227 Interview with Argyll Soldier 1 (Private Soldier), April 2014.

the British Army had ever faced'.[228] Argyll interviewees had a much more 'professional respect' for the South Armagh IRA than other IRA units. The IRA on the border in the early 1970s often wore combat gear and berets. They even occasionally patrolled rural areas. Interestingly, an Argyll officer observed that soldiers from rural backgrounds did better in South Armagh.[229] The South Armagh IRA thought the same about their Volunteers; Belfast IRA Volunteers Martin Meehan and Terence 'Cleeky' Clarke were thought to be brave but clueless when operating in a rural environment. It was soon made clear to them in 1972 that they should leave the area.[230]

An Argyll soldier described a rare 'live and let live' encounter, an agreement to disengage without either side opening fire, between an Argyll patrol and an IRA unit in Jonesborough, South Armagh during the autumn of 1972.

> I remember we were out on a night patrol with Moose [Corporal Campbell, 6 Platoon, B Company], in the top end of Jonesborough. We got the old double tap on the magazine. You could nae see hand signals ... And the word came back that there was another fighting patrol on the other side of us. We were up the top end of Jonesborough and we were on the left-hand side and they were on the right-hand side. We didn't know which patrol it was, an Army patrol or what. But it shouldn't have been there. The Section Commander, Moose, said, 'Right, I'm going to go for them'. He went up and spoke to the guy. They went back that way and we went our way. It was later Moose says, 'Aye, you were lucky tonight boys.' And that was when we found out that it was one of their patrols. He more or less said that 'If we all start shooting, then most of us will get killed here because we were so close.' Moose comes walking down, 'Come on, let's go.' And we walked down the hill.[231]

The IRA on the border frequently intercepted the British Army's communications. The IRA also had their own radio communications,

228 Interview with Argyll Soldier 5 (Officer), May 2014.
229 Interview with Argyll Soldier 5 (Officer), May 2014.
230 Harnden, *Bandit Country*, 45–47.
231 Interview with Argyll Soldier 8 (Private Soldier), November 2013.

to which British Army wireless operators in turn could listen in.[232] One Dundalk-based Republican could do a passable imitation of B Company's OC, Major Buchanan, in an attempt to lure the Argylls into an ambush.[233] Although the Argylls clearly despised the IRA, their 'shoot and scoot' ambushes, their bullying treatment of young girls such as Nancy McCumiskey, they could at the same time admit some professional respect for their rural enemy. The Scots Guards were much less impressed by the IRA units they encountered in the urban areas of West Belfast and Londonderry.

Retribution:
'Giving Some Back'

Visiting Derry at the end of 2 Scots Guards' tour in November 1972, Alan Cameron of West Scotland's *Oban Times* captured some of the frustration expressed by the guardsmen he met. A guardsman in Left Flank told the reporter that the Rossville flats 'stank with hostility'. Another guardsman was quoted as saying:

> These people in the Bogside are always trying to make fools of us. They curse and swear at us and are always making filthy gestures in our direction. Even the little kids chuck bricks at us. If we could only get stuck into them it would not be so bad, but we are not allowed.[234]

A D Company, 1 Argylls, soldier, the target of yet another border ambush, admitted that he did 'get stuck in'. An Argyll vehicle near the border had been shot at, and it ended up in a ditch – four soldiers lay dazed or unconscious. The Argyll soldier interviewed was the first on the scene. Furious, he looked around and saw a local young man standing watching them from a field; he shouted at him and the young man started running. That was enough for the soldier, who ran after him and proceeded to beat him up:

---

232 Interview with Argyll Soldier 1 (Private Soldier), April 2014.
233 Interview with Argyll Soldier 3 (NCO), September 2014.
234 'The Bogside Where Snipers Lurk in Darkened Streets', *Oban Times*, November 9, 1972.

We bounced him all the way back to the bloody PIG [Army patrol vehicle]. 'Where's the gun that you used? We'll bring you back to Newry and we'll test you for gunpowder traces so you might as well tell us anyway.' I hugely believed that he was responsible for firing that shot. It later turned out that he wasn't but there was nothing I could do about that. I went to court for assault and was let off by the judge because of the circumstances. It was not one of my proudest moments. It's not being shot at. It's when you see your mates lying there and they're injured.[235]

Here the soldier in question acknowledged that he needed to vent his anger; because the local man was nearby, he was possibly the gunman, but his immediate desire for vengeance overwhelmed any possible doubts. Either this man *was* the gunman, or at least he knew who was; the soldiers treated him accordingly. A number of soldiers were indeed charged with assaulting a local man, Thomas Mullan, on October 2, 1972, who claimed he was merely returning some cattle to a field near Killeen, County Down. The presiding magistrate, John Petrie, later dismissed the case due to 'a conflict of evidence'.[236]

The experiences of other units in Northern Ireland also provide similar incidents of the overwhelming need for immediate retribution in the aftermath of a shooting or a bombing incident. Indeed, the same sentiment is mirrored in accounts of soldiering during the Iraq war.[237] In the immediate aftermath of a fatal explosion in 1973 that killed two of their comrades, soldiers from 2nd Battalion, Parachute Regiment (2 PARA) shot local farmer Martin Walsh in the head near his farm in Belleeks, South Armagh. The soldiers claimed that Walsh was shot as he ran away and failed to stop when challenged. Soldiers saw Walsh carrying a bag, which they alleged was fertiliser used for explosives (it was found

---

235 Interview with Argyll Soldier 8 (Private Soldier), November 2013.
236 'Charges Dismissed Against Soldiers', *Newry Reporter*, April 26, 1973.
237 'And while you are sitting there the anger builds as you review what just happened. Somebody, not far from this spot, someone right around here – it could be him, him or him – just tried to kill you ... Somebody tried to kill you, he got away and all of these people know something, yet they aren't saying anything. How could you not want to kill them, too, for protecting the person who just tried to kill you? How could you contain that rage?' Frederick, *Black Hearts*, 85.

to contain cattle feed). Martin Walsh later described being taken to a nearby lake where he had his head immersed in water after he was unable to answers questions about who had carried out the bombings. Walsh claimed he was then shot: 'He told his mother that an officer ordered him to climb a fence and he was shot in the head as he did so. He alleged he heard one soldier say, "Will I finish him off, sir?" and the officer replied, "No, there are too many watching".'[238] Walsh's account is disputed; however, the account resonates with that of the Argyll incident in that soldiers, lifting their heads in the disorientating aftermath of an IED attack, quickly fastened guilt upon the nearest available suspect.

Soldiers knew that they had to account for every round, not only to the battalion but also to the RMP. They sometimes found ways around this. For example, in 1973, when 2 Scots Guards took over their area of operations from 3 Royal Green Jackets in West Belfast, Scots Guards NCOs were alarmed to discover that individual Green Jacket riflemen were passing on 'Buckshee' ammunition (extra rounds not listed as Army ordnance) to guardsmen: 'I got the platoon together and told them – "right we have an amnesty, give me all your rounds" – and eventually they handed over 120 for a platoon of 30. Which is a lot of ammunition. You could do a lot of damage with that.'[239] Only for the diligence of Scots Guards NCOs, guardsmen could have fired rounds that were impossible to trace. It was a recipe for atrocity.

The Scots Guards and the Brandywell

The death of individually charismatic and popular soldiers could also have a profound influence on how soldiers viewed and treated the local population. One such soldier for 2 Scots Guards was 26-year-old guardsman John Van Beck. Van Beck was shot in the back by a sniper while on patrol with Right Flank on September 17, 1972: 'Van was larger than life. And if anybody was going to survive it was going to be him. Not only physically but also mentally.'[240] A patrol later found graffiti on a Bogside corner, 'Van Beck is dead. Ha Ha.'[241] At 17.00 on September 23,

---

238 'Two Soldiers Die in Horror Blast', *Newry Reporter*, April 12, 1973.
239 Interview with Scots Guards Soldier 16 (NCO), January 2014.
240 Interview with Scots Guards Soldier 3 (Guardsman), November 2013.
241 TNA: WO 305/4272 2nd Battalion Scots Guards, Operational record of battalion net communications, September 1972.

another Right Flank soldier, Guardsman George Lockhart, was shot while on patrol on the Lecky Road, also in the back. Lockhart was enormously popular, even if not the most effective combat soldier. He was a type of mascot for 2 Scots Guards – the commanding officer even called him by his first name. Lockhart, who worked in the Company stores at Bridge Camp, had frequently begged to go out on patrol; he was shot on his first one.[242]

Morale in Right Flank's bridge camp plummeted after the death of Van Beck, the shooting of Guardsman Fee on September 22 and the mortal wounding of George Lockhart the following day, all by snipers whom Right Flank struggled to identify, let alone kill. On a phone call home to Aberdeen a Right Flank guardsman's conversation about mounting 2 Scots Guards casualties was interrupted: 'A voice broke in [on the line] which said, "and you'll be next".'[243] The guardsmen in Right Flank wanted revenge: a Right Flank officer recalled how challenging it was to keep the guardsmen in line, 'It wasn't easy – I remember going into the barrack room afterward and the men were asking me "Who is going to be next sir?"'[244] Another officer recalled Colonel Boam having 'some difficult conversations with Right Flank. Some of the guardsmen were saying, "Come on sir, let's go and rip them apart".' Boam took to visiting Right Flank more frequently, listening to his guardsmen and telling them how counter-productive a more aggressive approach would be.[245] A guardsman later revealed (during a court case taken against a local woman for her participation in a riot) that on the afternoon of September 21, 1972, he and other guardsmen baited a crowd of local protestors with a song celebrating the shootings of Bloody Sunday in the city earlier that year.[246]

Right Flank thought they had a reasonably good idea of names of the IRA men most likely to have shot Guardsman Lockhart. Alleged IRA Volunteers, John 'Gurky' Gallagher, James 'Yinty' Coyle and possibly

---

242 Interview with Scots Guards Soldier 17 (NCO), November 2013.
243 TNA: WO 305/4272 2nd Battalion Scots Guards, Operational record of battalion net communications, August 1972.
244 Interview with Scots Guards Soldier 19 (Officer), December 2014.
245 Interview with Scots Guards Soldier 13 (Officer), December 2014.
246 'Soldiers Sang "We Shot 13 More Than You", Court Told', *Derry Journal*, November 7, 1972.

William McGuinness, had been seen in the area where the single shot was fired, on the corner of Quarry Street and Lecky Road.[247] Battalion HQ, meanwhile, were convinced that Martin McGuinness had been the sniper who killed Lockhart, 'We thought he shot George Lockhart. We were told afterwards we missed him by around 50 seconds. We had a very good follow-up. Martin McGuinness was very much [the CO's] opposite number! To this day I believe that he shot one of our guardsmen.'[248]

Local Republicans were quick to complain about the Scots Guards' 'good follow-up':

An hour after a British soldier had been shot by a sniper in Lecky Street, a hoard of Scotch soldiers screaming obscenities, invaded the streets, pushing the people in from their doors and not allowing them out of shops; which were full of busy Saturday evening shoppers. They even began a house-to-house search of the area, shouting that the district was full of 'fucking Fenian gunmen'. The district was sealed off for four hours. Some people were beaten up. 'Needless to say, the British Army made it quite clear that they regarded the people as a lot of Fenian bastards and Irish pigs, and promised to be back, "to take it out on them".'[249]

The tone of the article is predictably hostile. But some of the basic details are indisputable; Right Flank did indeed seal off the area, searching 62 houses. And relations, as soldiers agree, between the Scots Guards and the people of the Brandywell had reached a new low.[250]

As Guardsman George Lockhart lay dying in the Royal Victoria Hospital in Belfast, Right Flank decided to 'give some back' to the people of the Brandywell. At 06.00 on the morning of September 25, local political activist, Ivan Cooper, called 2 Scots Guards Battalion

247 TNA: WO 305/4273 Intsum, 2nd Battalion, Scots Guards, September 25–October 1, 1972.
248 Interview with Scots Guards Soldier 13 (Officer), December 2014.
249 'British Army Pogrom in Brandywell', *Volunteer: Voice of Republican Derry*, October 1972.
250 Adjutant's Diary, 2nd Battalion, Scots Guards, 1971–1972.

Headquarters to complain about a Saracen dragging a piece of tin around the Brandywell.[251] Later that day an angry crowd assembled at bridge camp (Right Flank's HQ):

> [W]ith a REP [representative] from every st [street] in the Brandywell. They said martial law had been declared in the Brandywell. Called the Saracen 'the tank' and that it had been towing 6 metres of corrugated iron for 2 and half hours this morning at 30 miles per hour. Children get no sleep and in addition soldiers were swearing at them.[252]

Republican activists took full advantage of the further deterioration in relations between the 2 Scots Guards and the people of the Brandywell. The *Derry Volunteer* wrote:

> The retaliation [after the death of Lockhart] ... took the form of midnight patrols kicking doors, ringing door bells, while a Saracen armoured car trailing corrugated sheeting drove around the streets. The Army patrols next day went about shouting that the 'Irish pigs did not get much sleep last night'. Others sealed off the area and began house-to-house search operations. This was as much as the people could stand and men, women and children came out and sat down on the street in protest. A chorus of jeering from the British soldiers was answered by the younger element with a hail of stones. The British replied with baton charges ... That night the windows of an old age pensioner were broken and a 'Bloody Sunday' memorial cross and other articles were stolen. Many residents woke in the morning to find slogans scrolled 'Fucking Irish Pigs', 'Fenian Bastards – we will get you', and a large slogan on Lone Moor Road, 'Fuck the Pope'.[253]

251 TNA: WO 305/4273 Commander's Diary of 2nd Battalion, Scots Guards, August 31, 1972–September 30, 1972.
252 TNA: WO 305/4272 2nd Battalion Scots Guards, Operational record of battalion net communications, August 1972.
253 'British Army Pogrom in Brandywell', *Volunteer: Voice of Republican Derry*, October 1972.

Nationalist leader, Eddie McAteer, also condemned the actions of Right Flank in the Brandywell: 'I have been shocked at the reports of the Glasgow Rangers' language and general Catholic-baiting behaviour of British troops in the search of the Brandywell area … I just wish that the old dears at Darlington [Whitelaw-brokered Unionist–Nationalist power-sharing negotiations] would put down their tea cups and face the crude realities of Britain's last colonial war.'[254] The local civil rights association also reported allegations of harassment by Right Flank in Brandywell at the end of September:

> They [the Scots Guards] drive along the footpaths and the people have to run for their lives. When the soldiers see that nobody takes them on they circle the estate and try to get the young lads going. The colonel of this regiment said that he wanted to have good relations with the people of this area … We say to you now colonel and to you Willie Whitelaw, control your troops, investigate these incidents and publish the facts.[255]

One Right Flank officer acknowledged that he knew what was going on but that he tactfully went to bed on the nights in question. He described how Right Flank Guardsmen painted 'Up Rangers' and other offensive slogans on pieces of corrugated iron and hung these from their vehicles and then drove around the Brandywell 'to piss off' the locals. This led to three days of rioting, which, in the view of the officer, was no bad thing – guardsmen were able to let off some steam.[256]

The response from battalion HQ was one of surprise and confusion. They didn't know which story to believe and presumed that the complaints were exaggerated. Meanwhile, the officers and NCOs of Right Flank were not going to tell them otherwise.[257] Despite the ramped-up atmosphere after the death of Lockhart, this was not the first time that graffiti on Saracens and other vehicles had been used to antagonise the

254 'Tension as Army Seals Off Derry Streets', *Derry Journal*, September 26, 1972.

255 '"Continuous Harassment" at Shantallow, CRA Says', *Derry Journal*, October 13, 1972.

256 Interview with Scots Guards Soldier 18 (Officer), June 2013.

257 Interview with Scots Guards Soldier 18 (Officer), June 2013.

local population. On August 6, 1972, Brigade Headquarters sent the following message to 2 Scots Guards and other units: 'All graffiti and soldier inspired writings to be taken off all Saracens.'[258] The communication by graffiti or baiting very much went both ways; Republicans had been quick to mock the death of Van Beck and other soldiers.

On September 22, Guardsman Fee was badly wounded by a sniper in Deanery Street.[259] Forty minutes later, a G Company patrol was also shot at, after which a quick follow-up saw the arrest of Charlie McSheffrey and Brian Ward at a house in Durra Street. The soldiers succeeded in recovering an Armalite rifle and transferring the two men to RUC Victoria Station, while being harassed by a small crowd of local men who threw stones and bottles at the patrol. 2 Scots Guards believed that McSheffrey was a senior member of the Derry IRA. An internee, he had been released by William Whitelaw following an appeal by his wife – to the considerable annoyance of the Army.[260] On the night of their arrest by 2 Scots Guards, at approximately 04.00, McSheffrey and Ward alleged that they received a visit from the G Company arresting soldiers at the Strand Road RUC Station, where they were being detained. McSheffrey gave his version of what occurred:

> I was made to stand in the corner with my hands on my head. A soldier then hit me under the throat with his fist. I fell to the floor He then put his hands around my neck and nearly choked me. I thought I was going to pass out. I was then dragged to another corner by the neck and all three soldiers started to kick and punch me. After about 15 minutes I was made to stand in the corner with a blanket over my head. I was made to stand like that for about one hour. All the time I could hardly breath because of a pain in my chest. The next day I asked to see a doctor but it wasn't until my wife came to see me at 7 pm that I asked her to get my own doctor who sent me to hospital for an x-ray.[261]

258 TNA: WO 305/4272 2nd Battalion Scots Guards, Operational record of battalion net communications, August 1972.
259 Adjutant's Diary, 2nd Battalion, Scots Guards, 1971–1972.
260 Adjutant's Diary, 2nd Battalion, Scots Guards, 1971–1972.
261 'Derry Remand Prisoners – "We Were Brutally Ill-treated by Army"', *Derry Journal*, October 13, 1972.

Brian Ward alleged similar treatment but added another detail, that one of the soldiers told him that 'his cousin had been blown up in Crossmaglen by us bastards'.[262] Local Sinn Féin representatives later reported that the doctor who treated McSheffrey complained to the Army and to the RUC. 'Following a strong protest made to Inspector Frank Lagan of the RUC and to British Army officers, an assurance was made that no military personnel would be allowed near McSheffrey during the period he would be at the RUC barracks in Strand road.'[263]

The end of 2 Scots Guards tour brought a welcome last day 'bonus' for the soldiers: two would-be IRA bomb-makers, John Brady and James Carr, were killed. At 11.40 on November 28, 1972, a G Company patrol was passing a house along Meenan Drive when it suddenly exploded. The soldiers temporarily lost their hearing; when the dust finally cleared they saw that the house had completely disappeared. Nothing but rubble and strewn body parts remained.[264] Colonel Boam went to view the damage and couldn't resist walking back through the area.[265] It was revenge, of a sort.

The Scots Guards and West Belfast

Only occasionally did soldiers have the satisfaction of arresting the men they strongly believed had killed their comrades. At 16.20 on October 4, 1971, a house at 240 Cupar Street in Ballymurphy was destroyed by a bomb of 70–100 lb that had been placed in a Butcher's shop next door. The house at 240 Cupar Street was an OP for 1 Scots Guards. One guardsman was killed: Guardsman Brian Hall, who lay trapped beneath the rubble for an hour and a half and died from the inhalation of carbon monoxide fumes.[266] Several other guardsmen were badly wounded – Lance Sergeant Whittle lost his right eye. An NCO described the explosion and the immediate, chaotic aftermath:

262 'Derry Remand Prisoners – "We Were Brutally Ill-treated by Army"', *Derry Journal*, October 13, 1972.

263 'Derry Man Beaten up by British Soldiers', *Volunteer: Voice of Republican Derry*, November 1972.

264 Interview with Scots Guards Soldier 11 (Officer), December 2013.

265 Interview with Scots Guards Soldier 13 (Officer), December 2014.

266 'Fumes Killed Soldier After Explosion', *Fermanagh News*, August 26, 1972.

We were in one of these four-man patrols; we were heading towards it, when the thing went up. And, like, if you are caught in an explosion, things move in slow motion, as you get thrown up in the air and come down. We found this guy [Guardsman Brian Braun] – his legs were on fire. He was burning. His legs were really bad. So we managed to put it out. We put water on his legs.[267]

The same NCO was also on the scene during another explosion at an OP located in a house, 217 Springfield Road, at 12.30 on October 30, 1971. Two men, believed to be bricklayers, went into the house next door, claiming that that they had to block up the windows.[268] The 'brickies' were searched but succeeded in concealing their explosives. Guardsman Norman Booth, a cook attached to 1 Platoon, Right Flank, 1 Scots Guards, was killed immediately:

Wee laddie, I had just been speaking to him. I walked upstairs. Up it went. And when I went downstairs, he was lying there and he was dead. He looked fine, just full of dust. I grabbed an arm – we got an arm each – and I put my hand around his head and, well, the concussion had just blown his head in. A lovely wee guy, do anything for you, talking to him five minutes earlier.[269]

Some of the Scots Guards soldiers were angry at the vulnerability of such OPs, referring to them as 'death houses'.[270] They also believed that Official IRA senior Volunteers Eamon 'Hatchet' Kerr and Jim Sullivan were responsible. The NCO who witnessed both incidents had the satisfaction of arresting Sullivan on a street just off the Springfield Road later in the tour. 'We knew they were tooled up. So I got my lad Ferguson to search him. He didn't find anything. So I searched him myself and there was a Luger [pistol]. We got him for possession.'[271]

Problems with discipline also beset 1 Scots Guards. A platoon sergeant recalled how one of his section commanders had beaten up a local man,

---

267 Interview with Scots Guards Soldier 4 (NCO), November 2013.
268 Interview with Scots Guards Soldier 4 (NCO), November 2013.
269 Interview with Scots Guards Soldier 4 (NCO), November 2013.
270 Interview with Scots Guards Soldier 1 (Officer), May 2014.
271 Interview with Scots Guards Soldier 4 (NCO), November 2013.

182

an event of which he had no knowledge until contacted by another unit.[272] According to the officers and NCOs from 1 Scots Guards that were interviewed, the battalion was normally very firm about clamping down on such behaviour if it could be proved beyond doubt to have taken place. 'There were some who got above their station. Cowboys who wanted to have a go at somebody ... One guy was taken to Springfield Road, held for two days and then sent back to Britain. They were really a problem. If you got a clown like that, it can affect the whole company.'[273] Criminal charges did not necessarily follow; the soldier was normally sent home and discharged from the regiment at the first available opportunity.[274]

Local man Thomas Sinclair later claimed that he was assaulted, together with his friend Mick Murphy, by soldiers from 1 Scots Guards when they went to buy beer in Ballymurphy. He was knocked unconscious and woke up in the Vere Foster School, HQ of Right Flank, 1 Scots Guards. Upon regaining consciousness, he alleged that he was beaten up again. Sinclair's wife later enlisted the help of the warden of the Crumlin Road prison to make a complaint.[275]

Another West Belfast man, George Burt, also made allegations of mistreatment by 1 Scots Guards. On December 11 1971, Burt was arrested following an alleged shoot-out with soldiers. He was treated in the Royal Victoria Hospital, where he said that soldiers ordered the doctors and nurses out of his room and then proceeded to beat him up. Burt claimed that the soldiers kept asking him about whether he had shot a soldier on St James' Street, a possible reference to Guardsman Paul Nicholls who was shot dead by a sniper on November 27, 1971, at St James's Crescent in West Belfast.[276]

Some reports of abuse were dismissed out of hand, particularly because they came, not from the police, but from the civil rights association or others seen to be close to the Republican movement. A Northern Irish Minister of State, Peter Mills, believed that such complaints were part of, 'a Republican/IRA campaign to denigrate the Army or police in NI ... launched by Fr. [Denis] Faul.'[277] Under difficult operational

272 Interview with Scots Guards Soldier 16 (NCO), January 2014.
273 Interview with Scots Guards Soldier 16 (NCO), January 2014.
274 Interview with Scots Guards Soldier 16 (NCO), January 2014.
275 PRONI: CJ 4/241 Denis Faul Complaints of Brutality against Troops/RUC.
276 PRONI: CJ 4/241 Faul Complaints.
277 PRONI: CJ 4/241 Faul Complaints.

circumstances, many conscientious Scots Guards officers and senior NCOs did try to investigate such allegations. But they could be met by a wall of silence from the group of guardsmen believed to have been involved in an incident: 'NTR [Nothing to Report] was a very frequent report if such an event happened.'[278]

The Argylls in South Armagh: The Death of Edmund Woolsey

One Argyll officer believed that his battalion began to 'get personal' in Northern Ireland after taking a number of casualties in September 1972: 'The soldiers would have been cross about that and there would have been a bite to their business afterwards.'[279] A soldier from B Company described in an interview how the Argylls had found an abandoned car on a road near Crossmaglen, but did not investigate further. When a man returned to collect the car, he was 'blown to bits'. The Argylls who arrived on the scene saw an opportunity for further retribution. Having found the man's feet some distance from the explosion, they picked them up and tied them to the front of a Saracen armoured personnel carrier. They then placed a sign above the man's limbs that read, 'Here's one who won't run away'.[280]

There was only one such explosion near Crossmaglen during the Argylls' 1972 tour. Edmund Woolsey, the 32-year-old owner of the Ulster Hotel in Warrenpoint, was killed when a bomb went off as he opened the door of a car near Crossmaglen. Woolsey was alleged to have had contacts with the Official IRA in South Down and across the border in County Louth; it was also later alleged that 'dark forces' working for the British State deliberately targeted Woolsey.[281] However, there is some confusion in the narrative – the Argyll soldier interviewed said that the car belonged to a 'known IRA man' who was later killed in the explosion, and that the Argylls had allowed him to approach the car knowing that it was booby-trapped.[282] But Woolsey did not own the car: he was merely accompanying two friends, Michael O'Reilly and Jack Tinnelly, to recover the car, a Ford

278 Interview with Scots Guards Soldier 16 (NCO), January 2014.
279 Interview with Argyll Soldier 5 (Officer), May 2014.
280 Interview with Argyll Soldier 20 (Private Soldier), April 2014.
281 B. Hanley and S. Millar, *The Lost Revolution: The Story of the Official IRA and the Workers' Party* (London: Penguin, 2010), 185.
282 Interview with Argyll Soldier 20 (Private Soldier), April 2014.

Cortina 1600E, for another Warrenpoint man and a friend of the group, Tim Morgan.[283] Morgan was closely linked with Official Sinn Féin (the political wing of the OIRA) and was very active in Republican circles in South Down.[284] The car was stolen on the night of September 9 while Morgan, O'Reilly and a group of friends were at a dance at the Derryhale Hotel in Dundalk, a town across the border in the Republic of Ireland. O'Reilly, on behalf of his friend Tim Morgan (and possibly because of Morgan's Republican connections),[285] reported the stolen car to the local Gardaí who, in turn, passed on the description of the vehicle to the RUC in Newry.[286] In the days after the incident, Tim Morgan travelled to Dublin, where he was staying on the day of Edmund Woolsey's death. O'Reilly, Woolsey and Tinnelly took it upon themselves to recover Morgan's car, which the group of friends often used.[287] The OIRA in South Down and South Armagh alleged that Woolsey was 'slain by British Forces in mistake for another person whom they had hoped to lure to the booby-trapped car'; the Officials were probably referring to Tim Morgan.[288]

The events leading up to Woolsey's death occurred as follows: in the days after the dance at Derryhale, Michael O'Reilly told his employer,[289] the owner of an engineering works in Newry, about the theft of Morgan's car and described it to him.[290] At approximately 09.00 on Monday, September 18, 1972, O'Reilly's employer told him that, while driving in

283 'Hotel Owner Dies in Border Booby Trap Explosion', *Newry Reporter*, September 21, 1972.

284 Interview with a former Official Sinn Féin Representative, Dundalk, August 15, 2015; 'Bank Raid – Two Sent for Trial', *Newry Reporter*, May 24, 1973.

285 Incidentally, a man called Tim Morgan was charged with committing a bank robbery in Rostrevor in early 1973. 'Jury Fail to Agree', *Newry Reporter*, July 5, 1973.

286 PRONI: ARM/6/1/1/26/17 Coroner's inquest into death of Edmund Woolsey, March 23, 1973.

287 Interview with a former Official Sinn Féin Representative, Dundalk, August 15, 2015.

288 'British Killed Woolsey', *Irish Independent*, September 23, 1972.

289 Per an agreement between the author and PRONI, the names of individuals not already in the public domain – through newspaper/other media reports – including Mr Michael O'Reilly's employer, the RUC Duty Constable at Forkhill RUC Station on the morning of September 18, 1972, have been omitted.

290 Interview with a former Official Sinn Féin Representative, Dundalk, August 15, 2015.

the South Armagh area the previous day, he had seen the car described by O'Reilly parked on a rural road near Ballsmills.[291] O'Reilly's employer then spoke to the police at Forkhill RUC station. An RUC Constable told him that the car was not in their area of responsibility but that they would contact Crossmaglen RUC station and call Michael O'Reilly back directly.[292] The RUC then investigated further. According to the witness deposition of the Forkhill RUC station duty officer at the coroner's inquest into Edmund Woolsey's death, because there was no RUC presence in Crossmaglen that morning, he had spoken to a soldier – Warrant Officer Alex Muir, the B Company NCO responsible for intelligence – who informed him that the car had been checked out by an Army helicopter and that the owner could now proceed to take it.[293] However, Alex Muir should have known that standard procedure for dealing with a suspected booby-trapped car and declaring it safe to move did not involve merely checking it from the air. Muir later clarified in his inquest witness deposition that 'The procedure for checking whether a vehicle is booby-trapped internally is to have the bonnet and boot blown off by an expert.'[294] The Forkhill RUC constable subsequently rang Michael O'Reilly and confirmed that it was the car he was looking for and that he should ring Crossmaglen RUC station himself prior to travelling to the area.[295] Later the same day, on the afternoon of September 18, Michael O'Reilly telephoned Crossmaglen RUC station from his place of work and spoke to 'a Scotchman',[296] later identified at the inquest as Warrant Officer Alex Muir.[297] As O'Reilly appeared to have some problems making himself understood, his employer later told the inquest that he again intervened on his behalf. Muir also told O'Reilly's employer that a helicopter had checked out the car. According to the employer's statement, he then asked, "'Is there any chance of a bomb or a bobby-trap [sic] in the car?" He told me, "No, the car has been checked out.'"[298]

291 PRONI: ARM/6/1/1/26/17 Woolsey.

292 'Hotel Owner Dies in Border Booby Trap Explosion', *Newry Reporter*.

293 PRONI: ARM/6/1/1/26/17 Woolsey; 'Open Verdict on Hotel Owner', *Newry Reporter*, March 29, 1973.

294 PRONI: ARM/6/1/1/26/17 Woolsey.

295 PRONI: ARM/6/1/1/26/17 Woolsey.

296 'Hotel Owner Dies in Border Booby Trap Explosion', *Newry Reporter*.

297 PRONI: ARM/6/1/1/26/17 Woolsey.

298 PRONI: ARM/6/1/1/26/17 Woolsey.

Another friend of Edmund Woolsey's, Jack Tinnelly, described how, between 17.30 and 17.35 on the evening of Monday, September 18, 1972, he went for a drink in the Ulster Hotel in Warrenpoint and there agreed to accompany his friends Michael O'Reilly and Edmund Woolsey to collect the missing Ford Cortina. Michael O'Reilly later told the *Newry Reporter* that on the way to the Ballsmills/Glassdrumman area of South Armagh, the three men called at the RUC station in Forkhill, where O'Reilly told a constable that he was on his way to collect the car. The constable told him he would accordingly make a log entry at the station. Finding the car at a crossroads near Ballsmills, O'Reilly told the journalist what happened next:

> 'We got out of our own car. We went over and looked inside the car. There did not seem to be anything in it. We opened the boot. There was nothing in it. We did notice that there was a cassette stolen out of the car.' He said Jack Tinnelly was standing between five and ten yards in front of the car. Mr. Woolsey was going to open the driver's door. 'I was standing behind him. As soon as he opened the door all I could remember was a bang and black smoke in front of me. I was blown back. Then Tinnelly shouted, "God it has blown up!"' Mr. O'Reilly said he and Tinnelly then ran down the road and later they saw that the car had disintegrated.[299]

The two survivors also recounted that they had been joking moments before the explosion that the car might be booby-trapped.[300] There was a discussion as to who would open the driver's door. Edmund Woolsey volunteered to do it.[301] The last remark Woolsey made was to tell them that there was a cassette missing.[302] At the inquest one of the two men who accompanied Mr Woolsey went on to describe the aftermath of the explosion:

> We ran down the road maybe fifty yards. Down the road a piece there was people coming out of a house. I shouted to them,

---

299 'Hotel Owner Dies in Border Booby Trap Explosion', *Newry Reporter*.
300 PRONI: ARM/6/1/1/26/17 Woolsey.
301 Interview with a former Official Sinn Féin Representative, Dundalk, August 15, 2015.
302 PRONI: ARM/6/1/1/26/17 Woolsey.

'For Christ's sake come up and give us a bit of help.' They came anyway and some man came over to me and I told him that my mate was opening the car door and she blew up. Him and I walked up towards the car and when we got up to it I could see pieces of debris, but I could see no sign of Edmund. We walked up the side of the road and looked in the drain on my right. This man said, 'That looks like something there.' I looked in and saw this part of the body. There were no clothes on it so I turned and walked away. This chap jumped into the drain and came back to me in a few minutes and he said to me, 'Your friend's dead.'[303]

Prior to submitting his witness account to the inquest, the Argyll NCO responsible for B Company intelligence amended his statement to read, 'I said that the car had been checked out', crossing out the words 'from the air'.[304]

Why would WO Muir tell the RUC and O'Reilly's employer that the car had been checked out, when he knew that the abandoned car was regarded as suspicious and had not been inspected by an ATO? The Argylls may have been happy that a local Republican was killed – it did not matter that Woolsey was suspected of being connected to the Official IRA, which was on ceasefire. But such 'retribution' was probably unplanned; the Argyll private soldier's account somewhat exaggerated. According to an Argyll officer, relying upon written accounts from the time, the Argylls only discovered Woolsey's identity and suspected OIRA links after the explosion. Woolsey did not own the car, he had not borrowed it, and he was not on the Argylls' list of suspected IRA or OIRA activists; more importantly, it was simply chance that he was the first of the three men to open the door of the car.[305] According to the Argyll officer's contemporaneous notes, a foot patrol from Crossmaglen had reported finding the car on September 13, 1972. The patrol conducted a brief but careful examination of the car, but did not touch it, and reported not seeing any wires or anything else suspicious (such as the smell of explosives). There were no RUC constables in Crossmaglen for much of this period and the Argylls had not received any report that the

---

303 PRONI: ARM/6/1/1/26/17 Woolsey.
304 PRONI: ARM/6/1/1/26/17 Woolsey.
305 Interview with Argyll Soldier 14 (Officer), May 2014.

car in question had been reported stolen. According to the officer: 'They wouldn't have gone too close, mind you, or poked around. They would have given it a wide berth. The ATO wasn't called. He would have been called if there was a strong suspicion that it was wired. It would have been pretty low down the league tables of the many suspicious vehicles we were dealing with.'[306]

A helicopter check on the vehicle was completed on the morning of September 18 and nothing suspicious was reported. There is no doubt that an ATO should have been called; the car was located in the middle of an area with a high level of insurgent activity and the IRA was occasionally known to leave such devices in South Armagh (even if most of them were defused or failed to explode). However, the failure to do so is probably more down to a communication failure between B Company, 1 Argylls and the RUC, compounded by a combination of complacency and fatigue on the part of the Argylls. The Argylls were also under pressure: if the car was not a direct threat to their soldiers, they had more immediate things to be doing than securing a vehicle that was potentially left as a 'come on' for an IRA ambush – or so the logic went.[307] If soldiers from B Company in Crossmaglen had found out that the car belonged to or had been stolen from Tim Morgan, a much more active figure in the Official Republican movement than Woolsey, they may also have been less inclined to 'clean up' after what appeared to be potentially one group of Republicans (IRA) targeting another (OIRA). One well-placed Official Sinn Féin representative interviewee believed that it was very possible that the IRA, despite later denial, had stolen Tim Morgan's car, booby-trapped it and used it as a lure for an aborted ambush on an Argyll patrol (stealing an Official Sinn Féin supporter's car may even have been an added 'bonus' for the Provisional IRA).[308]

Brian Hanley and Sam Millar in their book *Lost Revolution* have suggested that more sinister elements, including possibly a link with the British State, might have deliberately conspired to bring about the death of Woolsey because of his links with the OIRA.[309] Based on the evidence presented here, chance, complacency and error seem to be more likely

---

306 Interview with Argyll Soldier 14 (Officer), May 2014.

307 Interview with Argyll Soldier 14 (Officer), May 2014.

308 Interview with a former Official Féin Representative, Dundalk, August 15, 2015.

309 Hanley and Millar, *The Lost Revolution*, 185.

explanations. However, what Edmund Woolsey's death does reveal is a casualness or disregard towards the welfare of the local population. The Argylls were primarily concerned with their own survival; they should have properly considered the risk to the local population. If they, the soldiers, were not to approach the car, neither should any local civilians have been cleared to do so until an ATO had been called. In the aftermath of the explosion local people told the *Newry Reporter* that the car had been in the area for eight days.[310] Unfortunately, the inquest into Edmund Woolsey's death seems to have been conducted in some haste, beginning at 16.30 on Friday, March 23, 1973 and concluding that same day with an 'open' or inconclusive 'verdict' on Woolsey's death. Important questions seem not to have been posed to the Army, which might have revealed some of the errors that led to the explosion.[311]

What about the Argyll interviewee's reference to Edmund Woolsey's legs being used as a sort of trophy? Would the Argylls even have had the opportunity to do such a thing? Half an hour after the explosion, after being attended to by a doctor for minor injuries, Tinnelly and O'Reilly left the Ballsmills area after securing a lift to Warrenpoint. The two men wished to inform Anne Woolsey of her husband's death before she heard it from other sources. Edmund Woolsey's body was taken away by ambulance. Both legs were missing below the knee, according to the ambulance driver and the RUC scene of crime officer.[312] The explosion that killed Edmund Woolsey occurred at approximately 19.00 on September 18, 1972. By the time the RUC Scene of Crime officer responsible for evidence collection arrived from Newry, it was getting dark. Due to the security threat in South Armagh he was unwilling to examine the scene by torchlight and left the area. Returning the next morning at 09.30 he took swabs from the car that later revealed traces of the explosive mix including nitrobenzene. He also reported that 'The method of initiation may have been the courtesy light switch connected

---

310 'Hotel Owner Dies in Border Booby Trap Explosion', *Newry Reporter*.

311 Kenneth Littlejohn, an English criminal and former paratrooper who had some contacts with the Secret Intelligence Service and the Official IRA, later claimed that the car was in his possession for a time prior to being used in the explosion. However, Littlejohn's account is so riddled with factual errors that it is difficult to discern facts from lies and distortion. M. Dillon, *The Dirty War* (London; Arrow, 1991), 95–115.

312 PRONI: ARM/6/1/1/26/17 Woolsey.

to an electrical detonator in intimate contact with a substantial charge of explosive substance placed inside the car'.[313] The constable found fragments of money, which he diligently handed over to Anne Woolsey two months later.[314] The RUC constable also found Edmund Woolsey's 'shattered pair of slip-on brown shoes' 27 yards from the scene of the explosion.[315]

No post-mortem was conducted on Edmund Woolsey's body due to a dispute at the time between pathologists and the government. However, the doctor who examined Mr Woolsey's body in Newry on behalf the RUC found that he had suffered catastrophic, 'multiple blast injuries'. The force of the explosion had propelled Woolsey's body into the roadside drain where he was later found. Given where his shoes were later discovered, 27 yards from his body, and that much of his legs appear not to have been recovered, it is indeed possible that his feet or part of his lower legs could have been separated from the rest of his body by the explosion, removed by Argyll soldiers from the scene before the collection of evidence around mid-morning the following day, when the RUC returned to investigate, having been absent for more than 12 hours.[316] The description of Argyll soldiers using Edmund Woolsey's feet as a trophy of sorts cannot therefore be discounted. Another Argyll interviewee, an officer, also confirmed that shortly after the incident he had heard such an account of soldiers 'mucking about' with Woolsey's legs, which they had found still in his shoes some distance from the explosion.[317] Edmund Woolsey's death occurred at a very difficult time for the Army, and particularly for B Company, 1 Argylls. Procedure and good judgement were clouded by the sheer tempo of operations in rural South Armagh and a hardened, resentful attitude towards the local populace.

The social anthropologist Simon Harrison has concluded that there are no examples of soldiers taking 'trophies' – posing with bodies or collecting body parts – in Northern Ireland. This can be explained, according to Harrison, by the cultural affinity between Britain and

313 PRONI: ARM/6/1/1/26/17 Woolsey.
314 PRONI: ARM/6/1/1/26/17 Woolsey.
315 PRONI: ARM/6/1/1/26/17 Woolsey.
316 PRONI: ARM/6/1/1/26/17 Woolsey.
317 Interview with Argyll Soldier 22 (Officer), March 2015.

Ireland, in contrast to some colonial theatres.[318] There is some evidence – in addition to the account of the taking of Edmund Woolsey's legs – to suggest that Harrison is mistaken: Antony Beevor has written how soldiers from the Royal Artillery, when recovering the body-parts of IRA bombers killed in an 'own goal' explosion, picked up a head and played catch with it.[319] Another Argyll soldier, on a later tour of Belfast, also described how soldiers collected body parts as 'trophies'; one soldier allegedly drilled a hole in a piece of skull he found in a car in which IRA men had been killed so that he could wear it around his neck.[320] Soldiers also claimed to have taken photographs of themselves shaking the hands with the corpse of Patrick McAdorey, an IRA Volunteer suspected of involvement in the murders of three Royal Highland Fusiliers in March 1971.[321] Such 'trophy taking' may have been more infrequent than in colonial conflicts, where there was a lot less public scrutiny and restrictions on violence, but it does appear to have taken place.

Intelligence

A lack of actionable intelligence – 'the most vital element in successful counter-terrorism' – was a constant problem for the Scots Guards and the Argyll and Sutherland Highlanders.[322] 1 Scots Guards made a considerable number of arrests in and around the Ballymurphy/Turf Lodge/ St James' area following the introduction of internment in August 1971; the addresses were occasionally wrong, some of the wanted men were dead: 'There was a lot of misunderstandings as to who was who in the area. We had only two or three RUC officers and they never went out.'[323] Meanwhile, the highly aggressive behaviour of 1 Scots Guards predecessors, 2 PARA, in the Ballymurphy area (culminating in the 'Ballymurphy massacre' between August 9 and 11, 1972; 1 Scots Guards took over responsibility for the area on August 26, 1971) saw relations

---

318 S. Harrison, *Dark Trophies: Hunting and the Enemy Body in Modern War* (New York: Berghahn Books, 2012), 162–163.
319 Beevor, *Inside the British Army*, 276.
320 M. Frankland, *Afterwards* (Dumfries: Glenmill, 2009), 12–13.
321 McCleery, *Operation Demetrius and its Aftermath*, 59.
322 R. English, *Terrorism: How to Respond* (Oxford: Oxford University Press, 2009), 131–133.
323 Interview with Scots Guards Soldier 2 (Officer), June 2014.

between the British Army and the people of West Belfast hit its lowest ebb.[324] Another Army intelligence unit, the Military Reaction Force (MRF), were regarded as errant 'cowboys'.[325]

Soldiers felt exceptionally vulnerable, surrounded by the watching eyes of the local, '100 per cent hostile' population. 'For us it was like a POW camp. Everybody was watching us all the time.'[326] Units lacked 'street-level intelligence' for their patch. Instead of relying upon others, they began to build this themselves, trying to observe 'patterns' in the streets they constantly patrolled. Observation Posts were critical; these were now placed on top of buildings, such as the Rossville Flats in Derry.[327] Soldiers were also allocated particular streets and patches for which they were expected to be the 'intelligence expert', remembering the names of families and studying pictures of wanted men who lived or operated in their area.[328] Left Flank, 2 Scots Guards also introduced 'squirrel patrols' in Londonderry. These were four-man teams led by a Corporal/Lance Sergeant and were outside the normal patrolling patterns. The intent was simple: 'They would just hang about, talk to as many people as possible and try to pick up information. They were not a huge success but we did get to know people and begin to understand the neighbourhood, who lived there, associations etc.'[329] 2 Scots Guards, in particular, watched for 'pressure points', pieces of information that would allow them possibly to turn IRA Volunteers into informers. An example of such information included the gathering of information on the movements of Bernadette Canning, the future wife of Martin McGuinness. Infidelity (not discovered in the case of Bernadette Canning) was a potential weapon.[330] Sometimes, however, battalions were passed misleading information that was designed to lure them into an ambush. In the case of 2 Scots Guards in Londonderry,

---

324 For an account of the Parachute Regiment during this period, see A. Sanders, 'Principles of Minimum Force and the Parachute Regiment in Northern Ireland, 1969–1972', *Journal of Strategic Studies* (2016).

325 Interview with Scots Guards Soldier 11 (Officer), December 2013.

326 Interview with Scots Guards Soldier 1 (Officer), May 2014.

327 Interview with Scots Guards Soldier 14 (Officer), May 2014.

328 Interview with Scots Guards Soldier 15 (Officer), May 2014.

329 Interview with Scots Guards Soldier 22 (Officer), May 2014.

330 TNA: WO 305/4273 Commander's Diary of 2nd Battalion, Scots Guards, August 31, 1972–September 30, 1972.

sources of such questionable information included ex-internee, Charlie McSheffrey, a local Republican who was later arrested by the battalion after a failed attack. In the days after their arrival, McSheffrey warned 2 Scots Guards that there were mines and booby-traps 'in the area south of Creggan Street and west of Little Diamond'. Such information may have been an attempt to slow down the advance on the morning of Motorman.[331]

The Tide Turns Against the IRA

By late 1972, the Army observed that the IRA was its best recruiting sergeant for informers; a trickle of tip-offs about IRA plans grew into a steady flow of actionable intelligence. IRA tactics increasingly outraged local sentiment: the punishment shootings and beatings, the tarring and feathering of local women and the blowing up of popular local amenities such as shops and restaurants. Towards the end of 1972, a weekly intelligence summary for 2 Scots Guards in Londonderry noted that, 'The residents of the north end of Stanleys Walk have openly told patrols they are fed up with Barney McFadden, and that since he has been "king of the gasworks" he has done nothing but cause trouble.'[332] After the Argylls helped to put out a fire started by the IRA in a school in County Armagh they were tipped off about a nearby booby trap by locals normally considered hostile to the Army (targeting a local school was immature and politically disastrous).[333] In the aftermath of an IRA bomb that exploded prematurely at the Newry customs station, killing three IRA Volunteers and six local men, including popular customs officials, the local civil rights association launched a 'Say No to the Provos campaign'. This bombing had been particularly horrific; a newspaper report of the time described the devastating aftermath of the explosion:

> The bodies of the dead were severely mutilated and firemen and ambulance crew had the gruesome task of picking up limbs and broken skulls, collecting the remains of the dead in plastic bags.

331 TNA: WO 305/4273 Intsum, 2nd Battalion, Scots Guards, September 25–October 1, 1972.
332 TNA: WO 305/4273 Intsum, 2nd Battalion, Scots Guards, September 25–October 1, 1972.
333 'Argylls Come Under Fire', *Oban Times*, August 17, 1972.

Blood covered a large portion of the main hallway and offices and pieces of flesh were found embedded in the ceiling. For those involved in the rescue operations it was a sickening sight.[334]

Soldiers from Support Company, 1 Argylls, were involved in recovering bodies and sealing off the area. The number killed in the explosion was originally listed as eight, later confirmed as nine; a single body part and torn driving licence confirmed that a third IRA bomber, Patrick Hughes, had also died, in addition to Oliver Plunkett Rowntree and Noel Madden.[335] The local IRA battalion commanding officer condemned those who questioned their tactics. They were, he said, 'the Irish Quislings of this generation … get the hell out our country'.[336]

Given the occasional examples of excessive violence and the generally acrimonious relationship between the Army and the Catholic population in 1972, it took extreme IRA insensitivity to push a sizeable number of local people in nominally 'green' areas into passing information to the military. Even in Londonderry, where relations between the Army and the inhabitants of Derry had reached a nadir, 2 Scots Guards now made most of their limited weapons finds because of local tip-offs.[337] In 1971, the situation for 1 Scots Guards was more challenging; the IRA had yet to lose the goodwill, or passive ambivalence, of much of the local population. Weapons finds often occurred due to 'hunch' searches and the intense observation of the movements of local inhabitants rather than specific intelligence. By the end of 1972, the IRA's campaign was seriously out of step with Catholic mainstream opinion in the urban areas of Northern Ireland. The IRA had contrived to squander the enormous opportunity of internment and the Bloody Sunday murders.[338]

334 'Slaughter – Eight Die in IRA Bomb Outrage', *Newry Reporter*, August 24, 1972.
335 'Open Verdict on Nine who Died in Customs Station Bomb Horror', *Newry Reporter*, February 15, 1973.
336 'CRA Calls for End of Bombing', *Fermanagh News*, August 26, 1972; 'Bomb Atrocity – Funerals of the Victims', *Newry Reporter*, August 31, 1972.
337 TNA: WO 305/4274 2nd Battalion Scots Guards, Operational record of brigade net communications, November 1972.
338 See, for example, E. McCann's account from this time of the revulsion felt by many Catholics towards the IRA's killing of civilians. McCann, *War and an Irish Town*, 105.

Misguided Tactics and the Persistent Problem of South Armagh

Armagh proved the hardest nut to crack in the intelligence game: 3 Brigade had almost no informants in South Armagh, apart from one or two beleaguered Protestant farmers, among an overwhelming Catholic majority; these Protestants were not in the 'information cycle'.[339] Visits to Crossmaglen and the border by 3 Brigade HQ were relatively infrequent, with one exception. Colonel Joe Starling, second-in-command of 3 Brigade, would disregard the Argylls' warnings and their careful, painstaking approach to clearing the roads of South Armagh of IEDs: 'You would suddenly find Joe Starling driving up the middle of all of this, right through south Armagh and arriving at battalion headquarters.'[340] The former Parachute Regiment officer was keenly interested in hearing details of Argyll fire fights but he had nothing to offer in terms of intelligence. The Argylls also had a problem in that the responsible military intelligence officer for the area was exceptionally rank-conscious and wanted only to pass on information to the commanding officer of the Argylls rather than the responsible intelligence officer.[341] The situation was steadily deteriorating in the rural areas along the border, most gravely in Armagh, West Tyrone (particularly in the heavily bombed town of Strabane) and South Fermanagh; the Argylls were running to stand still. The IRA was also increasing its bomb-making capabilities in the border region during 1972.[342]

Intelligence was much better in South Down, particularly in the town of Newry, where some IRA Volunteers had been correctly identified. The RUC in Newry were led by competent senior officers, sensitive to local opinion and concerns and broadly accepted by most of the Catholic community.[343] However, the Argylls could quickly whip up resentment through a less than judicious application of the law, such as when D Company confiscated civil rights literature, a tricolour and a song-book about Kevin Barry (a young man executed for his part in the IRA insurgency of 1919–1921) from a local woman on the basis that these were seditious materials.[344]

339 Interview with Argyll Soldier 16 (Officer), May 2014.
340 Interview with Argyll Soldier 13 (Officer), December 2014.
341 Interview with Argyll Soldier 17 (Officer), May 2014.
342 Interview with Argyll Soldier 17 (Officer), May 2014.
343 RSDGA: Mitchell, 'An Officer's Diary'.
344 'Lady Claims Theft by Army', *Mourne Observer*, October 10, 1972.

The Argylls also took advantage of Operation Motorman to crack down heavily on areas believed to harbour Republicans. Some locals saw their actions as collective punishment, an excuse to vent aggression. Civil rights activists in Castlewellan and Hilltown, County Down, reported what they alleged to have occurred; local people were assembled outside their houses and made to stand with their legs spread, hands outstretched against the wall. Soldiers swore at them and one 'Scottish soldier' allegedly told the residents of one area that they were being targeted because they were members of 'an inferior race'.[345] A few soldiers tied residents' hands and then made them lie face down on the street, allegations that resemble the Argylls' frequent treatment of suspects in Aden, but seldom seen in Northern Ireland. (The accounts sound somewhat similar to 'Portcullis' tactics – whole areas sealed off, everybody searched while lying either prone on the ground or with their legs spread, hands against the wall.) The soldiers involved in the search of Hilltown and Castlewellan were reportedly from D Company, 1 Argylls.[346]

Some abuse or excessive violence by 1 Argylls of the local population during their tour in 1972 did take place, as seen earlier, and this was enough for potentially exaggerated accounts of Army violence to be believed. Reports of such incidents had a negative effect upon the willingness of local people to cooperate with the Army. Misguided 'hearts and minds' initiatives also backfired: on August 2, 1972, the Argylls give local children a lift to school in their Saracen and Humber Pig[347] vehicles from the Derrybeg estate in Newry. They were quickly accused of using children as human shields, a charge angrily denied and ridiculed by the Argylls, but more plausible to a suspicious local population that knew that Army vehicles were frequently targeted by the IRA using IEDs.[348] Such incidents would probably have adversely affected the flow of intelligence volunteered by the local population to the RUC and the Army.

---

345 'Motorman in East Down: A Survey by the Association for Legal Justice and Castlewellan Citizens' Advice Centre' (undated), a pamphlet contained in a letter sent to Father Denis Faul by Pauline Foley dated November 10, 1972, included as part of the Cardinal Conway Papers, Cardinal O'Fiaich Library, Armagh. See also BBC News, 'Return to Aden – without Mad Mitch'.
346 Interview with Argyll Soldier 30 (Officer), November 2016.
347 FV1611A Humber Pig Mk 2.
348 'Jocks Clear the "No Go" areas and People Begin to Talk', *Oban Times*, August 10, 1972.

Lessons Not Learned

Some Argyll interviewees blamed their predecessors, the Duke of Wellington's Regiment, for the negligible amount of intelligence they received upon their arrival in Crossmaglen. Moreover, the training in Kent was also primarily aimed at preparing soldiers for operations in urban areas such as West Belfast. Although 1 Argylls also spent a few days in May 1972 at the Stanford training range in Norfolk, sharpening their rural patrolling skills, the IRA campaign in South Armagh was just beginning to escalate and Army 'lessons learned' and simulations on combating IRA tactics in the hilly terrain of the border counties were relatively limited.[349] The Argylls were also not adequately briefed on IRA tactics in the area, including the use of decoy incidents and roadblocks. They learned the hard way.

First Battalion, the Royal Hampshire Regiment, which replaced the Argylls in RUC H Division, also failed to learn from their predecessors, particularly from the deaths of Captain Bill Watson and Colour Sergeant Jimmy Struthers. An NCO from the Hampshire Regiment died in almost identical circumstances to Watson and Struthers in South Armagh:

> The night before [a message] on the confidential phone, and this message was taken by Captain Tim Glass, the Battalion Operations Officer, gave us some vague directions to an isolated outhouse building. And this message was passed down to the effect that there were some strange movements or suspicious circumstances. And on reflection of course this was 'a come on'. This message was related to the platoon in Forkhill with the instructions that the platoon should observe the building but go nowhere near it. Either that message wasn't properly passed or the Corporal [Section Commander Corporal Leahy] decided he should do more than his brief, went up to it with his section, found it locked and booted in the door with the effect that a booby-trap was set and Corporal Leahy suffered extremely damaging injuries to his face and body and died two or three days later.[350]

349 Interview with Argyll Soldier 5 (Officer), May 2014.
350 IWM: 13915 Audio Recording – Roger Coleman, Hampshires, Service in Northern Ireland.

Major Peter Morton of 3 PARA, would later complain of the same knowledge/intelligence deficit when his company arrived in South Armagh for a four-month tour in 1973, highlighting once again the apparent difficulty of maintaining operational knowledge; the Parachute Regiment does not seem to have had the opportunity to learn from the Argylls and the Hampshire Regiment's experiences:

> Although the Company had lots of Belfast experience it was almost totally unprepared for the rural area of South Armagh ... Regrettably but inevitably we learnt the hard way. Radio-controlled and electrically detonated landmines occurred with alarming frequency – often several in one day. Four of my soldiers were killed ... I felt their deaths very personally because I knew that with better training and less 'gung-ho' attitude at least some of those men would be alive today.[351]

The IRA in South Armagh and East Tyrone was a learning organisation. For example, IRA Volunteers observed that soldiers always came back to search for spent cartridges after a fire fight. When A Company did this after an incident in East Tyrone, the IRA rigged a mine among the cartridges. But for a cow becoming the unintended victim of the device, the IRA would most likely have inflicted more Argyll casualties.[352] An IRA Volunteer in Crossmaglen later reflected how they would think up different 'ruse' incidents, burning down a school, leaving a bomb in a car, so that they could then 'score a hit':

> There'd be a phone call or a car would drive into the street and one of the boys would say: right, there's a Brit patrol coming out of Crossmaglen heading down the Monog road ... Immediately, the operations officer would say: 'Look, I think they are heading there. Let's get there before them and have a reception committee meeting.' It was a war of wits.[353]

In South Armagh, and along much of the border, the IRA had the initiative, and they had intelligence. In such trying circumstances one

---

351 P. Morton, *Emergency* Tour, 2.
352 'Cow Killed by Bomb Meant for Soldiers', *Belfast Newsletter*, August 17, 1972.
353 Harnden, *Bandit Country*, 46–47.

Argyll officer opined that the best they could hope for was a 'score draw' – until the Army slowly mustered the resources and knowledge to hit back.[354]

Combat and Cohesion

Discipline

Soldiers often enjoy debating whether a good garrison soldier – neat, well-drilled, punctual – translates into a good combat soldier, or whether the 'bad boys' of peacetime make the best fighters during wartime.[355] Colonel Tony Boam of 2 Scots Guards had no doubts about where he stood on the matter. Writing to his soldiers in the days after assuming command for the Bogside, Boam began by telling them that, 'As guardsmen I believe that we start with a considerable advantage over most units. Our general bearing, smartness, behaviour, discipline and good manners are all qualities which impress the public.'[356] Bad drill, bad dress infected operational behaviour, including fire discipline. The Scots Guards officer and NCO hierarchy were notoriously tough when it came to dress discipline, an overbearing attitude that was occasionally resented by young guardsmen, but mostly accepted. Guardsmen liked to look smart, even on operations; it was part of the social image they had learned to project.[357] For Lieutenant Colonel Tony Boam, commanding officer to 2nd Battalion, Scots Guards, looking smart was a way of reassuring the local populace that they were the efficient representatives of law and order. A smart bearing discouraged the 'opposition' from having a go; if you did everything else efficiently, then you were also likely to kill efficiently.[358]

Unlike other units, such as the Parachute Regiment, Boam was not looking for a fight, especially against crowds of young, angry adolescents who were only a few steps away from being radicalised and joining

354 Interview with Argyll Soldier 15 (Officer), December 2013.
355 S. Junger, *War* (London: Fourth Estate, 2010), 14–15.
356 TNA WO: 205/4273 Notice from Lieutenant Colonel Tony Boam, commanding officer to 2nd Battalion, Scots Guards, on taking over operational control of the Bogside area of Londonderry, September 5, 1972.
357 Interview with Scots Guards Soldier 8 (Officer), March 2013.
358 Interview with Scots Guards Soldier 19 (Officer), December 2014.

the IRA if they got an unnecessary beating from a British soldier. On September 17, 1972, he pulled his troops back during a march by a crowd 300-strong, some of whom were carrying tricolour flags and improvised weapons such as bicycle chains, and wearing masks. After half an hour, with no punitive action forthcoming from the Army, the now bored crowd dispersed, to the considerable irritation of some of Boam's junior officers who wanted to 'get stuck in'.[359] Boam was instilling a valuable lesson: restraint – not stooping to unnecessary street brawls, careful observation and the efficient and highly selective use of violence, were the most valuable weapons the Army had in Northern Ireland. The 2 Scots Guards CO knew that local people were watching and listening; they were a captive audience, locked between insurgent and counter-insurgent, but they could actively support either side or at least not offer assistance. Boam's command style was not perfect – 2 Scots Guards made mistakes – but he was smarter than some. Northern Ireland Minister, Peter Mills, noted a similar, very selective approach to the use of force when he met Boam while 2 Scots Guards were on operations in Belfast at the beginning of 1974. Boam's strategy, he concluded, was one of 'winning the people over rather than having a "damn good kill" … he does not want the public to be influenced by genuine reports of Army harassment.'[360] The fact that 2 Scots Guards soldiers did harass the residents of the Brandywell in September 1972 is perhaps evidence of the complexity of command rather than any ill-intention on Colonel Boam's part.

Scots Guards officers and NCOs constantly reminded guardsmen of the need for exceptional fire discipline in Northern Ireland. On no account were soldiers to shoot without first locating a firing point. In urban areas, this was exceptionally difficult:

When you did come under fire it was just 'crack crack' from some flats a long way away. And if you didn't have a target you couldn't

359 TNA: WO 305/4273 Commander's Diary of 2nd Battalion, Scots Guards, August 31, 1972–September 30, 1972.
360 PRONI: CJ 4/668 Matters concerning the Security Forces, June 1973–January 31, 1974, Northern Ireland Office Memorandum prepared by Jean White for Jonathan Margetts, Permanent Secretary to Peter Mills, Minister of State for Northern Ireland, 'Mr. Mills' visit to the Scots Guards on 24 January 1974', dated January 29, 1974.

return fire … if you did fire back – the SLRs, they go straight through a block of flats anyway – and so you kill some granny. They would have got huge propaganda out of that.[361]

An example of good 1 Scots Guards fire discipline during the 1971 Belfast tour was heard during the inquest into the death of an 18-month-old baby girl, Angela Gallagher, at the junction between Iveagh Street and the Falls Road on September 3, 1971. Despite coming under fire from an IRA unit – four or five shots were fired in total – the patrol commander, a Lance Corporal, told his men not to shoot back as they were unable to locate a firing point. A ricochet from an IRA bullet killed Angela Gallagher, who was playing with her sisters on a nearby street. A Provisional Sinn Féin leader later described Angela Gallagher's death as 'one of the hazards of urban guerrilla warfare'.[362] The Scots Guards may not have 'got even' – the Army killed very few IRA gunmen even in this most violent of periods – but, by and large, they kept their discipline.

There were occasional exceptions to the good fire discipline of the Scots Guards: 1 Scots Guards in 1971 came under fire on a daily basis – sniping attacks were a constant feature of patrolling in West Belfast in the months after the introduction of internment. As the days wore on the frustration of not returning fire became almost intolerable. A guardsman who served in 1 Scots Guards recalled that, on one of his last patrols in Belfast in 1971, an NCO told him to take a 600 yards shot at a block of flats in the dark, the general area in which the NCO believed a sniper was operating.[363] Tired and frustrated, with a long list of casualties, 1 Scots Guards were not immune to 'last week syndrome'. Bishop Edward Daly recalled that the last week of every battalion's tour in the early was a dangerous time. According to Daly, soldiers wanted 'to settle the score. In the last week of every tour they took out their aggression. People were very scared of each battalion in its last week.'[364] A senior RUC officer also recalled being concerned about 'last week syndrome' on the part of rotating battalions in the early 1970s; everybody, particularly the local residents and the police, was on edge.[365]

361 Interview with Scots Guards Soldier 7 (Guardsman), November 2013.
362 McKittrick et al., *Lost Lives*, 96–97.
363 Interview with Scots Guards Soldier 7 (Guardsman), October 2014.
364 Interview with Bishop Emeritus Edward Daly, Derry, May 14, 2014.
365 Interview with RUC Officer 6, Belfast, November 2015.

'Player' Units

The Argylls prided themselves on being the British Army's most combat experienced regiment since the end of the Second World War. Many Argylls were exceptionally tough men, even by Army standards. Within 1 Argylls, D Company 'enjoyed' the reputation of being home to the hardest of the hard – one group of soldiers was known as 'The D Company Plastic Surgery Society'.[366] D Company relished the riot situations they encountered in Newry, 'What the Jock really liked being part of was the snatch squad. He would rush out with "gym shoes", light kit and a truncheon and lay about them. Both sides quite enjoyed that. First of all the Irish quite enjoyed throwing huge clods onto the Jocks and the Jocks quite enjoyed welting people over the head.'[367] B Company, 1 Argylls, were 'the nice guys' even though they had some discipline problems: 'B Company had a group in Germany called "the Bacardi boys". They were always in trouble, up to their neck in it, always in the shite.'[368] Some Argyll soldiers in Northern Ireland took to carrying personal weapons, such as knives, and there was also a noticeable slip in the rules regarding combat dress, which NCOs struggled to correct. An Argyll soldier allegedly carried a small hand axe when on patrol; he had reportedly used it against a Celtic fan in Glasgow and been charged for the offence.[369]

As in Aden, in Northern Ireland many soldiers divided infantry regiments into 'Players' and 'Crap-hats'. 'Players' were aggressive regiments who were willing to bend, or even break, the rules in order to get the job done. These were often the regiments who traditionally had most combat experience during the colonial counterinsurgency era (for example, Gurkha regiments, Highland regiments, the Royal Green Jackets, the Parachute Regiment). Or, as Brigadier Joe Starling put it, 'Battalions at that time divided naturally into "gentlemen", who kept a low profile and hoped to live a quiet life, and "Players", who sought to dominate their operational area and to confront the terrorists head on. 1 PARA was a

366 Interview with Argyll Soldier 6 (Private Soldier), May 2014.
367 Interview with Argyll Soldier 5 (Officer), May 2014.
368 Interview with Argyll Soldier 32 (Private Soldier), May 2014.
369 Description of Private Lowe included in Correspondence between author and Argyll Soldier 32 (Private Soldier), May 2014; PRONI: CRCT/3/2/2/159A Court file of Stanley Hathaway, John Byrne, Iain Chestnut and Andrew Snowball.

"Player" Battalion.'[370] Lieutenant A.F.N. Clarke, in his memoir about serving as an officer in the Parachute Regiment in Northern Ireland, recalled the hostility 'Player' battalions felt for 'Crap-hats': 'We arrive up at the Glosters, and stand sneering at them. Crap-hats.'[371]

The Argylls met the criteria for being a hard, 'Player' regiment in the British Army, even if not to the level of Clarke's paratroopers. The Argylls believed they had been severely let down by the Army hierarchy who had failed to back them in Aden and in preventing the breaking up of the regiment two years later. Deborah Norden has described how such a rupture in the 'parental duty' of the Army hierarchy can have a debilitating effect on discipline, respect for hierarchy and can lead to the hyper-investment of small units.[372] Although the Scots Guards produced a steady flow of SAS officers, they were sometimes mocked for being insufficiently aggressive, or 'gentlemen'.[373] Scots Guards officers and many NCOs wore their 'gentlemen' image with pride. One officer who served in Ballymurphy, Left Flank, 1 Scots Guards, recalled that, 'We were very gentlemanly. We weren't kicking in doors unless it was absolutely necessary. Michael Nurton [company commander, Left Flank] took the "hearts and minds" approach very seriously.'[374] The approach of 1 Scots Guards to patrolling in West Belfast was substantially 'toned down' compared with their 2 PARA predecessors, a deliberate and wise decision on the part of more cerebral officers such as Major Nurton.

---

370 Starling, *Soldier On*, 150–151.

371 A.F.N. Clarke, *Contact* (London: Pan, 1983), 63.

372 D. Norden, *Military Rebellion in Argentina: Between Coups and Consolidation* (Lincoln, University of Nebraska, 1996), 112–113.

373 The Parachute Regiment appears to have been an extreme 'Player Battalion', very aggressive and willing to take the law into their own hands, as Lieutenant A.F.N. Clarke recalled: 'Toms sitting in their overcrowded rooms putting more powder into baton rounds to give them more poke; some insert pins and broken blades into the rubber rounds. Buckshee rounds have had the heads filed down for a dum dum effect, naughty, naughty, but who's to know when there are so many spare rounds of ammunition floating about. Lead-filled truncheons, magnum revolvers, one bloke has even got a bowie knife.' Clarke, *Contact*, 44. Brigadier Joe Starling also recalled the Parachute Regiment's disdain for Foot Guards regiments: The PARA '"Toms" viewed the Guards with some disdain ... they had a poor opinion of the officers, whom they felt were epitomised by the caricature of the mythical guards officer "ffearfully-ffearfully-Chinless".' Starling, *Soldier On*, 53.

374 Interview with Scots Guards Soldier 2 (Officer), June 2014.

Contact: Automatism and Leadership under Fire

Both the Scots Guards and the Argylls were involved in prolonged fire fights with the IRA during 1971 and 1972, as well as also suffering from more frequent attacks from single-shot snipers. A young 2nd Lieutenant called John Holmes, who would later go on to command 22 SAS and become Director of Special Forces, was involved in a shoot-out in the Turf Lodge, West Belfast for six hours while serving as commander of 12 Platoon, Left Flank, 1 Scots Guards in 1971. Holmes was on patrol in the area with a half-section when he noticed a crowd building a roadblock and burning tyres at Turf Lodge Roundabout in West Belfast, which in the past had marked the prelude to an ambush on soldiers investigating such an incident. Lieutenant Holmes took cover near the roundabout and observed two British Army ferret scout cars approaching the roundabout. The cars saw the roadblock, stopped, did a three-point turn and proceeded to head back in the direction they came from. But the wheels of the last ferret in the convoy went over the edge of the roundabout; the vehicle tipped over, 'like a turtle on its shell'.[375] The commander of the ferret opened a hatch door, before slamming it shut again when he saw the crowd surge forward towards him. Holmes believed that things were about to turn very ugly; the soldiers in the Ferret were likely to be lynched, possibly burned alive. Lieutenant Holmes 'fired some shots over the crowd's head, shouted, "Let's do this", then ran forward and laid into the crowd'. The crowd scattered, and Holmes and his men were able to get the two men out of the Ferret.[376] At that point a number of gunmen, operating from the Turf Lodge flats, opened fire on the guardsmen, who had now been joined by the other half-sections from 12 Platoon who were patrolling nearby. The soldiers took cover in a nearby farmhouse (Turf Lodge was a partly rural area in 1971) and returned fire for almost six hours. Holmes contacted his company commander by radio; Major Michael Nurton asked him if he could handle the situation and decided not to send reinforcements, trusting Holmes 'to get on with doing his job'.[377] Although nobody seemed to have been hit in the exchange of fire, Holmes and his platoon thoroughly enjoyed the encounter. One soldier recalled that the family

---

375 Interview with Scots Guards Soldier 2 (Officer), June 2014.
376 Interview with Scots Guards Soldier 2 (Officer), June 2014.
377 Interview with Scots Guards Soldier 2 (Officer), June 2014.

at the farmhouse 'brought us tea and sandwiches at half-time. The IRA later burned it [the farmhouse] down, possibly in revenge.'[378]

Lieutenant Holmes was awarded a Military Cross for his actions. Holmes also met the criteria for good officership established by his men: he was brave and competent, a front-foot soldier constantly seeking to engage the IRA but he would not risk his guardsmen's lives needlessly. He was not 'a hero', the derogatory term used for a junior officer using his platoon simply to inflate his ego and for self-advancement.[379] Soldiers were confident in his professional skills and his loyalty towards the group's key interests: survival and positive, but not reckless, action. One guardsman recalled how, after the death of Guardsman George Hamilton (shot in the back by a sniper in Ballymurphy), Lieutenant Holmes gathered his men and told them that if they continued to do their jobs properly they would get revenge. The more professional they were, the more they relied upon their skills and discipline, then the more likely they were to get results. Twelve Platoon looked up to their young Lieutenant; Holmes was a new type of junior Scots Guards officer – middle-class: the Army was his chosen profession.[380]

The incident in Turf Lodge was relatively unique; in Belfast and Londonderry, engagements with the IRA tended to be 'short and sharp' affairs. Substantial British reinforcements usually arrived within seconds in urban areas and the IRA felt outmatched and at risk of encirclement in such circumstances. But in Armagh, along the border, the IRA was more confident of holding their own against isolated units of British soldiers. Most attacks still took the form of 'shoot and scoot', but in 1971 and 1972 a number of prolonged fire fights also took place. Not only (Provisional) IRA units were involved in these rural ambushes in South Armagh but also, until their ceasefire in May 1972, the Official IRA (especially around the Forkhill area where they enjoyed most support).[381]

One of the most significant fire fights with the IRA in 1972 occurred before the Argylls' arrival in South Armagh – a two-and-a-half-hour contact on the morning of January 27 between an IRA unit that included

378 Interview with Scots Guards Soldier 2 (Officer), June 2014.
379 Hockey, *Squaddies*, 167.
380 Interview with Scots Guards Soldier 7 (Guardsman), November 2013.
381 RSDGA: Major Scrivener, Royal Scots Dragoon Guards, 'N. Ireland War Diaries'.

Martin Meehan and soldiers from the Royal Scots Dragoon Guards and the Devonshire and Dorset Regiment. The detailed written accounts of the incident provided by both sides offer an instructive guide into combat experiences along the border. On the morning in question, a patrol of C Squadron, Royal Scots Dragoon Guards, operating out of Gosford Castle in County Armagh, under the command of Lieutenant McSwiney, travelled to an area south of Forkhill, near Dungooley in County Louth. Their task was to provide a Saladin escort for a patrol led by soldiers from S Company, Devon and Dorsets, who were operating out of the RUC Station at Forkhill. S Company wanted to check out a suspected claymore bomb that had reportedly been placed near two burned out vehicles (one lorry and one van).[382] Arriving at the border at approximately 08.10, an Intelligence Officer from the Royal Scots Dragoon Guards described what happened next:

> Sure enough, EOD [Explosive Ordnance Disposal] found a milk churn with 100 lb of gelly [gelignite] in it and the wires leading from it over the border. He cut the wires and that was the signal for the battle to start. Felix [the EOD officer] disappeared under a bush and stayed there … For the next three hours battle raged. Eight gunmen in a farmhouse [just south of the border near Dungooley] blazed away at our people who blazed back.[383]

The soldiers used good manoeuvring tactics, constantly seeking better fire positions throughout the contact (and staying just on the right side of the border).[384]

There was a lull in the fighting at 10.45 – the RSDG were running out of ammunition. Shortly afterwards, a helicopter arrived nearby, bringing with it Major Charles Ramsay, OC of C Squadron, Royal Scots Dragoon Guards and more ammunition, but the IRA unit seems to have retreated by 11.00. The Gardaí had arrived nearby but did not approach the farm (they were unarmed). Major Ramsay later reported that the IRA unit was intercepted by the Irish Army but let go; they were subsequently arrested in Dundalk the following day and, to the outrage of the RSDG, released

382 RSDGA: Mitchell, 'An Officer's Diary'.
383 RSDGA: Mitchell, 'An Officer's Diary'.
384 RSDGA: Mitchell, 'An Officer's Diary'.

following 'lack of evidence'.[385] The RSDG and the Devon and Dorsets went through a remarkable amount of ammunition during the contact at Dungooley, just under 3,700 rounds. Their officers were annoyed when 3 Brigade queried the large number of rounds used during the battle. In his diary, Lieutenant Mitchell of the Royal Scots Dragoon Guards wrote scathingly about, 'the idiots in brigade headquarters ... The rather tense suggestion that they come down and do better themselves shut them up, but honestly, how out of touch can these people get!'[386] The RSDG were relatively impressed by the IRA action: 'Again the IRA used extremely well-concealed fire posns [positions], and again the sun was in our eyes – damn it! It is probable that they had pre-recced their concealed escape routes, which they must have used after 10.45 hrs.' The RSDG were also deeply concerned that the IRA had used what they believed was some type of 'Anti-tank gun' and recommended to brigade that they be allowed to use their 76 mm ammunition – which would result in much greater IRA casualties if such an incident arose in the future.' This request was denied.[387]

C Squadron, RSDG thought they had inflicted multiple casualties on the IRA; this was not the case. Martin Meehan, one of the IRA gunmen, thought that he had also killed or wounded some soldiers.[388] Although there were no casualties on either side, the incident was, according to Major Ramsay, 'a classic example of an IRA staged border incident. They provide the bait, booby-trap it and ambush it, in the sure knowledge that the Army will investigate'. But Major Ramsay was generally pleased with these increasing border incidents, 'which have been very successful in: (1) Achieving a high attrition rate; (2) Demonstrating our potential force; (3) Raising our morale; (4) Retaining control of the actual border.'[389] Ramsay cautioned that radio communications were extremely poor in South Armagh. He also wrote of the need to 'avenge' previous attacks on British soldiers. Four days later, C Squadron was involved in

385 RSDGA: 'Operational Report 4/72 Forkhill Incident 27th January', C Squadron, Royal Scots Dragoon Guards, signed by Major C.A. Ramsay, Officer Commanding C Squadron, dated January 30, 1972.
386 RSDGA: Mitchell, 'An Officer's Diary'.
387 RSDGA: 'Operational Report 4/72 Forkhill Incident 27th January'.
388 'Meehan was in Notorious Dungooley Gun Battle', *Irish Independent*, November 7, 2007.
389 RSDGA: 'Operational Report 4/72 Forkhill Incident 27th January'.

another fire fight, at Narrow Water near Warrenpoint, in which 5,209 rounds of ammunition were fired across the border into a house in the Republic of Ireland.[390]

As well as demonstrating a relative contempt by the RSDG for 3 Brigade HQ, the above incidents also highlight some early lessons learned about IRA tactics in RUC H Division. These were somehow not passed on to the Argyll and Sutherland Highlanders, in the same way that, the Royal Hampshire Regiment and 3 PARA would subsequently also not learn from the Argylls in 1973. On August 8, 1972, approximately a week after arriving in South Armagh, 2 Section, 6 Platoon, B Company, 1 Argylls were ambushed for the first time. Patrolling near Cullaville, the Argylls were approached by a local woman who told Sergeant Jimmy Kilcullen that there was a burning butter lorry blocking the road near Drombue townland. Revved up, the Argylls ran down the road towards the incident: 'We could have been walking into an ambush but we were hyped up, our training almost taking over.'[391]

Private James Chestnut later recalled that the patrol stopped short of the burning lorry, but, seeing no enemy activity nearby, slowly approached the scene. They tried to radio B Company HQ to call for assistance, but the A41 radio was not working. Sergeant Kilcullen decided to head back towards base; however, on taking the most direct route from Drombue to Crossmaglen, Kilcullen's patrol found the road blocked by a burning car. The men had stumbled upon a 'classic' South Armagh ambush, except the IRA, expecting the burning lorry to be reported to B Company HQ in Crossmaglen, had not anticipated a patrol coming from the other direction. The IRA Volunteers waiting in a concealed fire point now hurriedly improvised upon seeing Kilcullen's section arrive at the burning car. Chestnut later recalled that a local man asked them to look at something in the ditch near the burning car:

> We were all crowded around this oil drum when someone shouted that it was a bomb. We scattered, maybe getting sixty feet from it, when there was an almighty explosion. Everything stood still; we were on the deck watching this cloud of dirt and rubble slowly rising. It was quite a sight. A falling rock snapped

390 RSDGA: 'Operational Report 4/72 Forkhill Incident 27th January'.
391 RMASH: Chestnut.

the pistol grip of one rifle and one man was knocked unconscious – we thought he was dead. We got up and stood around shocked and confused. Then the ground started kicking up around us and the Sergeant shouted that we were under fire.[392]

Despite the days of simulated explosions and ambushes in Lydd and Hythe, some of the soldiers of 6 Platoon became disorientated. One soldier recalled watching a telegraph pole shoot into the air like a javelin by the force of the explosion; he couldn't believe his eyes. Two key individuals helped the section snap out of their potentially fatal torpor. Sergeant Jimmy Kilcullen shouted at the soldiers, telling them that they were under fire, so that they remembered their training drills, took cover and returned fire. Kilcullen was also the first to return fire. Meanwhile, Corporal Alec Henderson, another Aden and Borneo veteran, shouted at Chestnut to follow him and proceeded to 'advance towards fire', using the infantry's fire and manoeuvre drill, moving along a wall, returning fire and covering each other, until they reached a farm building where they believed the firing was coming from.[393] Six Platoon reported that they returned 20 rounds to the 150 rounds fired at them by the IRA unit and the shooting stopped.[394]

The Argylls made a mistake in approaching the ambush site with such a lack of caution and by crowding around the suspected device, an example of raw enthusiasm rather than 'training kicking in'. Some soldiers were also struck by a sense of stunned disbelief when they came under fire from a 'real enemy' for the first time. However, they were quickly brought out of their stunned disbelief by their NCOs; their training worked and saved them from taking casualties. By moving towards the firing-position, they forced the IRA unit to retreat and got their unit out of the 'kill zone'. One soldier recalled Sergeant Jimmy Kilcullen constantly hammering home the fundamental message of why his sections needed to 'fire and manoeuvre': 'If we come under fire, you locate the fire. Advance towards the fire and clear it. If you sit down, you die.'[395] Others reported that the intense familiarity with this infantry drill was critically important

---

392 RMASH: Chestnut.
393 RMASH: Chestnut.
394 TNA: WO 305/4407 The Argyll and Sutherland Highlanders Battalion Diary, April 1969–March 1974.
395 Interview with Argyll Soldier 3 (NCO), September 2014.

– responses learned in training kicked in: 'All you think about is the next ten metres.'[396] An Argyll officer later noted that:

> People can function when they are kicked into it. Heat of the moment stuff is never a problem for soldiers ... The big problem is that they will do too much, they will loose off all their ammo at the general area. It's a common reaction. The instinct for the first time soldier in an ambush is that, 'I'm frightened, I'm going to frighten him more.' Well-trained soldiers, who've done it before – they're the ones who 'get down, crawl, observe, sights, fire.' It can happen in a flash. Good NCOs get others to do that. Not blaze away.[397]

In describing responses to coming under fire the Argyll officer elucidates the essential difference between 'forward panic', as defined by Randal Collins and observed in the murderous, chaotic waves of trench assaults by conscripts in the First World War, and professional soldiering – the controlled and very deliberate response to coming under fire, aimed at minimising losses and using a set of drills steadily to outmanoeuvre the enemy.[398] Wild-eyed heroism is not prized in such a situation if it interrupts the synchronisation of collective group movements; individual acts of 'glory hunting' can turn a set of movements instinctively understood by the group into chaos. However, fear and adrenalin could also be used to good purpose in the professional era, if controlled within a preordained and understood drill context:

> Fear kicks in. Big time. It can make you do a lot of things. You would be amazed at how quickly you can move your body over

396 RMASH: Chestnut.
397 Interview with Argyll Soldier 5 (Officer), May 2014.
398 'Typically in war it occurs when troops have been under intense pressure from their opponents for a long period: a forward panic starts with tension and fear in a conflict situation. This is the normal condition of violent conflict, but there the tension is prolonged and built up ... there is the shift from relatively passive – waiting, holding back until one is in a position to bring the conflict to head – to be fully active. When the opportunity finally arrives, the tension/fear comes out in an emotional rush.' R. Collins, *Violence: A Microsociological Theory* (Princeton, NJ: Princeton University Press, 2008), 85.

what looked like an impenetrable object. You can use that fear positively. It is not always negative. Adrenalin and fear are both important. In some regiments there is a fair degree of macho. And that can also be helpful as long as it is contained. A good officer is able to direct and channel these emotions.[399]

Again, the Argyll officer's observation chimes with research elsewhere, including by Anthony King. King draws upon a US Marines' colour scheme of emotional responses to events between white and black: 'white' represents boredom; 'yellow' signifies initial arousal; 'orange' indicates significant levels of concentration, while 'red' demonstrates some levels of adrenalin, complete concentration and substantial autonomy over thoughts and actions. 'Black', by contrast, was not desirable for professional soldiers since it was unpredictable: 'a state of panic or rage when individuals are overwhelmed by the situation which confronts them and are dominated by adrenalin-induced physical responses of flight or fight.' King notes that 'black' was the state often experienced by conscripts in trench warfare. 'Red' is the optimal level of arousal for professional soldiers.[400]

Moderate levels of fear can trigger positive levels of alertness; soldiers are in control and they reach for the drills or procedures they have learned and rehearsed endlessly. They can operate coherently as a group and there is no individual panic.[401] A Scots Guards NCO, who had been ambushed many times, believes that the key motivation to conducting professional, but dangerous, manoeuvres under fire is discipline and conditioning. In such situations soldiers do not weigh up relationships and look after their friends, rather they look to their leaders and collectively implement familiar manoeuvres designed to allow a group to advance and withdraw together as the situation requires. Performing a role within a rehearsed group motion is all that a soldier could think about.[402]

The weight and importance of the Argyll NCOs leadership is repeatedly apparent in accounts of the other fire fights the Argylls experienced along the border during their 1972 tour. On October 30, 1972, after setting up

399 Interview with Argyll Soldier 5 (Officer), May 2014.
400 King, *The Combat Soldier*, 326.
401 H. Strachan, 'Training, Morale and Modern War', *Journal of Contemporary History* 41 (2006), 212.
402 Interview with Scots Guards Soldier 6 (NCO), November 2013.

camp near the 'Southern Mushroom' mountain near Drumuckavall on the border, an IRA unit of approximately eight men opened fire on 1 Section, 6 Platoon, B Company. The IRA had driven a herd of cows in front of them in order to approach the Argyll position. Hearing the noise, the Argyll patrol put up a flare, which was answered by a barrage of accurate IRA fire. Seconds before coming under fire, 6 Platoon's commander, Colour Sergeant Jimmy Struthers, told his section to 'get down', possibly saving some of their lives. Struthers then immediately got his soldiers out of the 'kill zone' towards better cover, withdrawing half section by half section, again using a 'fire and manoeuvre drill'. B Company's second-in-command, Captain Bill Watson, was on the radio; GPMGs were brought into position and put down covering fire, and a lot of it. Another soldier admitted that he found the Garand armour piercing rifles, used by the IRA during this engagement, to be very unnerving, but only after the engagement when he had time to think about the prospect of being shot with such a round, 'That was scary. It made you a little wobbly.'[403]

On November 3, 1972, the Argylls decided to try to turn the tables on the IRA. A D Company platoon with a range of weaponry including sniper rifles and machine guns was flown into Drumuckavall together with a half a troop of 17th/21st Lancers who had taken over from the Royal Scots Dragoon Guards in Gosford Castle. They dug in along the Southern Mushroom during the early hours of the morning and then waited for an opportunity to ambush the IRA. A soldier from 6 Platoon, B Company recalled that, 'We were then set up as a sort of duck-shooting gallery in an area where everything happened. We spent a few hours walking up and down a road waiting for something to happen but hoping it wouldn't.'[404] The firing, when it came (at approximately 13.30), was from an unexpected direction. The Argyll ambush party had themselves been ambushed. The IRA had located the unit the previous evening and moved into the area under the cover of darkness. As different Argyll units moved towards the sound of the firing, there was some confusion and firing at each other. Meanwhile, up on the ridge, the Argylls had suffered a casualty; Private Ronnie Hewins was hit in the thigh in the initial burst of fire and lay exposed in the 'kill zone'. A soldier from 6 Platoon recounted the incident:

---

403 Interview with Argyll Soldier 3 (NCO), September 2014.
404 RMASH: Chestnut.

Ronnie was hit almost immediately. I looked at Jimmy McCormack. We didn't say anything. We just both stood up and moved forward, moving 'by fire' or 'fire manoeuvre'. Move, down, fast burst, move. We got to Ronnie; he was lying on the wrong side of the wall. Jimmy laid down fire and I managed to haul him over back on our side. We kept trying to stick morphine into him; it took us a few gos to do it properly but then we gave him too much. He went from screaming like a stuck pig to babbling like a baby.[405]

The interviewee distinctly recalled feeling empowered as the adrenalin kicked in: 'My hearing was so sharp. I felt I could see for miles. Time slowed down.'[406] By this time, at the end of their tour, the soldiers of 6 Platoon had been under fire on multiple occasions. Reactions kicked in much more quickly. It took another half an hour before a helicopter could get in to evacuate Private Hewins from the area. The Medical Officer, Captain Charles Boyle, was immediately pinned down; only by some remarkable flying by an Army pilot were the Argylls able to get Hewins off the hill and to Musgrave Hospital, Belfast where he made a partial recovery from his wounds (his time in the Army was effectively over).[407]

The Problem with 'Cold Kills'

Soldiers enjoyed the adrenalin of combat, even if these incidents could also be emotionally scarring. Too much adrenalin, the 'black' state described by King and Sebastian Junger, could, however, cause the soldier to miss his target. A sudden increase in heart rate causes the hands to tremble, with knock-on effects for a soldier's aim.[408] However, an Argyll officer noted another persistent, and unexpected, problem that affected soldiers in Northern Ireland – an inability to take life. Soldiers could respond to being under fire without much problem. Survival instincts and training drills would kick in reasonably quickly. But when presented with

---

405 Interview with Argyll Soldier 29 (NCO), September 2014.
406 Interview with Argyll Soldier 29 (NCO), September 2014.
407 Interview with Argyll Soldier 29 (NCO), September 2014.
408 Junger, *War*, 33.

an opportunity to kill an IRA gunman from an unseen position – taking the first shot – many soldiers froze. The same officer had run the British Army sniper's course:

> The final piece of sniper training would be up at the Duke of Argyll's estate, where he allowed us to cull deer. I decided that we weren't convinced that these guys who could hit a mark on a piece of paper target at 700/800 yards could actually kill something when faced with a live thing. And that proved to be absolutely the case. 'Buckfever' it's described as, is a very good description. It's when you face a large living creature. They freeze and the sights go all over the place. And so we used to only allow snipers to get their full qualification if they killed a living being; we would make them shoot a deer on the Duke of Argyll's estate, culling a hind usually. No great range; that was not the message. The message was can he actually do it ... 150 metres, 200 metres, easy shot. It was surprising how many couldn't, from Gurkhas to anybody else – they were just hopeless. They would miss or wound it.[409]

Unable to shoot a deer in a 'cold kill', soldiers could not be relied upon to do so in the case of a human being. The longer the range, the more likely a concealed sniper was to take the shot.[410] A distancing of the soldiers from identifying with the local population also became more important. It can be argued that a process of 'making an other' of the Irish was, to a degree, an inculcated survival mechanism, as well as a means of venting anger over casualties; if the soldier is to take life, it cannot be the lives of his kith and kin. One Argyll NCO from D Company – an Aden veteran – briefly left the Army to become a debt collector in Greenock in the West of Scotland. He found that he couldn't do it; he knew these people, he sympathised with them and the idea of using any threats or violence, even in self-defence, was too odious.[411]

A Royal Marine Captain and the future leader of the Liberal Democrats Party, Paddy Ashdown, later recalled that he felt out of step in

---

409 Interview with Argyll Soldier 18 (Officer), May 2014.
410 Interview with Argyll Soldier 18 (Officer), May 2014.
411 Interview with Argyll Soldier 24 (NCO), March 2015.

1971 with his fellow officers and marines in Northern Ireland (Ashdown has always been proud of his Irish identity, having spent much of his childhood in Comber in North Down):

> But for me it was different. This was my city as well as my theatre of operations. Suddenly I found the Irish jokes increasingly tiresome and the black-and-white certainties of our operational assumptions increasingly inappropriate. For the first time I was beginning to see military operations not just from the viewpoint of the soldier patrolling the street, but from that of the person living on the street as well. And I found it very uncomfortable.[412]

Captain Ashdown left the Royal Marines in 1972.[413]

Too much familiarity or affinity could be a threat to military performance; too little could lead to atrocity. The sociologist Erella Grassiani, in her work on the Israeli military in the Occupied Territories, has noted that it is particularly difficult for soldiers to take life when they are working among a civilian population in a low intensity operation: 'Seeing these people as "individuals" can make it harder for the soldier to carry out work.'[414] A separation of identity became a professional necessity. According to the Argyll officer involved in sniper training:

> I found the problem was to get guys to shake off the view – 'Am I really right to be doing this between W.H. Smith and a Marks and Spencers'. And, meanwhile, seeing granny pushing grandchild down the road in a pram. This makes a big difference. All the other places, wherever we had been had been peasant countries where you are in a different country, where natives are natives. Here they are not natives, they are your kith and kin. The topography is exactly as you recognise it at home. Yet you have a rifle in your hands. You are faced with a situation and your first instinct is, 'This can't be happening.' And that takes training and time; it made Ireland such a unique operation.[415]

---

412 Ashdown, *A Fortunate Life*, 140–141.
413 Ashdown, *A Fortunate Life*, 140–141.
414 Grassiani, *Soldiering*, 23.
415 Interview with Argyll Soldier 18 (Officer), May 2014.

In such circumstances, the separation of the Irish from 'us' becomes more than about casual dislike; moral distancing is also a professional necessity. Even so, the same Argyll officer reported his consistent disappointment that, after days of planning and execution, Argyll snipers in concealed positions would not be able to shoot IRA Volunteers. These were the same soldiers who would not hesitate to hit back if provoked or attacked.[416] The Argyll officer is convinced that such 'inefficiency' led to the death of more soldiers because of an inability to shoot IRA Volunteers in such circumstances:

> The ambush is set around a weapons hide. And you know that whoever is going to come to that weapons hide is going to be IRA to come to collect the weapons so they would stake these things out for days. And the after-action report shows that when asked why it was the IRA had escaped, they would say 'I had to challenge them first' rather than 'just shoot them dead.' So when they put their hands in and picked up the Armalite or the AK47 that was the moment where they were legally allowed to kill him. They couldn't do it, so they would say 'Halt' and the chap's reflexes were over the hedge and gone before they fired. That happened lots of time and it is because of this inability to kill somebody … You trained him, you gave him specific orders and he couldn't do it .[417]

The battalion log books and diaries of 2 Scots Guards have many accounts of missed shots, sometimes at close range. Adrenalin kicks in, some doubt creeps in and the target gets away. Typical of such an incident is the following account of an ambush in a 2 Scots Guards Intelligence summary report: 'On 22 Nov, an ambush was set up at GR43041701. At 2200 Z [Zulu time], a gunmab [sic] appeared at GR43071697; two rounds were fired at him, but he was seen to run away. A follow-up search of the buildings and around the slaughterhouse proved negative.'[418] And exactly the 'halt' situation described by the Argyll officer interviewee occurred on October 29, 1972:

---

416 Interview with Argyll Soldier 18 (Officer), May 2014.
417 Interview with Argyll Soldier 18 (Officer), May 2014.
418 TNA: WO 305/4274 2nd Battalion, Scots Guards, Intsum No.7, November 20–26, 1972.

On 29 0035 Oct, a patrol moving from the alley into the Lecky Rd saw a man with a weapon moving from Brandywell Ave into Quarry St. The gunman was ordered to stop but failed to do so, one round was fired, but no hits were claimed. The patrol was in no doubt that the man was carrying a weapon. This area had been the scene of a number of sniping attacks in the past.[419]

Embarrassed, soldiers would often claim a hit, perhaps even convincing themselves that their shooting had been more accurate, and it would be assumed that the IRA had 'spirited' their wounded across the border. The Knights of Malta were presumed to connive in the setting up of IRA 'field hospitals'.[420] Tiredness could also play a role. Eighteen-hour days or, in the case of the Argylls, seven-hour patrols would wear soldiers out quite quickly. Tired men began to see things; fatigue affected not only general performance, but also aim and decision-making. An exhausted B Company, 1 Argylls patrol once fell asleep as a group on a hill overlooking a farm of interest.[421]

Conclusion

Soldiers crave certainty, namely an identifiable, known enemy on whom they can exact revenge for their own casualties.[422] Northern Ireland was anything but certain; tip-offs about bombs by 'concerned locals' could be a lure towards a prepared ambush. The few locals who mocked the death of soldiers such as Trooper Ian Caie or Guardsman John Van Beck could stimulate a general hatred among soldiers towards the local population as a whole. And the more the desire for revenge, the less exacting soldiers became about who fit the classification of 'the enemy'. Operations in Northern Ireland contained a paradox: young men trained to dominate a situation overseas had to show remarkable, unprecedented restraint on a domestic operation. They enjoyed combat, but were uncertain of whether they really were inflicting the same level of losses on 'the opposition'. As

419 TNA: WO 305/4273 2nd Battalion, Scots Guards, Intsum, October 23–29, 1972.
420 Military Intelligence Captain, Bloody Sunday Inquiry Witness – Reference No. INQ 2225: Interview with Scots Guards Soldier 20 (Officer), June 2013.
421 Interview with Argyll Soldier 20 (Private Soldier), April 2013.
422 Neitzel and Welzer, *Soldaten*, 234.

casualties mounted, they occasionally engaged in punitive attacks on the local population. Individual companies and section commanders enjoyed significant autonomy. Competent and respected officers and NCOs were critical to 'keeping a lid' on such indiscipline, not only through fear of punishment but also out of mutual respect. As one experienced Scots Guards NCO put it, 'Young soldiers knew that if they did something wrong, it would hurt me more. They didn't want to disappoint you.'[423]

Soldiers could often tell when an officer was willing to turn a blind eye to abuses – such as when an officer in Right Flank, 2 Scots Guards in Londonderry went to bed while soldiers engaged in the harassment of the residents of Brandywell after the death of a number of guardsmen. In the absence of a functioning and respected police force in some Nationalist areas, it was often a case of a local civilian's word versus that of a soldier. Isolated, hated and taking casualties in a majority Catholic city of Londonderry, soldiers began to believe that even relatively benign movements such as the Knights of Malta, the Catholic Church and nominal allies, the US Navy, were working against them. Scots Guardsmen were convinced that the Catholic Church allowed the spire of St Eugene's Cathedral to be used as a sniper's nest. Priests in Derry were accused of hiding weapons for the IRA. A convent near Bridge Camp in the city was used as cover by snipers; Right Flank, 2 Scots Guards gave it a 'barrage of fire'. Occasionally they were right – some priests and US sailors were openly hostile to the Scots Guards and sympathetic to the IRA. The Knights of Malta ambulance service was reluctant overtly to cooperate with the Army, lest their members come under threat for being 'spies'. The behaviour of a few, however, came to be seen as representative of the whole of these institutions. Meanwhile, narrative descriptions of the local population tended to dwell particularly on the heinous behaviour of women and children, who would bait and assault the soldiers. Soldiers seemed to have expected a higher level of feminine passivity or sympathy. Local women could indeed be very hostile and even violent, but they weren't doing the shooting.

The retribution meted out by the Scots Guards to the residents of the Brandywell at the end of September 1972 was certainly not unprecedented; such behaviour occurred in other units during the early days of Operation Banner. A former Queen's Own Highlander described how his

---

423 Interview with Argyll Soldier 23 (NCO), March 2015.

regiment responded to the death of 21-year-old Private James Hesketh on December 10, 1973:

> 'Paddy bashing' took off for the next days. Our patrols would be in wait outside the church youth clubs and discos for when the boys came out and they got the shite beaten out of them. You can get in a fair head-butt with your helmet on and its visor down. One night some of them with a girl fought back outside a disco on Broadway. One of our lads hit the deck so one of my platoon used his rifle muzzle across the girl's face. He split it open right down the side. She'd not got a boyfriend for a while after that one.[424]

The antipathy shown by women (who dressed and looked like girls back in Scotland) to young, near-adolescent soldiers particularly hurt. The reference to the girl in question 'not having a boyfriend for a while' highlights such frustrations; the soldiers clearly enjoyed punishing the girl for her rejection, and aggression, towards them. A generalised, suspicious view of the population of an area as a whole had detrimental consequences; soldiers' empathy occasionally dropped to dangerously low levels.

A disregard for civilian lives arguably contributed to the very casual attitude of B Company, 1 Argylls in the events leading up to the death of Edmund Woolsey in South Armagh on September 18, 1972. There are some similarities between counterinsurgent symptoms experienced in Belgium 1914 and those in Northern Ireland in 1972. John Horne and Alan Kramer have described German soldiers' obsession with the idea that Belgian insurgent snipers were using church towers: 'Fear of the person was transposed onto his setting so that the church and its tower aroused particular suspicion as the site of the deadly machine-guns and of communication with the enemy.'[425] German soldiers also came to view the Red Cross as an enemy, wearing the symbols of goodwill and neutrality but in reality working with the insurgents, similar to accusations in Londonderry about the role of the Knights of Malta.[426]

---

424 Sanders and Wood, *Times of Troubles*, 173.
425 J. Horne and A. Kramer, *German Atrocities, 1914: A History of Denial* (New Haven, Conn.: Yale University Press, 2001), 107.
426 Horne and Kramer, *German Atrocities*, 107.

Horne and Kramer have also written about the extra weight given in soldiers' accounts of counterinsurgency to the alleged role played by women and children: 'Women and children thus symbolized the intrinsic treachery of the enemy civilian in its most extreme form, and served to warn German troops against trusting any inhabitants.'[427] The *Sunday Mail* noted a particular vitriol expressed by the wives of Scottish soldiers towards Derry activist, Bernadette Devlin, who was a high profile MP during the early 1970s. A soldier's wife told journalists that, 'I get so angry when I see what women and children in Ulster are doing to our men. If Bernadette Devlin walked down our street at this moment there wouldn't be anything left of her.'[428] Soldiers, and their families, expressed a deep hatred and contempt for 'cowardly snipers'. An Argyll private soldier's wife wrote a poem to express her hatred for the IRA:

> You hid behind the kids
> Who set up an ambush for you
> While their mothers rattled lids.
> You slunk in darkness at the rear
> A yellow sweating skunk
> Take a shot and disappear
> 'Some hero'...
> But here's a little food for thought
> That you may contemplate
> The British Army fear for nought
> And Rats Exterminate.[429]

In Belgium in 1914, accounts circulated of German soldiers being given water laced with arsenic; some soldiers in Northern Ireland believed that 'friendly' locals put ground glass in soldiers' tea.[430] Soldiers' hatred of Catholics living in 'hard' Republican areas was encouraged by local 'friends': for example, false atrocity stories were circulated in Northern Ireland about the alleged torture of three young Royal Highland Fusiliers soldiers, John and Joseph McCaig and Dougald McCaughey on March 9,

---

427 Horne and Kramer, *German Atrocities*, 110.
428 'The Women Who Wait and Dread That Awful Knock on the Door', *Sunday Mail*, December 7, 1971.
429 J. Glen, 'To a Sniper', *Glengarry Tales*, August 1972.
430 Horne and Kramer, *German Atrocities*, 17.

1971, claiming that they had been castrated before death. Individual Unionists and loyalists told the soldiers that the IRA were 'inhuman', 'bestial', the families of local children arrested for rioting were 'animals'.[431]

Horne and Kramer have also described the propensity for false accounts of the grotesque deaths, injuries and mutilation of soldiers.[432] But although the groups of soldiers examined here, especially in Derry, had their suspicions about the role of the Catholic Church and other local organisations, it is important to ask why matters did not get worse than they did. Whereas German soldiers in 1914 frequently acted upon their suspicions, committing large-scale atrocities, British soldiers in Northern Ireland only rarely carried out their more extreme desires for revenge. By and large, officers and NCOs in Northern Ireland curbed their soldiers' desire for revenge, keeping them the right side of the law. The best officers recognised the potential for revenge, particularly after the death of a charismatic officer, actions that would damage the reputation of a unit and the goals of the wider mission in Northern Ireland, and took steps to prevent punitive acts against the local population. When the OC of B Company, 1 Royal Hampshire Regiment was shot twice in the head in Newry (amazingly he survived and resumed his military career) during his battalion's 1972–1973 tour of RUC H Division, his CO moved quickly to limit the potential for retribution:

> He was extremely popular ... Of course the soldiers were very keen to go out to avenge their company commander. The Colonel, realising that this would happen, sent down the Battalion 2IC [second-in-command] ... who had won the Military Cross with the Devons, who then continued to command that Company until we left Northern Ireland.[433]

Soldiers were often disgusted by the intense bigotry they encountered in Northern Ireland. For Scottish soldiers, open sectarian violence at

---

431 NAI: TAOIS/ 2003/16/259 Letter from The Very Reverend Thomas Clements, Dean of Clogher, St Macartin's Cathedral, Enniskillen, September 27, 1972; Cardinal Conway Archives, Letter to Cardinal Conway dated April 24, 1972 (names of correspondents retained by author), Cardinal O'Fiach Library, Armagh.
432 Horne and Kramer, *German Atrocities*, 17.
433 IWM: 13915 Audio Recording – Roger Coleman, Hampshires, Service in Northern Ireland.

home amounted to clashes between Rangers and Celtic or Hibernian and Hearts twice a year; they had no desire to emulate Northern Irish conditions. Many had been brought up in socialist-voting households, where sectarianism was frowned on. Soldiers generally despised the IRA (although the Argylls had some admiration for the South Armagh IRA's military competence); they also disliked, and did not trust, the pseudo-military organisation of Loyalism.

The more restrained approach towards internment and arrest introduced by William Whitelaw took some of the sting out of Catholic grievances in Northern Ireland. But Whitelaw's policy was deeply resented by soldiers of all ranks. There was a temptation for soldiers to conclude that because 'the law' was not on their side; they needed to find other methods to get retribution. Only they *knew* who was guilty of crimes. The most egregious example of a 'Player' unit exacting frequent and brutal retribution from the local population is that of 1 PARA in both Loyalist and Nationalist/Republican areas.

Both the Scots Guards and the Argylls also had their incidents of retribution. But these were not a typical or regular feature of their behaviour. For the most part, the Argylls did not behave like they did in Aden. The crucial difference was good officership. Although some senior officers such as General Tuzo pushed for a return to some form of colonial tactics, mid-ranking officers such as Colonel Boam and Colonel Palmer knew that they were soldiering in a different era. They impressed on their officers and NCOs the need to act with restraint towards the local population. Sectarianism, although it occasionally reared its head, was generally discouraged among the ranks (lest it tear them apart). Verbal abuse of the local population occurred, but was frowned upon by many officers and NCOs alike. I have examined at length why singular transgressions happened, why sometimes company, platoon commanders and NCOs got it wrong. The domestic and global uproar that followed Bloody Sunday and the presence of British and international media left more perceptive officers in no doubt that such punitive acts would be counter-productive in the court of public opinion in Northern Ireland and abroad.

Coercion was no longer an option. As Colonel Palmer noted, the British public were far more squeamish when it came to punitive actions close to home than they had been during recent colonial wars. Something had changed: Palmer concluded that, like it or not, 'the enemy can only be fought by methods which public opinion at home, and indeed fair-minded opinion abroad, finds acceptable'.[434] Hard, colonial tactics quickly proved impossible in such an environment. And, although many soldiers grew to dislike Northern Ireland, mutual loathing between counterinsurgent and the local population never reached those levels seen in Aden or in Kenya. Although the Irish were often vilified and mocked, there was still an enduring sense of familiarity.

When 2 Scots Guards returned to Derry in 1976 they noticed a significant shift in operational initiative in their favour. If 1972 was about 'holding the line', 1976 was about consolidating gains. Royal Signals' observation and listening equipment was 'state of the art' and there was considerable assistance from police and military intelligence, which now had many active sources of information among the local population. Operations were much more targeted. Even by 1973, senior officers in 2 Scots Guards observed a shift in momentum – they were watching the IRA more than the IRA was watching them.[435] Sadly, however, by that time irreparable damage had been done to the social landscape of Northern Ireland; for example, virtually the entire Protestant population west of the Foyle in Londonderry had moved.[436] And many inhabitants, deeply angered by Bloody Sunday and successive interactions with 'player units', would never trust the British Army again.

A tired and sore 1 Argylls, carrying dogs and other pets adopted in Northern Ireland, disembarked from *The Sir Galahad* at Yorkhill Quay in Glasgow at 07.00 on November 29, 1972; they had been cheered all the way up the banks of the Clyde by different groups of dock workers.[437] Some found it a disorientating experience to find themselves very suddenly back in Britain, geographically so close to the hills of South Armagh or alleys of the Bogside, sometimes hours after being shot at in Northern Ireland. On their first night back in Scotland a group of soldiers from 2 Scots Guards decided to recreate Derry in Edinburgh. They stopped cars on Prince's Street, told the drivers to get out and then used the cars as roadblocks. They then began to conduct VCPs on oncoming vehicles as they would on the Lecky Road in Londonderry barely 24

---

434 C. Palmer, 'Public Opinion and the Armed Forces', *Seaford House Papers* (1977), 80–89.

435 Interview with Scots Guards Soldier 11 (Officer), December 2013.

436 O'Dochartaigh, *From Civil Rights to Armalites*, 287.

437 Interview with Argyll Soldier 2 (Officer), November 2013; Interview with Argyll Soldier 1 (Private Soldier), April 2014.

hours previously. The police dealt tactfully with the drunken guardsmen – who eventually abandoned their makeshift VCPs. The guardsmen were adjusting to their new surroundings, having fun but also reminding the people of Edinburgh of where they had just come from.[438] A few weeks earlier they had mocked a drunk Derry man who, with blood streaming down his face, had tried to construct a roadblock on Henrietta Street.[439] Northern Ireland had a way of leaving its mark.

438 Interview with Scots Guards Soldier 3 (Guardsman), November 2013.
439 TNA: WO 305/4274 2nd Battalion Scots Guards: Sitrep No. 113, November 17–18, 1972.

4

Murder:
The Killing of Michael Naan
and Andrew Murray

Vengeance is mine; I will repay, saith the Lord.[1]

On the night of October 24, 1972, the Battalion Watchkeeper for the 16th/5th The Queen's Royal Lancers, the 3rd Infantry Brigade unit with lead responsibility for security in RUC L Division (Fermanagh and South Tyrone), typed a simple but shocking entry into the Battalion Log: 'At 1830 a Mr. T P Hannah reported to the Newtownbutler RUC that he had found two bodies at NANN'S [sic] farm. The bodies found were that of: Michael Nann 31 (RC) Andrew Murray 24 (RC). Both had been stabbed to death with a hay fork.'[2] News of the 'pitchfork murders' of farmer, and occasional civil rights activist, Michael Naan

---

1 Romans 12:19, quoted by Newtownbutler Parish Priest, Fr Patrick J. Duffy, at the funeral masses of Michael Naan and Andrew Murray. Fr Duffy urged his congregation not to take revenge. Locally, Michael Naan and Andrew Murray's friends believed their neighbours, part-time Protestant UDR soldiers, were responsible for the killings. 'Vast Funeral Cortege at Burial of Newtownbutler Men', *Fermanagh Herald*, November 4, 1972. The same biblical quote was later also used by a Unionist councillor when he spoke of justice being done to those members of the IRA who escaped prosecution for the murder of Protestants in County Fermanagh during the Troubles. M. Gordon-McBride, 'Symbol, Barrier, Resource, Bridge: Narratives of Experiences on the Fermanagh Border', unpublished Queen's University Belfast thesis, 2009, 172.
2 TNA: WO 305/4251 16th/5th The Queen's Royal Lancers Commander's Diary, Northern Ireland 1972.

and farm labourer Andrew Murray at an isolated farm in the townland of Aughnahinch, just south of the rural village of Newtownbutler (population approximately 1,000), spread fear through Fermanagh and across the nearby border in Counties Cavan and Monaghan. Like the Lancers, locals believed that Naan and Murray had been murdered in a frenzied attack with a pitchfork. In the days after the murders, a local newspaper, the *Anglo-Celt*, reported that, 'As there was no sign of a struggle, it is believed that the two victims were surrounded by men with pitchforks and had no chance either to resist or escape.' Local Catholics initially believed that the killings were a Loyalist response to the fatal shooting in an IRA ambush of Michael Naan's neighbour and part-time UDR soldier, Private Robin Bell, on October 22.[3]

The murders of Michael Naan and Andrew Murray appeared to be eerily reminiscent of another dark chapter in Fermanagh's history, 'The Mackan Fight', an incident that has been handed down through the folklore and whispered warnings of successive generations. On that occasion, during a clash with Orangemen on their traditional annual celebration of the Battle of the Boyne on July 12, 1829, a local Catholic, Ignatius McManus, 'twice stabbed Robert Mealey with a pitchfork'. Four local Protestant men were killed at Macken: 'The affair has come down in tradition as a great Catholic victory.'[4] Were Naan and Murray now paying a belated debt in blood for this 'victory'? Was the choice of a pitchfork as the murder weapon deliberate? Even in an era marked by sectarian atrocity, the people of Newtownbutler were deeply shocked by the apparent brutality of Naan and Murray's deaths; some feared for their lives.[5]

An autopsy soon made clear that, although the two victims were subject to a vicious attack, neither had been stabbed to death with farm implements; indeed, the examining pathologist specifically ruled out 'pitchforks or graipes' as the murder weapon. According to deputy State pathologist, Dr Derek Carson, the men were repeatedly stabbed by a person(s) using a double-edged knife that was at least five and half inches

---

3 'Brutal Killing of Two Newtownbutler Men', *The Anglo-Celt*, October 27, 1972.
4 M. McManus, 'The Macken Fight', available at http://mexlist.com/mcmanus/macken.htm (accessed September 22, 2017).
5 Interview with former Fermanagh SDLP Councillor, Fergus McQuillan, Newtownbutler, November 28, 2016.

long.[6] Both had been stabbed in the heart multiple times. Dr Carson counted at least seventeen stab wounds to Naan's upper chest; some had run together to form gaping holes. One stab wound was five and half inches deep. Naan had also been stabbed in the neck and evidently been struck on the right side of his face where there was a marked abrasion. Murray too had been stabbed multiple times, mostly in the back; he had also been hit on the head at some point.[7] Despite the clear conclusion by Dr Carson that the murder weapon was a long knife (believed by some to be a bayonet), the misnomer, the 'Pitchfork murders', has found an enduring place in the annals of Irish atrocity.[8]

Frank McManus, the Nationalist MP for Fermanagh and South Tyrone, quickly concluded that soldiers had carried out the killings; this explained the 'almost casual' investigation carried out by the RUC: 'The only doubt is whether they were in or out of uniform. All opinion agrees that it was a professionally done job ... A double-edged weapon was used. The bayonet is the Army and the UDR possess a double-edged weapon.'[9] McManus was right to suspect that soldiers were behind the murders,

6 PRONI: CRCT/3/2/2/159A Hathaway, Byrne, Chestnut and Snowball, 'Report by the Deputy State Pathologist following a Post-Mortem on Michael Naan and Andrew Murray, October 25, 1972'. Trial document made available by Legal Professional 2. The author gained access to two court files, one held by PRONI – PRONI: CRCT/3/2/2/159A – and another, similar, but more substantial, case file held by a legal professional who preferred to remain anonymous but was centrally involved in the murder trial of January 1981. Because of an agreement reached with PRONI whereby the author would not identify any name, except for those convicted, in subsequent publications, reference has generally been made to the files provided by Legal Professional 2, who imposed no restrictions of access. However, the author has compared both files at length. In some of the witness statements it is possible to discern who took the statement or wrote up the interview transcript. In others, it is not possible to do so. Some documents are undated, but where possible a date and the person who recorded or witnessed the statement or interview are provided. Many of the soldiers referred to here were promoted after 1972; some left the Army. However, their respective ranks as held on the day of the murders of Michael Naan and Andrew Murray, October 23, 1972, have been used throughout so as to avoid confusion.
7 PRONI: CRCT/3/2/2/159A Hathaway, Byrne, Chestnut and Snowball, 'Report'; 'A Wrong Tip Led to the Solving of a Double Murder', Irish News, January 16, 1981.
8 'Funeral of Newtownbutler Men', Fermanagh Herald, November 4, 1972.
9 'Funeral of Newtownbutler Men', Fermanagh Herald.

but mistaken in believing that part-time UDR soldiers had carried out the killing. In January 1981, more than nine years after the killings took place, two serving soldiers and one former soldier, all of whom had served in 13 Platoon, D Company, 1 Argylls in 1972, eventually pleaded guilty to their roles in the murders of Michael Naan and Andrew Murray. Former Platoon Sergeant Stan Hathaway was convicted of two counts of murder and sentenced to life imprisonment (he was released from prison in 1992). Corporal John Byrne was convicted on one count of murder (Murray) and also received a life sentence (he was released in 1991). Both men had initially intended on pleading not guilty but later relented, entering a guilty plea, after their legal representatives made clear that they would not win their cases and would receive harsher sentences (Hathaway held out the longest, changing his plea midway through his trial). Lance Corporal Iain Chestnut, who already had a criminal record for firing pellets at local people in Newry in 1972, was also reluctant to plead guilty. He ultimately admitted to a reduced charge of manslaughter and was sentenced to four years' imprisonment relating to the death of Andrew Murray (he served less than two). The officer commanding 13 Platoon in 1972, 2nd Lieutenant Andrew Snowball, pleaded guilty to withholding information, receiving a one-year suspended prison sentence.[10]

Lieutenant Snowball came from a well-known Scottish military family. His father, Brigadier Ted Snowball, was a highly distinguished Argyll officer. Schooled at Harrow, Andrew Snowball would later marry the niece of Simon Maxwell, 13th Baron Farnham, an Irish peer whose family seat, Farnham House, was situated in County Cavan.[11] In 1978, when the RUC renewed its investigation into the Fermanagh murders, Snowball was serving as aide-de-camp to GOC Scotland, Lieutenant General Sir Michael Gow (a former Scots Guards officer; his father was a close friend of another former GOC Scotland, Lieutenant General Sir Henry Leask, also Scots Guards). Now a captain, Andrew Snowball's

---

10 'Judgment', *Fermanagh Herald*, January 24, 1981; Brian MacDonald, *The Pitchfork Murders* (Newtownbutler: Louis Leonard Sinn Féin Cumann, 2013), 45.
11 Entry for the Hon. Sheelin Virgina Maxwell, Royal Genealogy Archive, University of Hull; T. Wilson, 'The Strange Death of Loyalist Monaghan', in S. Paseta (ed.), *Uncertain Futures: Essays about the Irish Past for Roy Foster* (Oxford: Oxford University Press, 2016), 180.

career in the Army was progressing well; he had good prospects for future promotion.[12]

Andrew Snowball joined the Argylls in 1971 shortly after completing a six-month officer-training course at the military academy at Mons officer training academy (short of A-level qualifications, he was ineligible for training at Sandhurst). Aged only 18, he was posted with Balaklava Company to Gibraltar later that year, where his first platoon sergeant was Jimmy Struthers, a capable NCO who helped him manage the challenges of junior command.[13] He completed a platoon commanders' course in late 1971 before joining the freshly reformed 1 Argylls in the spring of 1972. In D Company he was reunited with a friend from Mons, 2nd Lieutenant Alistair McKillop, a Queen's Own Highlander 'borrowed' by an undermanned 1 Argylls. Snowball was 20 at the time of D Company's deployment to Fermanagh, making him one of the British Army's youngest officers.[14] According to the RUC, Snowball was not present on Naan's farm at the time of the murders; Sergeant Hathaway, Corporal Byrne, Lance Corporal Chestnut and Private John Mcguire made up the four-man unit the RUC claimed visited the farm. However, 13 Platoon's OC admitted learning that his soldiers had stabbed Naan and Murray to death on the same night as the murders took place.[15]

Up until the time of their arrests in June 1979 the other three convicted Argylls had also done well in the years after the killings: Stan Hathaway had gone on to become a Staff Sergeant in the Royal Electrical and Mechanical Engineers and was based in Germany for a number of years. John Byrne became a Sergeant in the Military Provost Staff Corps and was based at HM Prison Maze in Northern Ireland. After a dishonourable discharge and a six-month prison sentence for assaulting civilians in Newry in September 1972, former Lance Corporal Iain Chestnut began a career as a crane operator and crew supervisor on a North Sea oil-rig for Santa Fé. His employers thought highly of him (he was

---

12 'A Wrong Tip Led to the Solving of a Double Murder', *Irish News*, January 16, 1981.
13 As related in an earlier chapter, Struthers was killed in South Armagh in November 1972.
14 Interview with Argyll Soldier 5 (Officer), May 2014; Correspondence with Argyll Soldier 7 (Officer), December 2016.
15 PRONI: CRCT/3/2/2/159A Hathaway, Byrne, Chestnut and Snowball, 'Report'; 'A Wrong Tip Led to the Solving of a Double Murder'.

rehired by Santa Fé after his release from prison).[16] Lieutenant Snowball's sometime batman and radio operator, Private John Brennan Mcguire, who was present at Naan's farm on the day of the murder, had all charges against him dropped on November 30, 1979; he agreed to become a State witness. In 1988, Mcguire was promoted to serve as Regimental Sergeant Major of the Argyll and the Sutherland Highlanders.[17]

Military witness testimony at the trial confirmed that Hathaway and Byrne were excellent soldiers. Hathaway was known for 'strictness rather than aggressiveness'. According to Lance Corporal Chestnut, 'He had no reputation for being a good man in a rough house. He was straight down the line and formal in his attitudes as a sergeant.'[18] Byrne had been acting as a platoon sergeant at various periods during D Company's 1972 tour; he, Hathaway and Chestnut were tough and experienced.[19] The three NCOs were all Aden veterans; Chestnut carried both knife- and bullet-wound scars.[20] Like most non-commissioned officers, the three men came from working-class backgrounds. Unusually for the Argylls, Hathaway was a native of Morayshire in the far north of Scotland (historically a recruiting area for the Seaforth Highlanders) and grew up near the town of Forres; his family appear to have been involved in farming. It later emerged at the trial that when Hathaway was a child he witnessed the death of a man in a thrashing machine. At the age of 15 he joined the Merchant Navy, before enlisting in the Argylls in the early 1960s.[21] At the time of the murders he had just celebrated his 30th

---

16 PRONI: CRCT/3/2/2/159A Hathaway, Byrne, Chestnut and Snowball, 'Report'.

17 'Soldiers on Trial for Double Stabbing of Catholics on Farm', *Fermanagh Herald*, January 17, 1981.

18 Statement of Iain Fletcher Chestnut, dated June 12, 1979. Document made available by Legal Professional 2.

19 Statement of Major John Jeremy Mackenzie, witnessed by Corporal C.J. Pert, Royal Military Police Special Investigations Branch (RMP SIB), January 18, 1973, Form 266A (Military), Case No. 15549/3. Document made available by Legal Professional 2 involved in the trial of Hathaway, Byrne, Chestnut and Snowball. Document missing from the original PRONI file CRCT/3/2/2/159A.

20 PRONI: CRCT/3/2/2/159A Hathaway, Byrne, Chestnut and Snowball: Charge Sheets.

21 TNA: BT 372/2147/15R695441.002 Registry of Shipping and Seamen: Central Registry of Seamen: Seamen's Records: Hathaway S A 18/10/1942 Forre R695441;

birthday (October 18).[22] Byrne, aged 25 in October 1972, was from the Clydeside port of Greenock, a traditional Argyll recruiting area. Like many Greenock men he would have been expected to work on the docks, go to sea or join the Army. Iain Chestnut had strong family connections with Aberdeenshire (a Gordon Highlanders recruiting area), where he was living at the time of his arrest. However, his mother was Northern Irish; he had an aunt who lived in County Down, in the same area of operations as 1 Argylls in 1972. (His local contacts proved useful when it came to selecting his legal team, namely Wallace and Co., a solicitors' firm located in Banbridge, County Down.)[23]

Police officers at the trial outlined the sequence of events that led to the convictions: in May 1978, a former Argyll, horrified at the 'Yorkshire Ripper' killings, contacted police to report that the murders were being carried out by a serving soldier. The former soldier believed that one of the soldiers that killed Murray and Naan was now committing similar crimes in England. The horrific knife attack on 18-year-old prostitute Helen Rytka, including multiple stab wounds to the chest, were similar, or so the soldier believed, to accounts he had heard of the murders of Michael Naan and Andrew Murray.[24] After some hesitation on the part of the police, that information eventually prompted an RUC and RMP investigation that led police officers to the soldiers of 13 Platoon.[25]

The Argylls appear to have been already forewarned; Lance Corporal Chestnut related that a former Army friend, now an RUC police officer, told him the identity of the Argyll 'grass' at the outset of the investigation, in January 1979.[26] Indeed, an RUC detective later gave evidence at the

Statement of Lance Corporal Iain Chestnut, June 10, 1979. Trial document made available by Legal Professional 2.

22 It is notable that D Company's OC Major Jeremy Mackenzie (31), Sergeant Hathaway (30) and Michael Naan (31) were all of a similar age at the time of the murders.

23 PRONI: CRCT/3/2/2/159A Hathaway, Byrne, Chestnut and Snowball: Charge Sheets.

24 'A Conscience Betrayed Killers', *The Times*, January 16, 1981.

25 'A Wrong Tip Led to the Solving of a Double Murder', *Irish News*.

26 Statement of Iain Fletcher Chestnut, dated June 12, 1979. Document made available by Legal Professional 2 involved in the trial of Hathaway, Byrne, Chestnut and Snowball. Document missing from the original PRONI file – CRCT/3/2/2/159A.

trial that the informant now lived in fear of his life.[27] Upon hearing of the investigation, Chestnut wasted no time in contacting other soldiers, including his former platoon commander, 2nd Lieutenant Andrew Snowball.[28] Months of prepared obstruction, lies and denial followed, but in June 1979, evidence gathered from other soldiers in 13 Platoon led to a series of confessions. Two RMP SIB investigators, Staff Sergeant Malcolm Denton and Sergeant Robert Stronach, interviewed Sergeant Stan Hathaway in Germany. According to the SIB investigators' account (the RUC were not present), Hathaway broke down and confessed his crime and the involvement of two others, Corporal John Byrne and Lance Corporal Iain Chestnut.[29] The police had ascertained who had killed Naan and Murray; however, the reasons why the men died are less clear and deserve further exploration.

The 'Pitchfork murders' can be seen as a 'symptomatic event': According to Richard Bessel, a symptomatic event is a moment in history which, if properly analysed, offers an insight into some of the formal and informal power relationships that both cause and limit violence, including the ability of individuals with access to State institutions to advance their own interests or goals in ways that run contrary to accepted norms of justice and/or procedure.[30] An analysis of the investigation and punishment of the perpetrators highlights a number of issues for concern, namely that the inquiry into the circumstances of the killing of Naan and Murray was hindered at various turns by informal networks. This chapter will also draw upon the work of Peter Bachrach and Morton Baratz, who have argued that a study of key

---

27 'A Conscience Betrayed Killers', *The Times*, January 16, 1981.

28 Statement of Iain Fletcher Chestnut, dated June 12, 1979. Document made available by Legal Professional 2 involved in the trial of Hathaway, Byrne, Chestnut and Snowball. Document missing from the original PRONI file – CRCT/3/2/2/159A.

29 Transcript of an RMP/SIB interview on June 7, 1979 with Sergeant Stanley Hathaway, as recorded by RMP SIB Staff Sergeant Malcolm Denton, dated June 28, 1979.

30 The phrase 'symptomatic event' is taken from Richard Bessel's well-known 'The Potempa Murder' article which examined the murder of communist labourer Konrad Pietzuch by a group of local Sturm Abteilung members in a village on the Silesian border with Poland on August 10, 1932. R. Bessel, 'The Potempa Murder', *Central European History* 10(3) (1977), 241–254.

decisions, non-decisions or non-questions can reveal 'the prevailing mobilization of bias' in institutions to protect more powerful individuals. Non-decision-making here is defined as 'the practice of limiting the scope of actual decision-making to "safe" issues by manipulating the dominant community values, myths, and political institutions and procedures'.[31] Non-decision-making and the mobilisation of bias can be overt, as in the case of the 1953 War Office inquiry into alleged abuses perpetrated by British soldiers during the Mau Mau rebellion when General Sir George Erskine successfully applied pressure to limit the scope of the inquiry in order to preserve the 'good name' of the Army.[32] However, it can also be the product of what Bachrach and Baratz have described as 'latent power', namely deference shown towards a powerful actor or institution's real or imagined preferences.[33]

The military sociologist Erella Grassiani has pointed out how frequently militaries and governments seek to explain away military atrocities as the result of one or two 'rotten apples', thereby refusing to examine the wider group processes at play, effectively isolating the individual from his wider unit, the small, constant group of individuals whom he influences and is, in turn, influenced by.[34] In this case, the latent power of the British Army appears to have prevented the airing of difficult questions relating to the role of D Company's leaders in the events that led to the deaths of Michael Naan and Andrew Murray. The Naan and Murray case fits with a trend of deliberate, systematic dishonesty by military witnesses that have repeatedly thwarted proceedings aimed at examining allegations against the Army. Nevertheless, the murder of Naan was not representative of the British Army's campaign in Northern Ireland – it was an exceptionally violent and brutal incident. Compared with the sheer scale of violence seen in other insurgencies or civil wars, Stathis Kalyvas has noted that 'there has been considerable reciprocal restraint in Northern Ireland' (even if it does not appear that way to the conflict's victims).[35] Moreover, although D Company did show signs

31 P. Bachrach and M. Baratz, *Power and Poverty: Theory and Practice* (Oxford: Oxford University Press, 1979), 47.

32 H. Bennett, *Fighting the Mau Mau: The British Army and Counter-Insurgency in Kenya Emergency* (Cambridge: Cambridge University Press, 2013), 206–209.

33 Bachrach and Baratz, *Power and Poverty*, 26–27.

34 E. Grassiani, *Soldiering under Occupation* (Oxford: Berghahn, 2013), 1.

35 Kalyvas, *The Logic of Violence in Civil War*, 7.

of deviant behaviour before the murders – a contributory factor to the events that followed – it still took a dramatic catalyst, namely the suspected abduction of a soldier, to set the conditions for murder.

Finally, this chapter also examines the process that led to Michael Naan's denunciation by his neighbours as 'a known IRA man'. The murders of Naan and Murray reveal the occasionally excessive reliance of regular British units in Fermanagh on local part-time 4 UDR soldiers during the early years of Operation Banner.[36] The targeting of Michael Naan accords with Kalyvas's description of 'selective violence' during civil wars: 'Selective violence results from the *joint action* of local and supralocal actors, insiders and outsiders, civilians and political actors. It is the outcome of an *exchange* between them and entails, therefore, an intimate relation between denouncer and denouncee.'[37] Kalyvas notes that the production of blacklists for the targeting of neighbours is a typical manifestation of selective violence during civil wars. However, the motives for suspecting a neighbour may not be entirely political. Envy, perceived aloofness or marked difference, Kalyvas observes, is sometimes the tipping point for inclusion on a blacklist handed over to external armed actors who arrive in a community.[38] Kalyvas highlights the critical role of long-standing grudges between neighbours in explaining denunciation, how these motives are then opportunistically grafted onto the wider context of a civil war. He points out that, 'While political actors "use" civilians to collect information and win the war, it is also the case that civilians "use" political actors to settle their own private conflicts.' Put otherwise, civilians may effectively turn political actors into their own 'contract killers'.[39]

Kalyvas is not trying to suggest absolutes – he notes that a mix of motivations and suspicions, some political, others borne out of social malice, are often behind the denunciation of a neighbour to outsiders during a time of conflict and strain on the civil power.[40] I will suggest

---

36 TNA: CJ 4/1784 Paper entitled, 'The Future Role and Organisation of the UDR', TNA: WO 305/4251 16th/5th The Queen's Royal Lancers Commander's Diary, Northern Ireland 1972, Operation Instruction No. 3, Headquarters Squadron, October 6, 1972; Kalyvas, *The Logic of Violence in Civil War*, 340.

37 Kalyvas, *The Logic of Violence in Civil War*, 336.

38 Kalyvas, *The Logic of Violence in Civil War*, 379.

39 Kalyvas, *The Logic of Violence in Civil War*, 379

40 Kalyvas, *The Logic of Violence in Civil War*, 380.

that social malice, enduring resentment over the Naan family's purchase of a farm previously in Protestant hands, fused with suspicion regarding Michael Naan's family background and political activities, played a role in why the local, part-time UDR unit (C Company, 4 UDR), led by Major Albert Liddle, listed Michael Naan as being a senior IRA Volunteer, false information that led directly to Naan being targeted by D Company, 1 Argylls. Michael Naan was denied his rights in life and in death. He was targeted by locals, part-time soldiers from 4 UDR, subsequently killed by outsiders, D Company, 1 Argylls and the investigation into his murder was frustrated by a deliberate attempt to conceal evidence and by a deferential attitude towards the British Army on the part of investigators and the wider justice system.

Fermanagh Goes to War:
Internecine Suspicion and Atrocity

Memory and the Legacy of Violence in South Fermanagh

Tracing Upper Lough Erne from its south-western edge at the County Cavan town of Ballyconnell to the Earl of Erne's Crom Castle, near the town of Newtownbutler (a distance of just over six miles as the crow flies), allows for an appreciation of the long history of violence that has bloodied the banks of the Erne over the centuries, the result of inherited, internecine fears that played no small role in the deaths of Michael Naan and Andrew Murray. These were not 'mindless' or random killings; to understand why not it is necessary to examine the local historical spurs that shaped the course D Company subsequently followed in identifying, observing and then killing Michael Naan on the evening of October 23, 1972.

In the mid-eighteenth century, the traveller and Anglican clergyman William Henry wrote that, for a few miles, from the southern hills of Cavan to Crom Castle in County Fermanagh, Lough Erne 'observes the form of a large, silent, beautiful river'.[41] Snake-like rivulets run northwards from the south-west near Ballyconnell and from the south-east near Belturbert in County Cavan to Crom. Until the mid-twentieth century these were the highways of communication for many of the inhabitants

---

41 W. Henry, *Upper Lough Erne* (Whitegate: Ballinakella Press, 1987), 36.

of South Fermanagh. Fertile, curving, often wooded drumlins form islands that dot the Erne waters. In the seventeenth century, Scottish and English Protestant settlers arrived in South Fermanagh by boat from the plantation town of Enniskillen (itself built on an island that divides Upper from Lower Lough Erne) or the military garrison at Belturbet. The great Ulster Plantation estates on which they laboured, such as Florencecourt and Crom, clung to the banks of Upper Lough Erne. The settlers steadily cleared the thick oak, ash, birch and alder woods of south Fermanagh, burning and draining as they expanded their farmsteads. Fortified farmhouses were often built on top of drumlins. But travel by land was cumbersome and dangerous – the local Irish often attacked the outnumbered settlers – and was generally avoided. Crom Castle, billeted by the Crichton family, 'was a place of considerable strategical [sic] importance, commanding as it did the waterway between the two fortified towns of Enniskillen and Belturbet'.[42] It is also very beautiful. Shan Bullock, Fermanagh's best-known author (Bullock's father had been the Steward at the Earl of Erne's Crom estate at the end of the nineteenth century), etched the landscape as it can be appreciated from the slopes of nearby Slieve Rushen, near the village of Ballyconnell:

> Placid, irregular, the shores fringed with reeds and woods, rounded hills and little farms, at intervals fine residences of the gentry, a church, a tower, dim mountains far north and the peat smoke of a town, yachts tacking about, a ferry-boat crossing, someone fishing in a cot near the bulrushes for bream or perch, and between the shores many green islands.[43]

Ballyconnell or Belturbet to Crom is a short distance by boat but it is a space compressed with accounts of inter-communal strife over four centuries. From the seventeenth to the twentieth centuries, bouts of violence could periodically descend and damage otherwise practical, often cordial ties between neighbours in this thinly populated, agricultural region. Protestants and Catholics would retreat into familiar territory, clinging to institutions, which they believed would keep them safe, or

42 J. Crichton, 'An Account of Some Plantation Castles on the Estates of the Earl of Erne in the County of Fermanagh', *Ulster Journal of Archaeology* 2(1) (1895), 12.
43 S. Bullock, *After Sixty Years* (London: Sampson Low, Marston, 1931), 3.

even take revenge for past grievances. Memories of past outrages endured as living lessons for the present; a Fermanagh community relations officer, Mary Gordon-McBride, observed that 'social construction of historical events' as an interpretative prism for current events was particularly strong in the Fermanagh context, with 'highly selective' but deeply felt narratives being composed by both communities. The events narrated – such as the Mackan Fight – stretched back over decades and even centuries.[44]

The American anthropologist Henry Glassie, who conducted extensive research in South Fermanagh during the early 1970s, recalled hearing accounts of Mackan from both communities, 'Hushed, tense, they speak differently of Mackan Hill than any other event in their history. The voice is held back; now it races, confined and driven by the terrible relevance of the old Mackan fight.'[45] Glassie wrote about the complexity of intercommunal exchanges in South Fermanagh, where neighbours often had to cooperate out of necessity but where bloody narrative imagery and lingering fears of repeated violence and betrayal loomed large:

> That is why it matters where the dead of Mackan Hill died. They lived right here ... Larger conditions, dirt and rain and thundering storm, require neighbours to cooperate. They must stay engaged and in union despite ideological differences. Yet neighbour threatens neighbour. Visions rise of houses burned, of livestock destroyed, of eviction and famine. Neighbours are supposed to help build houses and help in the harvest of food, to join in preserving life. Then: neighbour murders neighbour. Deep evil is harrowed and scraped into view. The evil of politics, of distant leaders who care nothing for the little community's health, is alien no more. It has entered the neighbourhood, come into the breast, and soured the clay with blood.[46]

Since the partition of Ireland in 1921, an incongruous border, hurriedly drawn according to county lines, meanders through the lakes,

---

44 Gordon-McBride, 'Symbol, Barrier, Resource, Bridge', 147.
45 H. Glassie, *Passing the Time in Ballymenone: Culture and History of an Ulster Community* (Indianapolis: Indiana University Press, 1995), 223.
46 Glassie, *Passing the Time in Ballymenone*, 244.

promontories and islands of South Fermanagh. 'The neck', the Drummully salient, a sharp outcrop of County Monaghan in the Republic of Ireland, cuts through South Fermanagh. In the opinion of one former British Army officer who served in Fermanagh in the early 1970s, and previously in Malaya, the exposed situation in South Fermanagh, bisected at innumerable points by lightly policed counties in the Republic of Ireland (Monaghan, Cavan and Donegal) and its topography (innumerable lakes, thick woodlands, hills, islands etc.), meant that the county was 'made for insurgency'.[47]

The village of Ballyconnell at the south-west edge of Upper Lough Erne was synonymous among Protestants in South Fermanagh with the disaster that befell their co-religionists who were 'left behind' the new border, a stark and enduring warning should Northern Ireland's place in the UK be threatened in the future. In February 1923, Ballyconnell, newly part of the Irish Free State, was the scene of a sectarian raid by Republicans that was still recalled in shock by Protestants in neighbouring Fermanagh five decades later:

> The men jumped out and ran from house to house, hammering on the doors, demanding admission. Revolvers were fired at random to back up their demands. Doors were battered in. Windows were riddled with bullets, bombs exploded ... The principal business place, Messrs. Ovens and Richardson's, owned by Protestants, was selected for special attention because a raider had been killed a short time before when he was robbing the till in the shop. Indeed, it was felt that the entire raid was a reprisal.[48]

William Ovens was dragged outside and shot in the leg, crying out, "For God's sake boys, have mercy." His appeal was answered. Instead of firing a second time, they dragged Mr Ovens, bleeding and in pain, through the archway to the street and flung him into the hallway of a neighbour's house.[49] Ovens survived. A young shop assistant, Willie Ryan, 'a quiet,

---

47 Interview with a former UDR officer (4th Battalion), June 2014.
48 M. Dane, *The B Specials in Fermanagh* (Enniskillen: William Trimble Ltd., 1970), 14.
49 Dane, *The B Specials in Fermanagh*, 14.

inoffensive lad', was not so lucky. Upon giving the gunmen his name he was shot several times and left to die 'in great agony' in the street. Finally, the raiding party tried to set fire to the two shops but neighbours succeeded in dousing the flames after they departed.[50]

In 1970, Viscount Brookeborough, Northern Ireland's former wartime Prime Minister, recalled that such violence was the impetus for the establishment of the Ulster Special Constabulary, initially an irregular and illegal force, to protect Fermanagh's Protestant population. In an interview with a journalist from *The Impartial Reporter*, the then 82-year-old Brookeborough pointed to an oak tree on his Colebrooke estate, under which he sat waiting, rifle in hand, for the arrival of an IRA raiding party during the summer of 1920. From church towers and hills, and even the Cole Monument in Enniskillen town centre, local Protestant militia watched for raiding parties from the south.[51]

The attack in Ballyconnell was part of a campaign of violence against Protestants, broadly suspected as being hostile to the Republican cause, from 1919 to 1923. Some moved across the border, to settle in nearby Fermanagh. Mary Gordon-McBride, in her study of cross-border violence in Fermanagh, Cavan and Monaghan during the twentieth century, has estimated that 2,100 southern Protestants moved across the border to Fermanagh between 1920 and 1925.[52] Peter Leary in turn has observed that this period left an enduring legacy: Unionists who moved north across the border brought with them 'experiences of political and sectarian violence', while on the Nationalist side the 'terrorism' of the USC or 'B men' was added to 'Famine, penal laws, and dispossession'.[53] Ballyconnell also has a more immediate link with the deaths of Michael Naan and Andrew Murray; on the night of the murders, October 23, 1972, another group of soldiers crossed the border in order to observe the house of a suspected IRA Volunteer on the outskirts of the village.[54]

Moving two to three miles north-east from Ballyconnell, just across the border, the Erne–Shannon waterway passes the farms of two UDR

---

50 Dane, *The B Specials in Fermanagh*, 15.
51 Dane, *The B Specials in Fermanagh*, 3.
52 Gordon-McBride, 'Symbol, Barrier, Resource, Bridge', 94.
53 P. Leary, *Unapproved Routes: Histories of the Irish Border, 1922–1972* (Oxford: Oxford University Press, 2016), 50.
54 Interview with Argyll Soldier 5 (Officer), May 2014.

men targeted for assassination by the IRA on the night of September 13, 1972 – Privates Darling and Bullock. Tom Bullock and his wife were both murdered; Darling was not at home at the time. Just across the nearby Aghalane Bridge – an access point from the south used by the IRA to launch cross-border ambushes (and frequently closed by the Army) – a patrol from Chestnut Troop, RHA, was ambushed on the morning Naan and Murray were murdered. Another two miles further downstream, meandering along the eddies and narrow channels that make up Upper Lough Erne, boats pass by the Bloody Pass, named after a 1689 rout of Catholic soldiers loyal to James II, fleeing south-west after the Battle of Newtownbutler, in which they were defeated by local Protestant militia, 'Inniskilleners' and the garrison at Crom who were loyal to King William III (of Orange). The Crichton family, later the Earls of Erne, and their local tenants, cum militiamen, played a prominent role in the fighting, initially by refusing to surrender their besieged castle at Crom, being to the fore in the subsequent Battle of Newtownbutler and later in massacring the defeated Jacobites who found themselves pinned against the Lough, as recounted by the 4th Earl of Erne:

> A sally was made upon the fugitives, many of whom had taken refuge in the woods of Innisfendra [sic] Island by the garrison of Crom. From this they were driven by the Crom yeomen. The narrow neck of water at the south-east end of Innisfendra has ever since borne the name of the 'Bloody Pass' from the fearful slaughter of the flying men whose bodies bridged over the ford across which they tried in vain to escape.[55]

On the morning of October 23, in the hours prior to murdering Michael Naan and Andrew Murray, soldiers from 13 Platoon would conduct a search at Bloody Pass and throughout the island of Inisfendra.[56] The historian Darren Graham has recently identified the drumlin and ridge at Sandholes, adjacent to Naan's farm and where D Company

---

55 Crichton, 'Crom Castle'.
56 Statement of Major John Jeremy Mackenzie, witnessed by Corporal C.J. Pert, Royal Military Police Special Investigations Branch (RMP SIB), January 18, 1973, Form 266A (Military), Case No. 15549/3. Document made available by Legal Professional 2. Document missing from the original PRONI file CRCT/3/2 /2/159A.

Headquarters set up an Observation Post (OP) on the night of the murders, as the site for the Battle of Newtownbutler.[57]

Bloody Pass marks a crossroads on Lough Erne: a boat can turn its bow towards Belturbet (four miles to the south-east) – scene of a bomb attack that killed two teenagers (Paddy Stanley and Geraldine O'Reilly) on December 28, 1972, most likely carried out by Loyalist paramilitaries from Fermanagh – or continue northwards towards Crom (a few hundred yards away).[58] Just to the south and east of Bloody Pass, in the direction of Belturbet, is Galloon Island, near the townland of Derrydoon, the site of the killing of Private Robin Bell (4 UDR), Michael Naan's neighbour on October 22, 1972 (the Bells had recently purchased a farm in Derrydoon).[59] Galloon was also the location of a sectarian clash in 1858 between local Protestants and their Catholic neighbours. Catholic residents of Newtownbutler still recall handed-down narratives of the incident, when the construction of a Catholic Church in the parish, including the ringing of a newly purchased bell made in Dublin, apparently enraged local Protestants who rioted in Newtownbutler. A unit of Lancers, sent from Belturbet to put down the disturbances, charged the crowd, killing two local Protestant men.[60]

Continuing to the south-east along the banks of the Erne, a few hundred yards from Galloon, boats pass the townland of Cornacaghan, the former residence of the Latimer family who abandoned their farm in August 1972 after a series of attacks by IRA units. IRA snipers took full advantage of the higher ground and woodland in the old Lanesborough estate across the stretch of the Erne that represented the border to the south.[61] The largely desolate Lanesborough Lodge and estate was the work of an earlier IRA unit. On June 4, 1921, IRA Volunteers crossed the Erne from Fermanagh to raid and set fire to the ancestral home of

57 D. Graham, *Enniskillen and the Battle of Newtownbutler* (Farnham: Pike and Shot Society, 2011), 67.

58 'Final Report of the Commission of Investigation into the Dublin and Monaghan Bombings', published April 4, 2007, available at www.taoiseach.ie (accessed February 26, 2015).

59 The farm had previously belonged to the Beatty and Elton families. Land Registry of Northern Ireland, Folio 6513, County Fermanagh.

60 J. McCusker, *Memories of Newtownbutler and Canon Tom Maguire* (Lisnaskea: McBrien Printing, undated), 33.

61 'Shots Fired at Fermanagh UDR Man', *Impartial Reporter*, August 30, 1972.

the Earls of Lanesborough. Lord Lanesborough was burned out of his Irish home by some of his near neighbours and former tenants, including IRA commander Matt Fitzpatrick, who lived across the Erne channel that separates Lanesborough Lodge from the townland of Kilgarrow, a few hundred yards from Michael Naan's farm and close to where Andrew Murray lived with his mother at the time of his death.[62]

By a quirk of county geography, a twist of Lough Erne, Lanesborough Lodge was in a small piece of County Cavan jutting into Fermanagh. After partition, the 8th Earl of Lanesborough abandoned his burned-out Irish mansion and sold his remaining lands. A mile or so further south towards Belturbet is the Victorian mansion of Castle Saunderson, itself almost a mirror copy of Crom Castle, and the former home of Colonel Edward Saunderson (regarded as the father of Ulster Unionism). This stately gem was also left to ruin; but its demise was less sudden than Lanesborough Lodge, and came about due to IRA harassment and slow neglect, rather than burning. Remarkably, Wattlebridge primary school in County Fermanagh, frequently used for IRA recruiting and training in the 1920s, lay only a few hundred yards across a narrow stretch of water from Castle Saunderson.[63] At the turn of the twentieth century, the Earls of Erne (Crichtons), the Earls of Lanesborough (Butlers), the Barons Farnham (Maxwells) and the Saundersons were closely connected. Together they formed an elite society linked by the waterways of Lough Erne and the nucleus of competition between their rival yachts at the Lough Erne Yacht Club at Crom Castle, visited by viceroys and royalty alike. By the mid-twentieth century, only the Crichton family remained.

---

62 MAI, Bureau of Military History 1913–1921: Testimony of Lieutenant Colonel Francis Tummon, 'Recollections of Volunteer Francis Tummon of the Irish Republican Army', 45.

63 'Recollections of Volunteer Francis Tummon of the Irish Republican Army', 45. The local battalion was formed by IRA leader, Eoin O' Duffy, in or around the old schoolhouse in Wattlebridge in 1919. Francis Tummon later recalled the meeting, indirectly highlighting the fusion between the GAA and IRA recruiting practices during this time: 'In his talk, lasting roughly twenty minutes, [Eoin] O' Duffy outlined the objects of the Volunteers, how the organisation was built up and their ultimate aim, namely the overthrow of British rule in Ireland. Finally, he said that anyone present who was not prepared to use force should not join the Volunteers … Subsequent to this lecture a small group was assembled, mainly from the ranks of the GAA and elected Company officers as a first step.'

The ruin of these families served as a stark warning to those Protestant peers, including Lords Erne and Enniskillen, whose estates lay on the 'right side' of the border in 1921.[64]

IRA Volunteers from Newtownbutler who were 'out' in the Anglo-Irish war of the 1920s also fell victim to partition; they became targets for harassment and reprisal in Fermanagh. Leading Fermanagh IRA men such as Matt Fitzpatrick, Francis Tummon and James Smythe all moved across the border, where they received positions and pensions in the new Irish Free State; Smythe became an income tax collector at Clones, County Monaghan and Francis Tummon rose to the rank of Lieutenant Colonel in the newly formed Irish Army. Commandant Matt Fitzpatrick died on the evening of February 11, 1922, during a period of tit-for-tat violence between groups aligned with the nascent Free State government in Dublin and the Unionist administration of James Craig in Belfast. Fitzpatrick was the only IRA fatality in what Fermanagh Protestants regarded as a treacherous attack at Clones train station on a group of Special Constabulary policemen travelling from County Down to Fermanagh (Clones was a key junction for rail travel in Ulster). Four 'Specials' were killed; others wounded. Almost fifty years later, a former USC constable recalled the 'massacre':

> A man [Commandant Matt Fitzpatrick] with a Thompson gun came down the platform ... He stopped at the window of our compartment and demanded: 'Where are youse for?' We told him Enniskillen. He said, 'Youse are not for it tonight!' and he opened up on us with the machine-gun. He fired and shot a man named McMahon who was sitting beside me and he fell across my arm. I don't know how I escaped. He was sitting on the other side of me. We fell on the floor of the compartment and he fell on top of me. We lay there. My clothes were soaked with his blood. There was a lot more shouting and shooting. The next thing, one of the Specials, William Preston, who was further down the train, shot this man, Fitzpatrick, who was

---

64 The Maxwells had also co-founded Lough Erne Yacht Club, located at Crom Castle, the seat of the Earls of Erne and Arthur Maxwell. The 11th Baron Farnham played a leading role in the UVF in Cavan during the Home Rule crisis from 1912 to 1914. He was also for a brief period the leader of the Unionist Party south of the border after 1920. Wilson, 'The Strange Death of Loyalist Monaghan', 180.

Commandant of the IRA, and he rolled under the train ... If they had known he was dead, there would have been none of us left alive ... I was put with my face to the wall ... I felt sure they were going to shoot us all. Then the station-master came out and begged them not to shoot us and they didn't.[65]

The local Catholic narrative account was very different; the USC had opened fire first. Each community had their own version of the Clones 'massacre', which has been passed down to the present (an example of the polarised narratives observed by Gordon-McBride).[66] Protestants in nearby Lisbellaw were enraged. 'When the bullet-riddled, blood-stained train reached Lisbellaw, the appearance of it so incensed local Loyalists that they drove leading Sinn Féin figures from the village.'[67] Considering Lisbellaw was regarded as '99 per cent hostile' by the IRA, it is difficult to discern the identity of these 'Sinn Féin figures'. (Incidentally, during the 1970s, Lisbellaw was the home of Loyalist paramilitary leader Robert Bridges, suspected of being behind the Belturbet bombing and a number of other sectarian attacks.)[68]

To compound the 'massacre' perpetrated at Clones, at least in the eyes of border Unionists, the new Irish State renamed Erne Square (honouring the Earls of Erne) in Clones as Fitzpatrick Square to honour the man who orchestrated the attack on the Fermanagh-bound USC (Michael Naan's family owned a catering business in the same square).[69] A ballad was composed in Fitzpatrick's honour.[70] Michael Naan's uncle,

65 Dane, *The B Specials in Fermanagh*, 39; Gordon-McBride, 'Symbol, Barrier, Resource, Bridge', 109.

66 Gordon-McBride, 'Symbol, Barrier, Resource, Bridge', 147.

67 Dane, *The B Specials in Fermanagh*, 12.

68 MAI: Bureau of Military History 1913–1921, Testimony of Mr James Smyth, Battalion Adjutant, Lisnaskea Battalion, Leitrim Brigade, 1920–1921, 3; Houses of the Oireachtas, Joint Committee on Justice, Equality, Defence and Women's Rights, 'Interim Report on the Report of the Independent Commission of Inquiry into the Dublin Bombings of 1972 and 1973' (Dublin: Houses of the Oireachtas, November 2004), 125.

69 MacDonald, *The Pitchfork Murders*, 11.

70 The ballad begins as follows:
The fight at Clones Station, will long remembered be
where Commandant Fitzpatrick was sent to eternity

Alex Lynch, was an IRA Volunteer during the 1920s and a close friend of Matt Fitzpatrick. Naan's cousin, Seán Lynch, recalled as a child repeatedly questioning Alex Lynch about the Clones ambush, whose influence he later ascribed as central to the development of his own commitment to the Republican cause.[71] Michael Naan was also a friend of Dick Fitzpatrick, a descendant of the IRA leader and also a committed Republican.[72]

It is Crom Castle, less than a mile north, downstream from the Bloody Pass, that is the most northerly point of interest in the area of Upper Lough Erne under consideration; it requires closer examination, given its important role as the staging post for many D Company, 1 Argylls operations in late October 1972. Thomas Macaulay described Crom as 'the frontier garrison of the Protestants of Fermanagh'; indeed, the Castle maintained its own part-time infantry for much of the nineteenth century, a yeomanry tradition that would later be transferred to the Crichton family's patronage of the UVF and the North Irish Horse in the early to mid-twentieth century.[73] Shan Bullock recalled the enduring importance of Crom as a rallying point for Fermanagh Loyalists in his memoirs: 'Were it by unhappy chance to come that one day, as some foreboded, we should be threatened by insurgent bands, then from the Castle tower would fly the banner of England, and under it would fight shoulder to shoulder trained men from the garrison in Bunn [Belturbet] and gallant yeomen from the fields.'[74] The Crichton family maintained on display in Crom Castle the captured armour of Justin McCarthy, Lord Mountcashel, the defeated leader of the Jacobites at Newtownbutler in 1689. They also founded Crom Castle's own Loyal

---

without a moment's warning or time to breathe a prayer
but to meet his God in heaven, he was always well prepared.
The funeral from Clones town, was an inspiring sight to see
Midst pouring rain three thousand marched twelve miles to Drumalee
With General O'Duffy his oration it was grand
O'er the grave of Matt Fitzpatrick that true born Irishman.
McCusker, *Memories of Newtownbutler and Canon Tom Maguire*, 21.
71 'Interview: Seán Lynch – from Long Kesh to the District Policing Partnership', *An Phoblacht*, May 22, 2008.
72 Interview with James Naan, Newtownbutler, March 20, 2017.
73 Bullock, *After Sixty Years*, 183.
74 Bullock, *After Sixty Years*, 46.

Orange Lodge, whose meetings took place on the estate (Albert Liddle – OC of C Company, 4 UDR in 1972 – and his father Alexander were members of the lodge for a period spanning more than a century).[75]

There were occasional tensions between the Earls of Erne and their Protestant tenants, such as when the Enniskillen Methodist and social reformer Jeremiah Jordan aligned himself with the Land League and persuaded many rural Protestants to do likewise. But the making of common political cause between Catholic and Protestant tenants in South Fermanagh was short-lived. The 1881 Land Act did away with much of the abuses of landlordism and paved the way for the purchase of land by tenants in the ensuing three decades. The Land League, now co-opted by Irish Parliamentary Party leader, Charles Stewart Parnell, also took on a green, Nationalist tinge, and was renamed 'the National League'. Moreover, when it came to the ballot box, Protestants in South Fermanagh consistently voted for the Unionist candidate, including Henry, Viscount Crichton (son of the 4th Earl of Erne), despite his opposition to land reform. Frank Thompson has concluded that elections in Fermanagh in the late nineteenth century, 'demonstrated that landed and Orange influence and sectarian fears were still more pronounced in Fermanagh than in most other Ulster counties'.[76]

In 1881, John Crichton, 4th Earl of Erne formed the well-subscribed Fermanagh Defence Association, urging local Protestants to resist Nationalist invasion (represented by the Land League) of Ulster and not to employ Catholics.[77] At the beginning of the twentieth century,

75 'Obituary: Mr. Alexander Liddle', *Impartial Reporter*, August 16, 1973; 'Death of Respected Former Councillor', *Impartial Reporter*, July 26, 2007; Obituary: Mr. Joseph Albert Liddle, *Impartial Reporter*, August 30, 2007.

76 F. Thompson, 'The Land War in Fermanagh', in E. Murphy and W. Roulston, *Fermanagh: History and Society* (London: Geography Publications, 2005), 298.

77 Thompson, 'The Land War in Fermanagh', 300–312. However, relations between Fermanagh's gentry and their Protestants tenants were not straightforward. Shan Bullock recalled watching the Earl of Erne and his household going by boat to Sunday worship in the church of the holy trinity, Derryvore: 'Soon would come the great ones themselves – the lucky people – being rowed sedately to service, under a white awning, in their fine varnished boat, taking pride no doubt in all about them as became possessors in the land, conversing together as they passed us poor commoners in the tongue acquired at Oxford and the Schools.' Bullock, *After Sixty Years*, 45.

Lord Erne, now a senior member of the Orange Order, incarcerated a local Church of Ireland (Anglican) clergyman in a tower of Crom Castle when the latter announced his conversion to Catholicism.[78] The 4th Earl's son, Henry, Viscount Crichton, later took command of the UVF for the Newtownbutler area, organising weapons drills and other training on the Crom estate: 'When asked directly whether he would follow the traditions of his ancestors and lead the people of Fermanagh in resisting Home Rule by force if necessary should it become law, he [Major Crichton] replied unambiguously that he was prepared to do so.'[79] By joining the UVF, Viscount Crichton risked being dishonourably discharged from his regiment, the Royal Horse Guards. But in the turmoil unleashed by the 'Curragh mutiny' in 1914 (a signal by a number of officers stationed in Ireland that they would not enforce Home Rule even if ordered to do so), Viscount Crichton's UVF membership was overlooked. He was later killed in action in Belgium during the First World War.[80]

Crom Loyalists also played a role during the Anglo-Irish War of 1919–1921; men from Crom estate appear to have taken part in the burning of Catholic homes in Roslea on February 21, 1921, shortly after the 'Clones massacre' of USC men and in the immediate aftermath of the IRA shooting dead of George Lester as he opened his shop in Rosslea village. The 'burning of Rosslea' was later commemorated in a ballad that lauded such 'men from Crom'.[81] In the early 1920s, Protestant militias, drawing upon UVF structures and arms, were established to repel

---

78 PRONI, 'Introduction to the Earl of Erne Papers', 38, available at https://www. nidirect.gov.uk/sites/default/files/publications/erne-d1939.pdf (accessed September 22, 2017).

79 B. Barton, 'The Origins and Development of Unionism in Fermanagh, 1885–1914', in E. Murphy and W. Roulston, *Fermanagh: History and Society* (London: Geography Publications, 2005), 326.

80 Lowry Cole, 4th Earl of Enniskillen, also organised UVF training on his estate; important meetings were held in Florencecourt during 1912 and 1913 to discuss the importation of arms from Germany. Barton, 'The Origins and Development of Unionism in Fermanagh, 1885–1914', 326.

81 31 Catholic houses were attacked in Rosslea; 10 were burnt. 'From Cooneen and Ballagh, and from that down to Crom, From Inver and Shanro, and the robbers from Drum. They all marched in sections to the town of Rosslea. To put a full stop to ri-tor-al-aye-ay.' The ballad is reproduced in R. Maguire, R. Morton and J. Blacking, *Come Day, Go Day, God Send Sunday* (London: Routledge and Kegan

Republican attacks, leading to tension with the regular Army. A dispute between the Lincolnshire Regiment and Protestant militias took place in Lisbellaw in the aftermath of an IRA attack on the town in June 1920, as later recounted by a local participant: 'When the soldiers arrived in Lisbellaw they were going to disarm the local men, but they pointed out that they were fighting under the Union Jack and eventually after considerable discussion they were allowed to retain their arms.'[82] Ultimately, these militias, organised in part by the local gentry, particularly by Lord Brookeborough, were co-opted by the State to become the USC. The USC was, in effect, 'born in Fermanagh', emerging out of a long tradition of Protestant militias and vigilante groups, capable of resisting and targeting local IRA support. Albert Liddle's father, Alexander, joined the USC at its inception.[83]

Crom Castle was home to the Seaforth Highlanders and units of the US Army during the Second World War. West Ulster aristocrats, including the Brookes and Crichtons, dominated the North Irish Horse cavalry regiment (the 5th Earl of Erne, attached to another cavalry unit, was killed during the retreat to Dunkirk in May 1940). Although their economic power had waned, the political influence of the landed gentry still endured. Olwyn Purdue, in her study of Northern Ireland's peerage, has noted an unusual level of enduring political influence and resilience among the West Ulster aristocracy. Right up until the early 1970s, families such as the Dukes of Abercorn, the Dukes of Westminster and Viscounts Brookeborough served at various levels of government in Northern Ireland and represented Fermanagh in the House of Commons. Indeed, the narrow victory of the Nationalist candidate, Frank McManus, over the sitting Ulster Unionist MP, James, Marquess of Hamilton, the future Duke of Abercorn, shocked a Fermanagh peerage still accustomed to having a prominent, if not sometimes definitive, say in the political affairs of West Ulster.[84] The vice-chief of the general staff, General Sir Cecil 'Monkey' Blacker, a close friend of the Brookes who visited Fermanagh in October 1972, later recalled that 'Northern Ireland in its attitude to

Paul, 1973), 152. The author is grateful to Dr Tim Wilson for bringing this ballad to his attention.

82 Dane, *The B Specials in Fermanagh*, 12.

83 Dane, *The B Specials in Fermanagh*, 12.

84 O. Purdue, *The Big House in the North of Ireland: Land Power and Social Elites* (Dublin: University College Dublin Press, 2009), 198–208.

its ruling class – the gentry – was a good many years behind comparable attitudes across the Irish Sea.'[85]

In the 1960s and 1970s, the local aristocracy in Fermanagh continued to play an enduring role in the discussion of security matters. Military service was still the norm: the 6th Earl of Enniskillen, David Lowry Cole, was a serving major in 4 UDR; Harry Crichton, Lord Erne, had resigned his commission from the North Irish Horse in 1968. The future 2nd Viscount Brookeborough and Chairman of Fermanagh County Council, John Brooke, frequently advised Conservative MPs on security affairs in the county, including in October 1972 when John Biggs-Davison visited Fermanagh.[86] On November 8, 1972, John Brooke discussed with Conservative MPs the possible use of SAS patrols on the border.[87] Brooke's son, Alan, the present Viscount Brookeborough, was commissioned into the 17th/21st Lancers in 1970. (Alan Brooke was the same age as Andrew Snowball; the two young officers had been at Harrow together. 17/21 Lancers assumed responsibility for D Company's area of operations while the latter were in Fermanagh.)[88] According to a full-time UDR officer, the 49-year-old John Brooke tried to 'order local UDR men around like he had done with the B Specials [the USC]'.[89] In October 1972, Brooke, the son of Northern Ireland's wartime Prime Minister, the 1st Viscount Brookeborough, urged the Army to pursue the IRA across the border, citing Israeli military operations as a useful international precedent.[90]

A senior UDR officer recalled that the Earl of Erne invited him to dinner at Crom Castle in 1972 and proposed that some of his workers join the UDR. These men were already acting as a 'de facto' militia for Crom estate; Lord Erne had built pillboxes and had weapons at his disposal.

---

85 Blacker, *Monkey Business*, 171.

86 'UDR Murders "Action of Animals" Says British MP', *Impartial Reporter*, October 8, 1972.

87 CPA: CRD 3/18/1 Minutes of a Meeting of the Conservative Party Northern Ireland Backbench Committee, November 8, 1972.

88 See the announcement of the retirement of Henry Crichton, 6th Earl of Erne KCVO as Lord Lieutenant for the County of Fermanagh and the confirmation of Alan 3rd Viscount Brookeborough as the new Lord Lieutenant, 'Lord Lieutenant for County Fermanagh', 10 Downing Street, May 14, 2012.

89 Interview with a UDR Officer (4th Battalion) June 2014.

90 '"British Troops Should Pursue Gunmen across Border" – Brooke', *Derry Journal*, October 24, 1972.

He now proposed that these men should be included as part of the local C Company, 4 UDR, but that they should remain under his command, to protect the estate (an echo of the Crom Castle yeomanry of the nineteenth century). The UDR officer politely declined Lord Erne's offer.[91] During the investigation into the murders of Naan and Murray, Major Jeremy Mackenzie also described an 'eight-strong military organization', armed guards who answered to the Earl of Erne.[92] In an interview, Lord Erne recalled that he 'knew everybody', all the GOCs and secretaries of state for Northern Ireland during the 1970s, whom he met frequently and to whom he expressed his concerns. Lord Erne's connections were self-evidently impressive; he was the godson of George VI and his stepfather was the 5th Baron Terrington, Christopher Montague Woodhouse, a Conservative MP and former intelligence officer who served as SIS (MI6) Head of Station in Tehran and was one of the architects of the 1953 coup to get rid of Prime Minister Mohammad Mossadegh. At a local level, he would report on the identities of IRA men he 'knew' to be operating within his area; Army officers would come to take lists of names from him. According to Lord Erne, IRA gunmen generally 'shot in the back' before quickly disappearing innocently to 'sit by the fire in their cottages'.[93]

In April 1972, the Earl of Enniskillen wrote to the Secretary of State, William Whitelaw, from Florencecourt claiming that the 'enemy is clearly identified' and urging him to adopt colonial tactics in order to defeat the IRA.[94] Estates along the border occasionally resembled 'military bases' in the early 1970s as soldiers camped out, took refreshments and used them as staging posts for operations in the surrounding area (their owners were also regarded as vulnerable VIPs whom the Army wished to protect).[95] The exceptionally wealthy and well-connected Robert Grosvenor, 5th

---

91 Interview with a UDR Officer (4th Battalion), June 2014.

92 Statement of Major John Jeremy Mackenzie, witnessed by Corporal C.J. Pert, Royal Military Police Special Investigations Branch (RMP SIB), January 18, 1973, Form 266A (Military), Case No. 15549/3. Document made available by Legal Professional 2. Document missing from the original PRONI file CRCT/3/2/2/159A.

93 Interview with Henry Crichton, 6th Earl of Erne, Crom Castle, September 18, 2015.

94 PRONI: D1702/12/69/1–9 Earl of Enniskillen Papers, Letter from the 6th Earl of Enniskillen to the Secretary of State for Northern Ireland, William Whitelaw, dated April 6, 1972.

95 PRONI: D1702/12/69/1–9 Earl of Enniskillen Papers, Letter from the 6th Earl

Duke of Westminster, a resident at Ely Lodge near Enniskillen, former Royal Artillery officer, and Unionist MP for Fermanagh and South Tyrone, 1955–1964 (his maternal grandfather was the 4th Earl of Erne), kept up a correspondence with the Prime Minister, Edward Heath. Like his fellow peers in Fermanagh, the Duke was deeply unhappy with the Army's performance in Fermanagh and he urged Heath to take a much stronger hand against the IRA.[96]

The many meandering turns of Lough Erne initially formed an innocuous county boundary, and later, a deadly border, exploited by Republican groups and causing the upheaval of Loyalists and Republicans on both sides. Francis Tummon, an IRA veteran from Derrykerrib, Newtownbutler, recalled the shock of being arrested and abused by a party that included 'our own neighbours', members of the part-time USC.[97] Such violence between neighbours fostered a legacy of suspicion and, occasionally, smouldering hatred. Protestants believed that the IRA could not function without the active support of a wider network of sympathetic local people in South Fermanagh. There was some truth in this view; Francis Tummon ended his witness testimony to the Bureau of Irish Military History by thanking 'those who gave us lodging and food, who stood up against the raids of Crown Forces and denied any knowledge or information'.[98] Forty years on, Frank McManus, later the MP for Fermanagh and South Tyrone, recalled being told by his USC-serving neighbours to take his shoes off and stand in his socks in the snow, an incident McManus later described as 'deeply and deliberately humiliating'. Such incidents brought about a political awakening in McManus including a determination to end British rule in Northern Ireland.[99]

Stories of sectarian attacks lingered on in local memory. Catholics retold the perfidy of how local Protestants participated in the burning

of Enniskillen to the Secretary of State for Northern Ireland, William Whitelaw, dated April 6, 1972.

96 Letter from the 5th Duke of Westminster to Edward Heath, dated July 13, 1972, available at www.thebrokenelbow.com/2014/03/25/ (accessed March 12, 2015).

97 MAI, Bureau of Military History, 1913–1921: Testimony of Lieutenant Colonel Francis Tummon, 'Recollections of Volunteer Francis Tummon of the Irish Republican Army', 45.

98 MAI, 'Recollections of Volunteer Francis Tummon of the Irish Republican Army', 51.

99 Interview with Frank McManus, Enniskillen, May 30, 2016.

of Catholic homes and businesses in Roslea on February 21, 1972, while Protestants recalled the spate of assassinations and reprisal burnings, carefully orchestrated by IRA leader Eoin O'Duffy and the Monaghan Brigade of the IRA to avenge Rosslea.[100] O'Duffy also ordered raids on County Fermanagh to kidnap 100 prominent Unionists; forty were seized and held for a time south of the border. Although later released these captives carried with them stories of sectarian abuse and privation.[101] Glassie recalled the importance of culture and memory, the stories of men like Alex Lynch in fostering a new generation of Republicans in the early 1970s to continue a very old war. Leaving a pub one evening he observed a local member of the IRA:

> With people moving past, laughing, jamming in the doorway, a quiet handsome young man who has known the terror of midnight roads, the engine's hum, the feel of a makeshift bomb in his palms, stands, looking at no one, and says softly, 'When I hear the old men sing, I love Ireland more.'[102]

Memory and mythology spanning fifty years played a key role in highlighting grievance and ennobling violence by both Republicans and Loyalists in the early 1970s. Or as the IRA Volunteer Eamon Collins put it, such sentiments gave 'political legitimacy to the age-old pastime of spying on one's neighbours, turning neighbourhood vendettas into noble struggles'.[103]

The stuttering 1956–1962 IRA 'Border Campaign', which saw attacks on Fermanagh RUC stations in 1955 and 1956, did little to change the political status quo but a lot to harden political opinion among Protestants in the county. Many Unionists concluded that any moves to address Catholic grievances or improve relations with successive governments in Dublin should be resisted.[104] The attendance of up to 11,000 mourners and twenty priests at the Limerick city funeral of IRA Volunteer Seán South, killed in a failed IRA raid on Brookeborough police station in

100 See Wilson, 'The Strange Death of Loyalist Monaghan', 183–185.
101 Patterson, *Violent Frontier*, 5.
102 Glassie, *Passing the Time in Ballymenone*, 85.
103 Kalyvas, *The Logic of Violence in Civil War*, 339.
104 R. English, *Irish Freedom: The History of Nationalism in Ireland* (London: Pan, 2007), 361.

South Fermanagh on January 31, 1956, reaffirmed the view among Unionists that the Republic of Ireland was not to be trusted.[105]

Nationalist gatherings in Fermanagh, such as the Newtownbutler *Feiseanna*, founded to promote Gaelic culture and Irish unity, were banned in the mid-1950s.[106] These meetings, with large tricolour banners bearing slogans such as 'Ireland Gaelic, Ireland Free', were initially reluctantly tolerated by the local RUC. However, after high-profile visits by senior political figures from Dublin, such as that in 1952 when Taoiseach Éamon de Valera was greeted by a group of local IRA veterans (wearing their service medals from the 1919–1921 War of Independence/ Anglo-Irish War), the RUC decided to crack down on the *Feiseanna*, particularly when it came to the display of the flag of the Irish State, the tricolour, then a banned symbol in the North. In 1955, the local parish priest, Canon Tom Maguire, was hit by a police water cannon after he refused to take down a flag. Fights broke out between Newtownbutler's Catholics and their Protestants neighbours, who had been called up along with other USC units. By this time the *Feiseanna* had taken on a more militant hue, with the oration being given by Tomás Óg MacCurtain who had previously been interned by the Irish government and served on the IRA Executive Council during the Border Campaign (his father, a Lord Mayor of Cork and a senior IRA Volunteer, had been killed in a reprisal raid by members of the Royal Irish Constabulary in 1920).[107] Events such as the *Feiseanna* in Newtownbutler, filled with cultural contestation, Republican commemoration and occasional violence, would have played a significant role in the politicisation of young men such as Michael Naan. Meanwhile, Albert Liddle, a part-time USC constable, would have taken part in suppressing the *Feiseanna*.

Many Protestants also regarded the Gaelic Athletic Association (GAA), particularly its celebration of dead Republican and Fenian leaders, with considerable suspicion. The apparently ambiguous relationship between the promotion of Gaelic culture, the Catholic Church and the celebration of political violence, all represented at the 1955 Newtownbutler *Feis*, would not have been lost upon young Protestants, heightening their fears that the IRA and cultural events such as the Feiseanna/political

105 Patterson, *Violent Frontier*, 10.
106 MacDonald, *The Pitchfork Murders*, 11.
107 McCusker, *Memories of Newtownbutler and Canon Tom Maguire*, 52.

movements like the civil rights campaign were two sides of the same coin. These were all part of what the Anglican Bishop of Clogher, Robert Heavener, writing in the late 1970s using the pseudonym Robert Cielou, described as the IRA's 'Trojan horse'.[108] A number of the leading civil rights activists in Newtownbutler had common ties to the same townland, Cornabray (or Cornabrass), including Fergus McQuillan, John Joe McCusker and Seán Lavelle, although they ultimately chose separate political paths, from moderate Nationalism (McQuillan) to militant Republicanism (McCusker and Lavelle). Cornabray essentially became the new Derrykerrib, a nearby townland noted for the strong IRA sympathies of some of its inhabitants in the 1920s and, according to an account in Gordon-McBride's study, frequently raided by the RUC for decades afterwards due to the enduring perception that it was 'Republican territory'.[109] As elsewhere in Northern Ireland, political and military activism was often fostered and conditioned by minutely local circumstances and handed-down memories.

Low-level violence continued on into the 1960s in the border areas, including well-publicised incidents of police constables crossing the border to search houses and 'ambush the ambushers'. This was a continuation of a long-held premise of Loyalism and the USC, namely that 'the most effective way of defending Loyalist homes was *not* to stay in them. Ambushing the ambushers looked far more promising'.[110] The early 1960s were recalled by Frank McManus as a time of 'profound depression' for the Catholics of South Fermanagh. By contrast, the emergence of the civil rights movement in the later part of the decade marked an 'unstoppable awakening', a time of optimism when a new generation of Catholic university graduates, like McManus, returned home to challenge the old structures of Protestant political and institutional power in Fermanagh.[111] However, at least from the Unionist or Loyalist perspective, many civil rights activists in Fermanagh appeared to have direct or family ties to the IRA; Frank McManus (his brother Pat died in an IRA bomb attack in 1958) and Frank Maguire (elected as an independent MP in 1974

108 R. Cielou, *Spare my Tortured People* (Lisnaskea: Whitethorne Press, 1983), 185.
109 Interview with former Fermanagh SDLP Councillor, Fergus McQuillan, Newtownbutler, November 28, 2016; Gordon-McBride, 'Symbol, Barrier, Resource, Bridge', 147.
110 Wilson, 'The Strange Death of Loyalist Monaghan', 181.
111 Interview with Frank McManus, Enniskillen, May 30, 2016.

and previously an IRA Volunteer who was interned during the Border Campaign) both fell into this category.[112]

A Breakdown in Social Relations: Fermanagh in the Late 1960s and Early 1970s

In the late 1960s and early 1970s, Protestants in Fermanagh were a minority in the county; Catholics numbered just over 50 per cent. Catholics enjoyed an even greater majority in South Fermanagh, the poorer, more rugged half of the county. Cracks in community relations in South Fermanagh steadily widened as the civil rights protests of 1968 gathered momentum. Fermanagh was arguably the county most egregiously affected by gerrymandering and the discriminatory allocation of public services in favour of Protestants.[113] Crom, the electoral division of Lisnaskea Rural District Council which surrounded the Earl of Erne's Crom Castle, was carefully constructed to gain a Protestant majority – 181 to 105 – while the nearby Drumshimuck division was drawn up so as to limit the 'waste' of Protestant votes – hence the Catholic majority was 257 to 32 Protestants.[114] Such gerrymandering and discrimination persisted until the electoral and local government reforms of the 1970s.[115] Even as late as the 1960s, no Catholics were appointed to any senior position on the Fermanagh County Council; overall, the Council employed 338 Protestants to 32 Catholics.[116] At the end of the decade the Fermanagh Civil Rights Association accused the County Council, chaired by John Brooke, of 'a deliberate effort to eradicate the Catholic majority of County Fermanagh'.[117] It was grand rhetoric but it resonated with many Catholics in the county.

Civil rights activists in Newtownbutler condemned Fermanagh County Council's attempts to move a significant part of the growing Catholic population from the village – where Catholic and Protestant voter numbers in the local electoral division were closely balanced – to a new council housing area in the townland of Donagh, which already returned a comfortable Catholic majority. They argued that the latter site

---

112 E. Moloney, *A Secret History of the IRA* (London: Penguin, 2003), 245.
113 Patterson, *Violent Frontier*, 15.
114 'Fermanagh Facts', 8–9.
115 'Fermanagh Facts', 2.
116 Patterson, *Violent Frontier*, 15.
117 'Fermanagh Facts', 8.

was much more expensive than the Newtownbutler alternative, requiring the installation of new facilities readily available in the town; these activists also alleged that Protestants were disproportionately allocated social housing in Newtownbutler itself.[118] Social housing for Catholics in Protestant majority areas was infrequently provided; the Fermanagh Civil Rights Association pointed out that in the Florencecourt district only 1 council house out of 29 had been allocated to a Catholic family from 1945 to 1967, even though Catholics made up more than 40 per cent of Florencecourt's population and were generally more impoverished than their Protestant neighbours.[119] This trend was repeated across South Fermanagh, with varying degrees of severity; in total, Catholics received 40 per cent of council housing despite making up more than 57 per cent of the Lisnaskea Rural District area.[120] The years 1971 and 1972 saw the introduction of two local government reform acts of parliament that effectively ended gerrymandering and Ulster Unionist control of Fermanagh County Council. However, in late 1972, these changes had yet to address enduring Catholic grievances towards local government in South Fermanagh.[121]

Wider police–community tensions in Belfast and Derry also affected Fermanagh where the regular RUC had previously enjoyed a reasonably good relationship with the Catholic population. Now civil rights and Republican activist Tom Flatley accused the RUC of 'informing to the Army'.[122] Fermanagh's Catholics were outraged by the introduction of internment. Martin McCleery has observed that a one-day strike in September 1971 brought business to a standstill in Enniskillen when 1,000 people left work to march in protest. Catholic employees were allegedly sacked and victimised for taking part in the strike. Meanwhile, Frank McManus's brother, Fr Sean McManus, was fined £20 for obstructing the RUC (Fr McManus told the judge that he refused to recognise a British 'colonial' court).[123]

Once the IRA began its cross-border raids during 1971 and 1972, launching attacks on what it called 'military and economic' targets,

---

118 'Fermanagh Facts', 15.
119 'Fermanagh Facts', 35.
120 'Fermanagh Facts', 34.
121 'Fermanagh Facts', 34.
122 'Army Raids in North Fermanagh', *Impartial Reporter*, August 7, 1972.
123 McCleery, *Operation Demetrius and its Aftermath*, 133.

sectarian tensions in Fermanagh began to overflow. In Irvinestown, the local GAA club was blown up; shortly afterwards, the town's Orange Hall was bombed.[124] In Enniskillen, the local Alliance Party alleged that Catholic businesses were being intimidated and forced to close against their will by Loyalist paramilitary groups.[125] Meanwhile, after Bloody Sunday, Frank McManus led a campaign of civil disobedience, urging voters not to pay their rates and for councillors to boycott local government institutions and agencies. In the summer of 1972, McManus also withdrew from the House of Commons, in protest at 'military repression' in Northern Ireland.[126]

The Protestant population of Fermanagh were disorientated by the imminent end of Unionist dominance of Fermanagh County Council and gravely concerned at the disbandment of the USC and disarmament of the RUC, institutions that Protestants had relied upon to protect them in past periods of unrest along the border. The UDR was a more centralised force compared with the USC; part-time UDR men were expected to operate according to new standards with a strict chain of command. Former USC constables, now part-time UDR soldiers, criticised the relative lack of flexibility and local initiative compared with the USC.[127] This IRA campaign appeared more vicious and sustained than the previous border campaign (where, for the most part, local USC men were not directly targeted). As well as a spate of UDR assassinations, the IRA began planting bombs in Fermanagh's towns and villages, sometimes without warning (one VBIED in Enniskillen appeared to be deliberately disguised by placing a dummy in the front seat to avoid detection).[128]

Unlike the eastern counties of Northern Ireland where Presbyterianism was particularly strong, many of Fermanagh's Protestants were Anglicans, members of the Church of Ireland. However, those looking to the Church of Ireland for calm leadership were disappointed. In the 1970s, Bishop of Clogher, Robert Heavener (whose diocese included most of South Fermanagh), called for the transfer of

---

124 'Bomb Damage at Irvinestown', *Impartial Reporter*, April 9, 1972; Gordon-McBride, 'Symbol, Barrier, Resource, Bridge', 120.

125 'Enniskillen RCs "Forced to Close"', *Impartial Reporter*, September 2, 1972.

126 McCleery, *Operation Demetrius and its Aftermath*, 138.

127 'UDR Murders "Action of Animals" Says British MP'.

128 McCleery, *Operation Demetrius and its Aftermath*, 155.

'anti-British elements' among the Fermanagh population to the Republic of Ireland, asking, 'is it not the duty of the British Government to seek out the anti-British elements in Northern Ireland, especially those in areas that are noted for harbouring the IRA and INLA gunmen, deprive them of British citizenship and transfer them to Eire [*sic*]?'[129] The Very Reverend Thomas Clements, Dean of Clogher, shared similar sentiments. During a sermon at St Macartin's Cathedral in Enniskillen in August 1972, Clements claimed that the civil rights movement had unleashed a 'malignant evil'. The Dean was reported as saying that 'the worst fears of the most biased man had been fully justified and they were face to face with the spirit of inhuman evil'.[130] Clements, whose diocese extended south of the border, to parts of County Cavan, also wrote to Taoiseach Jack Lynch in September 1972 on behalf of the Association of Churches (Fermanagh), accusing him of harbouring criminals guilty of 'bestial conduct'.[131] According to Clements, the majority in Northern Ireland were now entitled to strike back, including at the civil rights movement.[132]

The IRA's Fermanagh Operations, 1971–1972

In Autumn 1971, Fermanagh was patrolled by approximately 160 full-time soldiers drawn from regular British Army units. (This later increased to more than 300 by early 1972 – a paltry number for a large, topographically challenging, area of operations.) From July to November 1971, an Artillery unit, 170th (Imjin) Battery, 45th Field Regiment, Royal Artillery, complained that they were, 'wholly responsible for an area of nearly eight hundred square miles comprising County Fermanagh and a small part of County Tyrone, an area enclosed by no less than 45 per cent of the entire Provincial border'. Imjin Battery had little experience of patrolling on foot or on water – suddenly they were thrust into RUC L Division and responsible for 135 miles of border lakelands. They were housed in Lisgoole School, three miles

129 Cielou, *Spare my Tortured People*, 185.
130 '"Black Evil" Facing Ulster: Proclamation from the Pulpit', *Impartial Reporter*, September 2, 1972.
131 NAI: TAOIS/ 2003/ 16/259 Letter from The Very Reverend Thomas Clements, Dean of Clogher, St Macartin's Cathedral, Enniskillen, September 27, 1972.
132 '"Black evil" Facing Ulster: Proclamation from the Pulpit'.

south of Enniskillen, '110 men crammed into classrooms'. Imjin Battery operated 'quite independently', although technically they fell under the operational command of 17th/21st Lancers, with detachments at RUC Stations in Belleek and Rosslea.[133]

As in February 1922, the IRA focused much of their campaign in Fermanagh against exposed 'salients' of Northern Ireland. Belleek was attacked; Rosscor Viaduct leading into the town was blown up at the end of 1971, in one incident in March 1972, 13 IRA Volunteers engaged 20 soldiers based at Belleek RUC Station. The soldiers fired over 1,000 rounds and an abandoned, blood-stained car was later found near Enniskillen. Soon the Army was forced to deliver supplies to the RUC Station in Belleek, and later in Roslea, by helicopter as an increasing flow of soldiers (mostly from Artillery Regiments) were killed and wounded by claymore mines and other IED attacks during the spring and summer of 1972.[134] For example, on June 2, 1972, Gunners Brian Robertson and Victor Husband, both from 29 Corunna Battery, 4th Field Regiment, Royal Artillery, were killed in an IED explosion while on a foot patrol near Rosslea; on August 7, 1972, Lance-Bombardier David Wynne and Gunner Leroy Gordon (also 29 Corunna Battery) were killed by another remotely detonated IED while travelling in a Land Rover near the South Fermanagh town of Lisnaskea.[135]

Imjin Battery had little operational intelligence but appears to have absorbed a profound mistrust of the local Catholic population in South Fermanagh:

[T]he many small towns and villages widely scattered throughout the area were predominantly Catholic and strongly Republican. It took some time to get used to the idea that a large number of these people, if not actively hostile, were quite prepared to give assistance to the IRA gangs, and the apparent peace of the countryside was no more than superficial.[136]

---

133 Major N.M. Pughe, RHA, 'Border Shellhounds', *Journal of the Royal Artillery* 99(1) (1972), 28.

134 Pughe, 'Border Shellhounds', 30–31.

135 Royal Artillery Museum, Woolwich: 1st Regiment, Royal Horse Artillery, Annual Historical Returns, January 1–December 31, 1972.

136 Annual Historical Returns, January 1–December 31, 1972.

The RUC in Fermanagh also believed that some local Catholics were informing on their neighbours: 'There is no doubt that the targeting was done by locals. The IRA units would spend very little time in the North.'[137] Such a prospect was deeply unsettling, to the soldiers and police officers who served in L Division, but even more so to the Protestant community of South Fermanagh. Frank McManus, MP for Fermanagh and South Tyrone in the early 1970s, maintained a close dialogue with the IRA during this time. He was able to meet with its Chief of Staff, Seán Mac Stíofáin, in Dublin on at least one occasion during 1972. McManus described himself as a Republican but one who did not agree with some of the IRA's methods. He later outlined the different layers of relations between South Fermanagh's Catholics and the IRA. The vast majority would not denounce them to the RUC or the Army; a smaller, but considerable number (perhaps in the hundreds) would offer them shelter, information or financial support; very few (some dozens) would take an active part in the armed campaign. According to McManus, a large proportion of Fermanagh's Catholics (the adult Catholic population in the Lisnaskea Rural District Council area, comprising much of South Fermanagh, was just under 6,000 in the late 1960s) would describe themselves as sympathetic to Irish Republicanism of some hue but this, contrary to the assumptions of some outsiders, did not necessarily translate into active support for the IRA.[138]

Many Catholics were also aware that the IRA's campaign was bringing Fermanagh to the precipice of full-blown sectarian war in which Catholics would be at a pronounced disadvantage. Frank McManus estimated that most Protestants had 'two to three guns per house'. This awareness led to two, somewhat contradictory conclusions. First, people should not overtly help the IRA because their tactics were pushing Fermanagh into a deeper civil war that broke down the bonds of cooperation and tolerance between neighbours. However, many Catholics also did not want to alienate the IRA entirely, most obviously because of a fear of retribution by local Volunteers but, more subtly, because of a lingering 'Defender' tradition, namely the perception that, if a doomsday situation arose, the only armed force that was likely to

---

137 Interview with RUC Officer 6, Belfast, November 2015.
138 Interview with Frank McManus, Enniskillen, May 30, 2016; McCusker, *Memories of Newtownbutler and Canon Tom Maguire*, 55.

intervene to prevent large-scale Protestant paramilitary violence in Fermanagh was the IRA. A number of Catholics had been murdered by Loyalist paramilitaries in Fermanagh in the early 1970s; some were overt supporters of the civil rights movement, others were not. The predominant military presence in Fermanagh was the UDR, not regular soldiers, and these were seen as being at the core of the problem, not the solution, when it came to Catholics fears about escalating sectarian violence.[139]

The IRA took advantage of the momentum generated by the civil rights movement, the limited presence of the Army, and the porous border to launch a hit-and-run campaign on the security forces and their alleged supporters. During 1972, the main street in Lisnaskea, South Fermanagh, was bombed on successive occasions, clothes shops and supermarkets were among the premises damaged (a mother and her baby were also hurt in one incident). Protestant businesses in and around Newtownbutler also came under attack. 'Economic targets' was a euphemism for a general campaign of sectarian attacks against local Protestant interests, a crude attempt to intimidate a community into acquiescence with Republican aims.[140] The IRA also targeted Crom estate; on July 29, 1972, IRA bombs destroyed the milking parlour, creamery and some other buildings. A month earlier, the IRA also blew up a fishing lodge belonging to Lord Erne.[141]

IRA assassinations of UDR part-time soldiers living in isolated areas along the border peaked during 1972.[142] Five UDR soldiers were killed in the months leading up to D Company's arrival in Fermanagh. In March 1972, after the killing of Private Thomas Fletcher, 4 UDR Headquarters in Enniskillen decided to move some families of part-time soldiers away from the border.[143] The situation further deteriorated in the summer and

---

139 Interview with Frank McManus, Enniskillen, May 30, 2016; F. McManus, *Ulster: The Future* (a pamphlet from the early 1970s in the author's possession).
140 'Another Explosion Rocks Lisnaskea', *Fermanagh Herald*, July 21, 1972.
141 TNA: WO 305/4251 16th/5th The Queen's Royal Lancers Commander's Diary, Northern Ireland 1972; 'Fermanagh Erupts in Widespread Pre-Truce Incidents', *Fermanagh Herald*, July 1, 1972.
142 'UDR Men Flee Homes after Threats', *Impartial Reporter*, March 16, 1972; Interview with a UDR Officer (4th Battalion), June 2014.
143 'UDR Men Flee Homes after Threats', *Impartial Reporter*; 'Decades on and the Tears are Still Falling', *News Letter Orange Order*, April 7, 2006.

autumn of 1972, beginning in July when a UDR part-time soldier, John Johnston, was shot in the hand and leg in Wattlebridge, not far from Michael Naan's farm.[144] On August 7, 1972, Lance Corporal William Creighton was shot dead by an IRA unit outside his home at Magheraveely near Newtownbutler. Two more UDR men, Lance Corporal Alfred Johnston and Private James Eames, were killed in Enniskillen on August 26 while inspecting a booby-trapped car. Private Francis Veitch was shot dead outside Kinawley RUC Station on September 3. Other part-time UDR soldiers had very near misses, including the Latimer brothers at their farm near Cornacaghan, Newtownbutler (a mile or so south-west from Aughnahinch); six shots were fired at their farm but one brother succeeded in returning fire from a bedroom window at their would-be killers (Richard Latimer would later be killed by the IRA at his shop in Newtownbutler in 1980). The Latimers left Cornacaghan following the attack and moved to Lisnaskea.[145]

On August 28, 1972, 57-year-old Protestant farmer William Trotter was killed by a booby-trap bomb left on his farm in the townland of Drumralla. Drumralla is directly opposite the entrance to Naan's farm; Trotter and Naan were immediate neighbours. Trotter was not a member of the UDR and it was difficult to explain away the murder as a 'political' assassination. Instead, the coroner described Trotter's death as effectively ethnic cleansing; the IRA was making 'a concerted effort to drive families from their homes'. This echoed the sentiments of many Protestants in the area, whether Trotter was the intended victim of the bomb or not (another local, Catholic account claimed that the bomb had been hidden on Trotter's farm for use elsewhere).[146]

The murder of a 53-year-old border farmer, Private Thomas Bullock and his wife, Emily, on September 21, 1972, particularly the callous shooting of Emily Bullock at the entrance to the couple's house, also profoundly shocked the Protestant community of South Fermanagh. The Bullock family lived in the townland of Killynick, an exposed promontory of Northern Ireland that was yards from the border. They were popular in the Newtownbutler, Derrylin areas of Fermanagh and across the border

---

144 'Fermanagh Erupted in Widespread Pre-Truce Incidents', *Fermanagh Herald*, July 1, 1972.
145 'Decades on and the Tears are Still Falling'.
146 McKittrick et al., *Lost Lives*, 257.

(their farm was only a few miles from the Cavan town of Ballyconnell). Shan Bullock, Tom Bullock's uncle, was Fermanagh's most celebrated author and the Bullock family had enduring ties to the Earl of Erne – Tom Bullock had often fished and attended the shoots on the Crom estate.[147] Indeed, Killynick had been the residence of the Crichton family, before their move to Crom Castle.[148]

The battalion log of the 16/5 Lancers provides a laconic but detailed account of the Bullock murders:

> 1830 – 2 cars, a black Hillman and a brown Ford Escort crossed the Aghalane border crossing from Eire. One car, the brown Ford Escort carrying three men drove to the house of Pte. Bullock (4UDR). His wife opened the door and was shot dead in the stomach by a .45 revolver. The remaining men then moved into the house and shot Pte. Bullock using a .303 and M1 carbine. The men then left. The other car, a black Hillman, carrying 5 men, went to the house of Pte. Darling [who was not at home]. His wife saw the other car approaching and hid the children under the bed and hid her husband's SMG. The raiders ransacked the house, stealing his combat suit and 2 × magazines containing 30 rounds each. They then left.[149]

The two cars met up in Newtownbutler before returning across the border, spending approximately 15–20 minutes in Northern Ireland. Less than a month later, the IRA blew up the petrol station of Stephen Bullock, a cousin of Tom, at Aghalane, a major crossing point along the border. Stephen was not a member of the UDR, but his criticism of the IRA after the death of Private Bullock had been noticed.[150]

Emily Bullock had long feared that, living so near the border, her husband would be targeted by the IRA; when he was on duty she would lie in a sleeping bag on the landing of their house in Killynick waiting for

147 'Bishop Warns of "Corrosive Hate" at UDR Funeral', *Impartial Reporter*, September 28, 1972.

148 T. Reeves-Smyth, *Crom Castle Demesne*, vol. 1 (Rowellane: National Trust, 1999), 35.

149 TNA: WO 305/4251 16th/5th The Queen's Royal Lancers, Commander's Diary, Northern Ireland 1972.

150 'Border Filling Station, Shop and Store', *Fermanagh Hearld*, October 7, 1972.

his return and vowed that the IRA would kill Tom 'over her dead body'. Dianne Woods, a niece of Tom Bullock, later recalled that in the days after the murder of her uncle, 'a vile call was made to an abattoir in the area telling them they had two bullocks for them to process'.[151] The brutality of the killing, and the further intimidation of the bereaved Bullock family, caused profound inter-community tension in Newtownbutler. According to Lord Erne, local Protestants believed that the IRA had vowed to keep the British flag on the Anglican church in Newtownbutler at half-mast until 'there wasn't a single Protestant left' in the surrounding area.[152] In early October 1972, Conservative MP John Biggs-Davison, together with leading Ulster Unionists Harry West and Captain John Brooke, toured Newtownbutler and the border area. Biggs-Davison described the attacks on UDR men as 'the acts of animals'.[153]

The Pressure to Retaliate against the IRA: Loyalist Mobilisation and Intelligence-Gathering in Fermanagh

By October 21, 1972, the day the Argylls arrived in Lisnaskea, the conflict in Fermanagh had escalated still further. Earlier that month, William Craig, the leader of the Unionist Vanguard Movement, spoke to a 3,000-strong rally of Loyalist supporters outside Enniskillen town hall. The Fermanagh UDA and local organisations such as the ex-USC Association were joined by 'a large contingent from Belfast, including members of the UDA, LAW [Loyalist Association of Workers], Orange Volunteers, UVF, Tartan gangs and bringing up the rear were members of the Loyalist Women's Action Association, dressed in blue uniform'.[154] Craig conveyed his congratulations to the UDA commander present, Billy Neill, on the recent Loyalist cross-border raids into the Republic of Ireland.[155] He went on to tell the people of Fermanagh that they must now take action: 'Throw away the inhibitions that have grown up. You are in a war situation.'[156]

---

151 C. Kilpatrick, 'IRA Victim Hits Out at Sick Hunger Strike Parade Through Derrylin', *Impartial Reporter*, July 16, 2014.
152 Interview with Henry Crichton, Crom Castle, September 18, 2015.
153 'UDR Murders "Action of Animals" Says British MP'.
154 'You are in a War Situation', *Impartial Reporter*, October 12, 1972.
155 'You are in a War Situation', *Impartial Reporter*.
156 'You are in a War Situation', *Impartial Reporter*.

The week after the Enniskillen rally, Harry West (a future UUP leader) claimed that Edward Heath's government had betrayed the Army in Fermanagh. Army sources had told him that:

> Their hands are tied … Government policy was designed to wear us (the majority) down. The evidence on the ground would appear to support this suggestion … So much for the concern of the Tory Party for their fellow British citizens living in this part of the United Kingdom, and being mercilessly murdered and terrorised daily.[157]

The forces of law and order had been winning, West claimed, until 'the disaster' of direct rule reversed those gains. West's colleague and former Stormont Minister, John Taylor, told the same gathering that, 'I have no doubt that civil war is now a probability and that any Loyalist not preparing for civil war is not prudent. It is prudent for people to realize that civil war is now a probability.'[158]

In such an atmosphere of fear and heated speeches by Fermanagh's leaders, the situation began to take a more sinister turn when Vanguard and other Loyalist leaders encouraged their supporters to, in Craig's words, 'build up the dossiers on the men and women who are a menace to this country, because one day … it may be our job to liquidate the enemy'.[159] In October 1972, Loyalist leader Basil Anderson established a club of Loyalist Defence Volunteers (LDVs) in Lisnaskea; its aim was to unite Loyalist paramilitary groups and associations in Fermanagh. The USC Association, some of whose members were now serving in the UDR, joined the LDV.[160] Anderson urged Protestant men in Fermanagh to 'Join Ulster Vanguard and come out from the comparative comfort and safety of your homes and join your brave and valiant neighbours in the UDR and Police Reserve.'[161] A duality is evident here; Basil Anderson

---

157 'Only a Unionist Alliance Can Save Ulster', *Impartial Reporter*, October 19, 1972.
158 'Taylor Says Civil War is Imminent', *Impartial Reporter*, October 19, 1972.
159 David McKittrick and David McVea, 'Making Sense of the Troubles' (London: Penguin, 2002), 80.
160 '"Volunteers" to Protect the Fermanagh Loyalists', *Impartial Reporter*, November 14, 1972; Interview with a UDR Officer (4th Battalion), June 2014.
161 '"Volunteers" to Protect the Fermanagh Loyalists', *Impartial Reporter*.

asked Loyalists to play a role simultaneously within the security forces while also remaining active in Loyalist paramilitary organisations, highlighting the dangerous potential for intelligence and/or blacklists flowing between the UDR and Loyalist paramilitary organisations. Anderson also told *The Impartial Reporter* that Loyalist paramilitaries had undertaken a 'serious and detailed study' of the IRA's cross-border attacks on Protestant homes near the border. A UDA representative added that:

> Intelligence files compiled by the Loyalist militant organisations in the county reveal a very strong gathering of known IRA men in Clones, Monaghan and Bundoran [in County Donegal]. A detailed and complete list, along with photographs of IRA and their supporters in Co. Fermanagh has been compiled and their movement noted.[162]

Another Loyalist paramilitary representative emphasised that Catholic neighbours of Protestant victims of the IRA played a key role in facilitating the cross-border attacks:

> It is known ... that local supporters of the IRA are used to compile a detailed list of the movements of an intended victim, probably a neighbour. This list is then passed to the murder squad in the South. The murder squad travel across the Border, commit their foul deed and retreat to safety in the South.[163]

Lists and counter-lists became an obsession on both sides, as both Loyalists and Republicans marked out their neighbours for retribution and even death. Anderson and other Loyalist leaders also told *The Impartial Reporter* that, following this border study, discussions took place between Loyalists and representatives of the security forces in Fermanagh.[164] In early October, Loyalist paramilitaries launched a number of raids across the border aimed at 'ambushing the ambushers'. These included the capture of an IRA arms dump in Redhills, County Cavan, just across the border from Newtownbutler. Similar raids, mostly with sound

---

162 '"Volunteers" to Protect the Fermanagh Loyalists', *Impartial Reporter*.
163 '"Volunteers" to Protect the Fermanagh Loyalists', *Impartial Reporter*.
164 '"Volunteers" to Protect the Fermanagh Loyalists', *Impartial Reporter*.

intelligence, also saw Loyalist paramilitaries venture into Monaghan and Donegal to capture or destroy IRA arms (on October 6, 1972, the UDA claimed to have seized four Armalite rifles and 'churns of explosives' in County Monaghan and on October 16, attempted to blow up a fertiliser store near Carrigans in County Donegal). On the same day, a car bomb exploded on Fermanagh Street in Clones, just across the border from Newtownbutler, seriously injuring a local man, Eugene Cumaskey.[165] The house of IRA Volunteer Philip McDonald, in the Drummully salient of County Monaghan (and not far from Michael Naan's farm), was also targeted by Loyalist paramilitaries.[166] Remarkably, UDA leader Billy Neill, unmolested by the RUC or the Army, was able to accept the congratulations for leading such incursions during the October Vanguard rally in Enniskillen. George Farrell, a part-time 4 UDR soldier, and a member of the UVF, was later convicted in a Dublin court of planting a bomb in the Donegal town of Pettigo on September 28, 1973.[167]

Brigadier Peter Bush, 3 Brigade's commander (with responsibility for Fermanagh) had been at pains not to provoke a wider conflict with the still-legal Ulster Defence Association and other Loyalist paramilitary groups affiliated with the Vanguard movement. On June 17, 1972, in a communication entitled, 'Directive on Security Forces Reaction to Protestant Activity', Brigadier Bush spelled out the Army's approach: 'Aim: The Security Forces will continue to avoid, to the greatest extent possible, confrontation with the Protestant community.'[168] Loyalist paramilitary groups operating in Fermanagh, and elsewhere along the border, were not being suppressed by the State even when they admitted to carrying out illegal activities, such as launching cross-border raids in the Republic of Ireland. Frank Steele, the SIS (MI6) representative in

---

165 TNA: FCO 87/120 Border, Letter from K.C. Thom to W.K.K. White, Republic of Ireland Department, dated October 6, 1972. For a timeline and discussion of UDA and UVF bombings in the Republic, see also, 'Final Report of the Commission of Investigation into the Dublin and Monaghan Bombings', published April 4, 2007, available at www.taoiseach.ie (accessed February 26, 2015); 'The Clones Bomb Blast', *Anglo Celt*, October 27, 1972.
166 TNA: WO 305/4209 3rd Infantry Brigade, Log Sheet, May 9, 1972; 'Fógraí Bháis', *An Phoblacht*, March 30, 2006.
167 'Border Bomb Made Woman a Terrorist', *Daily Telegraph*, September 1, 1982.
168 TNA: WO 305/4209 Directive on Security Forces Reactions to Protestant Activity, signed by Brigadier Peter Bush, CO 3 Brigade, June 17, 1972.

Ireland, was a key liaison with Loyalist paramilitaries during this time and took a close interest in Loyalist cross-border attacks, requesting updates on the Irish government's response. But little was done to curtail the still-legal UDA and other groups.[169]

After the murder of Michael Naan's Protestant neighbour, part-time UDR soldier and farmer Robin Bell, on October 22, 1972 (the day before the killings of Naan and Murray), Loyalist paramilitaries warned the security forces that, 'should another Loyalist be murdered or intimidated, immediate retaliatory action would be taken in their respective areas'. The Latimers and the Bells were both specifically mentioned in the statement – both families lived close to Michael Naan.[170] In fact, as we have seen, a Loyalist cross-border campaign had already begun and would escalate still further. At the end of December 1972, the UVF planted bombs in the border towns of Clones (County Monaghan), Belturbet, Swanlinbar (County Cavan) and Pettigo (County Donegal), killing two people in Belturbet. Between November 1972 and January 1973, four Loyalist bombs in Dublin would kill three people and injure 185.[171]

In October 1972, senior officers in the Gardaí were very concerned about the blurring of lines between the UDR, the RUC and Loyalist paramilitary groups affiliated with the wider Vanguard Movement that were operating in Fermanagh. Some officers in the RUC were also alarmed at intelligence collaboration between the security forces and Loyalist paramilitaries. Such concerns later emerged in the official inquiry chaired by Mr Justice Henry Barron into Loyalist bombings in Republic of Ireland in the early 1970s. Garda officers reported that the bombings had been carried out by a Vanguard and UVF-linked organisation called the Red Hand Commando. More troublingly, the Gardaí named a senior RUC officer who they believed was passing intelligence to Loyalist paramilitaries. This officer was apparently later 'sidelined' by more senior RUC officers so as not to pass on sensitive information.[172]

169 TNA: FCO 87/120 Border, Letter from K.C. Thom to W.K.K. White, Republic of Ireland Department, dated October 6, 1972.

170 '"Volunteers" to Protect the Fermanagh Loyalists', *Impartial Reporter.*

171 'Final Report of the Commission of Investigation into the Dublin and Monaghan Bombings', published April 4, 2007, available at www.taoiseach.ie (accessed February 26, 2015).

172 'Interim Report on the Report of the Independent Commission of Inquiry into the Dublin Bombings of 1972 and 1973', 136.

An RUC officer who served in Fermanagh during the 1970s also later recalled his mistrust of certain elements of the constabulary serving in the county. When, in the immediate aftermath of the sectarian murder of a Catholic man, Patrick O'Reilly, near Enniskillen on May 27, 1975, this RUC officer received information about the possible involvement of local Loyalist paramilitary leader, Robert Bridges, he moved quickly to prevent his RUC colleagues in Fermanagh hearing of this development, lest they tip off Loyalist paramilitaries who would then dispose of the evidence. A CID officer from outside Fermanagh was sent to conduct the investigation: the apparent outcome of the interrogation of Loyalist suspects was a list of police officers and local UDR soldiers suspected of being involved in a series of Loyalist plots, including a plan to seize weapons from Enniskillen UDR barracks.[173] The RUC officer, rather than trusting his report to the normal channels of communication, drove to RUC Headquarters in Belfast to present it by hand. Robert Bridges, who was also suspected of playing an important role in cross-border bombings in Monaghan, was ultimately tried and convicted of murder.[174]

The evident concern about security forces' collusion in facilitating, ignoring or covering up extra-judicial killings in Fermanagh and across the border, expressed in a number of reports sent to Garda Headquarters by Garda Chief Superintendent J.P. McMahon and other senior Garda officers, and the corroboration of such concerns by a well-placed senior RUC officer, leaves open the possibility of some knowledge or collusion among local RUC officers to conceal the circumstances of the deaths of Michael Naan and Andrew Murray. However, the police officer that initially took charge of the murder investigation on October 25, 1972, Inspector Paddy Gilligan, was, according to the same RUC interviewee, widely regarded as a fair-minded, professional officer.[175] Gilligan noted the unusual absence of farm implements and other possible evidence in the aftermath of the murders, suggestive perhaps of a well-organised clean up of the scene. The investigating RUC officers were troubled by the absence of military records for October 23, 1972, particularly

173 Interview with RUC Officer 6, Belfast, November 2015.
174 'Interim Report on the Report of the Independent Commission of Inquiry into the Dublin Bombings of 1972 and 1973', 125; Interview with RUC Officer 6, Belfast, November 2015.
175 Interview with RUC Officer 6, Belfast, November 2015.

with respect to D Company, 1 Argylls. During the course of 1973, a number of RUC officers travelled to Scotland and England to search for military Watchkeepers' log books and other operational paperwork, routinely compiled by military units in Northern Ireland. According to an RUC officer, there was nothing available for the night in question; he concluded that these records had been deliberately destroyed.[176] The disappearance of such files so soon after the event is striking, particularly because during the initial course of the RMP SIB investigation into the activities of D Company on the night in question, Major Jeremy Mackenzie and Corporal C.J. Pert, RMP, appeared to use D Company records to provide quite precise details of D Company operations in Fermanagh (location of multiple VCPs etc.). Why did the RMP SIB not retain a copy of these records? At any rate, sometime in 1973 the records were 'lost' and were not available when the RUC came looking for them.[177]

A large number of former USC police officers served in 4 UDR. A full-time British officer attached to 4 UDR recalled that his 'key challenge was to get them to switch from thinking as policemen to being soldiers in aid of the civil power. 90 per cent were former B Specials [USC]. Only five Catholics joined [4th Battalion, UDR] and they never went on patrol. The rest all reckoned they knew a Catholic at 50 paces.' Moreover, it was acknowledged that Loyalist paramilitaries in Fermanagh, as elsewhere, joined the UDR.[178] A report prepared by Military Intelligence in 1973, entitled 'Subversion in the UDR', noted that UDR collusion with Loyalist paramilitaries, the passing of information or equipment for the purposes of terrorism, mostly occurred at the company level:

> In many areas company headquarters are isolated, and the soldiers and NCOs are not well known to battalion headquarters staff: in such circumstances it would not be difficult to maintain contacts with or joint membership of a subversive group, and

176 Interview with RUC Officer 7, Belfast, November 2015.
177 Statement of Major John Jeremy Mackenzie, witnessed by Corporal C.J. Pert, Royal Military Police Special Investigations Branch (RMP SIB), January 18, 1973, Form 266A (Military), Case No. 15549/3. Document made available by Legal Professional 2. Document missing from the original PRONI file CRCT/3/2/2/159A.
178 Interview with a UDR Officer (4th Battalion), June 2014.

remain undiscovered. Indeed, in many areas where officers and men have known each other all their lives through church or social or Orange Order activities, membership of a Protestant para-military [*sic*] group might not be considered at all unusual or worth reporting to a higher authority.[179]

The report concluded by pointing out that although better vetting standards were introduced for new UDR recruits at the end of 1972 best estimates placed the number of paramilitaries that joined UDR and Loyalist subversive organisations at 5 per cent to 15 per cent of the more than 7,500 serving UDR personnel.[180]

October 1972 was a particularly low point in the UDR's history with respect to allegations of collusion. Clashes between Army units and Loyalist groups in Belfast combined with mounting frustrations at the increasing number of IRA attacks along the border prompted a sustained attempt by Loyalists to seize consignments of weapons from UDR armouries, including in County Londonderry and County Armagh. On the morning of October 23, 1972, the date of the murders of Michael Naan and Andrew Murray, a group of Loyalists 'overpowered' King's Park Camp in Lurgan and stole 85 SLRs and 21 SMGs that had principally been assigned to 11th Battalion UDR. The RMP later concluded that collusion in the raid by serving UDR soldiers was 'highly probable'.[181] UDR senior commanders, mostly drawn from regular British Army regiments, spent a lot of time trying to contain the suspicions and personal grievances that had built up among their UDR recruits.[182]

Two weeks before the arrival of D Company, 1 Argylls, in Fermanagh, 16/5 Lancers, with the support of Chestnut Troop, Royal Horse Artillery, launched an operation along the border to reassure the local population (using the Earl of Enniskillen's Florence Court estate as a key command post). Two squadrons, one on foot after being initially dropped by air near the border, the other mounted and pushing down towards the border

---

179 Document entitled 'Subversion in the UDR', dated August 1973, available at http://cain.ulst.ac.uk/publicrecords/1973/subversion_in_the_udr.htm (accessed April 5, 2016).
180 Document entitled 'Subversion in the UDR'.
181 Document entitled 'Subversion in the UDR'.
182 Interview with a UDR Officer (4th Battalion), June 2014.

from the north, had been involved in the operation.[183] The Lancers' CO advised his soldiers:

> Dump personal non-attractive items at a friendly farm since you are not issued with the correct equipment with which to walk long distances. You are to visit each farm and dwelling in your area of responsibility and speak with the occupier. Find out anything unusual and names of known gunmen. Try to re-establish public confidence.[184]

Not only did the Lancers lack the right equipment for long foot patrols but they were also trying to persuade local Protestants to denounce 'known gunmen' among their Catholic neighbours. It opened up the prospect for malicious denunciation on the part of local people, as observed by Kalyvas in his work on civil wars.[185] In 1972, 16/5 Lancers and other units also accepted an invitation to make use of Orange Order halls in County Fermanagh, including those in Newtownbutler, Faugh and Wattlebridge. Indeed, on October 27, 1972, the day of the Naan and Murray funerals, soldiers were apparently billeted in the Orange Hall in Newtownbutler. It left a profoundly negative imprint in the minds of the village's Catholic population: unlike the Lancers of 1858 or the Lincolnshire Regiment in 1920, here was a co-opted group of soldiers, seemingly working to the whim of local 'Orange' interests.[186]

In the broiling atmosphere of South Fermanagh in October 1972, the Lancers' casual attitude to intelligence gathering is questionable. Taking 'lists' of 'known IRA men' from Unionist sympathisers, including part-time UDR soldiers, could be a dangerous, irresponsible practice if not matched by rigorous intelligence grading and analysis.[187] Unlike

---

183 TNA: WO 305/4251 16th/5th The Queen's Royal Lancers Commander's Diary, Northern Ireland 1972, Operation Instruction No. 3, Headquarters Squadron, October 6, 1972.
184 TNA: WO 305/4251 16th/5th The Queen's Royal Lancers Commander's Diary, Northern Ireland 1972: Operation Instruction No. 3, Headquarters Squadron, October 6, 1972.
185 Kalyvas, *The Logic of Violence in Civil War*, 340.
186 'Newtownbutler News', *Anglo-Celt*, November 3, 1972; MacDonald, *The Pitchfork Murders*, 38.
187 Interview with a UDR Officer (4th Battalion), June 2014.

in parts of Belfast or even in large towns such as Newry, where the number of deployed regular soldiers allowed for the micro-surveillance of Republican areas, there was a notable absence of reliable intelligence in Fermanagh. Regrettably, D Company, 1 Argylls, had also left their NCO responsible for intelligence gathering and evaluation in Bessbrook, in order to provide 'some continuity' on their return to their normal area of operations.[188] Warnings had been consistently reiterated about treating UDR 'intelligence' with caution, not least by full-time officers attached to the UDR from other regiments.[189]

D Company failed to heed these warnings: Lieutenant Snowball's statement on intelligence and Naan's presumed guilt is particularly instructive:

> After our arrival at the site I became aware that a nearby farm was occupied by a man named Naan who was on our *suspect* list. Though it was *known* by then that Naan was a Provisional no instructions were ever issued by myself in relation to sightings or action to be taken in the event of meeting him. As *it was known that he was involved in everything* that went on down there his name was discussed on occasions. [Author's emphasis][190]

If Naan was *known* to be guilty, rather than merely a suspect, then Murray was guilty by association – as Lance Corporal Chestnut explained: 'I knew the farm was IRA and assumed that anyone connected with the farm would be suspected of terrorism.'[191] In Fermanagh, it appears that the Argylls were ready to accept UDR labelling of local men as 'known IRA' without question.

---

188 Interview with Argyll Soldier 12 (Officer), May 2014.

189 TNA: CJ 4/1784 'The Future Role and Organisation of the UDR'; Interview with a UDR Officer (4th Battalion), June 2014.

190 Statement of Andrew Snowball, as recorded by Chief Inspector William Scott, June 12, 1979. Document made available by Legal Professional 2.

191 'Iain Fletcher Chestnut Interview', dated November 5, 1980. Document made available by Legal Professional 2 involved in the trial of Hathaway, Byrne, Chestnut and Snowball. Document missing from the original PRONI file – CRCT/3/2/2/159A.

D Company Arrives in Fermanagh: A Different Approach

In October 1972, the Army in Fermanagh was under pressure: the appearance of Loyalist vigilante patrols along the border was a challenge to the Army's primary security role.[192] However, Loyalists had been very clear: if the Army failed to act, then they would. In late 1972, it appeared that Loyalists were rapidly losing patience with the Army and the RUC's claim to protect Protestants living in borders areas. Even when the Army in Fermanagh arrested an IRA unit it was mostly due to chance or an observant soldier rather than good intelligence.[193] Relations with Gardaí across the border were mixed, at best; the Gardaí at Clones in County Monaghan were regarded as 'extremely uncooperative'.[194] Indeed, it was widely believed in RUC and Army circles that a Garda sergeant in Clones was an IRA sympathiser or perhaps even a Volunteer.[195]

On October 21, 1972, D Company, 1 Argylls moved, in their capacity as Reserve Company, 3 Brigade, from Bessbrook, County Armagh (RUC H Division) to South Fermanagh (RUC L Division) for a period of a week. The Argylls were sent to Fermanagh to reinforce 16/5 Lancers and Chestnut Troop, 1st Regiment the Royal Horse Artillery. The aim was for the Argylls – a capable and experienced infantry company – to prevent further IRA attacks on local Protestants along the border, including on businesses, part-time UDR soldiers and VIPs (particularly Lord Erne). To reassure the local Unionist population they would significantly increase foot patrols in order 'to show a presence'. According to Major

---

192 For example, the Lancers received the following report from Wattlebridge in the summer of 1972: 'During the night reports were received from the RUC, that an eight man vigilante patrol had been moving around the village. They were masked, wearing combat jackets and carrying pickhelves.' TNA: WO 305/4251 16th/5th The Queen's Royal Lancers, Commander's Diary, Northern Ireland, 1972.

193 5/16 Lancers made such a discovery on June 11, 1972 when a suspicious soldier, Bombardier Dobson, stopped a car and discovered 240 lb of Co-op sugar in 16 polythene bags. The Lancers arrested four IRA men: Michael McManus, John Cannon, Desmond Leonard and James Lynch. TNA: WO 305/4251 16th/5th The Queen's Royal Lancers, Commander's Diary, Northern Ireland, 1972.

194 TNA: WO 305/4251 16th/5th The Queen's Royal Lancers, Commander's Diary, Northern Ireland, 1972.

195 Interview with RUC Officer 6, Belfast, November 2015; Interview with Argyll Officer 12 (Officer), March 2015.

Mackenzie, D Company also 'carried out OP work at night and this would have included watching likely roads [used by IRA ASUs moving across the border], watching RUC/UDR occupied houses, watching Crom Castle and that was about it'.[196] Although nominally under the operational command of 16/5 Lancers when they arrived in Lisnaskea on October 21 1972, in reality Major Mackenzie was free to plan operations at his own discretion.[197]

Jeremy Mackenzie's reputation for competency in Borneo – where he was deployed in the same area of operations as then Brigadier Harry Tuzo – may have further recommended D Company as a short-term solution to the Army's problems in Fermanagh, especially as Special Forces units were not yet deployed in Northern Ireland at this time. Borneo was the most fulfilling campaign in Tuzo and Mackenzie's careers – operations in Borneo involved aggressive patrolling, cross-border raids and infiltration, ambushes along rivers and in thick, mountainous jungle.[198] D Company's

196 Statement of Major John Jeremy Mackenzie (undated, 1979); Statement of Company Sergeant Major John Higgins, December 19, 1979, Trial document made available by Legal Professional 2.
197 According to Company Sergeant Major Higgins, the men of D Company 'were completely independent of these people but worked in conjunction with them'. Statement of CSM John Higgins, December 19, 1979, Trial document made available by Legal Professional 2.
198 Mackenzie's Kenyan background may also have worked in his favour. The 6th Earl of Enniskillen, David Lowry Cole, a former colonel in the Kenyan Police Reserve during the Mau Mau rebellion, had returned to South Fermanagh where he now served as a major in 4 UDR. The MI6 Representative for Northern Ireland in 1972, Frank Steele, also served in Kenya during this time, playing an important role, like David Cole, in the negotiation of Kenyan independence. General Harry Tuzo had served as the commanding officer of the 3rd Regiment, Royal Horse Artillery, when it was based in Alanbrooke Barracks in the small town of Gil Gil in central Kenya from 1961 to 1964, where the Coles (together with their cousins the Cholmondeleys) were the dominant landowners. Major Mackenzie was born and schooled in Kenya; his father served as an officer in the King's African Rifles and later as a senior colonial police officer. Meanwhile, the Earl of Erne's Crom Castle, where 13 Platoon, D Company would be based for much of its time in Fermanagh, had a recent connection with the Seaforth Highlanders – the regiment into which Major Mackenzie had followed his father. During the Second World War, officers of the Seaforth Highlanders had taken up residence in Crom Castle; non-commissioned officers (NCOs) and other ranks lived in Nissen

commander was ideally suited to missions that required resourcefulness and aggression. During pre-Northern Ireland training, Mackenzie insisted that he and his men in D Company would camp out under the stars, in 'bashas' – a word for a makeshift sleeping place used on operations – and would catch and cook their own food.[199] Fermanagh – its lakes, wooded hillsides and porous border – was his chance finally to claim more operational space. Even prior to their deployment to South Fermanagh, IRA ambushes of Argyll soldiers had been steadily increasing and the desire for positive action, to go on the offensive against an elusive enemy, had become increasingly attractive.

The Argylls' intensive operations in South Fermanagh included camping out at night in order to observe and search farms where suspected IRA activity took place.[200] The three D Company Platoons spread out: 13 Platoon under the command of 2nd Lieutenant Snowball was initially deployed to Lisnaskea on October 21, before being sent to 'camp out' along the border to the south-west of Newtownbutler, where it was for the most part based at Crom estate. Under 2nd Lieutenant Alistair McKillop, 15 Platoon patrolled the rural areas to the north and east of Newtownbutler.[201] Under Colour Sergeant Arthur Cairns,

huts on the grounds of Crom estate where the Seaforths conducted extensive training operations from 1941 and 1942 (and waited for a potential invasion of Ireland by Nazi Germany). PRONI: D1702/12/69/1–9 Earl of Enniskillen Papers, Letter from the 6th Earl of Enniskillen to the Secretary of State for Northern Ireland, William Whitelaw, dated April 6, 1972; PRONI: D1702/12/69/1–9 Earl of Enniskillen Papers, handwritten letter from Prime Minister Margaret Thatcher to the 6th Earl of Enniskillen, dated January 19, 1986; PRONI: D1702/12/69/1–9 Earl of Enniskillen Papers: A biography of the 6th Earl of Enniskillen, entitled 'A Manifesto: David Cole, Coalition Candidate', dated 1961; J. Powell, *Making Peace in Northern Ireland* (London: The Bodley Head, 2008), 67; 'Operation Green': Private/Lance Corporal Dennis March, 'Journey of the Globetrotters', Archive of World War Two memories, http://www.bbc.co.uk/history/ww2peopleswar/stories/61/a1109161.shtml (accessed October 5, 2015).

199 Interview with Argyll Soldier 11 (Officer), May 2014.

200 Interview with Argyll Soldier 5 (Officer), May 2014.

201 Like Mackenzie, Lieutenant McKillop was a Queen's Own Highlanders officer. He would later die in a helicopter accident in Belize in 1976. In April 1979, he was mentioned by Lieutenant Snowball in his police testimony as the other person who travelled with him in the Company 'q van' in Fermanagh on the way to an O group briefing. Statement of Lieutenant Andrew Snowball on April 6, 1979,

14 Platoon was sent to the west of Fermanagh, to patrol the border at and near the town of Belleek, a beleaguered promontory of West Fermanagh, which the IRA had tried, in a perhaps not coincidental repeat of a 1922 operation, to cut off from the rest of the county (bombing its police station, customs house, connecting bridges and viaducts). Company Headquarters was based at Lisnaskea RUC Station: Belleek was too far away for radio communication and had to be contacted via telephone and visited by helicopter (the other Platoons were in touch with Company Headquarters by C42 radio to Platoon Headquarters and from Platoon to Section level by A41 sets).[202]

Prelude to Murder:
A Breakdown in Command and Intelligence

'The Want Factor': Michael Naan, Albert Liddle and the Farm at Aughnahinch

Twenty-four-year-old Andrew Murray was 'quiet', a virtue in County Fermanagh: 'Like calm days, calm people bring no trouble to those living around them. They are "harmless".'[203] The fifth of a family of six, of modest means but widely respected, Andrew Murray lived at his mother's house in Derrykenny. He had been schooled at nearby Wattlebridge national school before joining the Rivers Council as a labourer in the late 1960s. He had been working for Michael Naan as a farm labourer for a few months. Like his mother Mary, Andy was known for his love of nature and gentleness.[204] He rarely drank; like many of the Argyll soldiers, he loved cowboy films. Andy was remembered by his friend Colm Caughey as 'a lovely person … I was fond of Andy. He would be there and we'd be after the cattle and Andy would say "don't hit them with the stick; you'll only put them mad." He didn't like that.'[205] In the

as recorded by Detective Inspector William McBurney; 'Two New War Names are Added to Inverness War Memorial', *Inverness Courier*, August 4, 2015.

202 Statement of Major Jeremy Mackenzie, December 17, 1979. Trial document made available by Legal Professional 2.

203 Glassie, *Passing the Time in Ballymenone*, 35.

204 'Obituary: Mary Ann Murray', *Impartial Reporter*, April 14, 2011; MacDonald, *The Pitchfork Murders*, 13.

205 MacDonald, *The Pitchfork Murders*, 13.

late 1960s, Murray's father died in unexplained circumstances in Belfast, where he went looking for work. Lord Erne employed Murray's sister, Kathleen, as a pantry maid at Crom Castle.[206] Andrew Murray was not under suspicion; Naan was the sole target on October 23, 1972.

Thirty-one-year-old Michael Naan was the youngest of ten children born to Joseph Naan and his wife Bridget (née Lynch). The Naan surname had deep historical links with Fermanagh ('Naan island' is situated on Upper Lough Erne). Until the end of the nineteenth century, Michael Naan's grandfather was a small tenant farmer in the townland of Ports, not far from Crom Castle, the seat of the Earls of Erne (although the Naan family's landlord was the Earl of Lanesborough).[207] The family later availed themselves of the Land Purchase (Ireland) Acts passed at the end of the nineteenth century to buy the family home and a five-acre farm from Lord Lanesborough. Other pieces of land were added to the family holdings in Ports and Killard, some of which were later farmed by Michael Naan's uncle Edward, or 'Wee Ned'.[208] For a number of years, Michael Naan's parents ran a successful accommodation and a catering and laundry service in Clones town (ten children demanded diverse sources of income). Michael, or 'Micky' as he was known to his friends, attended primary school for a time in Clones.[209]

The Naan connection with Ports was long-standing; the family had apparently forged good relations with many of their Protestant neighbours. Their farm hugged the demesne of Crom estate; the Naans would occasionally 'retrieve' a game bird that dropped onto their land during the frequent Crom shoots.[210] But bouts of sectarian tension were not unknown to Ports. James Naan recalls that his father, Enda Naan, and uncle Benny, were lucky to survive one encounter with their neighbours in the USC some time in the late 1940s/early 1950s:

> Benny and Enda Naan were living in Ports. They were coming home one night and the B Specials [USC] stopped them. They separated them and were obviously questioning them,

---

206 'Remembering the Victims', *Fermanagh Herald*, December 30, 1997.
207 Land Registry of Northern Ireland (hereafter LRNI), Folio 4525, County Fermanagh.
208 LRNI, Folio 4525, County Fermanagh.
209 Interview with James Naan, December 12, 2016.
210 Interview with James Naan, Newtownbutler, March 20, 2017.

threatening them ... They were both threatened that they were going to be shot. In the middle of it there was one shot fired. So they both went home thinking the other had been shot.[211]

Such incidents could live on in the memory of those involved and in the wider community. Albert Liddle would have been a young USC constable living nearby at the time.

During the 1940s, Joseph Naan, Michael's father, purchased two farms that had been in Protestant ownership for generations. In 1941, he bought a farm of just under 20 acres previously owned by John William Liddle in the townland of Killard, not far from Ports. Then, in 1944, he bought a farm of 48 acres in the townland of Aughnahinch, which lay a mile south from the village of Newtownbutler and three miles east of Ports. The Brooks family previously owned the farm at Aughnahinch, together with an adjacent 23-acre plot in the townland of Sandholes. The Brooks were reasonably prosperous farmers; like many other mid-sized or large Protestant farmers, they employed a Catholic maid to help with domestic chores. In 1923, 69-year-old William Brooks, having no son or daughter to inherit or work the farm, sold the Aughnahinch land to Luke Bogue from Brookeborough. According to local Catholic accounts, Luke Bogue was unknown to locals and the 'Bogue' name was confused for 'Pogue', an almost exclusively Protestant surname. The farm was unintentionally sold to a Catholic buyer.[212] William Brooks and his wife Charlotte later purchased a cottage and small farm on the outskirts of Newtownbutler.[213] Luke Bogue in turn subsequently sold the house and farm at Aughnahinch to Joseph Naan in 1944 – Michael was to spend much of his childhood at the farm before inheriting it in 1967.[214]

Whether deliberate or not it was unusual for Protestants in South Fermanagh to sell their land to Catholics. Rosemary Harris has observed

211 LRNI, Folio 140, County Fermanagh; Census of Ireland, 1911: Entry for the Brooks family, Aghnahinch, Newtownbutler; 'Obituaries: Mrs. Charlotte Brooks', *Impartial Reporter*, January 30, 1973.

212 MacDonald, *The Pitchfork Murders*, 12.

213 'Obituaries: Mrs. Charlotte Brooks', *Impartial Reporter*, January 30, 1973; LRNI, Folio 140, County Fermanagh.

214 LRNI, Folio 140, County Fermanagh; Interview with James Naan, Newtownbutler, March 20, 2017.

that along the border 'ownership of a farm meant the symbolic occupation of an area'; the purchase of farms owned by a person not of the same sect as the pervious owner was 'evaluated in terms of gain and losses for one or other side at the local level'.[215] Peter Leary has described how land ownership patterns in Fermanagh endured over centuries – in 1925, Colonel William Barton could explain why Catholics made up the majority in one particular townland on the island of Boa: 'It was deliberately done by my forebears … They drove the islanders into the townland.'[216] Leary concluded that 'the perpetuation of these patterns over generations kept these histories living in the moment'.[217]

Resentment endured locally that the farm at Aughnahinch had been 'lost' to Catholic ownership. Colm Caughey, a cousin of Michael Naan's, claimed that 'The Naan land seemed to have a want factor by some in the Protestant community.'[218] A story circulated among Newtownbutler's Catholics that two graves were dug near the Aughnahinch farmhouse as a message to the new owners.[219] In an interview with the author, James Naan remembered that a Union Flag frequently few from an island on the small lough adjacent to Naan's farm. He also recalled his uncle's annoyance when he gave a pair of oars to a local man – but not an immediate neighbour – who wished to visit the island (most likely to raise or replace the flag).[220]

Charlotte Brooks, the widow of William Brooks, outlived Michael Naan; she was Newtownbutler's oldest resident when she died at the age of 98 in 1975. She was born Charlotte Elizabeth Liddle in the townland of Killalahard, not far from Ports and Crom. Her family had

---

215 Bullock, *After Sixty Years*, 3; R. Harris, *Prejudice and Tolerance in Ulster: A Study of Neighbours and 'Strangers' in a Border Community* (Manchester: Manchester University Press, 1972), 168, 222.

216 Leary, *Unapproved Routes*, 49.

217 Leary, *Unapproved Routes*, 49.

218 MacDonald, *The Pitchfork Murders*, 13.

219 MacDonald, *The Pitchfork Murders*, 13.

220 Nevertheless, Michael Naan's relations with many of his immediate Protestant neighbours remained overtly friendly – he was on reasonably good terms with the Allens, Johnsons and Maguires, whose farms bordered his own. James Naan did not recognise the man who wished to visit the island on Lough Aughnahinch interaction – he was from the 'neighbourhood' but did not live adjacent to the Naans. Interview with James Naan, Newtownbutler, March 20, 2017.

strong connections with Lord Erne's Crom Castle – where her brother Alexander was a member of the castle's Loyal Orange Lodge and played in the Crom flute band, both of which had been established by the Earl of Erne. From 1921 to 1946, Alex Liddle served in the part-time USC, continuing to live in Killalahard with his wife Margaret and son Albert Joseph until his death in 1973 aged 88.[221] Albert Liddle later occupied an important political, civic and security role in Newtownbutler and South Fermanagh for many years. In 1972, at the age of 52, Major Liddle was OC C Company/Intelligence Officer, 4 UDR. A leading member of the local Royal Black Preceptory (a more exclusive chapter of the Orange Order), he was also the Worshipful Master of Crom Castle Loyal Orange Lodge in the early 1970s. Before his UDR service, Albert Liddle had previously served for eleven years as the Lisnaskea District Commander of the USC until its disbandment in 1969, commanding 14 sub-districts including Newtownbutler (he had joined the USC in the late 1930s and served in the Home Guard during the Second World War). Liddle was also elected as an UUP councillor from 1967 to 1997 and was appointed as a Justice of the Peace in 1969.[222]

Michael Naan was registered as the owner of the farm at Aughnahinch in June 1967. In June 1972, only four months before his death, Michael Naan acquired a 25-acre farm in the townland of Ports, formerly owned by 'Wee Ned' Naan, that was close to Albert Liddle's residence and Crom estate. This brought Naan's total land holdings to more than 90 acres. (He had already come into possession of approximately 20 acres of land in the townland of Killard, also a few hundred yards from Albert Liddle's farm.)[223] Naan was known as a diligent, 'tidy' farmer; in the late 1960s, he moved away from dairy farming in favour of keeping a suckler herd as the demand for beef continued to grow.[224]

Michael Naan's schooling across the nearby border in Clones, with its state-sponsored, strongly Nationalist teaching of Irish history and his enduring love of Fermanagh GAA, may have heightened his political

221 'Obituary: Mr. Alexander Liddle', *Impartial Reporter*, August 16, 1973.
222 Dane, *The B Specials in Fermanagh*, 31; 'Death of Respected Former Councillor', *Impartial Reporter*, July 26, 2007; 'Obituary: Mr. Joseph Albert Liddle', *Impartial Reporter*, August 30, 2007.
223 Interview with James Naan, December 12, 2016; 'Fermanagh News', *Anglo-Celt*, June 9, 1972.
224 MacDonald, *The Pitchfork Murders*, 11.

awareness with respect to politics in County Fermanagh, explaining his later activism in the civil rights movement. However, Naan's family may also have played an important influence in fostering his political views. Naan's mother, born Bridget Lynch, came from a strongly Republican family: a number of Naan's Lynch relatives had been IRA Volunteers. James Naan, Michael's nephew, later reflected that:

> His [Michael Naan's] strong political opinions came from the Lynches ... I can remember my granduncle sitting with Michael in the house in Aughnahinch talking about [a raid]. He was obviously a volunteer at the time but I remember him talking about them lying in the 'sioc' [frost]. There were two IRA columns attacking and I remember him talking about the bullets flying over his head.[225]

In the early 1970s, another generation of Lynches emerged as committed Republicans: Michael Naan's cousin, Seán Lynch, later became a senior Republican in County Fermanagh and was badly wounded after being ambushed by the SAS while on 'active service' in 1986. (IRA Volunteer Seamus McElwain was shot dead by the SAS shortly after being captured in the same incident.)[226] Michael Naan was a close friend of Seán Lynch's father.[227] Compared with his mother's family, the Naans were much less politically active. However, Enda Naan (James Naan's father) harboured harder, more overtly Republican, political opinions than his younger bother Michael. Although he predeceased Michael in 1967, Enda's family continued to live in Donagh, a well-known, largely Republican area near Newtownbutler, where they were close friends with the Leonard family (Desmond and Louis were both active IRA

---

225 Interview with James Naan, Newtownbutler, March 20, 2017.
226 In 1986, Lynch and Seamus McElwain were shot by the SAS while preparing an ambush near the border village of Roslea. Lynch was badly hurt but survived and was sentenced to twenty-five years' imprisonment for his part in the attempted ambush; a wounded McElwain was controversially killed a few minutes after he was apprehended by the SAS. Released under the terms of the Good Friday Agreement, Lynch is an elected Sinn Féin member of the Northern Irish Assembly for Fermanagh and South Tyrone. David McKittrick, 'Toll of Civilians and Terrorists Shot in Controversial Incidents', *Independent*, June 4, 1993.
227 M. Lynch, *The Long Road Home* (Dublin: Londubh, 2010), 21.

Volunteers – Louis was murdered in his butcher's shop in Derrylin by Loyalist paramilitaries in December 1972).[228]

At the time of his death, Michael Naan lived in the former residence of Albert Liddle's still-living aunt, Charlotte Brooks. Along the border the Orange Order has traditionally endeavoured to keep Protestant farms from being 'lost' to Catholics, particularly those families with strong Republican or Nationalist connections.[229] The loss of the farm at Aughnahinch to the Naan family – a farm that the Liddle family could have expected to inherit if William Brooks had not sold it – would have irked Albert Liddle, particularly since he was a senior member of the Orange Order/Royal Black Preceptory. Michael Naan and Albert Liddle would occasionally appear at the same court sessions that dealt with the electoral list for the Newtownbutler area – Naan, on behalf of the local civil rights association, to ensure that Catholic voters were officially registered in the electoral wards that made up the Newtownbutler area. Any objections had to be rebutted with documentary evidence; Liddle performed the equivalent task for the Unionist (almost exclusively Protestant) vote. The experience may have further hardened relations between the two.[230]

Michael Naan: From a Suspect to a 'Known' IRA Gunman

It did not take long for Major Jeremy Mackenzie to conclude that the RUC in Fermanagh had very little actionable intelligence or assistance to offer his company: 'The intelligence briefing on my arrival in Lisnaskea involved a short briefing by the RUC officer on previous incidents. There was no detailed intelligence briefing and the name Naan was not mentioned to me.'[231] Major Mackenzie subsequently appears to have met with Major Albert Liddle, OC C Company/Intelligence Officer, 4 UDR, and 'several local dignitaries'. These included the local general practitioner, Dr O'Flaherty, and the Earl of Erne, Harry Crichton. Lord Erne spoke with D Company's officers on a number of occasions including

---

228 Interview with James Naan, Newtownbutler, March 20, 2017.
229 Declan Lawn, 'Orange Order Says It Uses Land Funds to "Counter Republicans"' Illegal Proceeds', *BBC News*, February 15, 2015.
230 Interview with former Fermanagh SDLP Councillor, Fergus McQuillan, Newtownbutler, November 28, 2016.
231 Statement of Major Jeremy Mackenzie, January 18, 1973. Trial document made available by Legal Professional 2.

on the afternoon of October 23, and hosted a drinks reception for some officers and NCOs from D Company on the day after the murders, the evening of October 24, 1972.[232]

CSM John Higgins confirmed at the trial that the list of IRA Volunteers used by D Company in South Fermanagh came from the local C Company, 4 UDR.[233] This list should have been regarded as 'low grade' intelligence, pending verification and proper grading by the RUC and/or Military Intelligence at 3 Brigade and at HQNI. A senior 4 UDR officer observed that the RUC in Fermanagh were often 'stand-offish with the UDR. They were certainly careful with intelligence'.[234] The same officer claimed that he spent much of his time trying to get 4 UDR Intelligence Officers, including Majors Albert Liddle and Sam Foster, to look beyond their longstanding local prejudices towards certain individuals and to gather new intelligence on the largely adolescent IRA. Considering the tendency of part-time UDR officers to exaggerate local suspicions and the infiltration of the UDR by Loyalist paramilitary groups at the time, the Argylls should have also been circumspect in their treatment of 'blacklists' received from local part-time soldiers.[235] Instead, Naan, whose name was on the UDR 'blacklist', quickly became unquestioningly fixed in the minds of Lieutenant Snowball, Sergeant Hathaway and Corporal Byrne as a 'known IRA man', a quartermaster who was 'involved in everything that went down there'.[236]

No investigation or inquiry was ever undertaken by the Army to ascertain why Michael Naan was listed by the UDR as an IRA Volunteer/ quartermaster for Fermanagh and where/how the local UDR gained

232 Statement of Andrew Snowball, as recorded by RUC Detective Inspector William McBurney on April 6, 1979. Documents made available by Legal Professional 2; Statement of Major Jeremy Mackenzie, witnessed by Detective Chief Inspector William Scott and Detective Inspector William McBurney, August 11, 1979. Trial document made available by Legal Professional 2.

233 Document made available by Legal Professional 2. Document missing from the original PRONI file CRCT/3/2/2/159A.

234 Interview with a UDR officer (4th Battalion), June 2014.

235 Potter, The UDR, 82; Interview with a UDR officer (4th Battalion), June 2014.

236 Account by RUC Detective Superintendent Ernest Drew of his interview on June 12, 1979 with Lieutenant Andrew Snowball, OC 13 Platoon, D Company, 1 Argylls, dated August 11, 1979. Trial document made available by Legal Professional 2.

its information. IRA Volunteer Louis Leonard, murdered by Loyalist paramilitaries in his butcher's shop in Derrylin on December 15, 1972, was later revealed to be the IRA quartermaster in South Fermanagh at the time of Naan's death.[237] It is unlikely that Michael Naan was ever a member of the IRA; he was never claimed as an IRA Volunteer, unlike Louis Leonard. The IRA went so far as to put out a statement shortly after Naan and Murray's murders stating that both men 'were not connected in any way with the IRA'.[238] According to his nephew, Michael Naan enjoyed good relations with several local RUC men including reserve constable Bob Crilly – later murdered by the IRA – and Stanley Allen, his immediate neighbour and an RUC sergeant.[239]

Naan was heavily involved in the Fermanagh civil rights movement and for some that was very close to, if not equivalent to, being a member of the IRA. Naan was also an active supporter of Frank McManus (as were many Catholics in Newtownbutler), the MP for Fermanagh and South Tyrone and a leading figure in the Northern Resistance movement, a more radical fringe of the civil rights movement. McManus was tainted in Protestant eyes by his family connections to the IRA and his active dialogue with militant Republicans. On August 21, and again on October 9, Frank McManus had participated in meetings of *Dáil Uladh*, a nine county Ulster parliament, which was condemned by the local Church of Ireland bishop in Fermanagh, the Right Reverend Robert Heavener, as an IRA construct.[240]

237 According to a Republican memorial booklet commemorating Leonard, 'Louis joined B Company, South Fermanagh Brigade of the IRA. Louis swiftly moved through the ranks of the IRA, becoming the Company's quartermaster, a role which was to see him spend more and more time in the struggle.' Memorial booklet entitled 'Vol. Louis Leonard, South Fermanagh Brigade, Óglaigh na hÉireann, 1946–1972' (in author's possession).
238 Fergus McQuillan pointed out that Naan recognised the Northern Irish court system, repeatedly turning up to hearings to plead the case for a local Nationalist to be placed on the register, something an IRA Volunteer would not do. Interview with former Fermanagh SDLP Councillor, Fergus McQuillan, Newtownbutler, November 28, 2016; 'Newtownbutler News', *Anglo-Celt*, November 3, 1972.
239 Interview with James Naan, Newtownbutler, March 20, 2017.
240 Bishop Heavener also believed that the lay Catholic organisation, the Ancient Order of Hibernians, was a 'front' for the IRA – a longstanding belief among Protestants in West Ulster. Cielou, *Spare my Tortured People*, 108. Many Catholics

The anthropologist Rosemary Harris noted a contradictory attitude among border Protestants, many remarking that their Catholic neighbours were Janus-like: 'Catholics are great neighbours, till one day they could do a bad turn, and then they'll do it.' Or, 'All the time he's smiling at me I can feel the knife slowly turning.'[241] However, Harris also noted, 'just how careful the people were to try, in normal circumstances, to avoid any behaviour likely to cause hostility, in other words to keep the latent hostility latent'.[242] But this same avoidance of open disagreement in order to preserve cooperation and a semblance of neighbourliness also had the effect of reinforcing ignorance of the other community: 'Confrontation was avoided but at the same time so was the possibility of testing prejudices against reality.'[243]

The anthropologist Henry Glassie has noted that 'a neighbour' in rural Ireland is a term applied to individuals within a potentially wide area, often up to a mile in radius from a person's residence, sometimes even more.[244] During the tense days of 1972, the people of South Fermanagh, particularly from the farming community, often refused to believe that their immediate neighbours, those they cooperated with and interacted with on an almost daily basis, could be supporters of the IRA or of Loyalist paramilitaries. As a British officer in Fermanagh put it, 'It was always somebody over the hill' – in other words near enough in the neighbourhood to be a constant threat, but not close enough to know intimately. A senior RUC officer stationed in Fermanagh in the early 1970s reported the same trend – everyday familiarity was a great tonic for suspicion; a certain amount of physical distance and infrequent contact within the neighbourhood was required for demonisation.[245] Such a response was also a way to cope with the advent of neighbourly

had a similar suspicion regarding the true motives of the Freemasons and the Orange Order – the masons allegedly controlled who bought and sold property in the towns, while the Orange Order tried to ensure that farms remained in Protestant hands. Gordon-McBride, 'Symbol, Barrier, Resource, Bridge', 138.
241 R. Harris, *Prejudice in Ulster* (Manchester: Manchester University Press, 1972), 181.
242 Harris, *Prejudice in Ulster*, 199.
243 Harris, *Prejudice in Ulster*, 224.
244 Glassie, *Passing the Time in Ballymenone*, 292.
245 Interview with a former UDR officer (4th Battalion), June 2014; Interview with RUC Officer 6, Belfast, November 2015.

violence. Since violence could no longer be blamed on people far away in Belfast, Londonderry or even Enniskillen, but, in Glassie's words, 'has entered the neighbourhood, come into the breast, and soured the clay with blood', a closer culprit must be found without compromising the urgent daily need for economic and social cooperation with long-standing and immediate neighbours in a relatively isolated, rural area. Michael Naan lived close to, but not in immediate proximity to, the Bells and Albert Liddle.

Michael Naan was not 'quiet'. Glassie emphasised the gravity of breaking with your neighbours in South Fermanagh:

> It is 'a bitter kind of neighbour' who lets anger become spite or who lets political commitment stand in the way of decent sociability. Personal bitterness harms the community ... Politically bitter, the person breaks out of connection with great numbers of neighbours and becomes the channel through which the political force of the world beyond enters the community to destroy its own political structure.[246]

To a section of the Protestant population of Newtownbutler, Michael Naan had crossed a line. Naan was a vocal individual, committed to his political beliefs and unafraid to air grievances if he felt himself slighted or discriminated against.[247] In February 1972, Michael Naan had been arrested and convicted of taking part in an 'illegal but orderly' 150-strong demonstration in Newtownbutler to protest against the Bloody Sunday killings (He received a six months' suspended sentence and a £15 fine). Naan's co-accused included Fergus McQuillan, later a long-serving SDLP Councillor in Fermanagh.[248] But two other men in the dock with Naan, well-known Republicans John Joe McCusker and Seán Lavelle (Lavelle later became an RUC informant in the 1980s. McCusker's son, John Joe McCusker Jr, is currently a leading member of Republican Sinn Féin), were also convicted alongside Naan and McQuillan.[249] Among such company, in the bitter atmosphere of South

---

246 Glassie, *Passing the Time in Ballymenone*, 292.
247 MacDonald, *The Pitchfork Murders*, 13.
248 'Sequel to Derry Sympathy March', *Anglo-Celt*, March 24, 1972.
249 John Joe McCusker Jr. gave an oration from the steps of Dublin's General Post Office at the dissident Republican centenary commemoration of the 1916 uprising.

Fermanagh, rumours about Naan's alleged IRA membership and that of other civil rights activists, such as long-time SDLP councillor Fergus McQuillan, appear to have circulated among local Protestants.[250] There was a 'de facto boycott' of McQuillan's pub by many of his former Protestant regulars in the early 1970s; Crom estate, a valued customer, suddenly cancelled its orders.[251]

With approximately 90 acres, Naan held more land than most in 1972; as a bachelor, he had fewer outgoings, more to invest.[252] James Naan also recalls that at the time of his death his uncle hoped to go into 'contracting' – hiring out labour and machinery at harvest time. He hoped to leave much of the daily burden of farming at Aughnahinch to hired labourers like Andy Murray. Naan occasionally employed Jimmy Connolly from Wattlebridge to work at Aughnahinch – the Connollys were well-known Republicans in the Newtownbutler area.[253] Local people may have been suspicious about Michael Naan becoming more prosperous. The increasing presence of farm labourers at Aughnahinch may have also drawn attention and speculation, leading mistrustful (and possibly envious) local Protestants to conclude that Naan was acting as an IRA quartermaster. Local people who knew Naan remember that shortly before his death he was accused of buying extra food in Boyd's shop in Lisnaskea to feed IRA men on his farm. The implicit accusation here is clear; at least some of Naan's Protestant neighbours preferred to see Naan's increased prosperity as a result of his alleged IRA membership rather than hard work and shrewd investment.[254]

In the weeks before Naan's death, relations between Newtownbutler activists in the Fermanagh civil rights association and the local UDR C Company had become increasingly acrimonious. A group of civil rights activists travelled from the village to Enniskillen in early October

P. Smyth, 'Dissident Republicans Mark 1916 Rising Outside GPO' *Irish Times*, April 23, 2016. 'Special Branch Agent Safe at Home Says Sinn Féin', *Guardian*, October 20, 2006.

250 Interview with former Fermanagh SDLP Councillor, Fergus McQuillan, Newtownbutler, November 28, 2016.

251 Interview with former Fermanagh SDLP Councillor, Fergus McQuillan, Newtownbutler, November 28, 2016.

252 Glassie, *Passing the Time in Ballymenone*, 585.

253 Interview with James Naan, Newtownbutler, March 20, 2017.

254 Harris, *Prejudice in Ulster*, 222.

1972 to attend a Nationalist political meeting that was addressed by SDLP MPs Austin Currie and John Hume (Fergus McQuillan believes that Naan would have been among them).[255] The Newtownbutler group confronted Currie about his support for the UDR. According to a journalist writing in *The Impartial Reporter*, 'Mr. Currie was also heckled and there were shouts of "What about the UDR in Newtownbutler?"'[256] Worse for Naan, he was reportedly seen to fall out with Robin Bell a few days before Bell was ambushed and killed by the IRA (Naan was killed the day after Bell). 'Michael parked his car and they wanted to search it. Seemingly there were words between them, but people were watching and the UDR subsequently withdrew.' One of the UDR men was alleged to have struck Michael Naan's car with the butt of his rifle.[257]

Michael Naan's farm was situated close to that of William Trotter (murdered August 28, 1972) and Robin Bell (murdered October 22). He also lived near to the Latimer brothers, whose intimidation and subsequent move to Lisnaskea outraged and frightened local Protestants.[258] Local Loyalists were casting around for Catholic collaborators, those who betrayed the movements of their Protestant neighbours to the IRA. Naan was already firmly on Albert Liddle's radar; he certainly felt on edge. In the weeks before his friend's death, Fergus McQuillan recalled that Michael Naan, a fastidiously tidy person, told him that he had positioned certain items in the house so that he could monitor if they had been disturbed when he was absent and conclude that soldiers had been searching his farm again.[259] Such visits appear to have persisted after his death: James Naan remembered that the family found the name 'Robin' carved on the window-sill at the front of the Aughnahinch farmhouse with an arrow pointing across the farmyard to the byre where Michael Naan was murdered.[260]

255 Interview with former Fermanagh SDLP Councillor, Fergus McQuillan, Newtownbutler, November 28, 2016.

256 'Enniskillen Crowd Jeers SDLP MPs', *Impartial Reporter*, October 5, 1972.

257 MacDonald, *The Pitchfork Murders*, 13.

258 '"Volunteers" to Protect the Fermanagh Loyalists', *Impartial Reporter*, November 14, 1972.

259 Interview with former Fermanagh SDLP Councillor, Fergus McQuillan, Newtownbutler, November 28, 2016.

260 Interview with James Naan, Newtownbutler, March 20, 2017.

There were many vocal Republicans in the Newtownbutler/Donagh area in 1972 – others were much more radical and vocal than Michael Naan, including his Lynch cousins. Why then was he singled out? Here again it is worth turning to Stathis Kalyvas, who has emphasised 'the predominance of malice in denunciation' during civil wars.[261] Envy or resentment can be dressed up in political colours. Malice may not have been the unequivocal, predominant factor in the case of the blacklisting of Michael Naan, but it is a likely ingredient in a complex mix of local grievances. In the context of rural Fermanagh, where economic activities, such as the ownership of a farm, were frequently interpreted through a sectarian prism as a political or security threat, it is difficult to separate envy or personal malice from inter-communal political suspicion; rather, the two become blurred.

The local UDR company elevated Naan to become a primary target for co-opted outsiders, in this case D Company, 1 Argylls, not due to any significant intelligence about the violent threat that he posed, but because of sectarian antipathy. A combination of resentment over Naan's ownership of a traditionally Protestant farm in Aughnahinch, land closely connected to the family of the local UDR company commander, jealousy of his increased prosperity, and his public falling out with Robin Bell, would probably have earned Naan a dangerous degree of negative attention, especially in the turbulent days of 1972 when the potential for 'turning neighbourhood vendettas into noble struggles' was at its height. Naan had broken an unwritten rule about land ownership. Through his civil rights activism, Naan was merely adding insult to injury – he had become 'bitter'. His cousin Colm Caughey later recalled that shortly after the murders a Union Flag was raised on Lough Aughnahinch, bordering Naan's farm, echoing Harris's observation on symbolism and land ownership.[262]

D Company Operations: October 22–23, 1972

The day before the murders of Naan and Murray, at 02.53 on October 22, a patrol of Chestnut Troop, RHA, was ambushed along the border, not far from the site of the murders of Private Tom Bullock and his wife Emily in an IRA assassination a few weeks earlier, and near the southern

261 Kalyvas, *The Logic of Violence in Civil War*, 3.
262 Harris, *Prejudice in Ulster*, 222; MacDonald, *The Pitchfork Murders*.

town of Ballyconnell.[263] Chestnut Troop had attempted to intercept an IRA unit but had been ambushed in turn.[264] Five hours later, and two miles to the north-east, Private Robin Bell (4 UDR) was ambushed and shot in the head and arm while driving with his father and brother near Naan's farm, just off the Galloon Island road, on their way back from tending to the family's cattle. He later died in the Erne hospital in Enniskillen.[265] Thirteen Platoon and Chestnut Troop were involved in the follow-up cordon and search operation: 264 cars were stopped, 240 were searched, the hijacked car was located and Chestnut Troop fired three shots across the border at a suspected IRA unit.[266] CSM John Higgins recalled that later that evening Major Mackenzie convened an intelligence briefing at which D Company's three platoon commanders were present (the meeting took place at 15 Platoon's camp north of the village of Newtownbutler). At this briefing Michael Naan was identified as a senior IRA Volunteer in the South Fermanagh area.[267]

Major Mackenzie insisted on a high tempo of operations; 13, 14 and 15 Platoons had little time for sleep, conducting patrols along the border, searching farms, setting up ambushes and providing a security cordon for 4 UDR Private Robin Bell's funeral. On the night of 22 October 1972, 13 Platoon camped on Crom estate, nor far from the border. During the course of October 23, the day of the murders, Lieutenant Snowball and his platoon went by boat to search the island of Inisfendra that overlooked Crom.[268] Thirteen Platoon later visited a number of farms

---

263 TNA: WO 305/4251 16th/5th The Queen's Royal Lancers, Commander's Diary, Northern Ireland 1972, October 23, 1972.

264 An officer from Imjin Battery, 45 Field Regiment, Royal Artillery, described the logic of such an approach: 'More often than not the dominating ground was on the Republic's side of the border and it was a matter of course therefore for the Battery to move into their defensive fire positions before dawn and remain well concealed all day. Nevertheless, where the dominating ground was in our favour it was naturally seized either by stealth or vertical envelopment and occasional targets were presented to encourage the IRA to give away their positions.' Pughe, 'Border Shellhounds', 30.

265 TNA: WO 305/4251 16th/5th The Queen's Royal Lancers, Commander's Diary, Northern Ireland 1972, October 23, 1972.

266 Commander's Diary, Northern Ireland 1972, October 23, 1972.

267 'Naan's Name on Army List', *Belfast Telegraph*, January 15, 1981.

268 Statement of Major John Jeremy Mackenzie, January 18, 1973. Trial document made available by Legal Professional 2.

along the border, including the house that had been abandoned by the Latimers.[269] Lieutenant Snowball also met with Lord Erne during the course of the day. Later, around mid-afternoon, 13 Platoon moved camp to a second location, in an area close to Naan's farm.[270] An interviewee who served in 13 Platoon recalled a verbal confrontation between his section commander and Michael Naan at some point during the day; Naan demanded that the soldiers leave his property (an account of an earlier visit by soldiers to the farm is also recalled locally).[271] According to Naan's friend, Fergus McQuillan, locals who met Naan in a nearby shop that afternoon recalled that he was quite unsettled about the military activity around his farm.[272]

Hathaway and another NCO in 13 Platoon, Lance Corporal James Healey, recalled that Lieutenant Snowball briefed his platoon in the early evening of 23 October, stating that Naan was a quartermaster for the IRA.[273] Snowball later told the RUC that he tasked Hathaway to patrol the area near Naan's farm while he was simultaneously away at a company-level 'Orders Group' (O Group) meeting scheduled for 18.00. Snowball's statement places both him and his company commander away from the vicinity of Naan's farm at the time of the murders. (Major Mackenzie would normally take a leading role in a company-level O Group Meeting and, according to Snowball, did so on October 23, 1972.)[274] Snowball's version of events was contradicted by D Company's

269 'Shots Fired at Fermanagh UDR Man', *Impartial Reporter*, August 30, 1972.

270 The location of this camp appears to have been near a barn in an elevated, lightly wooded area immediately to the south of Lough Aughnahinch and a few hundred yards from Naan's farm (the grid reference given by Lance Corporal Chestnut was – GR H425239). Statement of Lance Corporal James Healey, December 16, 1979; Statement of Lance Corporal Ian Chestnut, June 10, 1979. Trial documents made available by Legal Professional 2.

271 Interview with Argyll Soldier 9 (Private Soldier), November 2013; 'Newtownbutler News', *Anglo-Celt*, November 3, 1972.

272 Interview with former Fermanagh SDLP Councillor, Fergus McQuillan, Newtownbutler, November 28, 2016.

273 Statement of Sergeant Stanley Hathaway, December 16, 1979. Trial document made available by Legal Professional 2; Statement of Lance Corporal James Healey, December 16, 1979. Trial document made available by Legal Professional 2.

274 Account by RUC Detective Superintendent Ernest Drew of his interview on June 12, 1979 with Lieutenant Andrew Snowball, OC 13 Platoon, D Company,

sergeant major, now Captain Higgins. In his testimony at Belfast Crown Court on January 15, 1981, Higgins recalled that D Company's O Group meeting was normally held at 18.00 every evening. However, on October 23 – the night of the murders – Higgins claimed that the briefing was held earlier. After the O Group meeting, at which he and Snowball were present, Higgins and Snowball then travelled to 13 Platoon's camp, close to Naan's farm. A briefing then took place at 13 Platoon's location. According to Higgins's testimony, both he and Snowball were in the vicinity of Naan's farm when the murders took place. (Lance Corporal Chestnut claimed that Private John Mcguire, who went with Hathaway, Byrne and Chestnut to Naan's, was acting as Snowball's batman and radio operator at the time of the murders.)[275]

Higgins recalled that he used a night vision device at a nearby OP to observe Hathaway and the other soldiers during their visit to Naan's. However, he claimed that he did not see the murders take place, only discovering what had happened on the evening of October 24. The most likely position for such an OP is a nearby drumlin in the townland of Sandholes, the site of the Battle of Newtownbutler, which afforded an excellent and discreet vantage point from which to observe Naan's farm. Thirteen Platoon's camp and the OP would then have been respectively placed on the two drumlins to the south and west of Naan's farm – a sound military disposition from which to detect, observe and counter any hostile activity. The OP at Sandholes would have been accessed from the Galloon Island road by means of an old track called Moore's lane.

Neither the Army nor the RUC, or even the DPP, appeared to be interested in anomalies between Snowball's and Higgins's testimonies. If Lieutenant Snowball was indeed in the approximate area of Naan's farm, as Higgins claimed, why not try to discover his exact whereabouts? Sergeant Hathaway also suggested that a fifth person was with the patrol when they visited Naan's farm. However, neither the RUC nor the Royal Military Police Special Investigation Branch officers put any pressure on

1 Argylls, dated August 11, 1979. Trial document made available by Legal Professional 2.
275 Contemporaneous notes made by a legal representative of the testimony given by Captain John Higgins, Belfast Crown Court, January 15, 1981. Trial document made available by Legal Professional 2.

Hathaway to reveal the identity of that person either during their initial interviews or afterwards.[276]

The urgent visit to Naan's farm was likely in response to the need for information to locate a missing D Company soldier. On the day of the murders, Private 'Fluff' Owens, a soldier in 15 Platoon, operating just to the north of the village of Newtownbutler, was declared missing for more than seven hours (14.00–21.15), before eventually turning up, 'unharmed but exhausted', at D Company Headquarters at Lisnaskea RUC Station. Owens had got lost while on patrol. Major Mackenzie recalled that the failure to locate Owens caused 'a considerable amount of concern'. (This part of OC D Company's statement was omitted from later versions prepared for the trial, in which the day of 23 October is recalled, like the rest of D Company's time in Fermanagh, as being relatively uneventful.)[277] According to CSM Higgins, the disturbing news of Private Owens's disappearance was reported at 'all levels' of military command in Northern Ireland.[278]

Capture by the IRA was every soldier's worst nightmare, meaning almost certain execution and possible torture beforehand.[279] Indeed, one of the questions Sergeant Hathaway put to Naan before he killed him related to Naan's whereabouts in the last 'two or three hours' (the Argylls were observing Naan's farm and would have known that he had left his farm during that afternoon, though the real purpose of his journey appears to have been to deliver firewood to Andrew Murray's mother).[280] If the IRA had captured Owens, then D Company urgently needed intelligence on

---

276 'Naan's Name on Army List', *Belfast Telegraph*.

277 Statement of Major Jeremy Mackenzie (undated, 1979), Trial document made available by Legal Professional 2. Document missing from the original PRONI file CRCT/3/2/2/159A. The document included in the PRONI file, dated December 17, 1979, appears to be an edited, shortened version of this longer statement.

278 Statement of Company Sergeant Major John Higgins, December 19, 1979: Trial document made available by Legal Professional 2.

279 TNA: WO 305/4251 16th/5th The Queen's Royal Lancers Commander's Diary, Northern Ireland 1972; Statement of Major John Jeremy Mackenzie (undated, 1979). Trial document made available by Legal Professional 2.

280 Interview with Sergeant Stanley Hathaway, as recorded by Detective Sergeant Henry Nixon and witnessed by Detective Sergeant Ronald Mathieson (undated), Trial document made available by Legal Professional 2; Statement of Mary Murray, December 30, 1979. Trial document made available by Legal Professional 2.

his whereabouts: Who better to ask than the man listed by D Company as the 'known' IRA quartermaster for Fermanagh, Michael Naan?[281]

During the period of Private Owens's absence another group of soldiers appear to have been sent across the border to observe another alleged IRA Volunteer's house in the village of Ballyconnell.[282] These soldiers were discovered by an off-duty Garda: in an incident report sent by a Colonel Dempsey of the Irish Army to the Department of Defence in Dublin, the Irish officer reported that, 'At 2345 hrs. an off-duty Garda on his way home met three armed British soldiers at Point A on sketch map enclosed. This point is about 0.8 miles from the border. The soldiers were heading back towards the border.'[283] An Argyll officer later recalled the incident, claiming it was an accident.[284] However, according to the Garda's account the soldiers 'stayed in the area for some time' – and 'may well have been observing a house or building'.[285]

Having already used boats to search islands on Upper Lough Erne on October 23, some soldiers could later have crossed Lough Erne to the church at Derryvore (also in the Crom estate) and continued on foot to the County Cavan side of Upper Lough Erne to observe another suspected IRA Volunteer's home before making their way back to camp that night. The narrow crossing-point over Lough Erne between Crom and Derryvore was frequently used by the Crichton family and the security forces (and a seasonal ferry service sometimes operated between the two points).[286] Even by the standards of Fermanagh in 1972, the night of October 23 appears to have been one of unusual operational intensity. Sending soldiers into a populated village south of the border was a bold, risky decision. It was probably taken at a time of considerable stress, during the period when Private Owens was missing.

---

281 Contemporaneous notes made by a legal representative of the testimony given by Captain John Higgins, Belfast Crown Court, January 15, 1981. Trial document made available by Legal Professional 2.

282 Interview with Argyll Soldier 5 (Officer), May 2014.

283 MAI: 2003/15/94-G2/C/1872 Pt 2. Border crossings and border incidents by British Army.

284 Interview with Argyll Soldier 5 (Officer), May 2014.

285 MAI: 2003/15/94-G2/C/1872 Pt 2. Border crossings and border incidents by British Army.

286 TNA: WO 305/4251 16th/5th The Queen's Royal Lancers Commander's Diary, Northern Ireland 1972.

The Killing of Michael Naan and Andrew Murray

Confession and Exculpation

At approximately 18.00 on October 23, Sergeant Stan Hathaway led a four-man unit (himself, Byrne, Chestnut and Private John Mcguire – the A41 radio operator)[287] into Naan's farmyard. Private Mcguire described what happened next:

> As we got to the edge of the farmyard Sergeant Hathaway told us to get behind a wall on the left of the farm. We got down behind a wall and we then heard a noise, which sounded like a tin bucket, in an adjoining building. Sergeant Hathaway handed his rifle to Corporal Byrne and went off round the corner of the building.[288]

The direct manner by which the soldiers approached the farmyard suggested that this was not a reconnaissance patrol; at the men's trial, CSM Higgins referred to the small size of the patrol as being similar to a 'clearance patrol', a sharp, aggressive operation to eliminate or capture a known enemy and seize a position.[289] It also seems likely that Hathaway had advance information that suggested that Naan was unarmed (to the Argylls, Naan was a dangerous terrorist) and that he, Hathaway, would not be surprised (suggesting a cordon of some sort, what the Army called an 'aggressive OP', ready to open fire if necessary).[290] Indeed, an OP had been set up to observe the farm in the hours preceding Hathaway's

---

287 Hathaway later insinuated that there may have been 'somebody else' with the patrol. It is unclear, however, if he was referring to the OP described by Company Sergeant Higgins or another soldier or soldiers who accompanied his unit to Naan's farmyard. Transcript of an RMP/SIB interview on June 7, 1979 with Sergeant Stanley Hathaway, as recorded by RMP SIB Staff Sergeant Malcolm Denton, dated June 28, 1979. Trial document made available by Legal Professional 2.

288 Statement of Private John Mcguire, December 18, 1979. Trial document made available by Legal Professional 2.

289 Contemporaneous notes made by a legal representative of the testimony given by Captain John Higgins, Belfast Crown Court, January 15, 1981. Trial document made available by Legal Professional 2.

290 M. Urban, *Big Boys' Rules: The Secret Struggle against the IRA* (London: Faber and Faber, 1993), 63.

arrival at the farm, as later described by CSM Higgins at the trial in Belfast in January 1981.[291] The military disposition of soldiers from D Company around Naan's farm, a 'clearance patrol' supported by other company elements including well-positioned cordons/OPs, appears to closely resemble the type of company-level operation (described in some detail in his interviews with police) that Major Mackenzie claimed he would have conducted if he had intelligence to suggest that Michael Naan was a senior IRA Volunteer or quartermaster with access to weapons and explosives. However, Mackenzie continued to insist that Naan was not a significant terrorist suspect, despite evidence given by his CSM (Higgins) and platoon commander (Snowball) to the contrary.[292]

In advance of the trial, Lance Corporal Ian Chestnut alleged that Major Mackenzie's orders were to intimidate Naan, to get information through rough methods if possible or, if not, to provoke Naan into a panicked response, either by contacting other IRA Volunteers or by moving weapons: 'He [Hathaway] was told to make their presence felt so that the OP [Mackenzie and Higgins] wld [would] then see him [Naan]. Under Mackenzie (an SAS man) we would do this kind of thing on an OP.'[293] By this logic it was no accident that men of the experience of Hathaway, Byrne and Chestnut were picked to go to Naan's farm – they would 'make their presence felt' against an IRA man if necessary. Hathaway was not known for casual rule-breaking. However, this was an operation that, if successful, could potentially save the life of a missing Argyll soldier. Rough methods were deemed necessary in the circumstances.[294]

Lance Corporal Chestnut and Private Mcguire apprehended Andrew Murray, who had been driving a tractor, near the entrance to the farm,

291 'Naan's Name on Army List', *Belfast Telegraph*.
292 Statement of Major John Jeremy Mackenzie (undated, 1979). Trial document made available by Legal Professional 2; Statement by Major John Jeremy Mackenzie, dated August 11, 1979, witnessed by Detective Chief Inspector William Scott and Detective Inspector William McBurney, RUC. Trial document made available by Legal Professional 2.
293 Interview with Lance Corporal Iain Fletcher Chestnut, dated November 8, 1980. Trial document made available by Legal Professional 2. Document missing from the original PRONI file – CRCT/3/2/2/159A.
294 'Iain Fletcher Chestnut – Amendment to Statement Made on 12th June 1979', dated June 13, 1979. Trial document made available by Legal Professional 2.

forcing him to lie on the ground (as was often standard practice in Aden) while Hathaway and Byrne proceeded further into the farmyard.[295] In a police interview, Hathaway later described how he went into a byre on the farm where he found Naan 'mucking out' near a cow and her calf. 'We started asking him questions about who he was, where he had been in the last two or three hours. He wouldn't answer the questions.'[296] Naan, according to Hathaway's account, became aggressive, brandishing a pitchfork at the soldiers:

> He then said he knew us and that he was going to get the IRA boys onto us. He knew people who were quite capable of knocking off troops. He knew where we were and could get quite a few of them to cause us trouble. He continued to be abusive and knew we couldn't harm him or lift him. I can't remember if he went for me. Byrne said, 'Do him in' or something like that. I had the knife in my pocket. I had taken it off one of the platoon who had it on his belt. I got it out and struck him in the stomach. He started screaming, 'I'll get the boys onto you.' He was still standing up. I must have carried on stabbing him. He was shouting for someone else. He tried to run out of the stable. Byrne blocked the door. I went after him to keep him quiet. He was shouting at someone to get the boys. He stopped screaming. He must have died on me.[297]

Hathaway's account is full of self-justification for the murder of Naan. Naan was a bad individual who was going to get the IRA to murder Argylls. Moreover, Hathaway emotionally distances himself from the actual killings. 'He died on me' – he was trying to 'keep him quiet', lest he alert the IRA. Byrne's recollection of Naan's death is also one of

295 'Mad Mitch and his Tribal Law'; Statement of Iain Fletcher Chestnut, as recorded by Chief Inspector William McBurney, June 10, 1979. Trial document made available by Legal Professional 2.

296 Statement of Sergeant Stanley Hathaway, as recorded by Staff Sergeant Malcolm Denton on June 7, 1979. Trial document made available by Legal Professional 2.

297 Statement of Sergeant Stanley Hathaway, as recorded by Staff Sergeant Malcolm Denton on June 7, 1979. Trial document made available by Legal Professional 2.

exculpation; Argylls soldiers were in imminent danger and he had to keep Naan quiet. After Hathaway finished stabbing Naan in the byre, there was a discussion about what to do with Andrew Murray. According to Byrne, 'We came outside and talked about it ... I remember us saying nobody is going to believe our story that Naan attacked us.'[298] They decided to kill Murray.

Private Mcguire, the soldier who had initially apprehended Murray at the entrance to the farmyard, described the second murder:

> I heard this terrible scream, a very high-pitched scream ... Hathaway and Byrne then came down the path towards us. At this time the man [Murray] at the gate was lying down in the path and nobody was touching him. Sgt. Hathaway then straddled this man. Sgt. Hathaway put his legs on either side of this man's head and started to stab him ... The second man [Murray] did not scream. I only heard grunts coming from him. During this time I also heard cows mooing and a dog barking.[299]

Chestnut also offered his account of the death of Andrew Murray:

> Hathaway was kneeling. Byrne sat across his back on his lower back or rump facing Hathaway. This left most of Murray's back exposed to Hathaway. There was some conversation between them and I heard the word 'Murray'. I surmised that Byrne and Hathaway were asking him his name. I was half across the lane then. Murray had his legs together. Originally I thought Mcguire had held an arm but I think Byrne had pinned Murray's arms to his side. There were mumbled words of two or three sentences – I thought he was going to be given a beating. Hathaway said, 'Come over Chestnut and hold his legs'. I came across and squatted down and held his heals [sic]. Mcguire was 4 or 5 feet away ... Murray offered no resistance. There were a couple of thumps and grunts out of Murray and on the second or third thump there was a grating noise. I could not see what was

---

298 Interview with Corporal John Byrne, as recorded by Detective Sergeant Henry Nixon, June 9, 1979: Trial Document made available by Legal Professional 2.
299 Statement of Private John Mcguire, December 18, 1979. Trial document made available by Legal Professional 2.

happening as Byrne was in the way. I looked round Byrne to his right and saw a knife in Hathaway's hand and saw blood on the man's back. I stood up and backed off to the other side of the lane and turned my back.[300]

Chestnut then heard what he called a 'death gurgle' from Murray. Hathaway summoned Chestnut back to help move Murray's body to a bog near the lane leading up to Naan's farm. Chestnut, as in the evidence provided by Hathaway and Byrne, was keen to emphasise that Mcguire did not play a role in the murder of Andrew Murray, lest the young soldier also be implicated.[301]

Hathaway told the SIB that, in the immediate aftermath of the murders, he encountered his platoon commander, Lieutenant Snowball, who, according to Sergeant Hathaway, later got rid of the murder weapon.[302] Yet Lieutenant Snowball does not appear to have been pressed on the whereabouts of the knife.[303] The two SIB NCOs who interviewed Hathaway had different accounts of what happened to the murder weapon. Sergeant Robert Stronach recorded Hathaway's account as:

Snowball was there. He said 'What's happened?'... He then said, 'It'll be all right.' He then took the knife away from me and said, 'We must get rid of this' ... I don't know what happened [to] it. I think it was chucked away in the water the next day. We were then moved out after 2 or 3 hours, it was still dark, to the Castle [Lord Erne's Crom estate – 13 Platoon Headquarters on October 24, 1972]. The OC [Major Mackenzie] was there.[304]

300 Statement of Iain Fletcher Chestnut, dated November 5, 1980. Document made available by Legal Professional 2.

301 Statement of Iain Fletcher Chestnut, dated June 12, 1979. Trial document made available by Legal Professional 2. Document missing from the original PRONI file – CRCT/3/2/2/159A.

302 Interview with Sergeant Stanley Hathaway on June 7, 1979, as recorded by Sergeant Robert Stronach, RMP SIB, on January 7, 1980. Trial document made available by Legal Professional 2.

303 Statement of Andrew Snowball, as recorded by Chief Inspector William Scott, June 12, 1979. Trial document made available by Legal Professional 2.

304 Interview with Sergeant Stanley Hathaway on June 7, 1979, as recorded by Sergeant Robert Stronach, RMP SIB, on January 7, 1980. Trial document made available by Legal Professional 2.

Staff Sergeant Malcolm Denton recorded Hathaway as saying that 'Somebody chucked the knife from a vehicle into the water when we were on the move. I was in one vehicle and the knife was thrown out into the water.'[305] Lance Corporal Chestnut recalled the knife being thrown towards the lough that lay on the edge of Naan's farm, immediately after the murders had been committed. If indeed this was the case, the knife should have been found by the RUC, unless it was removed in the intervening period. (The small lough in question, Aughnahinch Lough, was searched for the murder weapon.)[306] The knife was later described by Hathaway as: 'A dagger type, blade four or five inches long. Crossed pattern on the shaft and a finger guard on one side. I remember my hand slipped off once.'[307] But if the knife was thrown away 'the next day', as Hathaway suggested, after 13 Platoon returned to Lord Erne's Crom estate during the early morning of October 24, then the murder weapon could still be in the waters near the shores of Crom.

At the trial in January 1981, Dr Martin Whittet, a psychiatrist occasionally employed by the military in Scotland, offered mitigating circumstances for the murders. Hathaway claimed that Naan had attacked him with a pitchfork; according to Dr Whittet this could have triggered a childhood trauma for Hathaway who had witnessed a man falling into a thrashing machine when he was a boy of eight or nine in Morayshire in the north of Scotland. Hathaway now had 'a pathological fear of spikes, prongs and knives'.[308] Hathaway's former D Company comrades do not recall such a fear of knives; their Platoon Sergeant frequently handled bayonets. Hathaway was known as an exceptionally tough soldier, 'not a man you would cross'.[309] Moreover, Hathaway and Byrne's version of events – that Naan attacked the Argylls first with a pitchfork – was

305 Interview with Sergeant Stanley Hathaway on June 7, 1979, as recorded by Sergeant Malcolm Denton, RMP SIB, dated June 7, 1979. Trial document made available by Legal Professional 2.

306 Statement of Iain Fletcher Chestnut, dated June 12, 1979. Trial document made available by Legal Professional 2. Document missing from the original PRONI file – CRCT/3/2/2/159A.

307 Interview with Sergeant Stanley Hathaway on June 7, 1979, as recorded by Sergeant Robert Stronach, RMP SIB, on January 7, 1980. Trial document made available by Legal Professional 2.

308 'Judgment', *Fermanagh Herald*, January 24, 1981.

309 Interview with Argyll Soldier 8 (Private Soldier), November 2013.

later dismissed by the Deputy State Pathologist, Dr Derek Carson, who noted that 'the absence of wounds to the hands and forearms of the two victims seemed to indicate that they had not fought or struggled with their attacker.' The implication was that another soldier had probably restrained Naan while Hathaway repeatedly stabbed him.[310] A lawyer in the trial of the soldiers at Belfast Crown Court in January 1981 recalled observing the men in the dock: 'I remember thinking he [Hathaway] had a very lined face. He looked like a hard man, a man who had lived a hard life. He and Byrne were both hard, strong men. Hathaway was the man in charge.'[311] The depiction of Hathaway as a man who simply went berserk because he was threatened with a pitchfork while on a routine search is a neat conclusion, but it is less than convincing.

D Company Closes Ranks: The Open Secret of the Murders of Naan and Murray

In a cruel coincidence, Kathleen Murray served her brother's killers tea in Crom Castle less than 16 hours after the murders (on October 24, 13 Platoon was again camped out on the Castle grounds). She recalled the soldiers 'laughing and joking' at the time.[312] When D Company returned to their base in Bessbrook on October 27, 1972, the following entry was made in the battalion diary: 'D Company came back from their sojourn in Fermanagh, tired, but apparently happy and full of war stories.'[313] What these 'war stories' were is not clear. The only act of violence to take place during their time in Fermanagh in which the Argylls were directly involved was the murders of Naan and Murray. D Company did not locate any IRA arms, despite searching a number of farms and businesses. The only find of note was a military hand torch and a Schermuly flare found by 13 Platoon at the farm of local man, Michael McManus. Nor did they engage in any fire fights with IRA units.[314]

---

310 'Soldier's Illness Halts Murder Trial', *Belfast Telegraph*, January 13, 1981.
311 Interview with Legal Professional 1, Belfast, September 30, 2014.
312 'Remembering the Victims', *Fermanagh Herald*, December 30, 1997.
313 RMASH: File Reference D71, 'Historical Record 1 ASH', 1972–1973.
314 TNA: WO 305/4251 16th/5th The Queen's Royal Lancers, Commander's Diary, Northern Ireland 1972: situation report from 16/5 Lancers to HQ 3 Brigade, dated October 24, 1972.

Murder: The Killing of Michael Naan and Andrew Murray

John Hanna, an oil company representative, called to Naan's farm to collect a bill at 18.05 on October 24, almost 24 hours after the murders. Getting out of his van, he noticed a lot of blood near the entrance to the farm yard. Michael Naan's car was parked in the yard with a jacket thrown over the bonnet. Looking back down towards the lane he saw a body (later identified as that of Andrew Murray), face-up and half-buried in a bog thirteen yards from the right side of the lane leading up to Naan's farm. According to the RUC, this was the first report they received about any incident taking place at Naan's farm. Sergeant Desmond Cecil-Brown and two other Constables (Nixon and McBrien) from the RUC station at Newtownbutler then accompanied Hanna back to the farm. Initially, the two RUC constables detailed to search the farm could not locate Michael Naan. However, Sergeant Cecil-Brown appeared confident that Naan was there and told the Constables to search again; they found Naan's bloodied body in a byre lying face upwards beside a tethered cow and her calf.[315] Approximately two hours after being discovered by Hanna, the bodies were removed from the scene and taken to Erne Hospital mortuary in Enniskillen.[316] When Inspector Paddy Gilligan, an RUC CID officer, arrived at Naan's farm at 10.15 on the morning of October 25 to collect evidence, he found no trace of 'graipes, pitchforks or farm implements'.[317] The account of a pitchfork murder as recorded by 16/5 Lancers would later be found to be false, but Gilligan was not to know this when he was initially looking for a murder weapon. Dr Carson carried out a post-mortem on the bodies later that evening at the Erne Hospital in Enniskillen.

It is difficult to trace the origin of the account that Naan and Murray were stabbed with a pitchfork and how such a detail was relayed to 16/5 Lancers Headquarters in Omagh (operationally, if somewhat distantly, in command of D Company, 1 Argylls) within 24 hours of the murder. It is unusual that there were no such implements at the farm by the time the RUC arrived on the scene, especially since the Argylls responsible for the murders later described finding Hathaway 'mucking out' a byre

315 MacDonald, *The Pitchfork Murders*, 36.
316 There is a sad irony here; Michael Naan and other civil rights activists had long condemned Erne Hospital of being guilty of the most 'egregious discrimination'– its failure to employ Catholics. 'Fermanagh Facts', pamphlet published by the Fermanagh Civil Rights Association, Enniskillen, 1969, 29.
317 Statement of Inspector Patrick Gilligan, August 16, 1979. Trial document made available by Legal Professional 2.

where a cow and newborn calf were kept, the place where he died. The most persistent reference to a pitchfork came from D Company itself, including Sergeant Hathaway, who claimed Naan used it as a weapon.[318] Since soldiers are already armed, the suggestion of a pitchfork as a murder weapon may have led the casual observer initially, and wrongly, to conclude that the two men died following an internecine or sectarian dispute. That may have been the deliberate intention behind the origin of the rumour and the disappearance of the farm tools.

Hanna, the local oil company representative, does not appear to have been the first person to visit Naan's farm after the murders. Lance Corporal Joe Burke of 13 Platoon, D Company, 1 Argylls recalled in his witness statement that, on the night of October 23, 1972, he was tasked by Lieutenant Snowball and Sergeant Hathaway to seal off the entrance to Naan's farm because there had been a murder there. Burke's half-section set off for the farm and mounted a cordon at the entrance, as per his platoon commander's instructions. The men had orders not to allow anybody into the farm and were in direct radio communication with D Company Headquarters at the RUC Station in Lisnaskea at the time. But, according to Burke, a car and a group of men wearing work overalls did gain access:

> Sometime during the night I stopped and checked a shooting brake [an estate vehicle], I don't know the make, coming up the laneway towards the farm. There were four male occupants of the shooting brake, they were dressed in light overalls and said that they were from Clones. The particulars were circulated to Company Headquarters and I was informed to allow them to proceed to the farm. The shooting brake left the farm again after 10/15 minutes. I stopped and searched the occupants and vehicle before allowing it to leave the area. After first light we were withdrawn back to base camp.[319]

318 Interview with Sergeant Stanley Hathaway on June 7, 1979, as recorded by Sergeant Robert Stronach, RMP SIB, on January 7, 1980. Trial document made available by Legal Professional 2.

319 Statement of Lance Corporal Joe Burke, December 17, 1979. Trial document made available by Legal Professional 2. For 'shooting brake', see W. Diem, 'The Shooting Brake Makes a Comeback', New York Times, November 26, 2006, http://www.nytimes.com/2006/11/26/automobiles/26BRAKE.html?_r=0 (accessed April 27, 2015).

Another soldier, Private Frederick Clarke, who told police he was also on the cordon at the entrance of Naan's farm on the night of October 23, remembered a group of men dressed in overalls arriving at the cordon in a white-coloured shooting brake vehicle and that they were cleared by D Company Headquarters to gain access to Naan's farm. However, he did not recall searching the car; instead, he told the RMP SIB/RUC that he recognised the passengers. Strikingly, despite this report of a highly relevant visit of another party to the murder scene hours after the death of Naan and Murray (with their bodies still in situ), neither the RUC nor the RMP appears to have asked Clarke the names of this second group of men who were in Naan's farm on the night of the murders. The reference to 'Clones' is also unusual; Clones was a nearby County Monaghan town, just across the border and approximately six miles from Naan's farm. Clones was known to the Army as a 'hotbed' of IRA activity.[320] During the murder trial Private (now Sergeant) Clarke remembered that the men he recognised were 'IRA terrorists' before going on to withdraw most of his testimony under cross-examination because his memory had now become 'hazy'.[321]

The lack of farm implements and the visit of this group of men to the farm suggest some sort of tampering with the scene of the murders. According to the sentries who were there, the cordon on the night of the murders was ostensibly set up, with the knowledge of D Company Headquarters, to preserve a murder scene. This in itself is remarkable since Major Mackenzie, Sergeant Major John Higgins and the RUC gave evidence that they had not been informed that any crime had taken place until the subsequent day (when John Hanna made his report). Major Mackenzie later made reference to a cordon set up on the night of October 24.[322] The police do not appear ever to have attempted to resolve the discrepancy in timing (or whether there were indeed 13 Platoon cordons on the farm on both nights). However, if there was a cordon on the night of October 23, as the accounts of Lance-Corporal Burke and Private Clarke suggest, then why were the RUC not aware of the murders? The

320 Statement of Private Frederick Clarke. Trial document made available by Legal Professional 2.
321 Statement of Private Frederick Clarke.
322 Statement of Major John Jeremy Mackenzie (undated, 1979). Trial document made available by Legal Professional 2. Another, shorter version of this longer statement seems to have been produced, which is included in the PRONI court file.

sentries at the cordon also told police that they had radioed D Company Headquarters with the identities of the four men and they were cleared to enter the farm.[323] If the particulars were circulated to RUC Station Lisnaskea, then the number plate of this shooting brake vehicle and the identities of the occupants should have been recorded in the D Company log-book and possibly by the RUC duty officer.[324]

At 19.30 on the night of the murders, a local woman driving to Newtownbutler saw a group of soldiers very near to the lane to Naan's farm talking to two occupants of a black Morris Minor car. Thinking she was going to be searched she dipped her lights and slowed down, only to be waved on by one of the soldiers standing by the car. The Morris Minor car then moved out onto the road in front of the woman before turning off down the nearby Galloon Island road (to the immediate north-west of Naan's farm).[325] In his police statement Private Mcguire recalled that, upon leaving the farm, he had seen a 'young girl', later identified as Dympna Brady, stopping her car near Naan's farm and that she was told to continue by either himself or another soldier. However, investigating officers from the RUC and RMP SIB do not seem to have asked Mcguire about the parked Morris Minor seen by Dympna Brady at this time, a very obvious question to pursue.[326] Lieutenant Snowball also remembered that D Company had access to a 'q van' – a transit van – during their time at Fermanagh. A 'q van' was generally a civilian vehicle used for intelligence operations or moving troops discreetly into dangerous areas. However, Major Mackenzie rejected any suggestion that D Company had a 'q van'.[327]

---

323 The names of the four men in Clones should also have been noted in the Watchkeepers' Logbook for D Company, normally available in the TNA WO 305 files series. However, the whereabouts of D Company, 1 Argylls Watchkeeper's entries (and that of the rest of 1 Argylls in 1972) is unknown. It does not appear to be in the National Archives at Kew.

324 Statement of Private Frederick Clarke. Trial document made available by Legal Professional 2.

325 Statement of Dympna Brady. Trial document made available by Legal Professional 2.

326 Statement of Private John Mcguire, December 18, 1979. Trial document made available by Legal Professional 2.

327 Statement of Major Jeremy Mackenzie, witnessed by Detective Chief Inspector William Scott and Detective Inspector William McBurney, August 11, 1979. Trial document made available by Legal Professional 2.

Investigators do not appear to have attempted to discover which D Company officer – Snowball or Mackenzie – was telling the truth. They also did not follow up on the suggestion by Sergeant Hathaway that there may have been 'somebody else', a fifth member of the patrol that went to Naan's farm on the night of the murders.[328] A series of obvious questions were not posed to key witnesses; anomalies and inconsistencies in accounts were not investigated. It appears that the investigation was being kept deliberately narrow in order not to implicate or pose awkward questions to more senior individuals, suggestive of a mobilisation of bias or 'non-questioning' as described by Bachrach and Baratz.[329]

The Missing Major: Confusion over the Role and Location of D Company's Commander

Major Jeremy Mackenzie, contradicting the evidence of CSM Higgins and Lieutenant Snowball, initially claimed that Michael Naan was a 'non-entity' and that the first time he heard Naan's name mentioned was when he learned that he had been murdered.[330] Later he told police that it was possible that Michael Naan was on a list of suspects and that he may have given permission for a reconnaissance visit to Naan's farm. He also now recalled that the shooting brake or estate vehicle encountered by the soldiers on the cordon contained suspected members of the IRA: instead of being allowed access to the farm, the men should have been arrested for questioning as their names were known to D Company.[331]

328 A RMP SIB transcript of an interview between Staff Sergeant Malcolm Denton, RMP SIB, and Sergeant Hathaway proceeds as follows: Denton: 'Who all was there?' Hathaway: 'Self, Byrne, Chestnut and Mcguire.' Denton: 'Anyone else?' Hathaway: 'There may have been someone else. Denton: 'Who?' Hathaway: 'I don't know.' Denton: [does not press point] 'Who found Naan in this stable?' Hathaway: 'Me and Byrne.' Transcript of an RMP/SIB interview on June 7, 1979 with Sergeant Stanley Hathaway, as recorded by RMP SIB Staff Sergeant Malcolm Denton, dated June 28, 1979. Trial document made available by Legal Professional 2.
329 Bachrach and Baratz, *Power and Poverty*, 26–27.
330 Statement of Major John Jeremy Mackenzie, dated August 11, 1979, witnessed by Detective Chief Inspector William Scott and Detective Inspector William McBurney, RUC. Trial document made available by Legal Professional 2.
331 Statement of Major John Jeremy Mackenzie (undated, 1979). Trial document made available by Legal Professional 2. Another, shorter version of this longer

This was an extraordinary claim; why would Major Mackenzie and/or D Company Headquarters allow anybody but the police – particularly suspected IRA terrorists – to access an area being preserved as a murder scene? Remarkably, more than forty years later, the identity of these men remains unknown.

Sergeant Hathaway informed the RMP SIB and the RUC that D Company's Sergeant Major, John Higgins told him that both he and Major Mackenzie were observing Naan's farm when the murders took place. Hathaway also told investigators that Major Mackenzie arrived at 13 Platoon's camp near Naan's farm in the immediate period after the murders and told them to move to the Crom estate.[332]

In his interviews with police, Corporal Byrne also claimed that CSM Higgins told him that he was watching the farm on the night of the murders. Hathaway and Byrne believed that the regiment had taken steps to ensure that the murders were covered up.[333] On June 13, 1979, Lance Corporal Chestnut requested that his earlier statements be amended to include the following information:

> According to Mcguire, Hathaway and Byrne, they say that as well as Lt. Snowball being implicated, Sergeant Major Higgins and Major McKenzie [sic] were also involved. The special patrol was

statement seems to have been produced, which is included in the PRONI court file. The shorter version omitted certain details such as that describing the visit by four unidentified men to the farm; Statement of Major John Jeremy Mackenzie, dated August 11, 1979, witnessed by Detective Chief Inspector William Scott and Detective Inspector William McBurney, RUC. Trial document made available by Legal Professional 2.

332 Transcript of an interview with Sergeant Stanley Hathaway, as recorded by RMP SIB Sergeant Malcolm Denton, dated June 28, 1979; Transcript of an interview with Sergeant Stanley Hathaway, as recorded by RUC Detective Sergeant Brian Taylor, dated August 21, 1979. Trial documents made available by Legal Professional 2; PRONI: CRCT/3/2/2/159A Hathaway, Byrne, Chestnut and Snowball: Exhibit No. 5, MOD Form 266C (Military), dated June 7, 1979.

333 Interview with Corporal John Byrne, as recorded by Staff Sergeant Malcolm Denton, RMP SIB, dated June 18, 1979; Transcript of an interview with Sergeant Stanley Hathaway, as recorded by RMP SIB Sergeant Malcolm Denton, dated June 28, 1979; Transcript of an interview with Sergeant Stanley Hathaway, as recorded by RUC Detective Sergeant Brian Taylor, dated August 21, 1979. Trial documents made available by Legal Professional 2.

set up by them ... Byrne told me that Sergeant Major Higgins
and Major McKenzie were viewing the Naan farm all night with
the aid of night sights ... While I might have expected a bit of
roughing up I had never been told nor suspected assassination.[334]

'Assassination' appears to suggest that the aim of the visit to Naan's farm
may have involved not only an interrogation or 'a bit of roughing up', but
also possibly a plan to kill Naan. Could the desperate situation – losing
a soldier, believed to be possibly captured by the IRA – have prompted
a decision to send a brutal message to the IRA, similar to the reprisals
carried out against suspected IRA Volunteers by British units from 1919
to 1921? Such a suggestion appears reckless, almost unthinkable, but it
cannot be ruled out. One Argyll officer later justified the killings of Naan
and Murray as an effective 'means to an end' – there was a downturn in
IRA activity after the killings; D Company had got the right guys – the
IRA was intimidated and on the back foot.[335] Another Argyll officer
believed that there was a direct order given to Hathaway to kill Naan,
that the murder was not an accident, a case of Sergeant Hathaway going
'berserk': rather, this was a company-instigated operation and the killing
of Naan was the 'desired outcome'.[336]

During police questioning, CSM John Higgins initially could not
recall if anybody was watching the farm (and Hathaway's patrol) on the
night of October 23, 1972. But Higgins later admitted at the trial that
he was at Naan's farm on the night of the murders; he had been at an OP
situated on a slightly elevated position in a nearby field to watch Naan's
farm at the time of the murders. According to the *Belfast Telegraph*:

Captain Higgins said that on the night before the bodies of Mr.
Naan and Mr. Murray were discovered, he travelled to a hill
overlooking Naan's farm and viewed it through a night sight. He
told the court he could remember seeing what appeared to be a
four man patrol on the roadway in front of Naan's farm, but he
could see nothing else suspicious.[337]

334 Iain Fletcher Chestnut – Amendment to Statement Made on 12th June 1979,
dated June 13, 1979. Trial document made available by Legal Professional 2.
335 Interview with Argyll Soldier 15 (Officer), December 2013.
336 Interview with Argyll Soldier 33 (Officer), March 2015.
337 'Naan's Name on Army List', *Belfast Telegraph*.

CSM John Higgins does not appear ever to have been asked, either during the investigation and the subsequent trial, about the whereabouts of his company commander on the night of the murders.[338] By his own account, Higgins almost invariably accompanied his company commander when Major Mackenzie travelled to different locations during D Company's time in Fermanagh.[339] It would have been highly unusual (and very unwise) for a single soldier to occupy an OP, even more so in the case of CSM Higgins since he was supposed to be in charge of 'the company commander's escort and patrol group'.[340] It is reasonable to assume that Higgins was part of a D Company Headquarters group of soldiers observing Naan's farm at the time of the murders. Yet Higgins appears never to have been asked who was with him in the OP overlooking Naan's farm on the night of the murders.[341]

Investigators also seem to have accepted Higgins's claim that he did not see anything unusual from the OP overlooking Naan's farm. Considering Murray was stabbed to death in the farmyard, his body then carried down Naan's lane and thrown in a nearby bog, this part of Higgins's account is difficult to believe. D Company's CSM also did not recall being stopped by a UDR patrol on his way back from the area around Naan's farm. The reference to being stopped by a UDR patrol is important; the RUC evidently had information that such an encounter had taken place.[342] If Higgins was in a military vehicle such as a Saracen, it is unlikely he would have been stopped, but if he travelled in a civilian car – such as a transit van or a Morris Minor – he would have encountered the UDR roadblock.

A few days after the murders Lance Corporal Joe Burke recalled that 'the whole of No. 13 Platoon were paraded by Sgt Hathaway. I was present

---

338 Trial documents made available by Legal Professional 2.

339 Company Sergeant Major Higgins confirmed that he was in charge of his company commander's escort, travelling with him to various locations during their time in Fermanagh. Statement of Company Sergeant Major John Higgins, December 19, 1979. Trial document made available by Legal Professional 2.

340 Statement of Company Sergeant Major John Higgins, December 19, 1979. Trial document made available by Legal Professional 2.

341 This is not to imply that Major Mackenzie was undoubtedly with his Company Sergeant Major at the OP overlooking Naan's farm at the time of the murders but merely to suggest that the absence of questions clarifying the whereabouts of OC D Company, both to Mackenzie and Higgins, is difficult to explain.

342 'Naan's Name on Army List', *Belfast Telegraph*.

at the time. Sgt. Hathaway instructed everybody to keep their mouths shut or else they would be next in line.'[343] Such a description seems unusual, if not unlikely. According to other accounts, Sergeant Hathaway 'cared' for his Platoon; threatening to kill them was not in character. Another 13 Platoon soldier emphatically denied in an interview that any such incident or threat ever occurred and he could not understand why any soldier would give such an erroneous statement to police.[344] Such an account might have been useful, however, if the aim is to prove that 'unlucky' 13 Platoon were a group apart from the rest of the D Company, one that had been corrupted by their maverick sergeant, so that others are not implicated.

Lieutenant Andrew Snowball and 13 Platoon: A Question of Command

In January 1979, an agitated Lance Corporal Chestnut claimed to have rung his former platoon commander (now Captain Snowball) in order to discuss the reopened investigation into the Fermanagh killings. Chestnut had apparently received a phone call from an RUC friend (who had also served in the Army) identifying the former Argyll 'grass' who had informed the police about D Company's involvement in the 'Pitchfork murders'. According to Chestnut, Snowball reassured his former NCO, telling him that he 'should have a bad memory and sing dumb'. Two months later, after being extensively interviewed by the RUC, Chestnut said that he called Snowball again – leaving a message at the officers' mess in Catterick (where 1 Argylls were based). Snowball called him back a few hours later, Chestnut recalled:

> He seemed frightened and worried in case the call would be tapped. I told him the RUC had been to visit me and I was not of much help. He said 'That's fine. No-one else here is of much help to them. If you have any problems contact my father.' He gave me a telephone number. I believe his father is a very influential General.[345]

343 Statement of Lance Corporal Joe Burke, December 17, 1979.
344 Interview with Argyll Soldier 8 (Private Soldier), November 2013.
345 Interview with Iain Fletcher Chestnut, dated November 5, 1980. Document made available by Legal Professional 2 involved in the trial of Hathaway, Byrne, Chestnut and Snowball.

Major Mackenzie told investigators that Snowball came to see him in his house in early 1979 to discuss the Fermanagh killings (although, according to the account offered by Mackenzie, he did so in a vague, evasive manner). Mackenzie also observed that he did not think that Snowball had 'the strength of character' to cover up the murders of Naan and Murray, a strangely worded criticism of his former subordinate ('strength of character' should involve showing the requisite 'moral courage' to admit the crime in the first place).[346] Snowball also appears to have talked to his father, Brigadier Ted Snowball and former GOC Scotland, General Sir Henry Leask.[347]

After Hathaway's confession in June 1979, RUC Detective Superintendent Ernest Drew, who does not seem to have interviewed Hathaway, Byrne and Chestnut, met with Snowball on August 3, 1979 (Snowball is continuously referred to in his notes as 'Mr Snowball', unlike Hathaway et al. who are simply 'Hathaway' etc.). When Lieutenant Snowball initially did not respond to questioning, Superintendent Drew told him what he thought the latter's actions were on the day of the murders:

> When he did not reply I again drew attention to the fact that Sergeant Hathaway had already admitted his involvement as had other members of the patrol. It was furthermore alleged that he had been informed as to what had occurred and had in fact been present when some of the patrol washed blood off themselves on their return to camp.[348]

Snowball now broke his silence, saying, 'Did he say that?' He then requested that the RUC leave the room so that he could talk to an RMP

346 Statement of Major Jeremy Mackenzie, witnessed by Detective Chief Inspector William Scott and Detective Inspector William McBurney, August 11, 1979. Trial document made available by Legal Professional 2.
347 Account by RUC Detective Superintendent Ernest Drew of his interview on June 12, 1979 with Lieutenant Andrew Snowball, OC 13 Platoon, D Company, 1 Argylls, dated August 11, 1979. Trial document made available by Legal Professional 2.
348 Account by RUC Detective Superintendent Ernest Drew of his interview on June 12, 1979 with Lieutenant Andrew Snowball, OC 13 Platoon, D Company, 1 Argylls, dated August 11, 1979. Trial document made available by Legal Professional 2.

SIB Staff Sergeant Malcolm Denton alone. The RUC complied with this request. Twenty minutes later, when the RUC officers came back into the meeting room, Snowball admitted that he had known about the murders. Ultimately, and quite remarkably, the RUC told Snowball what they understood to have been his crime, instead of keeping an open mind as to whether he was more deeply involved in planning, being present during, or covering up, the murders (which is not to say that he was) or had more knowledge to that effect. Snowball simply had to concur with Detective Superintendent's Drew's understanding of what happened (which would ultimately enable him to avoid a custodial sentence). No more difficult questions were asked, including about his alleged disposal of the murder weapon, his own location during the murders, that of Major Mackenzie and the orders given to Sergeant Hathaway.[349]

Sergeant Hathaway had also been 'led' during police questioning; shortly before he confessed to killing Naan and Murray, he was informed by Staff Sergeant Malcolm Denton that '13 Platoon [were] the only members of your unit in that area [Naan's farm]'. Hathaway assented.[350] This casually stated 'fact' later emerged to be false when CSM Higgins confirmed in the witness box at the trial that he had also been at an OP at Naan's farm. According to Denton's own record of the conversation he also asked Staff Sergeant Hathaway to confirm that he, not any officer, was 'in charge' during the events that led to the murders.[351]

> I said [Staff Sergeant Malcolm Denton, RMP SIB]: 'Am I right in saying the platoon sergeant is the boss and the platoon commander does what he's told?'
> He said [Sergeant Stan Hathaway]: 'Not quite like that but it is

349 Account by RUC Detective Superintendent Ernest Drew of his interview on June 12, 1979 with Lieutenant Andrew Snowball, OC 13 Platoon, D Company, 1 Argylls, dated August 11, 1979. Trial document made available by Legal Professional 2.
350 Transcript of an RMP/SIB interview on June 7, 1979 with Sergeant Stanley Hathaway, as recorded by RMP SIB Staff Sergeant Malcolm Denton, dated June 28, 1979. Trial document made available by Legal Professional 2.
351 Transcript of an RMP/SIB interview on June 7, 1979 with Sergeant Stanley Hathaway, as recorded by RMP SIB Staff Sergeant Malcolm Denton, dated June 28, 1979. Trial document made available by Legal Professional 2.

expected that the sergeant looks after the platoon commander who is usually a young officer.'

I said: 'And Snowball was a young officer?'

He replied: 'Yes'.

I said: 'Therefore, it would have been you who knew where you were going and why.'

Hathaway resisted a little but ultimately failed to see the trap: only after the police interviews did he realise that he was being loaded with complete responsibility for the events that preceded Naan's murder. According to the SIB narrative, Hathaway's visit to Naan's farm was a decision he had taken alone; the patrol was routine. Denton was playing the rank card and inviting Hathaway to repeat the age-old myth beloved of the Sergeants' mess – NCOs are the ones who are really in charge. Staff Sergeant Denton does not appear to have been interested in exploring the wider context, the chain of events or orders that could have preceded Hathaway's arrival at Naan's farm. Denton also, somewhat impatiently, told Hathaway what he was doing in the period immediately preceding the murders, 'I [Staff Sergeant Denton] said: "Look, Hathaway, you were out and about int. [intelligence] gathering weren't you?" He [Sergeant Hathaway] replied: "Yes".' Denton also informed Hathaway that he alone had selected the members of the group that visited Naan's farm.[352] Denton was making some questionable assumptions, which narrowed the focus and scope of the police investigation: (1) that no officer or more senior NCO played a role in tasking, planning or commanding the operation around Naan's farm and (2) he consequently assumed, or professed to believe, that Hathaway was merely 'out and about' on the evening of October 23 in the vicinity of Naan's farm on a general, self-tasked 'int [sic] gathering' sweep of the local area. A good soldier like Stan Hathaway merely had to follow the SIB Staff Sergeant's lead.

Lance Corporal Chestnut claimed that Lieutenant Snowball brought a pellet gun to Northern Ireland, which he kept in his vehicle. Chestnut insisted that he used Snowball's pellet gun only on one occasion. However, at Chestnut's trial for malicious wounding at Down County

---

352 Transcript of an RMP/SIB interview on June 7, 1979 with Sergeant Stanley Hathaway, as recorded by RMP SIB Staff Sergeant Malcolm Denton, dated June 28, 1979. Trial document made available by Legal Professional 2.

Court on February 2, 1973, crown counsel claimed that 13 Platoon's Sergeant, Stan Hathaway, owned the pellet gun, not Lieutenant Snowball.[353] This is an anomaly since, by Chestnut and other soldiers' accounts, Hathaway was strict, 'by the book', when it came to standard dress and equipment in his platoon, confiscating the knives that 13 Platoon soldiers had taken to wear in their belts in Northern Ireland.[354] According to his soldiers, bringing a pellet gun to Northern Ireland was not in Hathaway's character.

Ted Snowball had apparently concluded that the Army, abetted by the RUC, was trying to scapegoat his son for a wider failure of command; other Argyll officers had known about the murders in 1972 and had failed to act both at the time and in the years prior to 1979. In the immediate aftermath of Andrew Snowball's admission to his part in concealing the murders for almost seven years, the Snowballs' wider circle of family and friends moved to manage the situation, including reminding the Army of its duty of care to its young officer. General Sir Henry Leask travelled to London on behalf of the Snowball family and met with the Adjutant General, General Sir Robert Ford. Twenty-four hours later, Andrew Snowball received free legal aid and the full support of the Army Legal Service (ALS); Major John Venn of the ALS later proved to be instrumental in preparing Andrew Snowball's case before it went to trial.[355]

Lieutenant Andrew Snowball was not the officer to bring decisive, ethical leadership to 13 Platoon. He was both young and inexperienced, wedged between a company commander who served on special operations in Borneo and a group of platoon NCOs proud of their record of suppressing an insurgency in Aden, occasionally through brutal means.

---

353 'Soldier Fired Air Rifle in Street', *Newry Reporter*, February 8, 1973; Interview with Iain Fletcher Chestnut, dated November 5, 1980. Document made available by Legal Professional 2 involved in the trial of Hathaway, Byrne, Chestnut and Snowball; Interview with Sergeant Stanley Hathaway, as recorded by Detective Sergeant Henry Nixon and witnessed by Detective Sergeant Ronald Mathieson (undated), Trial document made available by Legal Professional 2.

354 Interview with Iain Fletcher Chestnut, dated November 5, 1980. Trial document made available by Legal Professional 2 involved in the trial of Hathaway, Byrne, Chestnut and Snowball; Interview with Argyll Soldier 9 (Private Soldier), November 2013.

355 Author's correspondence with Argyll Soldier 4, November 2016.

Although quick to provide evidence when it came to prosecuting those IRA men who tried to kill him at Dromintee on September 10, Andrew Snowball initially deceived investigators about the murders of Michael Naan and Andrew Murray. He did so in a case of misplaced loyalty, 'for the good of the regiment'.[356] However, in mitigation, Snowball did not have many good options. If, as his co-accused believed, more senior officers knew about (or even planned) the violent interrogation of Naan, would he, as the regiment's most junior officer, be able to persuade the police if he decided to tell the truth? It would be his word against a number of very influential officers. Even if the police did believe him, the cost to his career and his entire social and support network would have been devastating (and his family regiment could possibly have been disbanded). Snowball put his regiment first; it would have taken considerable moral courage to do otherwise.

The questioning of both Major Mackenzie and Lieutenant Snowball appears to have been exceptionally polite, to the extent that the investigating RUC officers even agreed to leave the room so that Andrew Snowball could make his confession alone to SIB Staff Sergeant Malcolm Denton. Major (now Lieutenant Colonel) Mackenzie had also suffered a personal tragedy on August 27, 1979 when his close friend, Lieutenant Colonel David Blair, the CO of 1 Queen's Own Highlanders, was killed along with 17 other soldiers in a double bombing at Narrow Water, near Warrenpoint (Prime Minister Margaret Thatcher was presented with Colonel Blair's epaulette; little else remained). Mackenzie flew back from Hong Kong to assume command of 1 QOH. The period from 1979 to 1980 was a time of exceptional strain between the RUC and the Army as a direct consequence of the Warrenpoint bombings (the RUC's lack of intelligence and alleged 'soft tactics' were called into question by HQNI). Grilling Army officers, including the new CO of 1 QOH, who had been appointed to command in Northern Ireland in such shocking circumstances and was now due to take his battalion to Hong Kong, may have been too big a step for the RUC to take, offering a possible explanation for a deliberate or latent avoidance of difficult

---

356 Statement of Lieutenant Andrew Snowball, as recorded by Chief Inspector William Scott, June 12, 1979. Trial document made available by Legal Professional 2; Statement of Lieutenant Andrew Snowball as recorded by Inspector William McBurney, April 6, 1979. Trial document made available by Legal Professional 2.

issues and questions relating to the command of D Company, 1 Argylls in Fermanagh in October 1972.[357]

The Trials of Hathaway, Byrne, Chestnut and Snowball

The Ministry of Defence provided legal representation for Hathaway, Byrne and Snowball. Chestnut – dishonourably discharged in 1973 – was also given free legal assistance (although not by the Ministry of Defence as he had left the military). Chestnut was adamant that he would pick his own legal representation; he did not trust the State to appoint a solicitor on his behalf. He selected a County Down firm to represent him – Wallace and Co. (his legal team also included Daphne Trimble, later The Lady Trimble, and the mercurial but brilliant Desmond Boal QC as his barrister). His co-defendants, Hathaway, Byrne and Snowball were represented by the State appointed Lisburn firm, W.G. Maginess & Son.[358]

When formally charged with the murder of Naan in Belfast on January 11, 1980, Hathaway and Byrne remained silent; when accused of the murder of Murray both men replied 'No!' (I have not been able to find any explanation for their emphatic denial of the murder of Murray).[359] At their trial at Belfast Crown Court in January 1981, Hathaway, Byrne and Chestnut initially entered pleas of 'not guilty' to the charges (Hathaway and Byrne were charged with two counts of murder; Chestnut with one count). Given that the men did not deny that the victims died at their hands, such a plea may seem difficult to explain, particularly in the case of Hathaway who had been responsible for most of the violence. Two legal professionals involved in the case understood that Hathaway, Byrne and Chestnut did not want to take 'the fall' for the killings, which they claimed had been the outcome the Army, in this case their immediate superiors, wanted.[360] Hathaway's barrister, Richard Ferguson

---

357 Harnden, *Bandit Country*, 212.

358 Trial document made available by Legal Professional 2. Document missing from the original PRONI file – CRCT/3/2/2/159A.

359 PRONI: CRCT/3/2/2/159A Deposition of RUC Superintendent (undated). Per an agreement with PRONI, all names relating to the trial not already in the public domain have been omitted.

360 Interview with Legal Professional 1, Northern Ireland, September 30, 2014; Interview with Legal Professional 2, Northern Ireland, October 9, 2015.

QC, a former Unionist MP in Stormont, one of the outstanding British advocates of his generation and a Fermanagh man, pleaded with the judge for more time to consult with his client who was suffering from 'hysteria'.[361] Hathaway eventually agreed to plead guilty.[362]

Sergeant Hathaway's initial insistence on pleading not guilty to the charges before the court was not accepted by his own barrister; indeed, the court twice went into recess while Richard Ferguson sought to persuade his client to enter a guilty plea. Legal scholar Paddy Hillyard has observed that in Northern Ireland, due to the sheer volume and seriousness of criminal cases and the relatively small size of the Northern Irish bar, plea-bargaining was encouraged and practised at an unusual intensity compared with the rest of the UK.[363] Writing in 1981, one of Britain's most distinguished human rights lawyers, Richard Harvey QC, also noted that in Northern Ireland:

> Defence lawyers, both solicitors and barristers, are under their own professional, institutional and financial pressures to co-operate with the prosecuting authorities and avoid judicial disapproval. The smaller the bar the greater the pressure on its members to avoid a reputation for contesting cases with little likely chance of success.[364]

Unfortunately for Hathaway, Byrne and Chestnut, the charges were narrowly focused, with little attention paid to the wider circumstances and

---

361 A. Williams, *A Very British Killing: The Death of Baha Mousa* (London: Jonathan Cape, 2012), 200; 'Soldier's Illness Halts Murder Trial', *Belfast Telegraph*, January 13, 1981.

362 'Soldier's Illness Halts Murder Trial'. In 2009, the Fermanagh Unionist newspaper, *Impartial Reporter*, interviewed Richard Ferguson about his legal career. He had represented alleged IRA bombers and SAS soldiers accused of murder; he also discussed representing Rose West. However, possibly due to local sensitivity, he omitted to mention his representation of Sergeant Stan Hathaway. 'High Profile QC Richard Ferguson Dies', *Impartial Reporter*, July 30, 2009.

363 P. Hillyard, 'The Normalisation of Special Powers: From Northern Ireland to Britain', in N. Lacey, *Criminal Justice* (Oxford: Oxford University Press, 1994), 81–82.

364 R. Harvey, *Diplock and the Assault on Civil Liberties* (London: Haldane Society, 1981), 6.

chain of command in which the accused soldiers were operating. Ferguson, even if he understood Hathaway's insistence on the wider culpability of the organisation in which he served, may have simply concluded that his client's not guilty plea was simply 'unwinnable'. Even if Ferguson succeeded in proving that there was a wider conspiracy to do violence to Naan, his client had still admitted to killing Naan and Murray and would accordingly be convicted of murder; he was guilty of the charge presented to the court. Nevertheless, it is notable that Ferguson never attempted to point the finger at D Company's commander. If Major Mackenzie, as alleged by the accused, had some role in the operation on Naan's farm, then Richard Ferguson could have argued in mitigation that negligent command was an important determining factor in the murders. He chose not to, even though blame for all aspects of the operation, – planning, command and execution – was being wholly apportioned to his client.

In 2006, Richard Ferguson was again employed by the Ministry of Defence to represent a soldier, Lance Corporal Wayne Crowcroft, who was accused along with six other soldiers of playing a part in the 2003 murder of Iraqi hotel receptionist Baha Mousa, who had been detained by 1st Battalion, Queen's Lancashire Regiment (1 QLR). Crowcroft's Platoon Commander, Lieutenant Craig Rodgers, was initially implicated by a number of soldiers as being present during, and even participating in, the abuse that led to the death of Baha Mousa. According to these witnesses, officers present in Battle Group Main camp in Basra ordered soldiers to 'soften up' prisoners prior to interrogation.[365] Later in the trial, the same soldiers became sullen and resentful, suffering from extreme memory loss; these soldiers, like Hathaway et al., came to believe that in the Army 'shit rolls downhill'.[366] Once again, Richard Ferguson never pursued the argument that failings in command had placed his client in an adverse position. Instead, he very successfully focused his attention on casting doubt on the characters and testimonies of the Iraqi witnesses and a private soldier, Jonathan Lee, who particularly implicated his client, Lance Corporal Crowcroft. A succession of soldiers who witnessed the events that led to the death of Baha Mousa claimed that they could not remember any details of the events in question. The trial subsequently

---

365 Williams, *A Very British Killing*, 130.
366 Private Gary Reader, Queen's Lancashire Regiment, quoted in Williams, *A Very British Killing*, 289.

ended in only one soldier being convicted. Corporal Donald Payne was sentenced to twelve months' imprisonment for 'inhuman treatment'. Payne became the, albeit very lightly punished, 'rotten apple' of the QLR; other soldiers, including officers, were quick to apportion blame to Payne as he had already confessed to a role in killing Baha Mousa.[367]

Richard Ferguson's reasoning in both cases – that any attempt to shift blame onto officers or more senior NCOs was unlikely to succeed given the specificity of the charges – may well have been sound. In 2006, as in 1981, key military witnesses' memories had become 'hazy'. In the Naan/Murray case, records for D Company had been lost and the RUC and RMP SIB appeared to be uninterested in possible wider command culpability beyond charging Lieutenant Snowball with withholding information. There is a trend here: barristers may go for the most 'winnable' strategy, which can involve piling blame on one individual soldier – Staff Sergeant Hathaway in 1981, Corporal Donald Payne in 2006. But such an approach comes at a price; the specific command responsibility and culture of the unit concerned are not fully considered. It is each man for himself.

Both the Naan/Murray and Baha Mousa cases reveal a worrying trend of investigators being unable or unwilling to get to the bottom of the chain of events and/or orders that led to murder in both instances. The same can also be said for a succession of other cases, such as the investigation into Bloody Sunday, the killing of teenager John Boyle in 1978,[368] the murder of Kevin Heatley in 1975. In each instance, the judiciary noted persistent obstruction on the part of serving or ex-military witnesses. Obstruction on the part of serving soldiers yielded few consequences; indeed, many soldiers prospered in their military careers afterwards. In the case of the Bloody Sunday Inquiry, Lord Saville concluded that many soldiers 'knowingly put forward false accounts'.[369]

---

367 Williams, *A Very British Killing*, 254.

368 Boyle's family had tipped off the army about an IRA arms cache in a graveyard near Dunloy in County Antrim. However, the curious 16-year-old could not resist going back for another look at the weapons. Arriving at the site, he was fatally shot by soldiers from the SAS. Although the two soldiers who killed John Boyle were cleared of murder, the judge in the case, Lord Lowry, criticised the 'untrustworthy' testimony he received from the soldiers during the course of the trial. Urban, *Big Boys' Rules*, 63–65.

369 BBC News, 'Saville Report: Key Findings', June 10, 2010, http://www.bbc.co.uk/news/10319881 (accessed November 2, 2016).

In summing up his judgment in the case against Hathaway, Byrne, Chestnut and Snowball, Mr Justice John MacDermott told the court that he was confused by many aspects of the events surrounding the deaths of Naan and Murray, 'My knowledge … of what happened is little better than those who may have read the [news] papers about this case.' He expressed sorrow for the victims and their families and also went on to sympathise with the four Argylls standing in the dock: 'It [October 23 1972] was also a sad and tragic day for each of you who have destroyed your careers and brought grief on your families, and it was also a sad and tragic day for your Regiment.' MacDermott praised the men for pleading guilty and for showing remorse.[370] The judge then addressed Captain Andrew Snowball directly, saying that he was pleased that Snowball accepted that he should have informed the police of the murders but that many others faced with 'the enormity of that dilemma as it appeared to you, and if so tested, would be found wanting'. The soldiers were in 'a wartime situation' and the strain of the circumstances should be understood.[371] In the aftermath of the trial, instead of trying to resolve the inconsistencies of different soldiers' accounts of the events of October 23, 1972, and explain the circumstances that led to the brutal killings of two British citizens, the State decided to let the matter rest.

Comparison with the Mahé Affair

There are some similarities between the Naan/Murray killings and the 'Mahé affair', the 2005 murder of a prisoner by a French soldier in Côte d'Ivoire. In that year French soldiers deployed on Operation Licorne were sent to the lawless disengagement zone that had been established between the warring north and south of the country, with orders to prevent further killings and lootings in this ungoverned area. After French soldiers shot and wounded Fermin Mahé, the leader of a notorious gang, Colonel Eric Burgaud ordered Chief Warrant Officer Guy Raugel to kill the wounded prisoner, Mahé; Raugel smothered Mahé with a plastic bag on the way to the city of Man. Colonel Burgaud claimed that he had been implicitly instructed to kill Fermin Mahé by his superior, General Henri Poncet. Poncet had told him that, 'You bring him back to

370 'Judgment', *Fermanagh Herald*, January 24, 1981.
371 'Judgment', *Fermanagh Herald*.

Man, he does not escape, you drive slowly, you understand what I mean.' Burgaud did not quibble; the summary killing of Mahé would serve a military purpose and his 'moral code' had been altered by what he had experienced in Côte d'Ivoire.[372]

Ultimately, because the order was an oral one and implicit, the case against Poncet was thrown out by the judge due to lack of evidence. Under persistent police questioning, Burgaud only admitted to giving the order to his subordinates when it became evident that a number of his subordinates would be found guilty. At every stage of the investigation the police met organised obstruction on the part of the units involved, including the widespread falsification (and destruction) of military reports (including cause of death) relating to the murder of Fermin Mahé. The cover-up, based on a perceived need to avoid embarrassment and remain loyal to the group and the institution, was an important aspect of the 'Mahé affair' but by no means unique. The individuals concerned were convinced that no officer would report what they had seen or heard, out of either unit or, more broadly, military loyalty.[373]

Pascal Vennesson has described this incident as an example of when 'deviant cohesion supports operational goals at the tactical and operational level but contradicts the self-identity promoted by the Army as a whole and has negative strategic and political consequences'.[374] The same could be said for the murders of Michael Naan and Andrew Murray. A number of Argylls were convinced, and some still believe, that they had eliminated an important IRA leader. In their view, the operation in Naan's farm was, for a time at least, militarily effective. Moreover, as in the Mahé incident, the Argyll soldiers believed that murder would be effectively covered up. Another similarity is the subsequent dispute over what was, or was not, ordered by officers. Sergeant Stan Hathaway and Corporal John Byrne appear to have entered pleas of 'not guilty' at the outset of the trial because they believed that there was a wider context, including a responsibility of the chain of command that was not being acknowledged in the trial. Byrne reportedly refused to socialise with ex-Argyll 'criminals' while in prison. According to his own logic,

372 Vennesson, 'Cohesion and Misconduct', 240.
373 Vennesson, 'Cohesion and Misconduct', 243.
374 Vennesson, 'Cohesion and Misconduct', 236.

he had been a loyal soldier and did what his officers wanted; he was no criminal.[375]

Lance Corporal Chestnut told police that the reason he had not cooperated with the investigation was out of fear of his former institution, the Army. According to the RUC's notes, 'He [Chestnut] believed that the killing of the two men was Army orientated and that anything he said would have been twisted by the army.'[376] Hathaway, Byrne and Chestnut did not trust the justice system. From their perspective, the leaking of the informer's name by the RUC, the narrow scope of the investigation including the lack of interest in the visit to Naan's farm in the hours after the murders, the leading questions that this was a 13 Platoon NCO planned operation and the anomalies or deliberate omissions in witness statements, all seemed to point to a mobilisation of bias against their interests. They were convinced that the Army was out to protect its officers and its reputation by limiting the scope of the investigation; the police and DPP were either directly or implicitly involved in furthering that aim or simply uninterested in uncovering the series of events that led to the murders taking place. However, there is a significant divergence between the Mahé and the Naan/Murray cases. The Mahé case saw the investigating authorities test the assertions of Chief Warrant Officer Raugel that the murder of Fermin Mahé had been ordered by a higher authority and that evidence had later been tampered with, which subsequently transpired to be case. In the case of the murders of Naan and Murray, the same claims were never tested. Rather they were actively avoided.

375 Transcript of an RMP/SIB interview with Sergeant Stanley Hathaway, as recorded by Staff Sergeant Malcolm Denton, RMP SIB, dated June 28, 1979; Interview with Sergeant Stanley Hathaway on June 7, 1979, as recorded by Sergeant Robert Stronach, RMP SIB on January 7, 1980. Trial document made available by Legal Professional 2. Interview with Corporal John Byrne, as recorded by Detective Sergeant Henry Nixon, June 9, 1979. Trial documents made available by Legal Professional 2; Interview with Argyll Soldier 29 (NCO), September 2014.
376 Account of an interview between Detective Chief Inspector William Scott, Detective Inspector W.A.M. McBurney and Staff Sergeant M. Denton, RMP, SIB with Iain Fletcher Chestnut, June 1979 (as recorded by Detective Chief Inspector Scott). Trial document made available by Legal Professional 2.

Conclusion

Why did Michael Naan and Andrew Murray die? One Argyll soldier put the blame squarely on the Argylls' experiences in Aden; a 'hard core' in the battalion still celebrated the 'atrocious things' they had done on that operation and had reverted to that mind-set.[377] Yet the scale of violence perpetrated by the Argylls in Northern Ireland was much lower than in Aden, even though the Argylls suffered more casualties on Operation Banner. But unlearning tried tactics and behaviour – putting into practice Major David Thomson's message about eradicating 'Aden tendencies' – took time. It was especially challenging in the case of D Company:

> D Company in Aden was the hard, cutting edge of the Argyll and Sutherland Highlanders, commanded by Ian Mackay, one of the best soldiers I ever served with. To some extent Mackay's aura, his attitudes, lived on, particularly with the NCOs.[378]

D Company found it more difficult to cast off the shadow of Aden. Aden was something to be proud of, not rejected; the reputations of Sergeant Hathaway, Corporal Byrne and Lance Corporal Chestnut had been made there. D Company had an image to project: uncompromising, unorthodox but got the job done, *the* 'Player' company in a battalion that prided itself on being one of the toughest in the British Army. Jeremy Mackenzie, despite not being an Argyll officer, was an officer who embraced such an attitude rather than resisting it.

D Company was out for revenge after a period of mounting casualties. In the preceding months, Major Mackenzie's soldiers appear to have made several deliberate border incursions, including by helicopter.[379] A few days before the murders, Corporal John Byrne gave an interview to Les Wilson, a visiting journalist from Byrne's home town of Greenock. Byrne had been involved in two near-miss ambushes: the second ambush occurred when he was travelling in a mobile patrol near the village of

---

377 Sanders and Wood, *Times of Troubles*, 183.
378 Interview with Argyll Soldier 15 (Officer), December 2013.
379 MAI: 2003/15/94-G2/C/1872 Pt 2. Border crossings and border incidents by British Army: Increp 14/8/1972 signed by Commandant M. Fogarty, 1st Infantry Company Group, Eastern Brigade, Dundalk.

Killeen in South Armagh. His driver, Private Paul Carson, swerved off the road to avoid the bullets, crashing the vehicle and breaking his arm in the process. On both occasions, Byrne never saw the gunman.[380] (Nevertheless, other 13 Platoon soldiers then assaulted Thomas Mullan as recounted earlier.)

A need for retributive action, 'to do something physical', meant that D Company soldiers 'took more risks', including visiting South Armagh pubs such as the Three Steps in order to 'irritate the IRA'.[381] Major Mackenzie was one of the first (in the days before the deployment of the SAS) to set up ambushes to target suspected IRA men along the border.[382] D Company was prepared to stretch, and even occasionally break, the official rules in order to take the war to the IRA. In Major Mackenzie, D Company had a much-admired leader, one who relentlessly wanted to 'get in the face' of the IRA. But for all his considerable talents, Mackenzie ultimately failed to restrain the aggression and desire for revenge unleashed in D Company. There were already a number of warning signs before the Fermanagh murders: several soldiers in D Company, including Lance Corporal Chestnut, had assaulted civilians; units had deliberately crossed the border. But Major Mackenzie received no indication that HQNI, 3 Brigade or his battalion CO were in any way unhappy with his performance or that of his company. On the contrary, Mackenzie was regarded as an outstanding officer in Northern Ireland; sending D Company to Fermanagh may even be interpreted as a vote of confidence. A more rigorous assessment of D Company might have concluded that this was the Argyll unit that needed to 'throttle back', to be more judicious and less punitive in its dealings with the local population.

A persistent problem with violent, criminal behaviour dogged 1 Argylls throughout the 1970s and into the early 1980s. Less than two months after the Naan and Murray murder trial, a 19-year-old man, Colin Taggart, was stabbed to death after a brawl with Argyll soldiers outside a disco in north Antrim (1 Argylls was now the resident battalion in nearby Ballykelly).[383] Nevertheless, there is a contradiction here: the person of Sergeant Hathaway does not seem to fit with a depiction of

---

380 'IRA Fears Eagle Eyes in the Sky', *Greenock Telegraph*, October 26, 1972.
381 Author's correspondence with Argyll Soldier 7 (Officer), November 2016.
382 Interview with Argyll Soldier 14 (Officer), May 2014.
383 'Soldiers on Murder Trial in Ulster', *The Times*, March 10, 1981.

wanton indiscipline; all interviewees and witnesses who knew him or served with him paint the opposite picture. But Argyll officers had used hard, even brutal tactics in Aden, and Hathaway, like many other soldiers, had followed unquestioningly. This may have caused some confusion in Northern Ireland about desired outcomes. How do NCOs in a 'player' unit interpret their officers' sometime implicit instructions? Hathaway may have drawn on his previous experiences in Aden in believing his superiors wanted him to do violence to Michael Naan. Phrases like 'soften up', 'make their presence felt', 'roughing up' or 'drive slowly' are vague in their meaning, but can be interpreted as instructions sanctioning violence that goes beyond nominal military rules and norms, leading to an excessive, sometimes fatal, application of force.

For every act of Argyll indiscipline there were also many others of courage and humanity. The day after Hathaway and his co-defendants received their sentences in Belfast Crown Court, an Argyll medic saved the life of Bernadette McAliskey (née Devlin) and her husband after they were shot multiple times by Loyalist paramilitaries in the bedroom of their Coalisland home in County Tyrone (a unit from 1 Argylls was first on the scene).[384] D Company's previous operations and general reputation for being an uncompromising unit does not fully explain what went wrong in Fermanagh. Murder was an extreme anomaly, even for such a hardened unit. Another trigger was necessary, and that was the disappearance of Private Owens; such an event would have brought barely suppressed fear and emotions exploding to the surface. More than three decades later, an American airborne soldier described what happened when two soldiers in his company went missing, suspected of being abducted by insurgents, south of Baghdad on June 16, 2006 (the badly mutilated bodies of Privates First Class Kristian Menchaca and Thomas Tucker were discovered three days later):

> You're not supposed to tactically question somebody unless you're an interrogator. We were straight up interrogating people. Beating people's asses with weapons, threatening to kill them if they didn't talk. It was thug style, like a gang war, because

---

384 C. Thomas, 'Bernadette McAliskey is Badly Wounded', *The Times*, January 17, 1981.

we wanted our guys back alive and the chances of that were dwindling every second that went by.[385]

Such circumstances called for unorthodox, even brutal, means to gain information, unleashing a deviant cohesion that may have been unthinkable a few hours previously, behaving essentially 'like a gang'; and the Argylls were (far too easily) convinced that Naan was a senior IRA Volunteer. The justification of the killing of Naan as an effective, if ultimately regrettable, 'means to an end' has endured for decades.[386] One officer recalled that the security forces in Fermanagh 'knew exactly who had done things a lot of the time but trying to prove it was another question'.[387] Stanley Cohen's work on perpetrator mechanisms of excusing atrocity guilt helps illuminate why this might be the case. Cohen points out that perpetrators, or those closely linked to them, often acknowledge the unseemly nature of the deed but argue that it was practically necessary.[388] However, the assumption that the local security forces, particularly the part-time UDR, knew precisely who was guilty, or innocent, was a dangerous one. Major Albert Liddle continued to serve in his local UDR battalion and was mentioned in despatches for 'gallant and distinguished service' in October 1981.[389]

The murders of Naan and Murray were the culmination of a group process in D Company that fixed Naan's guilt and left no room for his possible innocence. D Company never stopped to question why Naan's neighbours, including those serving in 4 UDR, were so quick to denounce him and whether they were right to do so. Naan's political views, his desire for a united Ireland, his admiration for Republicans such as Frank McManus, were vocally expressed and disliked by local Unionists, but these were hardly uncommon in South Fermanagh at this time.[390] Naan's lack of deference, his commercial success and ownership of land linked to the Liddle family appear to have been resented. A living historical legacy of violence, the denunciation of Naan arising from a combination of social malice, political suspicion and, critically, the co-option of

385 Frederick, *Black Hearts*, 304.
386 Interview with Argyll Soldier 15 (Officer), December 2013.
387 Interview with Argyll Soldier 31 (Officer), May 2014.
388 Cohen, *States of Denial*, 59.
389 'Supplement to the London Gazette', *London Gazette*, October 6, 1981.
390 Interview with Frank McManus, Enniskillen, May 30, 2016.

outsiders, D Company, to cause harm to a neighbour, fits with Kalyvas's account of 'intimate violence' during civil wars.[391]

Fermanagh, its isolation, the resurgent suspicions of local Unionists and part-time UDR officers towards their Catholic neighbours, and a breakdown in leadership and intelligence structures in D Company, 1 Argylls and, more widely, in 3 Brigade/RUC L Division, provided the essential context behind the murders of Michael Naan and Andrew Murray. October 23, 1972 was the end of a process. Restraint, the management of violence – the particular vocation of a commissioned officer – was absent in D Company in Fermanagh during October 1972. Sergeant Hathaway very likely went out to hurt Michael Naan from the outset, to 'make his presence felt'. Lance Corporal Chestnut immediately reverted to Aden tactics upon seizing Andrew Murray, making him lie flat on the ground.[392]

The 6 foot 2 inch Lance Corporal Iain Chestnut (a relative giant among the generally diminutive Argyll Private soldiers and NCOs), or 'C/Nut' as he was known by other Argylls, had a reputation for enjoying violence, meeting what anthropologists would describe as a 'self-image promoter', men who 'are sensitive to attempts to question their claims to precedence and habitually precipitate violent situations in which they can demonstrate their power, courage and importance'.[393] Yet it is striking that he was not the man to inflict most violence on Naan and Murray – like Mcguire, he played a relatively peripheral role in the killings (at least by the accounts offered by Hathaway and Byrne). His more disciplined, 'straight down the line and formal', platoon sergeant took it upon himself from the outset violently to interrogate Michael Naan.

To his soldiers, Hathaway did not seem a man 'on edge'. He was a man in control and they looked up to him. According to one of his private soldiers, 'You respected him very quickly and when he said something you did it at the double. I liked him and the more into the tour the more I liked him. He was genuinely human. But hard. He could enjoy a laugh with the boys.'[394] Hathaway was charismatic; he was also loyal and efficient. A tough, uncompromising man, but one who clearly cared for

---

391 Kalyvas, *The Logic of Violence in Civil Wars*, 379.
392 Statement of Iain Fletcher Chestnut, as recorded by Chief Inspector William McBurney, June 10, 1979. Trial document made available by Legal Professional 2.
393 Horowitz, *Honor and the American Dream: Culture and Identity in a Chicano Community*, 89.
394 Interview with Argyll Soldier 8 (Private Soldier), November 2013.

his Platoon, fits more under the category of a 'self-image defender' – men who are 'sensitive to any actions that appears to discredit their image of themselves as persons with whom others do not trifle'.[395] Challenges or resistance to that notion of physical supremacy could not be permitted and would be severely punished, which could explain the rapid escalation of violence against Michael Naan.

Andrew Snowball had a degree of respect from his men; he was seen as a good, albeit a very young and inexperienced, junior officer.[396] However, the sentencing of 13 Platoon's commander, a one-year suspended sentence, despite his deliberate attempts to obstruct the investigation, seems quite lenient. Unlike the other accused, he could draw upon a powerful network of senior military officers to help prepare his defence. The investigation was hindered by organised obstruction but also by the RUC's apparent deference to authority. The future Lord Lieutenant of Fermanagh, Lord Erne, does not appear to have been questioned despite being in close contact with 13 Platoon in the immediate hours before and after the murders. The former COs of 1 Argylls, Major General Paddy Palmer and Brigadier Ted Snowball, also do not appear to have been interviewed in order to discover the extent of their knowledge about the murders (and when they learned about them).

Uncomfortable questions for the Army (and possibly the RUC) were not pursued, including: who were the individuals Lance Corporal Burke and Private Clarke claimed to have seen on the farm in the estate car on the night of the murders (the same persons identified over the radio to Company Headquarters for which records would have been kept)? What happened to the murder weapon and the missing implements at Naan's farm? Who was in the Morris Minor car seen talking to a group of Argyll soldiers on the road outside Naan's farm at the approximate time of the murders? What happened to the missing D Company operational records for October 23, 1972? CSM Higgins claimed that the suspected

---

395 Interview with Argyll Soldier 8 (Private Soldier), November 2013.

396 Interview with Argyll Soldier 8 (Private Soldier), November 2013; Transcript of an RMP/SIB interview Sergeant Stanley Hathaway, as recorded by Staff Sergeant Malcolm Denton, RMP SIB, dated June 28, 1979; Interview with Sergeant Stanley Hathaway on June 7, 1979, as recorded by Sergeant Robert Stronach, RMP SIB, on January 7, 1980. Trial document made available by Legal Professional 2; Interview with Corporal John Byrne, as recorded by Detective Sergeant Henry Nixon, June 9, 1979. Trial documents made available by Legal Professional 2.

abduction of Private Owens by the IRA was reported up the military chain of command to the highest level. If this was the case how did General Tuzo, Brigadier Bush and other senior officers respond to this alarming information? What instructions did they pass down to D Company?

The focus of the investigation was kept extremely narrow; obvious and significant questions appear to have been actively avoided in a manner – a mobilisation of bias – suggestive of that described by Bachrach and Baratz. Sergeant Hathaway was prompted into a series of statements regarding his decisions and actions on October 23, 1973 which served effectively to isolate him from more senior leaders in D Company. A sizeable group of soldiers in 1 Argylls were aware that soldiers from 13 Platoon had committed murder. A number of these could have joined Snowball in the dock for withholding information, had the DPP been so inclined. CSM Higgins's statement that he did not know about the murders, despite being at an OP overlooking Naan's farm at the time they occurred, is unconvincing. D Company's commander, Major Jeremy Mackenzie gave contradictory and confusing accounts in interviews with police. It is still unclear where he was on the night of October 23, 1972.

Whether the convicted NCOs had a genuine case to make about the complicity of D Company's command is very difficult to ascertain; however, there were certainly inconsistencies and anomalies in Major Mackenzie, Lieutenant Snowball and CSM Higgins's accounts that should have been teased out. In sum, more questions should have been put to D Company's leadership in order to substantiate or exclude the accounts put forward by the three NCOs and to investigate the claims of other soldiers such as Lance Corporal Burke and Private Clarke. Even if such questions could not have been asked in court, given the narrowness of the charges, it should have been incumbent upon the government and the Army to try to get to the bottom of the series of events and orders surrounding the murders of two British citizens. Instead, no investigation into a possible failure of command in D Company during October 1972 ever took place. Major Mackenzie's meteoric career continued unblemished and he went on to become a four-star general, Britain's most senior soldier in NATO. The circumstances of how a group of soldiers came be at Naan's farm and the concealment of evidence were not explored. Hathaway, Byrne and Chestnut were simply 'rotten apples'.[397]

---

397 Grassiani, *Soldiering*, 1.

Conclusion

> Patrolling, searching, arresting, those were our duties
> ... we were fairly rough with them. They began to
> get a bit frightened of us, the civilians did. We got a
> lot of information out of the civilians in the end until
> the Black and Tans [Royal Irish Constabulary Special
> Reserve] arrived and they were rougher than we were.
> Of course they frightened the civilians and our sources
> of information just dried up.[1]

The challenge of selecting and managing appropriate levels of violence to be used to put down insurgencies drew incoherent and strategically damaging responses among units that served in Ireland during the Anglo-Irish War of 1919–1921 and during the early part of Operation Banner in the 1970s. Charles Townshend's work on British counter-insurgency operations in Ireland from 1919 to 1921 offers a valuable account of reprisals, the hardening of attitudes and the collective punishment of the local population among certain Army and police units during that time, a diversity of behaviour that falls outside general instructions and standard procedures.[2] In the early 1970s, although

1 Brigadier Robert Anderson, formerly 2nd Battalion, Argyll and Sutherland Highlanders, who served with his battalion in East Galway and North Mayo during the Anglo-Irish War, from 1920 to 1921. IWM: Oral Recording – 5251, Robert Charles Beckett Anderson.
2 'The Brigade Major of the 17th Brigade in Cork frankly remarked after the conflict, "I think I regarded all civilians as 'Shinners', and I never had any dealings with any of them". Such an approach, though understandable, offered few roads to success in internal security work.' C. Townshend, *The British Campaign in Ireland, 1919–1921* (Oxford: Oxford University Press, 1975), 205.

'exemplary counterinsurgency' was officially at an end, different units and officers could still hold starkly contrasting views on what constituted 'firmness' or resolve and excessive violence or punishment of an area. Senior officers often failed to recognise patterns of behaviour that caused serious damage to community relations, police work and the gathering of intelligence.

On May 11, 1992, a soldier from 3 PARA was badly injured in an explosion near Cappagh in East Tyrone. The following day soldiers from his battalion decided to vent their anger on the nearby village of Coalisland. They 'sealed off the town' and ransacked two bars in the village, shooting three local men, one of whom who had tried to close the door of his bar, the Rossmore, to prevent the soldiers from gaining access.[3] The local RUC were incensed; in a few hours, 3 PARA was undoing years of increasingly successful police work in the area, including beating up sources that were providing vital information against the IRA. At a meeting with the local RUC, the CO of 3 PARA was told that, 'his men were now the best recruiting sergeant for the East Tyrone IRA'.[4] Although the Coalisland incident initially appears similar to accounts of grievance, polarisation and vengeance described in earlier chapters, the aftermath of the 'Coalisland riots' demonstrate how fundamentally the security relationship in Northern Ireland had changed. The RUC had steadily increased its capabilities over 20 years; well trained and with a sophisticated intelligence capability, the police were now unquestionably the senior security partner. Senior RUC officers demanded that 3 PARA be replaced in the area. Not only was the unit withdrawn but the commander of 3 Brigade, Brigadier Tom Longland, was also removed from command. The RUC, with the assistance of other Army units, were able to regain control.[5] It was a different, much less violent era; the security forces were confident enough to recognise the damage a single overly aggressive unit could do in a few days or weeks if unchecked. Unlike in the early 1970s, the complaints of local people were listened to; mistakes could be acknowledged.

In the preceding chapters I have advanced four arguments. First, I have concluded that small units of infantry soldiers enjoyed considerable

3 Sanders and Wood, *Times of Troubles*, 198; *Fortnight*, June 1992.
4 Interview with RUC Officer 8, December 2016.
5 Interview with RUC Officer 8, December 2016.

autonomy during the early years of Operation Banner and could behave in a vengeful manner towards the local population. When asked about the possibility of variations in operational conduct, the bulk of interviewees pointed to the company commander as having most influence. It was he, more than the CO, who set the local operational tempo and restraints on his soldiers. He could initiate his own operations (as long as they were limited in scale), set his own patrol routine, standard procedures and collect intelligence as he saw fit. He could become the 'Reverend Bastard' over an area, or he could send his Catholic soldiers to Mass and salute IRA cortèges as gestures of goodwill. Both approaches – the punitive and the conciliatory – coexisted simultaneously; HQNI and respective brigade headquarters failed to ensure operational consistency among its rotating battalions in Ulster. The Army also failed to prevent 'hyper-investment', those units whose aggressive self-image was out of step with the Army's purported values, general aims and rules of engagement in Northern Ireland.[6] Although many individual officers (including battalion COs examined here) grasped the political complexity of waging war at home in the UK, GOC General Harry Tuzo pushed for an approach that reverted to internal security practices that had been employed in the colonies. Meanwhile, handovers between battalions, particularly in South Armagh, remained inadequate; mistakes were repeated and command oversight was often absent (particularly in 3 Brigade). The Army's own 2006 'end of mission' report into Operation Banner hinted at such a 'laissez-faire' relationship between '9 to 5' brigade officers on a two-year deployment and the 'four-month, 24 hour' battalions under their command.[7] This research has confirmed such a finding.

---

6 Bernd Greiner, in the context of the Vietnam War, has described the divergence in US Army unit behaviour but also the capacity of senior officers to check inconsistency/the collective punishment of the local population by aggrieved soldiers: '1st Infantry Division ("The Big Red One") ... Commander William E. DePuy reputedly ruled with a rod of iron and knew how to check infringements by his units. As Harry G. Summers said of his time under DePuy, "If an artillery round landed within a hundred yards of a shrine or temple, the battalion commander could count on being relieved ... What I'm trying to get across is that the command climate in that unit was what protected it from these kind of atrocities. In contrast the 9th Infantry Division had a reputation for unbridled ruthlessness."' Greiner, *War Without Fronts*, 90.

7 British Army, *Operation Banner*, 2.10.

Second, I have also concluded that, although King is right to stress professional training and ethos as important factors in determining soldiers' combat behaviour, soldiers were also strongly motivated by a desire for vengeance. Richard English has argued that the deaths of three Royal Highland Fusiliers in 1971, murdered off-duty by the IRA, also saw a shift in soldiers' behaviour; shock and disgust found expression in a punitive approach towards the local population in general.[8] Both accounts, how emotional responses by soldiers to events changed the conflict by leading to further polarising acts of vengeance and violence, offer an invitation for further research, and were part of the rationale for this study. Retributive violence and grievance have been well documented in the case of paramilitary organisations in Northern Ireland, including by English.[9] But similar motivations on the part of soldiers have been largely ignored. Operations in the Bogside or Crossmaglen could quickly descend into very local confrontations between groups of young men, eager to provoke, escalate and react. Participation in violence for both groups was seen as highly desirable, if not status defining. New soldiers were fascinated by 'mythic violence'; as in gangs, combat is an initiation for 'real soldiers'.[10]

The temptation for cohesive, small units of soldiers – fuelled on a hyper-masculine, aggressive self-image – to challenge rival groups, including the local constabulary or even other soldiers during peacetime, is obvious. Again, a gang analogy comes to mind: once Loyalist paramilitaries in the Shankill Road challenged the authority of the Argylls on what the Scottish soldiers regarded as their 'patch', the Argylls took a particular relish in punishing them. Similarly, the Scots Guards hated the US Navy; indeed, British Army fights against US sailors were commonplace in Londonderry in the early 1970s. Although senior officers at HQNI did not directly sanction small infantry units taking out their grievances against the local population or collectively punishing the areas in which they operated, some did share an engrained contempt for the people who lived in those working-class areas where the IRA operated. The failure of the RMP SIB to conduct what it called 'normal standard' investigations in Northern Ireland in the early 1970s also led

---

8 English, *Armed Struggle*, 115–116.
9 English, *Armed Struggle*, 115–116.
10 Decker and Van Winkle, *Life in the Gang*, 69.

to confusion over what was acceptable behaviour among soldiers. An examination of the investigation into the murders of Michael Naan and Andrew Murray also reveals the latent power of the Army in Northern Ireland. The Argylls were able to conceal two murders for more than six years. Pertinent questions appear to have been avoided, suggestive of a mobilisation of bias. Although forced to take ultimate command responsibility for failing to expose the murders, D Company's most junior officer, Lieutenant Andrew Snowball, was able to draw upon an influential network and avoid spending time in prison.

Senior officers betrayed a disbelieving, even callous attitude to allegations of abuse. General Harry Tuzo was furious with the two Legion of Mary victims that were abducted and assaulted by the Parachute Regiment because they did not make their complaints through the security forces. His ire focused on the victims, who were only interested in 'propaganda', not the perpetrators. General King's contempt for the Creggan area of Londonderry – the inhabitants knew who the gunmen were and could have thrown them out – was symptomatic of a trend whereby soldiers began to widen the definition of guilt or culpability to the inhabitants of whole areas. The same trend can also be seen in other counter-insurgency campaigns. An American NCO serving in Iraq in 2005 observed, 'if your neighbour's up to something, you're going to know. And that's how they are. Everybody that you see knows or has participated in some kind of insurgency, or if they haven't participated, they've supported it in some way.'[11]

HQNI's own attitudes, mirrored at an operational level, were not conducive to good discipline, as soldiers came to regard whole areas through a prism of complicity in the deaths of soldiers. Almost nobody was presumed innocent in the Creggan or the Bogside in Derry. In South Armagh, even victims such as Majella O'Hare's father could be regarded as somehow culpable. The American author Leon Uris, who stayed with B Company, 1 Argylls in Crossmaglen on October 2–3, 1972, compared South Armagh to a 'leper colony', such was the polarisation between the soldiers and the local community.[12] The death of Edmund Woolsey in South Armagh on September 18, 1972 also demonstrated a lack of consideration for the local population. In 1971 and 1972, except for the

---

11 Frederick, *Black Hearts*, 83.
12 RMASH: File Reference D71, 'Historical Record 1 ASH', 1972–1973.

most egregious cases of abuse, battalions looked after and disciplined their own. Successive governments also failed to respond to complaints of Army excesses; pre-existing and complacent notions of inherent Irish dishonesty meant the government consistently dismissed complaints of abuse in Northern Ireland. Ireland was, after all, 'a land of clinging mythology'.[13] Much of the Catholic population in Northern Ireland came to believe that London either deliberately encouraged such behaviour or failed to prevent and investigate it. Both conclusions were damaging for the Army and for British strategy in Ulster.[14] Even today, many important questions about the events leading up to the deaths of Michael Naan and Andrew Murray remain unanswered; indeed, they were never asked in the first place.

The fundamental distinction between gangs and the military is that the military adheres to, and should act on behalf of, the law. Without such restraint and punishment, 'player' or hyper-invested units can come to resemble gangs, out for retribution using methods that go against the standards of the wider institution and state they are supposed to serve. Ruth Horowitz has described how the extreme violence and collective punishment meted out by US soldiers in Vietnam fascinated gang members in Chicago: 'Vietnam seemed to some of the younger males a glorified extension of their world in the streets.' Some gang members who enjoyed violence found the Army an attractive opportunity, but others noted that it carried risks – you didn't always get away with it: 'Calley [Lieutenant William Calley, a platoon commander convicted for his role in the 1968 My Lai massacre in Vietnam] ended up in jail, just like us.'[15] But the punishment of such deviancy is by no means straightforward, as can be seen from the numerous cases examined in this study.

---

13 Letter from the British Ambassador in Dublin, Adrian Galsworthy, to Kelvin White, Republic of Ireland unit, dated May 25, 1973, quoted in Patterson, *Violent Frontier*, 57.

14 In the aftermath of the 'Falls curfew' in 1970, Paddy Devlin, a labour activist in West Belfast and later an outspoken opponent of the Provisional IRA, tried to get support from the Labour Party for an official independent investigation into the behaviour of certain regiments in Belfast: 'I was disappointed to realise that Westminster MPs, of whatever party, did not like their army criticised, even when the criticism was true. That was the reality of a colonial empire in action – "our boys" – right or wrong.' Devlin, *Straight Left*, 131.

15 Horowitz, *Honor and the American Dream*, 84.

Soldiers in small units such as battalions or companies could, and did, become too exclusively loyal to the immediate group rather than the institution that employed them. In Fermanagh, Argyll soldiers' desire to achieve quick results and get revenge for casualties and other grievances meant that they could also mistake local resentment and low-grade intelligence for actionable information.

Unchecked cohesion had a way of turning on its master. Too often a detrimental, excessive and ultimately deviant loyalty to the regiment or its sub-units could seriously damage government policy and the reputation of the British Army in Northern Ireland. The fear of ostracism from the group, away from leaders that have taken on a charismatic role of influence, is often too great for young soldiers to refuse to carry out collective tasks or stand witness against other soldiers. As an NCO in 1 Scots Guards observed, a deviant but charismatic Sergeant could 'ruin' a Platoon in weeks, as young soldiers began to emulate him. Only sound officership and a strong sergeants' mess can stop such a rot. But a 'hyper-invested' group, one that contains soldiers with proven combat records, can sometimes be confused for a high-functioning one in aggressive units. It takes a good commander to know the difference.

Third, this study has concluded that soldiers' use of anti-Irish sentiment and, more rarely, sectarian language was a means of retaliation to physical attack and abuse; such abuse was also symptomatic of a perceived need to create some moral distance between soldiers and the local population. Anti-Irish sentiment was indulged in at all levels and, at least to some degree, mirrored sentiments occasionally heard at home in Britain. But rather than exhibiting entrenched sectarian or anti-Irish attitudes before deployment, Scottish soldiers were surprised and very often appalled by the scale of inter-communal hatred and violence they encountered in Northern Ireland. Creating a moral distance between them and the local population was partly utilitarian. A soldier does not want to take the life of 'kith and kin', better 'an other'; it took time for soldiers to adjust to the occasional need of killing people 'between a W.H. Smith and a Marks and Spencer'. The Parachute Regiment dismissed the Loyalist population as 'Irish bastards' during clashes in October 1972. However, the deaths of soldiers were also sufficiently gruesome for many to loathe the IRA and the people who supported them – the slow, lingering end of Lance Corporal Billy McIntyre (A Company, 1 Argylls), blown up near Benburb on September 10, 1972, being a case in point.

The Army could occasionally exhibit some limited signs of sectarian language or behaviour; it was not completely immune from being affected by the tensions of Ulster. This was apparent in the case of 2 Scots Guards in Derry, a 'rabid Catholic' city in the words of its CO. The contempt of one company commander for the decisions of Brigadier Mostyn, CO of 8 Brigade, led him to question whether loyalty to his Catholic faith had superseded his obligations as an officer, an interesting correlation with the behaviour of 2 Argyll officers towards their CO in Mayo in 1922 (that resulted in an informal ban on Catholic officers). Such reasoning also had a purpose; it helped justify the company commander's resistance to orders from 8 Brigade for 2 Scots Guards to go 'softly' in its dealings with the local population. Sectarian language was, very occasionally, used to 'bait' the local population in an area where soldiers had taken casualties. Given the large number of Catholic soldiers in Scottish regiments, it is not surprising that anti-Irish sentiments were the preferred means of venting abuse against the local population.

Fourth, British Army operational leadership and combat training worked. Hew Strachan has defined the aims of infantry combat training as 'the inculcation of battle drills, a set of procedures, so that when exhaustion makes rational thought impossible, or when fear has taken over, individuals react without thinking.'[16] Under fire, soldiers generally responded well, using drills to repress fire, move out of the 'kill zone' and work as teams to advance towards firing points. Training may even have been too intense; many soldiers were hyper-vigilant after the realistic training in Lydd and Hythe, expecting trouble from every quarter, not necessarily a reassuring posture to local residents. Nevertheless, when it came to initiating contact, shooting a suspected IRA Volunteer, some soldiers hesitated. 'Buckfever' was not uncommon; the cultural similarities between Britain and Northern Ireland meant that a deliberate process of emotional distancing became a practical, informal, but also potentially dangerous, response to the need to occasionally take life.

Despite the occasional instances of abuse examined, many mid-ranking and junior officers distinguished themselves in Northern Ireland during the early years of Operation Banner. This study has described such officers, among them Colonel Tony Boam and Major David Thomson. Good officers and NCOs recognised that to prevent criminal retribution after taking casualties they needed to manage soldiers' desire for revenge.

16 Strachan, 'Training, Morale and Modern War', 211.

Lieutenant John Holmes, 1 Scots Guards, catered to his men's need and desire for combat, insisting on good discipline and refusing to risk their lives unless he had a positive objective in sight. After the death of Guardsman George Hamilton, Lieutenant Holmes told his soldiers that they would have revenge, but they would do so within the limits of the law. An Argyll senior NCO who served in the Royal Highland Fusiliers during 1971 took firm action in the aftermath of the killing of the three Fusiliers by the IRA on March 9, 1971, murdered by the IRA after an evening's drinking in a Belfast pub, 'I had to disarm the soldiers and prevent them from going out the gate. I told them to wait, to wait for the right moment. There will be an opportunity to get even and when it comes along, we will be sure to take it.'[17] Junior officers and NCOs were critical in channelling and restricting soldiers' desire to do violence against a perceived threat.

The major and the corporal were the ranks that most defined combat experiences at the tactical level in Northern Ireland during 1971 and 1972. Section commanders and more junior NCOs (half-section commanders) were the patrol leaders who got soldiers through fire fights. NCOs helped soldiers overcome shock and disorientation under fire to reach for readily available skills and mechanisms that helped them fight they way out of an ambush. The remarkable forbearance shown by 1 Scots Guards on many occasions in West Belfast in 1971, not returning fire because they could not positively identify a firing point, provides a clear illustration of motivated, disciplined and soldiery behaviour, the type of response that separates soldiers from gangs.

It is impossible to speculate exactly what trajectory the conflict in West Belfast might have taken if 1 Scots Guards had been in Ballymurphy at the beginning of operation Demetrius, instead of arriving shortly afterwards. But the Scots Guards' general comportment and fire discipline does appear to have been markedly better than that of 2 PARA during August 1971, when the now infamous 'Ballymurphy massacre' took place. Clear-cut discipline was everything; soldiers had to know that excessive use of firepower or other forms of violence were not only frowned upon but would be punished. Revenge was an important motivation for many soldiers but it could be controlled, its range limited and directed. The murders of Naan and Murray by soldiers from D Company, 1 Argylls

17 Interview with Argyll Soldier 23 (NCO), March 2015.

offer an exceptional lesson on the dangers of hyper-investment among small infantry units. They also highlight the warning offered by Kalyvas about intelligence collection during civil wars, when counterinsurgents crave information in order to find and punish an elusive enemy, but end up as misinformed outsiders taking part in long-standing neighbourhood vendettas.[18] In an institution like the Army, which demands and rewards unceasing momentum, that lesson can easily be forgotten.

18 Kalyvas, *The Logic of Violence in Civil War*, 14.

Bibliography

Archives

British Library
British Army Cartoonists, 'By'eeee the right ... Laugh' (undated).
Ulster Defence Association, 'The 1972 Shankill Disturbances: A Series of Eyewitness Accounts Compiled by an Ulster Defence Team'.

Cambridge University Special Collections, Churchill College, Cambridge
GBR/0014/WLAW, William Whitelaw Papers.

Cardinal Tomás Ó Fiaich Library, Armagh
Cardinal William Conway Papers.
'"Motorman in East Down": A Survey by the Association for Legal Justice and Castlewellan Citizens' Advice Centre' (undated).

Conservative Party Archive, Bodleian Library, Oxford University

Diocese of Derry (Roman Catholic) Archives, St Columb's College, Derry
Bishop Edward Daly Papers.

Land Registry of Northern Ireland
Folios 140, 4325, 1733, 6513, County Fermanagh.

Liddell-Hart Centre for Military Archives, King's College London
GB0099 KCLMA Sir Frank Cooper Papers.

Military Archives of Ireland, Cathal Brugha Barracks, Dublin
SCS/29/71/1 – Border Operations.
2003/15/94 – G2/C/1872 Pt 2 – Border Crossings and Border Incidents by the British Army.

National Archives of Ireland, Dublin
Census of Ireland, 1911.

Department of Foreign Affairs: DFA 2000/5/33, DFA 2001/43/1407, DFA 2010/19/1618.
Department of the Taoiseach: TAOIS 2003/16/259.

National Archives of the United Kingdom, Kew
Board of Trade: 372.
Foreign and Commonwealth Office/Foreign Office: FCO 87.
Northern Ireland Office: CJ 3, CJ 4.
War Office/Ministry of Defence: WO 305, WO 373, DEFE 24.

National Army Museum, Chelsea
NAM 1999-12-140: S.F. Strichen, 'Soldier-Boy – Reminiscences of Scott Farrell Strichen, 3 RRF', unpublished manuscript.

Public Record Office of Northern Ireland, Belfast
Cabinet Secretariat, Records of: CAB/9G/27/6.
Community Relations Commission: CREL 4.
Crown Courts Records: CRCT/3/2/2/159A.
Political and Personal Papers of G.B. Newe: D3687.
Earls of Enniskillen, Papers of: D1702.

Regimental Museum of the Argyll and Sutherland Highlanders, Stirling Castle
N-J.1.CHE – 'Memories of Pte. James Chestnut, 22 Bravo, Crossmaglen, South Armagh, 1972'.
D71, 'Historical Record 1 ASH', 1972–1973.

Royal Artillery Museum, Woolwich
1st Regiment Royal Horse Artillery: Annual Historical Returns, January 1– December 1972.

Royal Scots Dragoon Guards Regimental Headquarters, Edinburgh Castle
R12, RB09: Lieutenant Colin Mitchell, 'An Officer's Diary: Scots Dragoon Guards, Northern Ireland, 1971–1972', unpublished diary.
R301, RB42, Entry Number 648: Police Service of Northern Ireland Historical Enquiries Team, 'Report on Tpr Ian Caie, Killed by IRA Bomb Northern Ireland, August 24, 1972'.
Major Scrivener, Royal Scots Dragoon Guards, 'N. Ireland War Diaries', 1971.

Royal United Services Institute, London
'Internal Security – A Neglected Aspect of Defence', Summary of RUSI Conference Proceedings, April 7, 1976.

Bibliography

Scots Guards Regimental Headquarters, Wellington Barracks, London
Adjutant's Diary, 1st Battalion, Scots Guards, 1970–1971.
Adjutant's Diary, 2nd Battalion, Scots Guards, 1971–1972.

Interviews and Correspondence

The Argyll and Sutherland Highlanders (Princess Louise's)
Argyll Soldier 1 (Private Soldier), April 2014.
Argyll Soldier 2 (Officer), November 2013.
Argyll Soldier 3 (NCO), September 2014.
Argyll Soldier 4 (Officer), November 2016.
Argyll Soldier 5 (Officer), May 2014.
Argyll Soldier 6 (Private Soldier), May 2014.
Argyll Soldier 7 (Officer), December 2016.
Argyll Soldier 8 (Private Soldier), November 2013.
Argyll Soldier 9 (Private Soldier), November 2013.
Argyll Soldier 10 (Officer), May 2014.
Argyll Soldier 11 (Officer), May 2014.
Argyll Soldier 12 (Officer), March 2015.
Argyll Soldier 13 (Officer), December 2014.
Argyll Soldier 14 (Officer), May 2014.
Argyll Soldier 15 (Officer), December 2013.
Argyll Soldier 16 (Officer), March 2015.
Argyll Soldier 17 (Officer), May 2015.
Argyll Soldier 18 (Officer), May 2014.
Argyll Soldier 19 (NCO), September 2014.
Argyll Soldier 20 (Private Soldier), April 2014.
Argyll Soldier 21 (Officer), November 2013.
Argyll Soldier 22 (Officer), March 2015.
Argyll Soldier 23 (NCO), March 2015.
Argyll Soldier 24 (NCO), March 2015.
Argyll Soldier 25 (Officer), November 2013.
Argyll Soldier 26 (Officer), November 2013.
Argyll Soldier 27 (Officer), May 2014.
Argyll Soldier 28 (Private Soldier), November 2013.
Argyll Soldier 29 (NCO), September 2014.
Argyll Soldier 30 (Officer), December 2016.
Argyll Soldier 31 (Officer), May 2014.
Argyll Soldier 32 (Private Soldier), May 2014.
Argyll Soldier 33 (Officer), March 2015.

An Army of Tribes

Crom Castle

Henry George Victor John Crichton, 6th Earl Erne KCVO, Crom Castle, September 18, 2015.

Enniskillen

Frank McManus (Former MP, Fermanagh and South Tyrone, 1970–1974; former leader Irish Independence Party and Northern Resistance Movement), May 30, 2016.

Legal Profession of Northern Ireland

Legal Professional 1, September 2014.

Legal Professional 2, October 2015.

Legal Professional 3, September 2015.

Military Intelligence, HQNI Lisburn

Military Intelligence Officer, May 2014.

Newtownbutler

Fergus McQuillan, Former SDLP Councillor, November 28, 2016.

Interview with James Naan, March 20, 2017.

Phone Interview with James Naan, December 12, 2016.

Royal Ulster Constabulary

RUC Officer 6, November 2015.

RUC Officer 7, November 2015.

RUC Officer 8, December 2016.

St Columb's College, Derry

The Most Reverend Edward Daly, DD., Lord Bishop Emeritus of Derry, Londonderry, May 16, 2014.

The Scots Guards

Scots Guards Soldier 1 (Officer), May 2014.

Scots Guards Soldier 2 (Officer), June 2014.

Scots Guards Soldier 3 (Guardsman), November 2013.

Scots Guards Soldier 4 (NCO), November 2013.

Scots Guards Soldier 5 (Officer), November 2013.

Scots Guards Soldier 6 (NCO), November 2013.

Scots Guards Soldier 7 (Guardsman), November 2013.

Scots Guards Soldier 8 (Officer), March 2013.

Scots Guards Soldier 9 (NCO), October 2013.

Scots Guards Soldier 10 (Officer), May 2014.

Bibliography

Scots Guards Soldier 11 (Officer), December 2013.
Scots Guards Soldier 12 (Officer), December 2014.
Scots Guards Soldier 13 (Officer), December 2014.
Scots Guards Soldier 14 (Officer), May 2014.
Scots Guards Soldier 15 (Officer), May 2015.
Scots Guards Soldier 16 (NCO), January 2014.
Scots Guards Soldier 17 (NCO), November 2013.
Scots Guards Soldier 18 (Officer), June 2013.
Scots Guards Soldier 19 (Officer), December 2014.
Scots Guards Soldier 20 (Officer), June 2013.
Scots Guards Soldier 21 (Officer), June 2014.
Scots Guards Soldier 22 (Officer), May 2014.

Ulster Defence Regiment (4th Battalion – County Fermanagh)
UDR Officer, June 2014.

US Naval Communications Station, Derry
Phone interview with US Navy Sailor 1 (Able Seaman), February 2015.
Email correspondence with US Navy Sailor 2 (Yeoman), February 2015.

Official Publications and Parliamentary Records

Barron Report, *Final Report of the Commission of Investigation into the Dublin and Monaghan Bombings* (Dublin: Department of the Taoiseach, 2007).
British Army, *Operation Banner: An Analysis of Military Operations in Northern Ireland* (London: Ministry of Defence, 2006).
Cameron Report, *Disturbances in Northern Ireland: Report of the Commission Appointed by the Governor of Northern Ireland* (Belfast: HMSO, 1969).
Compton Committee, *Report of the Enquiry into Allegations against the Security Forces of Physical Brutality in Northern Ireland Arising out of Events on 9th August 1971* (London: HMSO, 1971).
Houses of the Oireachtas, 'Committee on Finance – Adjournment Debate: British Army Border Infringement', Oireachtas Records (vol. 266, no. 4), June 14, 1973.
Office of the Prime Minister of the United Kingdom of Great Britain and Northern Ireland, 'Lord Lieutenant for County Fermanagh', Press Release issued by 10 Downing Street, May 14, 2012.
Parker Committee, *Report on the Committee of Privy Counsellors Appointed to Consider Authorised Procedures for the Interrogation of Persons Suspected of Terrorism* (London: HMSO, 1972).
Report of the Bloody Sunday Inquiry [Saville Inquiry] (London: HMSO, 2010).

Scottish Government: Justice and Analytical Services, *An Examination of the Evidence on Sectarianism in Scotland* (Edinburgh: Scottish Government Publications, 2013).

UK Defence Academy, *Seaford House Papers* (London: UK Defence Academy, 1978).

Wessely, S., 'Psychiatric Disorders, Psychiatric Injury and the Royal Ulster Constabulary (RUC)', dated December 1, 2004 (unpublished report in author's possession).

Winslow, D., *The Canadian Airborne Regiment in Somalia: A Socio-Cultural Inquiry. A Study Prepared for the Commission of Inquiry into the Deployment of Canadian Forces to Somalia* (Ottawa: Ministry of Public Works, 1997).

Regimental Magazines, Newspapers and other Media

Alloa Advertiser
Ardoyne Freedom Fighter
BBC News
Belfast Newsletter
Belfast Telegraph
The Broken Elbow (brokenelbow.com)
Crossmaglen Examiner
Daily Ireland
Daily Telegraph
Derry Journal
Falkirk Herald
Fermanagh Herald
Fermanagh News
Fortnight
'Foyled Again' – The Operational Journal of the Coldstream Guards in Northern Ireland, 1971–1972
Glengarry Tales – The Operational Magazine of The Argyll and Sutherland Highlanders
Greenock Telegraph and Clyde Shipping Gazette
Guardian
Impartial Reporter
Independent
Inverness Courier
Irish Independent
Irish News
Journal of the Royal Artillery
Londonderry Sentinel
Lower Falls Street Bulletin

Bibliography

Mourne Observer
New York Times
Newry Reporter
News Letter Orange Order
Oban Times
An Phoblacht
Queen's Own Highlander
Red Hackle
Rose and Thistle – The Operational Magazine of 2nd Battalion, Scots Guards
Saoirse – The Newspaper of the St James's and District Sinn Féin Robert Emmet/ Francis Liggett Cumman
Scarlet and Green Journal – 16/5th The Queen's Own Lancers
Scots Guards Magazine
Scottish Protestant View
Soldier Magazine
Sunday Mail (Glasgow)
Thin Red Line – The Regimental Magazine of the Argyll and Sutherland Highlanders
The Times
Volunteer – the Voice of Republican Derry
White Lancer and the Vendette

Published Memoirs

Adams, G., *Before the Dawn: An Autobiography* (London: William Heinemann, 1996).

Ashdown, P., *A Fortunate Life* (London: Aurum Press, 2009).

Blacker, C., *Monkey Business: The Memoirs of General Sir Cecil Blacker* (London: Quiller Press, 1993).

Bloomfield, K., *A Memoir: Stormont in Crisis* (Belfast: Blackstaff Press, 1994).

Bullock, S., *After Sixty Years* (London: Sampson Low, Marston, 1931).

Callaghan, J., *A House Divided: The Dilemma of Northern Ireland* (London: Collins, 1973).

Carver, M., *Out of Step: Memoirs of Field Marshal Lord Carver* (London: Hutchinson, 1989).

Clarke, A.F.N., *Contact* (London: Pan, 1983).

Conroy, J., *War as a Way of Life* (London: Heinemann, 1988).

Conway, K., *Southside Provisional* (Dublin: Orpen Press, 2014).

Devlin, B., *The Price of My Soul* (New York: Alfred Knopf, 1969).

Devlin, P., *Straight Left* (Belfast: Blackstaff Press, 1993).

Faulkner, B., *Memoirs of Statesman* (London: Weidenfeld and Nicolson, 1978).

Heath, E., *The Course of My Life* (London: Hodder and Stoughton, 1999).

Hermon, J., *Holding the Line: An Autobiography* (London: Gill and Macmillan, 1997).

Jackson, M., *Soldier* (London: Bantam, 2007).

Kitson, F., *Bunch of Five* (London: Faber and Faber, 2010).

Lynch, M., *The Long Road Home* (Dublin: Londubh, 2010).

McCann, E., *War and an Irish Town* (Harmondsworth: Penguin, 1974).

McKearney, T., *The Provisional IRA: From Insurrection to Parliament* (London: Pluto Press, 2011).

MacStíofáin, Seán, *Memoirs of a Revolutionary* (London: Gordon Cremonisi, 1975).

Mitchell, C., *Having Been a Soldier* (London: Hamish Hamilton, 1969).

Peck, J., *Dublin from Downing Street* (London: Gill and Macmillan, 1978).

Starling, J., *Soldier On! The Testament of a Tom* (Tunbridge Wells: Spellmount, 1992).

Whitelaw, W., *The Whitelaw Memoirs* (London: Aurum Press, 1989).

Books, Articles, Theses and Documentaries

Andrew, C., *Defence of the Realm: The Authorized History of MI5* (London: Allen Lane, 2009).

Arthur, M., *Northern Ireland: Soldiers Talking* (London: Sidgwick and Jackson, 1987).

Ashworth, T., *Trench Warfare, 1914–1918: The Live and Let Live System* (London: Macmillan, 1980).

Bandura, A., 'Selective Moral Disengagement in the Exercise of Moral Agency', *Journal of Moral Education* 31(2), 101–119.

Barker, D., *Soldiering On: An Unofficial Portrait of the British Army* (London: Andre Deutsch, 1981).

Barton, B., 'The Origins and Development of Unionism in Fermanagh, 1885–1914', in E. Murphy and W. Roulston, *Fermanagh: History and Society* (London: Geography Publications, 2005).

Barzilay, D., *The British Army in Ulster*, vol. 1 (Belfast: Century Services, 1973).

Bassford, C., 'Primacy of Policy and Trinity in Clausewitz's Thought', in H. Strachan and A. Herberg-Rothe (eds), *Clausewitz in the 21st Century* (Oxford: Oxford University Press, 2007), 74–90.

BBC (television documentary), 'Marine A: Criminal or Casualty of War', first broadcast on BBC One, April 9, 2014.

BBC (television documentary), 'Mad Mitch and his Tribal Law', released as part of a DVD collection, *Empire Warriors* (London: BBC, 2004).

Beattie-Smith, W., *The British State and the Northern Ireland Crisis* (Washington, DC: US Institute for Peace, 2011).

Bibliography

Bechofer, F. and L. Paterson, *Principles of Research and Design in the Social Sciences* (London: Routledge, 2000).

Beevor, A., *Inside the British Army* (London: Corgi Books, 1991).

Ben-Ari, E., *Mastering Soldiers* (New York: Berghahn, 1998).

Benest, D., 'Aden to Northern Ireland, 1966–76', in H. Strachan (ed.), *Big Wars and Small Wars: The British Army and the Lessons of War in the Twentieth Century* (London: Routledge, 2006), 115–145.

Bennett, H., *Fighting the Mau Mau: The British Army and Counter-Insurgency in the Kenya Emergency* (Cambridge: Cambridge University Press, 2013).

—— 'From Direct Rule to Motorman: Adjusting British Military Strategy for Northern Ireland in 1972', *Studies in Conflict and Terrorism* 23(6) (2010), 511–532.

—— 'The Other Side of the COIN: Minimum and Exemplary Force in British Army Counterinsurgency in Kenya'. *Small Wars and Insurgencies* 18(4) (2007), 638–664.

—— '"Smoke Without Fire"? Allegations against the British Army in Northern Ireland, 1972–5', *Twentieth Century British History* 24(2) (2013), 275–304.

Bentham, J., *The Works of Jeremy Bentham* (London: William Tait, 1838).

Bessel, R., 'The Potempa Murder', *Central European History* 10(3) (1977), 241–254.

Bew, P., *Ireland: The Politics of Enmity, 1789–2006* (Oxford: Oxford University Press, 2007).

Bew, P. and G. Gillespie, *Northern Ireland: A Chronology of the Troubles, 1968–1993* (Dublin: Gill and Macmillan, 1993).

Bew, P. and H. Patterson, *The British State and the Ulster Crisis* (London: Verso, 1985).

Bew, P., P. Gibbon and H. Patterson, *Northern Ireland, 1921–1996: Political Forces and Social Classes* (London: Serif, 1996).

Blacker, C. and H. Woods, *The Story of the 5th Royal Inniskilling Dragoon Guards, 1928–1978* (London: Spottiswoode Press, 1978).

Bourdieu, P., *Outline of a Theory of Practice* (Cambridge: Cambridge University Press, 1977).

Bourke, J., *An Intimate History of Killing* (London: Granta, 2000).

Bowen, E., *The Last September* (London: Vintage, 1998).

Bowyer Bell, J., *The Secret Army: The IRA* (Dublin: Poolbeg, 1989).

Bryman, A., *Social Research Methods* (Oxford: Oxford University Press, 2004).

Bushell, C.A.H., 'Insurgency and the Numbers Game', *Army Quarterly and Defence Journal* 84(1) (1969), 61–64.

Charters, D., 'The Changing Forms of Conflict in Northern Ireland', *Journal of Conflict Studies* 1(2) (1980), 32–39.

Cielou, R., *Spare my Tortured People* (Lisnaskea: Whitethorne Press, 1983).

Clark, H.S.W., 'Border Patrol', *British Army Review* 44 (1973), 25–28.

Clausewitz, C. von, *On War*, edited and translated by M. Howard and P. Paret (Princeton, NJ: Princeton University Press, 1989).

Cohen, S., *States of Denial: Knowing About Atrocities and Suffering* (Oxford: Blackwell Publishers, 2001).

Collins, R., *Violence: A Microsociological Theory* (Princeton, NJ: Princeton University Press, 2008).

Craig, A., *Crisis of Confidence: Anglo-Irish Relations in the Early Troubles, 1966–1974* (Dublin: Irish Academic Press, 2010).

Crawford, S., 'Race Relations in the Army', in H. Strachan (ed.), *The British Army, Manpower and Society into the Twenty-First Century* (London: Frank Cass, 2000), 119–138.

Crichton, J., 'An Account of Some Plantation Castles on the Estates of the Earl of Erne in the County of Fermanagh', *Ulster Journal of Archaeology* 2(1) (1895), 7–16.

Cunningham, M., *British Government Policy in Northern Ireland, 1969–1989* (Manchester: Manchester University Press, 1991).

Daase, C., 'Clausewitz and Small Wars', in H. Strachan and A. Herberg-Rothe (eds), *Clausewitz in the 21st Century* (Oxford: Oxford University Press, 2007), 182–195.

Dane, M., *The B Specials in Fermanagh* (Enniskillen: William Trimble Ltd., 1970).

De Baróid, C., *Ballymurphy and the Irish War* (London: Pluto, 2000).

Decker, S.H. and B. Van Winkle, *Life in the Gang: Family, Friends and Violence* (Cambridge: Cambridge University Press, 1996).

Dewar, M., *The British Army in Northern Ireland* (London: Arms and Armour, 1985).

Dillon, M., *The Dirty War* (London: Arrow, 1991).

Dixon, P., 'Hearts and Minds? British Counter-insurgency from Malaya to Iraq', *Journal of Strategic Studies* 32(3) (2009): 353–381.

—— 'Hearts and Minds: British Counterinsurgency Strategy in Northern Ireland', in P. Dixon (ed.), *The British Approach to Counterinsurgency: From Malaya to Northern Ireland* (London: Palgrave Macmillan, 2012), 265–290.

Donnan, H. and K. Simpson, 'Silence and Violence among Northern Ireland Border Protestants', *Ethnos: Journal of Anthropology* 72(1) (2007), 1469–1588.

Downes, C., *Special Trust and Confidence: The Making of an Officer* (London: Frank Cass, 1991).

Durkheim, E., *The Elementary Forms of Religious Life* (New York: The Free Press, 1995).

Bibliography

—— 'The Normal and the Pathological', reprinted in E.J. Clarke and D.H. Kelly (eds), *Deviant Behaviour: A Text Reader in the Sociology of Deviance* (New York: Worth, 2003), 80–84.

Edmonds, M., *Armed Services and Society* (Leicester: Leicester University Press, 1988).

Edwards, A., *Mad Mitch's Tribal Law: Aden and the End of Empire* (Edinburgh: Mainstream Publishing, 2014).

—— 'Misapplying Lessons Learned? Analysing the Utility of British Counterinsurgency Strategy in Northern Ireland, 1971–1976', *Small Wars and Insurgencies* 21(2) (2010), 303–330.

—— *The Northern Ireland Troubles: Operation Banner, 1969–2007* (Oxford: Osprey Publishing, 2011).

Ellison, G. and J. Smyth, *The Crowned Harp: Policing Northern Ireland* (London: Pluto Press, 2000).

English, R., *Armed Struggle: The History of the IRA* (London: Pan Macmillan, 2004).

—— *Irish Freedom: The History of Nationalism in Ireland* (London: Pan, 2007).

Evelegh, R., *Peace Keeping in a Democratic Society: The Lessons of Northern Ireland* (London: McGill–Queen's University Press, 1978).

Finer, S., *The Man on Horseback: The Role of the Military in Politics* (New York: Transaction, 2002).

Ferguson, T.A., *8th Battalion (Co. Tyrone), Ulster Defence Regiment* (Dungannon: Dungannon Branch of the Ulster Defence Regiment Association, 1995).

Foley, C., *Legacy of Strife: Cyprus From Rebellion to Civil War* (Harmondsworth: Penguin, 1962).

Frankland, M., *Afterwards* (Dumfries: Glenmill, 2009).

French, D., *The British Way in Counterinsurgency, 1945–1967* (Oxford: Oxford University Press, 2011).

Gallagher, T., *Divided Scotland: Ethnic Friction and Christian Crisis* (Glasgow: Argyll Publishing, 2013).

Galula, D., *Counterinsurgency Warfare: Theory and Practice* (Westport, Conn.: Praeger Security International, 2006).

Gat, A., *The Origins of Military Thought* (Oxford: Oxford University Press, 1989).

Glassie, H., *Passing the Time in Ballymenone: Culture and History of an Ulster Community* (Indianapolis: Indiana University Press, 1995).

Goffman, E., *An Essay on the Organization of Experience* (Boston: Northeastern University Press, 1986).

Goldsmith, R.F.K., 'Editorial', *Army Quarterly and Defence Journal* 103(1) (1971), 1–3.

Gordon-McBride, M., 'Symbol, Barrier, Resource, Bridge: Narratives of Experiences on the Fermanagh Border', unpublished Queen's University Belfast thesis, 2009.

Graham, D., *Enniskillen and the Battle of Newtownbutler* (Farnham: Pike and Shot Society, 2011).

Grassiani, E., *Soldiering under Occupation* (Oxford: Berghahn, 2013).

Greiner, B., *War without Fronts: The USA in Vietnam* (London: Random House, 2009).

Hamill, D., *Pig in the Middle – The Army in Northern Ireland, 1969–1984* (London: Methuen, 1985).

Hanley, B. and S. Millar, *The Lost Revolution: The Story of the Official IRA and the Workers' Party* (London: Penguin, 2010).

Harnden, T., *Bandit Country: The IRA and South Armagh* (London: Hodder and Stoughton, 2000).

Harries-Jenkins, Gwyn, 'Role Images, Military Attitudes, and the Enlisted Culture in Great Britain', in D.R. Segal and H.W. Sinaiko (eds), *Life in the Rank and File: Enlisted Men and Women in the Armed Forces of the United States, Australia, Canada, and the United Kingdom* (Washington, DC: Pergamon-Brasseys, 1986), 254–271.

Harris, H.E.D., 'The New Irish Rangers', *Army Quarterly and Defence Journal* 98(2) (1969), 195–197.

Harris, R., *Prejudice in Ulster* (Manchester: Manchester University Press, 1972).

Harrison, S., *Dark Trophies: Hunting and the Enemy Body in Modern War* (New York: Berghahn Books, 2012).

Hastings, M., 'Veterans and Mental Health in Contemporary Britain', *RUSI Journal* 159(6) (2014), 34–40.

Healey, D., 'British Defence Policy', *RUSI Journal* 114(4) (1969), 1–4.

Hennessey, T., *The Evolution of the Irish Troubles, 1970–1972* (Dublin: Irish Academic Press, 2007).

—— *Northern Ireland: The Origins of the Northern Ireland Troubles* (Dublin: Gill and Macmillan, 2005).

Henry, W., *Upper Lough Erne* (Whitegate: Ballinakella Press, 1987).

Hobbes, T., *Leviathan* (Cambridge: Cambridge University Press, 1996).

Hockey, J., *Squaddies: Portrait of a Sub-culture* (Exeter: Exeter University Publications, 1986).

Holdaway, S., 'Race Relations and Police Recruitment', *British Journal of Criminology* 31(4) (1991), 365–382.

Honig, J., 'Clausewitz's *On War*: Problems of Text and Translation', in H. Strachan and A. Herberg-Rothe (eds), *Clausewitz in the 21st Century* (Oxford: Oxford University Press, 2007), 57–73.

Horne, A., *A Savage War of Peace* (New York: New York Review of Books Publications, 2006).

Horne, J. and A. Kramer, *German Atrocities, 1914: A History of Denial* (New Haven, Conn.: Yale University Press, 2001).

Bibliography

Horowitz, R., *Honor and the American Dream: Culture and Identity in a Chicano Community* (New Brunswick, NJ: Rutgers University Press, 1992).

Howard, M., 'Mistake to Declare this "a War"', *RUSI Journal* 146(6) (2001), 1–4.

Huntington, S., *The Soldier and the State: The Theory and Politics of Civil–Military Relations* (Cambridge, Mass.: Belknap Press of Harvard University Press, 1957).

Hutchinson, S., 'The Police Role in Counterinsurgency', *RUSI Journal* 114(4) (1969), 21–25.

Ignatieff, M., 'Handcuffing the Military? Military Judgment, Rules of Engagement and Public Scrutiny', in P. Mileham and L. Willett (eds), *Military Ethics for the Expeditionary Era* (London: Royal Institute of International Affairs, 2001), 25–33.

Iron, R., 'Britain's Longest War: Northern Ireland, 1967–2007', in D. Marston and C. Malkasian (eds), *Counterinsurgency in Modern Warfare* (London: Osprey Publishing, 2008), 167–185.

Irwin, A. and M. Mahoney, 'The Military Response', in J. Dingley (ed.), *Combating Terrorism in Northern Ireland* (London: Routledge, 2009), 198–226.

Janowitz, M., *The Professional Soldier* (Glencoe: The Free Press, 1961).

Jeffery, K., *'An Irish Empire?': The Aspects of Ireland and the British Empire* (Manchester: Manchester University Press, 1996).

—— 'Security Policy in Northern Ireland: Some Reflections on the Management of Violent Conflict', *Terrorism and Political Violence* 2(1) (1990), 21–34.

Jolly, R., *Military Man, Family Man* (London: Brassey's, 1987).

Junger, S., *War* (London: Fourth Estate, 2010).

Kalyvas, S., *The Logic of Violence in Civil War* (Cambridge: Cambridge University Press, 2006).

Kennedy-Pipe, C., *The Origin of the Present Troubles in Northern Ireland* (London: Longman, 1997).

King, A., *The Combat Soldier: Infantry Tactics and Cohesion in the Twentieth and Twenty-First Centuries* (Oxford: Oxford University Press, 2013).

Kitson, F., *Directing Operations* (London: Faber and Faber, 1989).

—— *Low Intensity Operations: Subversion, Insurgency, Peace-keeping* (Dehradun: Upendra Arora for Natraj Publishers, 1992).

Lacqueur, W., *Guerrilla Warfare: A Historical and Critical Study* (New York: Transaction, 1998).

Leach, E., *Rethinking Anthropology* (London: Athlone Press, 1961).

Leary, P., *Unapproved Routes: Histories of the Irish Border, 1922–1972* (Oxford: Oxford University Press, 2016).

Ledwidge, F., *Losing Small Wars: British Military Failure in Iraq and Afghanistan* (New Haven, Conn.: Yale University Press, 2011).

Lindsay, O., 'Do Not Pass "GO" – Ulster 69', *British Army Review* (34) (1969), 42–48.

—— *Once a Grenadier* (London: Pen and Sword, 1996).

Kirk-Smith, M. and J. Dingley, 'Countering Terrorism in Northern Ireland: The Role of Intelligence', *Small Wars and Insurgencies* 20(3–4) (2009), 551–573.

McCleery, M., *Operation Demetrius and its Aftermath* (Manchester: Manchester University Press, 2015).

—— 'A Re-examination of the Use of Internment without Trial in Northern Ireland in the Early 1970s', Queen's University Belfast thesis, submitted 2013.

McCusker, J., *Memories of Newtownbutler and Canon Tom Maguire* (Lisnaskea: McBrien Printing, undated).

MacDonald, B., *The Pitchfork Murders – Uncovering the Cover-up* (Newtownbutler: Sinn Féin Cumann, 2013).

McFate, M., *Pax Britannica: British Counterinsurgency in Northern Ireland, 1969–1982* (New York: Wilberforce Codex, 2014).

McKittrick, D. and D. McVea, *Making Sense of the Troubles* (London: Penguin, 2001).

McKittrick, D., S. Kelters, B. Feeney and C. Thornton, *Lost Lives* (Edinburgh: Mainstream, 1999).

McManus, M., 'The Macken Fight', available at http://mexlist.com/mcmanus/macken.htm (accessed September 22, 2017).

Maguire, R., R. Morton and J. Blacking, *Come Day, Go Day, God Send Sunday* (London: Routledge and Kegan Paul, 1973).

Mileham, P., *Fighting Highlanders: The History of the Argyll and Sutherland Highlanders* (London: Arms and Armour, 1993).

Miller, L. and C. Moskos, 'Humanitarians or Warriors? Race, Gender and Combat Status in Operation Restore Hope', *Armed Forces and Society* 21(4), 613–637.

Moloney, E., *A Secret History of the IRA* (London: Penguin, 2007).

—— *Voices from the Grave: Two Men's War in Ireland* (London: Faber and Faber, 2010).

Morrison, D., *West Belfast* (Cork: Mercier Press, 1989).

Morton, P., *Emergency Tour: 3 Para in South Armagh* (Northampton: William Kimber, 1989).

Mulholland, M., *The Longest War: Northern Ireland's Troubled History* (Oxford: Oxford University Press, 2002).

—— *Northern Ireland at the Crossroads: Ulster Unionism in the O'Neill Years 1960–9* (Basingstoke: Palgrave Macmillan, 2000).

Mumford, A., *The Counterinsurgency Myth: The British Experience of Irregular War* (London: Routledge, 2011).

Bibliography

Nagl, J., *Learning to Eat Soup with a Knife: Counterinsurgency Lessons from Malaya and Vietnam* (Chicago: University of Chicago, 2005).

Naylor, M., *Among Friends: The Scots Guards, 1956–1993* (Barnsley: Pen and Sword, 1995).

Neitzel, S. and H. Welzer, *Soldaten* (London: Simon and Schuster, 2012).

Neumann, P., *Britain's Long War: British Strategy in the Northern Ireland Conflict, 1968–98* (Basingstoke: Palgrave Macmillan, 2003).

Newsinger, J., *British Counterinsurgency: From Palestine to Northern Ireland* (London: Palgrave Macmillan, 2002).

—— 'British Security Policy in Northern Ireland', *Race and Class* 37(1) (1995), 83–94.

Ní Aoláin, F., *The Politics of Force: Conflict Management and State Violence in Northern Ireland* (Belfast: Blackstaff Press, 2000).

Norden, D., *Military Rebellion in Argentina: Between Coups and Consolidation* (Lincoln: University of Nebraska Press, 1996).

O'Brien, C.C., *States of Ireland* (London: HarperCollins, 1974).

O'Callaghan, M., *British High Politics and a Nationalist Ireland* (Cork: Cork University Press, 1994).

O'Dochartaigh, N., 'Bloody Sunday: Error or Design?', *Contemporary British History* 24(1) (2010), 89–108.

—— *From Civil Rights to Armalites: Derry and the Birth of the Irish Troubles* (Cork: Cork University Press, 1997).

O'Halpín, E., *Defending Ireland: The Irish State and its Enemies since 1922* (Oxford: Oxford University Press, 1999).

O'Leary, B., *The Politics of Antagonism: Understanding Northern Ireland* (Oxford: Blackwell, 1995).

Otley, C.B., 'The Social Origins of British Army Officers', *Sociological Review* 18(2) (1970), 213–219.

Palmer, C.P.R., 'Public Opinion and the Armed Forces', *Seaford House Papers* (1977), 80–89.

Paret, P., *Clausewitz and the State: The Man, His Theories, and His Times* (Princeton, NJ: Princeton University Press, 2007).

Patterson, H., *Ireland's Violent Frontier* (Basingstoke: Palgrave Macmillan, 2013).

Porter, P., *Military Orientalism: Eastern War Through Western Eyes* (London: Hurst, 2009).

Potter, J., *The UDR: A Testimony to Courage* (London: Pen and Sword, 2001).

Prince, S., *Northern Ireland's '68: Civil Rights, Global Revolt and the Origins of the Troubles* (Dublin: Irish Academic Press, 2007).

Prince, S. and G. Warner, *Belfast and Derry in Revolt* (Dublin: Irish Academic Press, 2012).

Purdue, O., *The Big House in the North of Ireland: Land Power and Social Elites* (Dublin: University College Dublin Press, 2009).

Reeves-Smyth, T., *Crom Castle Demesne*, vol. 1 (Rowellane: National Trust, 1999).

Richardson, F., *Fighting Spirit: A Study of Psychological Factors in War* (London: Leo Cooper, 1978).

Richardson, L., 'Britain and the IRA', in R. Art and L. Richardson (eds), *Democracy and Counterterrorism: Lessons from the Past* (Washington, DC: United States Institute for Peace, 2007), 63–95.

Roberts, A., 'The Civilian in Modern War', in H. Strachan and S. Scheipers, *The Changing Character of War* (Oxford: Oxford University Press, 2011), 263–280.

Roberts, S., 'Fit to Fight: The Conceptual Component – An Approach to Military Doctrine for the Twenty-First Century', in H. Strachan (ed.), *The British Army, Manpower and Society into the Twenty-First Century* (London: Frank Cass, 2000), 191–200.

Rose, P., *How the Troubles Came to Northern Ireland* (Basingstoke: Palgrave Macmillan, 2001).

Ruane, J. and J. Todd, *The Dynamics of Conflict in Northern Ireland: Power, Conflict and Emancipation* (Cambridge: Cambridge University Press, 1996).

Ryder, C., *The Ulster Defence Regiment: An Instrument of Peace* (London: Methuen Press, 1991).

Sanders, A., 'Northern Ireland: The Intelligence War, 1969–1975', *British Journal of Politics and International Relations* 13(2) (2011), 230–248.

—— 'Principles of Minimum Force and the Parachute Regiment in Northern Ireland, 1969–1972', *Journal of Strategic Studies* (2016), 1–25.

Sanders, A. and I. Wood, *Times of Troubles: Britain's War in Northern Ireland* (Edinburgh: Edinburgh University Press, 2012).

Sarkesian, S., *Unconventional Conflicts in a New Security Era* (Westport, Conn.: Greenwood Press, 1993).

Scheipers, S., *Unlawful Combatants: A Genealogy of the Irregular Fighter* (Oxford: Oxford University Press, 2015).

Schmid, A.P. and A.J. Jongman, *Political Terrorism* (New Brunswick, NJ: Transaction Publishers, 2005).

Seu, B., '"Your Stomach Makes You Feel that You Don't Want to Know Anything about it": Densensitization, Defence Mechanisms and Rhetoric in Response to Human Rights Abuses', *Journal of Human Rights* 2(2) (2010), 183–196.

Shalit, B., *The Psychology of Conflict and Combat* (New York: Praeger, 1988).

Sharpe, L., 'Discipline', *British Army Review* 42 (1972), 39–43.

Shay, J., *Achilles in Vietnam* (New York: Touchstone, 1995).

Bibliography

Shils, E. and M. Janowitz, 'Cohesion and Disintegration in the Wehrmacht in the Second World War', *Public Opinion Quarterly* 12(2) (1948), 280–315.

Slim, H., *Killing Civilians: Methods, Madness and Morality in War* (London: Hurst, 2007).

Smith, M., *Fighting for Ireland? The Military Strategy of the Irish Republican Movement* (London: Routledge, 1995).

Sprung, G., *The Soldier in our Time* (Philadelphia: Dorrance, 1960).

Strachan, H., *Clausewitz's 'On War': A Biography* (London: Atlantic Books, 2007).

—— *The Politics of the British Army* (Oxford: Clarendon Press, 1997).

—— 'Training, Morale and Modern War', *Journal of Contemporary History* 41(2) (2006), 211–227.

Swinton, J., *A Short History of the Scots Guards, 1642–1962* (London: Gale and Polden, 1962).

Taylor, P., *Brits: The War against the IRA* (London: Bloomsbury, 2002).

Thompson, C.A.L., 'The British Army at Home', *British Army Review* 29 (1968), 71–75.

Thompson, F., 'The Land War in Fermanagh', in E. Murphy and W. Roulston, *Fermanagh: History and Society* (London: Geography Publications, 2005).

Torrance, D., *George Younger: A Life Well Lived* (Edinburgh: Berlinn, 2008).

Townshend, C., *The British Campaign in Ireland, 1919–1921* (Oxford: Oxford University Press, 1975).

Turner, A., *Crisis? What Crisis? Britain in the 1970s* (London: Aurum Press, 2008).

Urban, M., *Big Boys' Rules: The Secret Struggle Against the IRA* (London: Faber and Faber, 1993).

Vennesson, P., 'Cohesion and Misconduct: The French Army and the Mahé Affair', in A. King (ed.), *Frontline: Combat and Cohesion in the Twenty-First Century* (Oxford: Oxford University Press, 2015).

Vetlesen, A., *Evil and Human Agency: Understanding Collective Evildoing* (Cambridge: Cambridge University Press, 2005).

Walker, G., *A History of the Ulster Unionist Party: Protest, Pragmatism and Pessimism* (Manchester: Manchester University Press, 2004).

—— *Intimate Strangers, Political and Cultural Interaction between Scotland and Ulster in Modern Times* (Edinburgh: John Donald, 1995).

—— 'Ulster Unionism and the Scottish Dimension', in W. Kelly and J. Young, *Ulster and Scotland, 1600–2000* (Dublin: Four Courts Press, 2004), 33–42.

Walker, J., *Aden Insurgency: The Savage War in South Arabia, 1962–7* (Staplehurst: Spellmount, 2005).

Walker, W., 'Borneo', *British Army Review* 32 (1969), 11–17.

Weber, M., *Essays in Sociology* (London: Routledge, 1970).

White, R., *Provisional Irish Republicans: An Oral and Interpretative History* (Westport, Conn.: Greenwood Press, 1993).

Williams, A., *A Very British Killing: The Death of Baha Mousa* (London: Jonathan Cape, 2012).

Wilson, T., *Frontiers of Violence: Conflict, Identity in Ulster and Upper Silesia, 1918–1922* (Oxford: Oxford University Press, 2010).

—— 'The Strange Death of Loyalist Monaghan', in S. Paseta (ed.), Uncertain Futures: Essays about the Irish Past for Roy Foster (Oxford: Oxford University Press, 2016), 174–188.

Witherow, T., *Derry and Enniskillen in the Year 1689: The Story of Some Famous Battlefields in Ulster* (Belfast: 1873).

Wong, L., T.A. Kolditz, R.A. Millen and T.M. Potten, *Why They Fight: Combat Motivation in the Iraq War* (Carlisle, Pa.: US Army War College, 2003).

Wood, I., *Crimes of Loyalty: A History of the UDA* (Edinburgh: Edinburgh University Press, 2006).

Zuleika, Z., *Basque Violence: Metaphor and Sacrament* (Reno: University of Nevada Press, 1988).

Index

Page numbers in **bold** refer to maps and those with an 'n' refer to notes. Ranks and titles given are those held during the operations or periods under discussion. Authors are not given ranks or titles.

Index